Employment in Schools: A Legal Guide

Second Edition

Employment in Schools: A Legal Guide

Second Edition

Oliver Hyams

Published by
Jordan Publishing Limited
21 St Thomas Street
Bristol BS1 6JS

Whilst the publishers and the author have taken every care in preparing the material included in this work, any statements made as to the legal or other implications of particular transactions are made in good faith purely for general guidance and cannot be regarded as a substitute for professional advice. Consequently, no liability can be accepted for loss or expense incurred as a result of relying in particular circumstances on statements made in this work.

© Jordan Publishing Limited 2007

All rights reserved. No part of this publication may be reproduced, stored in a retrieval system, or transmitted in any way or by any means, including photocopying or recording, without the written permission of the copyright holder, application for which should be addressed to the publisher.

Crown Copyright material is reproduced with kind permission of the Controller of Her Majesty's Stationery Office.

British Library Cataloguing-in-Publication Data

A catalogue record for this book is available from the British Library.

ISBN 978 1 84661 016 5

Typeset by Letterpart Ltd, Reigate, Surrey

Printed in Great Britain by Antony Rowe Limited

PREFACE

This book is intended to be a comprehensive guide to the law of England and Wales as it affects employment in schools. The first edition of the book was a little sketchy in some places in relation to the law of employment generally, more sketchy in others about that law, but detailed about the regulation of employment in schools. Some parts of the first edition aimed to be a succinct but accurate statement of the principles of general employment law.

This second edition is in many ways the same in those regards. However, the statutory regulation of employment in (in particular maintained) schools has grown considerably since the first edition. Furthermore, there has been a need for a wholesale revision and rewriting of the chapter on the law of discrimination and human rights (although the part relating to human rights has not required much change, the law of human rights having had little direct effect on the law of employment). All of the rest of the text has been thoroughly revised and reconsidered. At least half of the text is new.

One chapter was not repeated: the chapter in the first edition on the history of the law of employment. The inclusion of that chapter was something of an indulgence on the part of Jordans, and in any event, there was a need for a completely new chapter, describing the statutory grievance procedures and the statutory dismissal and discipline procedures introduced by, or under, the Employment Act 2002. At the time of writing, however, the repeal of those provisions, or at least parts of them, had been indicated by the Government, so the new chapter (Chapter 2) may have a relatively short useful life.

The rest of the book will almost certainly start to be out of date as soon as it is published – if not before. I have attempted to state the law as it stood on 10 August 2007, but inevitably some developments will have occurred before then which were not reported.

I have been fortunate to benefit from the help of several expert solicitors, two of whom read through parts of the text when it was in draft form. Sarah Morgan (of the National Union of Teachers' Wales office) read through and commented very helpfully on Chapters 3 and 4. Elisabeth Griffiths (of Northumbria University) read through and commented helpfully on Chapters 2, 6 and 8. Komal Ladva (of Haringey London Borough Council) suggested a useful addition to Chapter 5. In addition, several colleagues in Devereux Chambers (Alison Padfield and Talia Barsam) read through draft chapter 6, reassuring me that it made sense in general terms. David Mangan, a research student at the London School of Economics, also read through drafts of chapters 3 and 4 and commented on them. Responsibility for any errors, infelicities of language, or lack of clarity, nevertheless rests firmly with me.

It often occurs that an author's family time suffers during the process of writing. I owe an enormous debt of gratitude to my wife, Gill, and daughters Sarah and Katy, who have with much good humour put up with my absences in that regard for some time now.

Finally, thanks are due as ever to the courteous and friendly staff of Jordans. Tony Hawitt and Deborah Saunders in particular have been both encouraging and forbearing while the text of this book was awaited and then in preparation.

Oliver Hyams
Devereux Chambers
28 August 2007

CONTENTS

Preface	v
Abbreviations	xvii
Glossary	xix
Table of Statutes	xxi
Table of Statutory Instruments	xxvii
Table of Cases	xxxv

Chapter 1
Introduction and Overview 1
Introduction 1
Employment law generally 1
   The development of the law 1
   Who is the employer? 2
   Who are employees? 2
   Prospective employees 3
What law is applicable to employment, both generally and in schools? 3
   General employment law 3
   Employment in a state school 4
   Employment in an independent school 6
The doctrine of precedent 6
Who determines employment disputes? 8
   Employment tribunals 8
   Employment Act 2002 grievance procedures 9
A practical factor: the rare award of costs 9
A further practical factor: restrictions on appealing 10
The aim of this book 11

Chapter 2
Dispute Resolution Procedures in the Employment Act 2002 13
Introduction and overview 13
   New statutory procedures 13
   Sanctions for non-compliance 13
The statutory grievance procedures 14
   Introduction 14
   The grievance procedures 15
      General requirements of the procedures in Schedule 2 16
   What is a grievance for the purposes of Schedule 2 to the Act? 16
   What is required from an employee who appeals? 18

When does the modified procedure apply?	18
What amounts to non-compliance with a grievance procedure in Schedule 2 to the Act?	19
General circumstances affecting the application of the statutory grievance procedures	19
Particular circumstances affecting the application of the statutory grievance procedures	21
The effect of a failure to follow the applicable grievance procedure	23
Effect on the employee	23
Effect on the employer	24
Extension of time where employee complies with statutory grievance procedure within primary time limit	25
The statutory dismissal and discipline procedures	25
Introduction	25
In what circumstances will the statutory dismissal and discipline procedures apply?	25
What are the statutory dismissal and discipline procedures?	26
When does the modified procedure apply?	28
Circumstances in which the parties are treated as having complied with the dismissal and discipline procedures	28
Effect of a failure to follow all or part of the statutory dismissal and discipline procedures	28
What is required for compliance by the employer with the dismissal and discipline procedures?	29
Without prejudice negotiations	30

Chapter 3
The Regulation of Employment in Schools — **31**

Introduction	31
Prohibition on the doing of specified work in a maintained school or a non-maintained special school	31
Qualified teacher status	32
Requirement (subject to exceptions) to be registered as a teacher	33
Conditions as to health and physical capacity	34
The barring of persons from teaching or otherwise working with children in relation to the provision of education	36
Introduction; Secretary of State's guidance	36
The statutory framework	36
Grounds for giving a direction	37
Procedure for giving a direction	38
Circumstances in which a direction must be given	38
Appeals, revocations and power to vary directions	39
Effect of a barring direction under section 142	41
Information to be given when an employee is dismissed or might have been dismissed from employment at a school	43
The General Teaching Councils	45
Introduction	45
Advice	45

Register of teachers	46
The GTCS' disciplinary powers in relation to teachers	48
Supply of information relating to teachers	52
Induction period to be served satisfactorily by a school teacher	53
Length of induction period	54
Supervision and training during the induction period	56
Completion of an induction period	56
Effect of failure satisfactorily to complete induction period	57
Charges for independent schools and sixth form colleges	58
Secretary of State's and National Assembly's Guidance	58
Qualification to be a head teacher	59

Chapter 4
Recruitment and Staffing of Schools   **61**

Introduction	61
The need for caution in relation to recruitment	61
Criminal Records Bureau and other checks	62
Obligation to keep a register of checks made	63
The legal issues which can arise when recruiting staff	65
Statement of terms and conditions	67
Rehabilitation of Offenders Act 1974	68
Pay and conditions	68
Introduction	68
To which teachers do the pay and conditions documents apply?	69
The school teachers' pay and conditions documents	70
Issues concerning the application of the school teachers' pay and conditions documents	71
Reviews of determinations concerning performance thresholds, advanced skills teacher standards, the excellent teacher standards and the fast track teacher standards	71
Is temporary safeguarding of pay lawful?	73
Issues relating to the Burgundy Book	74
Dorling v Sheffield City Council	74
Is an employee entitled to the full amount of sick pay under the Burgundy Book before he is dismissed because of the incapacity?	75
The required notice period	75
Appointment of a member of the staff of a maintained school	75
Introduction and overview	75
The staffing situation in a maintained school in England with a delegated budget	77
Local Education Authority concerns about the head teacher	77
Conduct, discipline and capability of staff	77
Appointment of staff	77
Appointment of staff in a community, voluntary controlled, community special or maintained nursery school where there is a delegated budget	78

Appointment of staff in a foundation, voluntary aided or foundation special school	81
Collaborating governing bodies	82
Delegation of powers	83
The staffing situation in a maintained school in Wales with a delegated budget	83
Significant additional powers and duties	84
Sufficiency of staff	84
Independent investigation of child protection matter	84
Acting head teachers and deputy head teachers	84
Selection panels	84
Requirement to advertise post of head teacher or deputy head teacher	85
Right to give advice in relation to appointments	85
The framework of the regulations relating to the staffing of maintained schools in Wales	86
Requirement to review staffing structure	86
Staffing for non-school activities	87
School teacher appraisal	87
Teachers, religious education and religious opinions	88
Protection of staff in certain maintained schools regarding religious opinions, and permitted positive discrimination in voluntary aided and foundation schools with a religious character	89
Discrimination in certain independent schools in favour of persons whose religious opinions are in accordance with the tenets of a particular religion or religious denomination	91

Chapter 5
Employment Rights and Duties — 93

Permanent or temporary employees?	93
The obligation to give notice	93
The obligation to comply with the contract of employment	94
Full-time or part-time employees?	94
Implied terms in the contract of employment	95
Trust and confidence	95
Good faith	95
Safe place and system of work	96
Grievances	96
Hours	96
Annualised hours	96
Maximum hours	97
Pension arrangements	97
Probationers	97
Contractual disciplinary procedures	97
Time off for public duties	100
Time off for trade union duties and activities	101
Employer's common law obligations after the contract has ended	101
Health and safety law	102

The Working Time Regulations 1998	102
Pay and other benefits	103
The right to be paid	103
National minimum wage	103
Deductions	104
Statutory sick pay	105
Right to be suspended with pay on medical grounds	105
Maternity pay	105
Statutory paternity pay	106
Statutory adoption pay	107
Promotions and other contractual variations	107
Pensions	108
Maternity rights	109
Time off for ante-natal care	109
Suspension with pay or suitable alternative work	109
Right to maternity leave	109
Dismissal on maternity grounds	111
Parental leave	111
Paternity and adoption leave	112
Paternity leave	112
Adoption leave	113
Time off for dependants	113
Protection from detriment	115
Employees' obligations	115
Express terms of a teacher's contract of employment	115
Implied obligations of teachers	117
Implied obligations of all employees	118

Chapter 6
Discrimination and Human Rights — 121

Introduction	121
The manner in which discrimination law protects employees	122
The relationship between national and international prohibitions on discrimination	122
Introduction	122
Human rights	122
Direct effect of European Community law	124
Indirect effect of European Community Law	125
Direct and indirect discrimination	126
Direct discrimination	126
Indirect discrimination	126
Proving direct discrimination	127
Introduction	127
Burden of proof directive	127
Employer's intention	132
Is unreasonable behaviour always discrimination?	132
Approach to be taken by employment tribunals	134
Harassment	135

Victimisation	135
Current prohibitions of European Community law	137
UK legislation concerning discrimination in employment	137
The legislation: an overview	137
The Sex Discrimination Act 1975	138
Direct discrimination	138
What is 'less favourable treatment'?	138
How should the comparison be made?	139
Handling complaints appropriately	139
Discrimination on the ground of pregnancy	140
Victimisation	144
Indirect discrimination	144
Definition of 'indirect discrimination'	144
Discrimination on the ground of marital status or civil partnership	147
The application of the definition of discrimination to employment	147
Harassment including sexual harassment	148
Agency workers and certain self-employed workers	149
Genuine occupational qualifications	149
Liability of employer for employees and agents; liability of secondary parties	149
Time limit for claiming compensation for discrimination contrary to the Sex Discrimination Act 1975	151
Compensation	154
Right to request flexible working	155
Discrimination against part-time workers	157
Discrimination against fixed-term workers	158
Racial discrimination	159
Discrimination on grounds of religion or belief	160
Discrimination on the ground of sexual orientation	160
Discrimination on the ground of age	160
Introduction	160
Salient features of the age discrimination regulations	161
Retirements	162
Procedure to follow in relation to retirement	162
Unfair dismissal on retirement	164
Fairness of a dismissal for retirement	165
Disability discrimination	166
Introduction	166
Definition of 'disability'	167
Long-term effects	167
Severe disfigurement	168
Normal day-to-day activities	168
Progressive conditions	169
Effect of medical treatment	169
Past disabilities	169

Discrimination in relation to employment	169
Deciding whether an employer has treated an employee less favourably for a reason related to the employee's disability	170
The duty to make reasonable adjustments	171
Code of practice	173
Equal pay	173
Introduction	173
Equal Pay Act 1970	173
Equal pay for equal work	174
Establishments with which comparisons can be made	174
Genuine material factor: justification generally	175
Remedies and time limit for claims	176
Human rights	176
Relevant Convention rights	176
Application by the European Court of Human Rights of Convention rights	178
Article 8: right to respect for private and family life	178
Article 9: right to freedom of thought, conscience and religion	178
Article 10: freedom of expression	179

Chapter 7
Redundancy **181**

Introduction	181
Definition of redundancy	181
Requirement for continuous employment	182
Losing the right to a redundancy payment	183
Calculation of a redundancy payment	184
Method of calculation	184
Calculation of redundancy pay	184
Time off to look for alternative work or undergo training	185
Unfair dismissal	186
Right to claim unfair dismissal	186
Substantive fairness	186
Selection for redundancy	186
Method of selection	186
Reasonable efforts to redeploy	187
Consultation	187
The application of the statutory dismissal and discipline procedure to redundancies	188
Automatically unfair selection	189

Chapter 8
Discipline and Dismissal **191**

Unfair dismissal	191
Introduction	191
Conditions for claiming unfair dismissal	192
Employee or self-employed?	192

Continuity of service	193
Illegality	195
Waiver of right to claim unfair dismissal	195
Was the employee dismissed?	197
Termination of the contract	197
Ending of a limited-term contract	197
'Constructive' dismissal	198
Changing of terms of employment	199
Mutually agreed termination or resignation	200
Frustration	201
When is a contract ended by frustration?	201
Imprisonment	201
Long-term illness	202
Alternative employment in a redundancy situation	203
Time limit for claiming unfair dismissal	204
Dismissals arising from a strike or other industrial action	204
Employer's burden of proof	205
Automatically unfair dismissal	205
Potentially fair reasons for dismissal	207
Was the dismissal reasonable?	208
Substantive fairness in capability dismissals	209
Proving incapability and offering an opportunity to improve	209
The competence of managers	210
Employees on probation	211
Incapability through ill-health	211
Dismissals of head teachers for incapability	212
Recognising poor performance	212
Tackling the problem	212
Substantive fairness in conduct dismissals	213
Adequate investigation	213
Warnings	214
Appeals	214
Relevance of criminal conduct	214
Redeployment	216
Was conduct misconduct?	217
Absence for religious worship	219
Refusal to attend a disciplinary interview	221
Substantive fairness: statutory bar	221
Substantive fairness: some other substantial reason	223
Sound, good business reason	223
Following a fair procedure	225
Personality clash	225
Procedural fairness	226
Relevance of contractual or statutory procedure	226
Witnesses in disciplinary hearings	226
Separating the roles of 'prosecutor' and 'judge'	227
Procedure to follow in a dismissal hearing	228
The opportunity to appeal	228

Time of determination of fairness of dismissal	228
Procedurally flawed dismissals may yet be fair	229
Remedies for unfair dismissal	229
The remedies available	229
Reinstatement or re-engagement	229
Orders for reinstatement	229
Orders for re-engagement	230
Circumstances in which orders may be made	230
Compensation	233
Normal awards	233
Additional awards	234
Maximum amount	235
Damages for breach of contract	235
Compensation for failure to give pay in lieu of notice	235
Discipline and dismissal in maintained schools	236
Employment powers and responsibilities where a maintained school has a delegated budget	236
Report by local education authority on performance of head teacher	237
Suspension of staff	237
Dismissal of staff	238
Delegation of the power to dismiss	238
Involvement of staff governors in decisions	239
Further procedural requirements	240
Employment tribunal proceedings where there is a delegated budget	245
Payments in respect of any member of staff of a maintained school with a delegated budget	246
Dismissals and resignations	246
Responsibility for payments in respect of claims where there is no dismissal or prior agreement to resign	247
Premature retirements	247
Problematic issues	248

Chapter 9
Staff Representation — **249**

Collective agreements	249
Right to time off for union duties and activities	249
Right not to be discriminated against in respect of trade union membership or activities	250
Strikes and other industrial action	251
Collective consultation	252
Definition of collective consultation	252
What does consultation involve?	253
Redundancy consultation	253
Consultation in relation to a TUPE transfer	254
Health and safety consultation directly with representatives or staff	255

Chapter 10
Transfers of Undertakings 257
Application of the Transfer of Undertakings (Protection of
 Employment) Regulations 2006 257
The effects of TUPE 258

Index 261

TABLE OF ABBREVIATIONS

a s 1 statement	a statement made under s 1 of the Employment Rights Act 1996
an LEA	a local education authority
Art	Article
CJCSA 2000	Criminal Justice and Court Services Act 2000
Community law	European Community law
CRB	Criminal Records Bureau
DDA 1995	Disability Discrimination Act 1995
DDR 2004	Employment Act 2002 (Dispute Resolution) Regulations 2004, SI 2004/752
EA 2002	Education Act 2002
EAT	Employment Appeal Tribunal
ECHR	European Court of Human Rights
ECJ	European Court of Justice
English Induction Regulations	Education (Induction Arrangements for School Teachers) (Consolidation) (England) Regulations 2001, SI 2001/2897, as amended
EPA 1970	Equal Pay Act 1970
ERA 1996	Employment Rights Act 1996
GMC	General Medical Council
GTCE	General Teaching Council for England
GTCW	General Teaching Council for Wales
HIV	human immunodeficiency virus
HRA 1998	Human Rights Act 1998
ICE Regulations 2004	Information and Consultation of Employees Regulations 2004, SI 2004/3426
LEA	local education authority
para	paragraph
paras	paragraphs
reg	regulation
regs	regulations
RRA 1976	Race Relations Act 1976
s	section
Sch	schedule
SDA 1975	Sex Discrimination Act 1975
SMP	Statutory Maternity Pay

ss	sections
SSAT	Social Security Appeals Tribunal
SSFA 1998	School Standards and Framework Act 1998
STPCA 1991	School Teachers' Pay and Conditions Act 1991
STPCD 2006	School Teachers' Pay and Conditions Document 2006
the Convention	the European Convention on Human Rights
the GTCs	the General Teaching Council for England and the General Teaching Council for Wales
THEA	Teaching and Higher Education Act 1998
TPCA 1987	Teachers' Pay and Conditions Act 1987
TULRA 1992	Trade Union and Labour Relations (Consolidation) Act 1992
TUPE	Transfer of Undertakings Regulations 2006, SI 2006/246
Welsh Induction Regulations	Education (Induction Arrangements for School Teachers) (Wales) Regulations 2005, SI 2005/1818 (W 146)

GLOSSARY

Two terms used in the text deserve explanation here.

First, except where the context indicates otherwise, the word 'he' includes 'she', the word 'his' includes 'hers', and the word 'him' includes 'her'. It is to be noted that Parliament adopts the same approach in statutory material.

Secondly, the term 'headteacher' is only rarely used in this book. This is because the term used in the applicable statutory provisions is 'head teacher'. Even though the term commonly used in the sector is 'headteacher', for the sake of consistency with the statutory provisions, the term usually used in the text to denote the head of a school is 'head teacher'.

It may also be helpful to state here that industrial tribunals and employment tribunals are the same tribunals under different names. Before the enactment of the Employment Rights (Dispute Resolution) Act 1998, the term 'industrial tribunal' was used. That Act renamed these tribunals 'employment tribunals'.

TABLE OF STATUTES

References are to paragraph numbers.

Civil Partnership Act 2004	6.63
Criminal Justice and Court Services Act 2000	3.19, 4.4, 4.18
s 28	3.25
s 30	3.19
s 35	3.27
s 35(1)	3.26
s 35(2)	3.25, 4.4
s 35(3)	3.26
s 35(4)	3.25
s 35(6)	3.26
s 36	3.27
s 36(1)	3.25
s 36(6)	3.28
s 36(13)(b)	3.28
s 42(1)	3.27, 3.28
Disability Discrimination Act 1995	1.8, 1.9, 2.11, 2.23, 3.9, 3.12, 6.42, 8.30, 8.56
s 1	6.127
s 2	6.137
s 3	6.126, 6.131
s 3(3)	6.131
s 3A	6.138
s 3A(6)	6.143
s 3B	6.139
s 4	6.139
s 4A	6.144
s 4A(3)	6.144
s 18B	6.145, 6.146
s 18D(2)	6.145
s 53A(8A)	6.149
s 55	6.124
s 56	2.11, 6.124
s 57	6.124
s 58	6.124
s 68(1)	6.124
Sch 1	6.127
para 2	6.129, 6.130
para 3	6.132
para 4	6.133
para 6(1), (2)	6.136
para 6A	6.135
para 8	6.134
Education Act 1996	1.4, 3.25, 3.61, 8.134
s 4	3.15
s 470	3.25
s 471	3.25

Education Act 1996—*continued*	
s 512A	8.134
s 512A(1)	4.54
s 512A(6)	4.54
s 579(1)	3.15, 3.61
Education Act 2002	1.12, 1.14, 3.3, 4.6, 5.73, 8.47, 8.79, 8.138, 8.148, 8.149, 8.151, 8.153
s 19	4.79
s 27	4.76, 8.151
s 27(1)	4.74
s 27(2)(d)	4.75
s 28	4.75
s 35	4.38
s 35(2)	4.38
s 35(7)	4.38
s 35(8)	8.124
s 36	4.38
s 36(2)	4.38, 4.57
s 36(4)	4.38
s 36(7)	4.38
s 36(8)	8.124
s 37	8.152
s 37(1)	8.148, 8.149
s 37(2)	8.148, 8.149
s 37(3)	8.148
s 37(4)	8.153
s 37(5)	8.148, 8.150
s 37(6)	8.150
s 37(7)	8.151
ss 119–121	4.22
ss 119–130	4.19
s 122	4.22, 4.23, 4.24, 4.25, 5.73
s 122(2)	4.20, 4.21
s 122(2)(a)	4.23
s 122(2)(b)	4.23
s 122(2)(c)	4.24
s 122(3)	4.20
s 122(3)–(5)	4.20
s 122(4)	4.20
s 122(5)	4.20
s 127	4.25
s 127(2)	4.25
s 128(2)	4.20, 4.21
s 128(3)	4.21
s 128(4)	4.21
s 128(5)(a)	4.21
s 128(6)	4.21
s 131	3.57, 4.77
s 132	3.37
s 133(1)	4.20

Education Act 2002—*continued*		Employment Rights Act 1996	1.9, 1.23, 1.29,
s 133(6)	3.3		3.64, 4.13, 6.106, 6.115, 8.13, 9.15
s 135	3.63	Pt 4A	2.12
s 140	3.15	s 1	4.13, 4.14, 4.15, 4.17
s 140(3)	3.15	s 4	4.14
s 141(5)	3.9	s 7A	4.14
s 142	1.14, 3.15, 3.17, 3.18, 3.19, 3.20,	s 7B	4.14
	3.22, 3.23, 3.24, 3.25, 3.29, 3.31,	s 11	4.16
	3.32, 3.33, 3.35, 3.48, 4.4, 4.6, 8.79	s 13	5.32, 5.35, 8.122
ss 142–144	1.14	s 14(1)	5.33
s 142(1)	3.15, 3.16, 3.17, 3.25, 8.47, 8.138	s 14(5)	5.33
s 142(1)(a)	3.18, 3.19, 3.37	s 23	4.27, 4.29, 4.30, 5.32
s 142(2)	3.15	s 25(4)	5.34
s 142(3)	3.15	s 43A	2.12, 8.113
s 142(4)	3.16	s 43B	8.40
s 142(5)	3.17	s 50	5.22, 5.23
s 142(8)	3.25, 4.4	s 52	7.15
s 142(9)	3.15, 3.29	s 57A	5.69, 5.70, 5.71
s 165	3.25	s 57A(1)	5.66
s 166	3.25	s 57A(2)	5.67
s 210	4.20	s 57A(3)	5.68
s 210(5)(c)	4.21	s 57B	5.69
s 212(2)	3.15	s 64	5.37
s 212(2)–(4)	3.15, 3.63	s 65	5.37
s 212(2), (3)	8.136	ss 66–68	5.41
s 212(3)(f)	3.15	ss 80F–80G	6.87
s 375(2)	4.80	s 80F(1)	6.87
Sch 2	4.38	s 80I	6.90
Education Act 2005	3.53	s 86	4.36, 5.2, 8.10
s 37(2)	3.53	s 95(1)	8.16
Education and Inspections Act 2006		s 95(1)(a)	2.38, 8.24
s 162	1.4	s 95(1)(b)	8.18, 8.84
Education Reform Act 1988	1.4	s 97	8.32
Employment Act 2002	1.25, 1.26, 2.1, 4.17,	s 97(2)	8.10
	5.62, 6.78, 7.27, 8.38, 8.95	s 98	8.79
s 31	2.32	s 98(1)	8.37
s 31(2)	2.32, 2.33, 2.45	s 98(1)(b)	8.43
s 31(3)	2.35	s 98(2)	8.43
s 31(4)	2.32, 2.34, 2.35, 2.45	s 98(2)(ba)	6.116
s 32(1)	2.29	s 98(4)	8.50, 8.72, 8.74, 8.79, 8.83, 8.85,
s 32(3)	2.31		8.91
s 32(4)	2.30	s 98(4)(a)	8.95
s 38	4.17	s 98A(1)	2.44
s 38(5)	4.17	s 98A(2)	2.48, 8.95
s 227	4.17	s 98B	8.41
Sch 2		s 98ZA	6.117
para 3	2.24	s 98ZB(1)	6.117
para 5	2.24	s 98ZB(3)	6.117
para 7	2.25	s 98ZC	6.118
para 7(1)	2.25	s 98ZD(1), (2)	6.119
para 7(3)	2.25	s 98ZD(3), (4)	6.119
para 7(4)	2.25	s 98ZE(1)	6.120
para 8	2.25	s 98ZE(1), (4)	6.119
Pt 2	2.7, 2.9, 2.29	s 98ZE(5), (6)	6.119
Pt 3	2.8	s 98ZF	6.121
Sch 3	2.5, 2.32	s 98ZG	6.122
Sch 4	2.5	s 99	5.58
Employment Relations Act 1999	1.7, 2.22,	s 100	8.113
	8.4	s 100(1)	8.39
s 10	2.22	s 100(1)(c)	8.38
s 10(4)	2.22	s 101A	8.41
s 23	1.7, 8.4	s 102	8.41
		s 103	8.39
		s 103A	8.40, 8.113

Employment Rights Act 1996—*continued*	
s 104(1)	8.39
s 104(4)	8.39
s 104A	8.41
s 104B	8.41
s 104C	8.41
s 105	7.28
s 105(1)(b)	7.28
s 105(3)	8.113
s 108(3)	8.42
s 108(3)(h)	7.28
s 109	6.116
s 114(1)	8.98
s 114(3)	8.98
s 114(4)	8.99
s 115(1)	8.101
s 116	8.102
s 116(1)	8.102
s 116(3)	8.103
s 116(4)	8.104
s 116(5)	8.105
s 116(6)	8.105
s 117(3)	8.118
s 119	2.44, 6.123
s 120(1A)	2.44
s 121	8.31, 8.112
s 122(4)	8.112
s 124(1A)	8.113
s 128	2.43
s 138	7.8, 7.9
s 139	7.2, 9.14
s 141	7.8
s 145	7.6
s 155	7.6
s 162	7.10
s 203	1.29, 8.12, 8.14, 8.15
s 203(3A)(d)	8.12
s 212	8.7
s 212(3)(b)	8.8
s 214(2)	7.6
ss 220–228	9.21
s 227	2.44, 6.89, 6.114, 7.11, 9.15, 9.21
s 227(1)	8.112
s 227(1)(za)	6.90
Sch 2	
para 15	2.12
Employment Rights Act 2002	
s 4	4.17
Employment Tribunals Act 1996	2.29, 8.121
s 3(2)	2.29
s 3(3)	8.121
Enterprise Act 2002	
s 35(7)	4.39
s 36(7)	4.39
s 144	3.20
Equal Pay Act 1970	2.11, 2.23, 6.5, 6.42, 6.56, 6.150, 6.154, 8.147
s 1	6.154
s 1(2)(a)	6.151
s 1(2)(b)	6.151
s 1(2)(c)	6.151
s 1(3)	6.154
s 2(5)	6.156
s 2ZA	6.156

Equal Pay Act 1970—*continued*	
s 2ZB	6.156
s 7B	2.11
s 8	6.65
s 74	2.11
Finance Act 1998	
s 142(7)	8.136
Health and Safety at Work etc Act 1974	1.10, 5.26, 5.51
s 2	5.26
s 3	5.26
s 16	5.51
Human Rights Act 1998	6.7, 6.158
s 3	6.7
s 6	6.8
Interpretation Act 1978	3.25, 3.26, 4.73
s 6(a)	4.73
s 11	8.136
s 17(2)(a)	3.25
Sch 1	6.63
Magistrates' Courts Act 1980	3.26
s 32	3.26
National Minimum Wage Act 1998	5.31
Pensions Act 1995	
ss 62–65	6.56
Police Act 1997	4.5, 4.7
Pt V	4.47
s 113B(6)	4.7
s 113B(6)(b)	4.7
Protection of Children Act 1999	3.16, 3.20
s 1	3.16, 3.19, 3.22, 3.25
s 9	3.20
Race Relations Act 1968	
s 12	6.76
Race Relations Act 1976	1.8, 1.9, 2.11, 2.23, 6.5, 6.21, 6.42, 6.100, 6.124
s 1(1A)	6.101
s 2	6.37
s 3	6.101, 6.102
s 4(2)(b)	6.34
s 33(1)	6.76
s 65	2.11
Rehabilitation of Offenders Act 1974	4.18
School Standards and Framework Act 1998	1.4, 3.63
s 20	3.63
s 21	4.79
s 22	4.76
s 50(3)	8.125
s 50(3)(b)	4.76
s 51A	4.76
s 51A(1)	4.76
s 51A(2)	4.76

School Standards and Framework Act
1998—*continued*

s 58	4.38
ss 58–60	6.103
s 58(1)	4.78, 4.82
s 58(1)(b)	4.80
s 58(2)	4.78
s 58(3)	4.78
s 58(4)	4.78
s 58(5)	4.79
s 58(6)	4.79
s 58(7)	4.80
s 58(8)	4.80
s 58(9)	4.78
s 59	4.81
s 59(2)	4.81, 4.82
s 59(3)	4.81
s 59(4)	4.81
s 60	4.82
s 60(2)	4.82
s 60(3)	4.82
s 60(4)	4.82
s 60(5)	4.82, 4.83
s 60(6)	4.83
s 69(3)	4.85
s 69(4)	4.78, 4.82, 4.83
s 124A	4.85, 6.103
s 124A(2)	4.84
s 124B	4.85
s 124B(2)	4.84
s 142(1)	4.79
s 142(8)	8.136
Sch 16	4.38, 4.40
Sch 17	4.38, 4.40
Sch 19	
para 3(3)	4.79

School Teachers' Pay and Conditions
Act 1991   4.19

s 1	4.22

Sex Discrimination Act 1975   1.8, 1.9, 2.11, 2.23, 6.1, 6.3, 6.5, 6.26, 6.36, 6.42, 6.44, 6.45, 6.46, 6.47, 6.57, 6.60, 6.65, 6.66, 6.78, 6.79, 6.95, 6.100, 6.124

s 1	6.58
s 1(1)(a)	6.45
s 1(1)(b)	6.58, 6.59, 6.61
s 1(2)(b)	6.58, 6.60, 6.61
s 2A	6.45
s 2A(3)	6.45
s 3	6.63, 6.64
s 3A	6.51
s 3A(3)(b)	5.58, 6.55
s 4	6.56
s 4A	6.67
s 4A(1)(a)	6.67
s 4A(1)(b)	6.67
s 4A(1)(c)	6.67
s 4A(2)	6.68
s 4A(3), (4), (6)	6.70
s 4A(5), (6)	6.69
s 5(3)	6.47
s 6	6.82
s 6(1)	6.65

Sex Discrimination Act 1975—*continued*

s 6(2)	6.66
s 6(2A)	6.67
s 7	6.72
s 7A	6.72
s 7B	6.72
s 9	6.71
s 9(3)	6.72
s 20A	6.57
s 20A(3)	6.57
s 20A(4)	6.57
s 41	6.26
s 41(1)	6.73
s 41(2)	6.74
s 41(3)	6.73
s 42	6.76
s 42(1)	6.75, 6.76, 6.77
s 42(2)	6.73, 6.74
s 63	6.82
s 63A(2)	6.26, 6.28, 6.29
s 66(4)	6.84
s 74	6.50
s 74(2), (2A)	6.50
s 76	6.78, 6.79, 6.82
s 76(1)	6.82
s 76(5)	6.78
s 76(6)	6.79, 6.81, 6.82
s 82(1)	6.71

Sexual Offences Act 2003   3.18
s 123	3.18

Social Security Contributions and
Benefits Act 1992   5.36, 5.38, 5.39, 5.40, 5.42, 5.44

s 35	5.40
s 155(1)	5.36
s 164	5.38
s 164(2)	5.38
s 164(4)	5.39
s 165	5.38
s 165(1)	5.38
s 171ZB(4)	5.42
s 171ZL(2)(b)	5.44
s 171ZL(4)(a)	5.44
s 171ZL(4)(b)	5.44
s 171ZN(2)	5.44
s 271ZN(2)	5.44

Tax Credits Act 2002   8.41
s 25	8.41

Teaching and Higher Education Act
1998   3.6, 3.34, 8.138

Pt I	
Ch 1	3.49
s 2	3.35
s 2(2)	3.35
s 2(3)	3.35
s 2(6)	3.35
s 2(7)	3.35
s 3	3.6, 3.36, 3.37, 3.39, 3.65
s 3(3)	3.37
s 3(3B)	3.37
s 3(4)	3.37
s 4	3.36
s 4(2)(g)	3.38

Table of Statutes

Teaching and Higher Education Act 1998—*continued*	
s 4(4)	3.38
s 4A	3.39
s 4A(1)	3.39
s 4A(3)	3.39
s 4A(4)	3.39
s 5(1)	3.47
s 8(1)	3.35
s 9	3.35
s 12	3.38
s 14	3.49
s 19	3.37, 3.50, 3.54, 3.59
s 19(7)	3.57
s 19(10)(b)	3.50

Trade Union and Labour Relations (Consolidation) Act 1992	1.9, 1.23, 8.13, 8.34, 9.1
s 21	8.35
s 137	9.8
s 140	9.8
s 146	9.5
s 152	9.6, 9.7
s 154	9.6
s 156	9.6
s 168	9.2
s 179	9.1

Trade Union and Labour Relations (Consolidation) Act 1992—*continued*	
s 188	2.38, 9.12, 9.14
s 190	9.15
s 190(5)	9.15
s 193	9.16
s 195	9.14
s 212A	8.13
s 219	9.9
ss 226–245	9.9
s 238A(2)	8.36
s 238A(3)	8.34
s 238A(4)	8.34
s 238A(5)	8.34
s 238A(6)	8.35
s 238A(7)	8.35
s 238A(7A)–(7D)	8.34
s 238A(8)	8.35
s 239(1)	8.36
s 239(2)	8.36
s 244	9.9, 9.10
s 298	9.14

Unfair Contract Terms Act 1977	5.14
Work and Family Act 2006	5.62

TABLE OF STATUTORY INSTRUMENTS

References are to paragraph numbers.

Civil Procedure Rules 1998, SI 1998/3132	1.30
Control of Lead at Work Regulations 2002, SI 2002/2676	
reg 10	5.37
Control of Substances Hazardous to Health Regulations 2002, SI 2002/2676	5.37
reg 11	5.37
Disability Discrimination (Meaning of Disability) Regulations 1996, SI 1996/1455	
reg 3	6.127
reg 4(1)	6.127
reg 4(2)	6.128
reg 5	6.132
Education (Head Teachers' Qualifications) (England) Regulations 2003, SI 2003/3111	1.12, 3.63
reg 2(2)	3.64
reg 3	3.64
reg 4(2)	3.63
reg 5(1)	3.64
reg 5(2)	3.64
Education (Health Standards) (England) Regulations 2003, SI 2003/3139	1.12, 3.9, 4.34
reg 6(1)	3.9
reg 6(2)	3.9
reg 6(3)	3.9
reg 7(1)(b)	3.11
reg 7(1)(c)	3.12
reg 7(2)	3.12
reg 7(3)	3.12
Education (Health Standards) (Wales) Regulations 2004, SI 2004/2733	1.12, 3.9
reg 7(1)(d)	3.12
Education (Independent School Standards) (England) (Amendment) Regulations 2007, SI 2007/1087	4.5
Education (Independent School Standards) (England) Regulations 2003, SI 2003/1910	1.14, 4.5
Education (Induction Arrangements for School Teachers) (Consolidation) (England) Regulations 2001, SI 2001/2897	1.12, 3.50, 3.51, 8.55, 8.81
reg 3(1)	3.51
reg 6	3.59
reg 7(2)(a)	3.53
reg 7(2)(b)	3.53
reg 8(2)(a)	3.53
reg 8(2)(b)	3.53
reg 9(1)	3.54
reg 9(2)	3.54
reg 9(3)	3.54
reg 10(1)	3.54
reg 10(3)	3.54
reg 11	3.55
reg 11(1)	3.55
reg 11(2)	3.55
reg 11(3)	3.55
reg 12	3.55
reg 13	3.56
reg 13(1)	3.56
reg 13(2)	3.56, 5.19, 8.81
reg 14	3.58
reg 15	3.58
reg 16	3.58
reg 16(1)	3.58
reg 16(2)(a)	3.58
reg 16(4)	3.58
reg 18(2)	3.59
reg 18(3)	3.60
reg 18(4)	3.60
reg 18(5)	3.60
reg 18A	3.55
reg 19	3.59, 3.60
reg 21	3.61
reg 22	3.52
Sch 2	3.51
Education (Induction Arrangements for School Teachers) (Wales) Regulations 2005, SI 2005/1818	1.12, 3.50, 5.19, 8.55, 8.138
reg 3(1)	3.54, 3.59
reg 5	3.54
reg 7(4)	3.54

Education (Induction Arrangements for
    School Teachers) (Wales) Regulations
    2005, SI 2005/1818—*continued*
reg 7(5)	3.58
reg 8(3)	3.54
reg 10(1)	3.55
reg 12	3.56
reg 13	3.58
reg 14(1)	3.58
reg 14(2)(a)	3.58
reg 14(4)	3.58
reg 16(2)	3.59
reg 16(3)	3.60
reg 16(4)	3.60
reg 16(5)	3.60
reg 17	3.59, 3.60
reg 19	3.61
reg 20	3.52

Education (Modification of
    Enactments Relating to
    Employment) (England) Order
    2003, SI 2003/1964   1.12, 6.152, 8.2,
        8.147, 8.154, 9.12, 9.14

Education (Modification of
    Enactments Relating to
    Employment) (Wales) Order
    2006, SI 2006/1073   1.12, 6.152, 8.2,
        8.147, 9.12, 9.14

Education (Non-Maintained Special
    Schools) (England)
    (Amendment) Regulations
    2007, SI 2007/1088   4.5

Education (Non-Maintained Special
    Schools) (England) Regulations
    1999, SI 1999/2257   4.5

Education (Prohibition from Teaching
    or Working with Children)
    (Amendment) Regulations
    2007, SI 2007/195   3.18, 3.19

Education (Prohibition from Teaching
    or Working with Children)
    Regulations 2003, SI 2003/1184   1.12,
        3.17, 3.18, 3.20, 3.21, 3.31, 3.48
reg 1(4)	3.29
reg 2	3.29
reg 4	3.29
reg 6(2)	3.17
reg 8(1)	3.19
reg 9(1)	3.22
reg 9(2)	3.22
reg 9(3)	3.22
reg 9(4)	3.22
reg 11(3)	3.21
reg 11(4)	3.21
reg 12	3.23
reg 12(1)	3.23
reg 12(2)	3.23, 3.24
reg 12(3)	3.23
reg 13(1)	3.20, 3.24
reg 13(2)	3.24
Sch 2	
para 2	3.19

Education (Provision of Information
    by Independent Schools)
    (England) Regulations 2003,
SI 2003/1934	3.29
reg 8	3.29

Education (Restriction of
    Employment) (Amendment)
    Regulations 2001, SI 2001/1269   3.48

Education (Restriction of
    Employment) Regulations 2000,
SI 2000/2419	3.48
reg 5A	3.48

Education (Review of Staffing
    Structure) (England)
    Regulations 2005, SI 2005/1032   1.12,
                                        4.72
reg 2(1)	4.72
reg 3(5)	4.72
reg 3(6)(a)	4.72
reg 3(6)(b)	4.72
reg 3(7)	4.72

Education (Review of Staffing
    Structure) (Wales) Regulations
    2005, SI 2005/1910   1.12, 4.72
reg 2(1)	4.72
reg 3(5)	4.72
reg 3(6)(a)	4.72
reg 3(6)(b)	4.72
reg 3(7)	4.72

Education (School Teacher Appraisal)
    (England) Regulations 2001,
    SI 2001/2855   4.77, 8.53

Education (School Teacher Appraisal)
    (Wales) Regulations 2002,
    SI 2002/1394   8.53

Education (School Teacher
    Performance Management)
    (England) Regulations 2006,
    SI 2006/2661   1.12, 3.57, 4.77, 8.53

Education (School Teachers' Pay and
    Conditions) (No. 2) Order 2006,
    SI 2006/2133   1.12, 4.26

Education (School Teachers'
    Prescribed Qualifications, etc)
    Order 2003, SI 2003/1709   1.12, 4.20

Education (School Teachers'
    Qualifications) (England)
    Regulations 2003, SI 2003/1662   1.12,
                                        3.5
reg 10	3.5
reg 10(1)	3.5
Sch 2	3.5

Education (School Teachers'
    Qualifications) (Wales)
    Regulations 2004, SI 2004/1729   1.12,
                                        3.5
reg 6	3.5
Sch 2	3.5

Education (Specified Work and Registration) (England) Regulations 2003, SI 2003/1663	1.12, 3.3, 3.6, 3.37
Education (Specified Work and Registration) (Wales) Regulations 2004, SI 2004/1744	1.12, 3.3, 3.6
Education (Supply of Information) (Wales) Regulations 2003, SI 2003/542	3.32, 3.48
reg 7	3.48
Education (Teachers' Qualifications and Health Standards) (England) Regulations 1999, SI 1999/2166	4.34
Education (Teachers' Qualifications and Health Standards) (Wales) Regulations 1999, SI 1999/2817	1.12, 3.5, 4.63
Employees (Prevention of Less Favourable Treatment) Regulations 2002, SI 2002/2034	8.84
Employment Act 2002 (Dispute Resolution) Regulations 2004, SI 2004/752	2.1
reg 2(1)	2.5, 2.23, 2.38, 2.40
reg 3(1)	2.38, 2.40
reg 3(2)	2.42
reg 4(1)(a)	2.38
reg 4(1)(b)	2.38
reg 4(1)(e)	2.38
reg 4(1)(f)	2.39
reg 4(1)(h)	2.39
reg 6(1)	2.5
reg 6(3)	2.15
reg 6(5)	2.5
reg 7(1)(a)	2.23
reg 7(1)(b)	2.24
reg 7(2)	2.24
reg 7(3)	2.23
reg 8(1)	2.25
reg 8(2)	2.25
reg 9(1)	2.26
reg 9(2)	2.26
reg 10	2.27
reg 11	2.18
reg 11(1)	2.20, 2.21
reg 11(4)	2.20
reg 12	2.17, 2.18
reg 12(1)	2.18
reg 12(2)	2.18
reg 12(3)	2.20
reg 12(4)	2.18
reg 13	2.18
reg 13(1)	2.22
reg 13(2)	2.22
reg 13(3)	2.22
reg 14	2.11
reg 15(1)(a)	2.37
reg 15(1)(b)	2.36
Employment Appeal Tribunal Rules 1993, SI 1993/2854	1.28
r 34A(1)	1.28
r 34A(2)(a)	1.28
Employment Equality (Age) Regulations 2006, SI 2006/1031	1.8, 2.23, 6.42, 6.116, 6.120, 8.45
reg 3(1)	6.106
reg 3(1)(a)	6.105
reg 3(1)(b)	6.105
reg 3(3)(a)	6.105
reg 30	6.106
reg 32	6.106
reg 32(2)	6.106
reg 33	6.106
Sch 6	6.117, 6.119
para 2	6.121
para 2(1)	6.107
para 2(2)	6.107
para 3	6.109
para 4	6.107, 6.122
para 5(2)	6.108
para 5(4)	6.108
para 5(5)	6.108
para 6	6.110, 6.122
para 7	6.121, 6.122
para 7(1)	6.110
para 7(2)	6.110
para 7(3)	6.110
para 7(4)	6.110
para 7(5)	6.110
para 7(6)	6.111
para 7(7)	6.111
para 8	6.112, 6.122
para 9	6.112
para 9(3), (4)	6.112
para 9(5), (6)	6.112
para 10	6.113
para 11(1)	6.114
para 11(3)–(5)	6.114
para 12(1)	6.114
para 12(3)–(5)	6.114
Employment Equality (Religion or Belief) Regulations 2003, SI 2003/1660	1.8, 2.11, 2.23, 4.78, 4.84, 6.42, 6.102, 6.103, 6.104
reg 2	6.102
reg 33	2.11
reg 39	4.78
Employment Equality (Sex Discrimination) Regulations 2005, SI 2005/2467	6.51
Employment Equality (Sexual Orientation) Regulations 2003, SI 2003/1661	1.8, 2.11, 2.23, 6.42, 6.45, 6.104
Employment Tribunals (Constitution and Rules of Procedure) Regulations 2004, SI 2004/1861	1.27, 2.31
r 38(1)(a)	1.27
r 40(1)	1.27
r 40(2)	1.27

Employment Tribunals (Constitution and Rules of Procedure) Regulations 2004, SI 2004/1861—*continued*	
r 40(4)	1.27
r 41(2)	1.27
Equal Pay (Questions and Replies) Order 2003, SI 2003/722	6.43
Fixed-term Employees (Prevention of Less Favourable Treatment) Regulations 2002, SI 2002/2034	1.9, 6.42
reg 1(2)	6.96
reg 3(5)	6.96
reg 4(1)	6.97
Flexible Working (Eligibility, Complaints and Remedies) Regulations 2002, SI 2002/3236	6.43, 6.87
reg 3	6.87
reg 3A	6.87
reg 3B	6.87
reg 6	6.90
reg 7	6.90
Flexible Working (Procedural Requirements) Regulations 2002, SI 2002/3207	6.43, 6.87
regs 3	6.89
reg 5(b)(ii)	6.90
reg 10(b)(ii)	6.90
reg 14	6.89
reg 15	6.89
General Teaching Council for England (Additional Functions) Order 2000, SI 2000/2175	3.36
General Teaching Council for England (Deduction of Fees) Regulations 2001, SI 2001/3993	3.38
General Teaching Council for England (Disciplinary Functions) Regulations 2001, SI 2001/1268	3.33, 3.41, 3.42, 3.48
reg 2	3.48
reg 7	3.47
reg 29	3.48
reg 29(2)	3.48
General Teaching Council for England (Registration of Teachers) Regulations 2000, SI 2000/2176	3.7, 3.36, 3.37, 3.38, 3.47, 3.49
reg 13	3.47
reg 14(1)	3.47
General Teaching Council for Wales (Additional Functions) Order 2000, SI 2000/1941	3.36
General Teaching Council for Wales (Disciplinary Functions) Regulations 2001, SI 2001/1424	3.33, 3.41, 3.42
reg 7	3.47

General Teaching Council for Wales (Disciplinary Functions) Regulations 2001, SI 2001/1424—*continued*	
reg 13	3.42
reg 18(5)	3.42
reg 24	3.42
reg 26	3.42
reg 26(2)(b)	3.42
General Teaching Council for Wales (Fees) Regulations 2002, SI 2002/326	3.38
General Teaching Council for Wales (Functions) Regulations 2000, SI 2000/1979	3.8, 3.36, 3.37, 3.38, 3.39, 3.47, 3.49
reg 3A	3.8
reg 4C	3.39
reg 13	3.47
reg 14(1)	3.47
Government of Maintained Schools (Wales) Regulations 2005, SI 2005/2914	
reg 50	8.128
reg 55(1)	8.130
reg 55(2)	8.130
reg 55(3)	8.139
reg 55(4)	8.130, 8.139
reg 55(4A)	8.139
reg 63	8.132
Head Teachers' Qualifications and Registration (Wales) Regulations 2005, SI 2005/1227	1.12, 3.65
Health and Safety (Consultation with Employees) Regulations 1996, SI 1996/1513	
reg 4	9.23
Independent School Standards (Wales) Regulations 2003, SI 2003/3234	1.14, 4.5
Independent Schools (Employment of Teachers in Schools with a Religious Character) Regulations 2003, SI 2003/2037	1.8
Independent Schools (Miscellaneous Amendments) (Wales) Regulations 2007, SI 2007/947	4.5
Independent Schools (Provision of Information) (Wales) Regulations 2003, SI 2003/3230	3.32
Industrial Tribunals Extension of Jurisdiction (England and Wales) Order 1994, SI 1994/1623	2.29, 4.28
art 10	8.121
Information and Consultation of Employees Regulations 2004, SI 2004/3426	9.12
reg 20	9.12

Ionising Radiations Regulations 1999,
    SI 1999/3232
    reg 24   5.37

Local Government Pension Scheme
    Regulations 1997, SI 1997/1612   5.49

Maternity and Parental Leave etc and
    the Paternity and Adoption
    Leave (Amendment)
    Regulations 2006, SI 2006/2014   5.53
Maternity and Parental Leave etc
    Regulations 1999, SI 1999/3312   3.55, 5.52
    reg 6(3)   5.52
    reg 7(1)   3.55, 5.52
    reg 7(5)   5.52
    reg 9   5.54
    reg 10   5.54
    reg 11   5.53
    reg 12A   5.55
    reg 13   5.59
    reg 14   5.59
    reg 15   5.59
    reg 17   5.60
    reg 19   5.72
    reg 20   5.54, 5.58
    reg 21   5.56
    Sch 2
        para 1(b)   5.61
        para 6   5.61
        para 7   5.61
        para 8   5.61
        paras 3–5   5.61

National Minimum Wage Regulations
    1999 (Amendment) Regulations
    2006, SI 2006/2001
    reg 11   5.31
National Minimum Wage Regulations
    1999, SI 1999/584   5.31

Occupational Pension Schemes (Equal
    Treatment) Regulations 1995,
    SI 1995/3183   6.42

Part-time Workers (Prevention of Less
    Favourable Treatment)
    Regulations 2000, SI 2000/1551   1.9, 6.42
    reg 1(2)   6.92
    reg 5(1)   6.91
    reg 5(2)   6.91
    reg 5(3)   6.92
    reg 5(4)   6.93
    reg 11   6.95
Paternity and Adoption Leave
    Regulations 2002, SI 2002/2788   5.62
    reg 12   5.64
    reg 13   5.64
    reg 14   5.64

Paternity and Adoption Leave Regulations
    2002, SI 2002/2788—*continued*
    regs 15–30   5.65
    reg 22   5.65
    reg 22(2)   5.65
    reg 28   5.72
Protection of Children and Vulnerable
    Adults and Care Standards
    Tribunal Regulations 2002,
    SI 2002/816   3.20

Redundancy Payments (Continuity of
    Employment in Local
    Government etc) (Modification)
    Order 1999, SI 1999/2277   7.7, 7.8
Rehabilitation of Offenders Act 1974
    (Exceptions) Order 1975,
    SI 1975/1023   4.18

Safety Representatives and Safety
    Committees Regulations 1977,
    SI 1977/500
    reg 9   9.23
School Budget Shares (Prescribed
    Purposes) (England)
    (Amendment) Regulations
    2004, SI 2004/444   4.76
School Budget Shares (Prescribed
    Purposes) (England)
    Regulations 2002, SI 2002/378   4.76
School Finance (England) Regulations
    2006, SI 2006/468   8.152
School Governance (Constitution and
    Procedures) (England)
    (Amendment) Regulations
    2003, SI 2003/1916   8.132
School Governance (Constitution)
    (England) Regulations 2007,
    SI 2007/957   4.79
    reg 8(1)(a)   4.79
    reg 8(1)(b)   4.79
School Governance (Constitution,
    Procedures and New Schools)
    (England) (Amendment)
    Regulations 2004, SI 2004/450   8.132
School Governance (Federations)
    (England) Regulations 2004,
    SI 2004/2042   8.132
School Governance (Federations)
    (England) Regulations 2007,
    SI 2007/960   4.6, 4.46, 4.47, 8.132
    reg 32   4.6, 4.47, 8.135
    Sch 9   8.135
School Governance (Procedures)
    (England) Regulations 2003,
    SI 2003/1377   4.61
    reg 14   8.132
    reg 16   4.61, 8.128

School Staffing (England) (Amendment) (No 2) Regulations 2006, SI 2006/3197	4.5, 4.6, 4.7	School Staffing (England) Regulations 2003, SI 2003/1963—*continued*	
		reg 24	4.59, 8.137
		reg 26	8.135, 8.137
School Staffing (England) Regulations 2003, SI 2003/1963	1.12, 4.5, 4.39, 4.40, 4.41, 4.61, 8.127, 8.154	reg 27	4.59
		reg 28	4.60
		reg 29	4.60
reg 3(3)(a)	4.6	reg 30(1)	4.60
reg 4(3)	8.129	reg 30(2)	4.60
reg 4(4)	8.129	reg 30(3)	4.60
reg 5(a)	4.42, 8.126	reg 32	4.46, 4.60
reg 5(b)	4.42	School Teacher Appraisal (Wales) Regulations 2002, SI 2002/1394	1.12, 3.57
reg 6(1)	4.43, 8.123		
reg 6(2)	8.125, 8.126		
reg 7	8.123	Social Security Benefits Up-rating Order 2007, SI 2007/688	5.43
reg 11	4.5		
reg 11(1)	4.47	Staffing of Maintained Schools (Miscellaneous Amendments) (Wales) Regulations 2007, SI 2007/944	4.5, 4.62
reg 11(1)(c)	4.51		
reg 11(2)	4.46, 4.47		
reg 11(3)	4.47		
reg 11(4)	4.5, 4.6, 4.47	Staffing of Maintained Schools (Wales) Regulations 2006, SI 2006/873	1.12, 4.5, 4.39, 4.41, 4.62, 4.63, 8.127
reg 11(5)	4.47		
reg 11(7)	4.6		
reg 11(8)	4.6		
reg 11(9)	4.6	reg 4(1)	4.63
reg 11(10)	4.6	reg 6(1)(a)	8.126
reg 11(11)	4.7	reg 7(1)	8.123
reg 11(12)	4.7	reg 7(2)	8.123
reg 11(13)	4.6	reg 7(3)	4.64, 8.139
reg 11(14)	4.6	reg 7(4)	4.64, 8.139
reg 12	8.135	reg 7(5)	8.125, 8.126
reg 12(1)	4.48	reg 7(6)	8.124
reg 12(2)	4.48	regs 9–15A	4.71
reg 13(1)	4.49	reg 11(1)	4.65
reg 13(2)	4.49	reg 17	8.123, 8.138
reg 13(3)	4.50	reg 17(1)	8.141
reg 13(3)(a)	4.50	reg 17(2)	8.142
reg 13(3)(b)	4.50	reg 17(3)	8.142
reg 13(3)(c)	4.50	reg 17(4)	8.143
reg 13(4)	4.50	reg 17(5)	8.143
reg 13(5)	4.51	reg 17(6)(a)	8.140
reg 13(6)	4.51	reg 17(11)	8.138
reg 13(7)	4.49	regs 20–27	4.71
reg 14(1)	4.53	reg 21(1)	4.68
reg 14(2)	4.53	reg 21(2)	4.68
reg 14(3)	4.53	reg 23(1)	4.69, 8.145
reg 15(1)	4.55	reg 23(2)	4.69
reg 15(2)	4.55	reg 23(3)	4.69
reg 15(4)	4.56	reg 23(4)	4.69
reg 15(5)	4.56	reg 23(6)	4.69
reg 15(6)	4.56	reg 29	8.138
reg 17	8.123, 8.135	reg 29(3)	8.144
reg 17(2)	8.135	reg 30(1)	8.145
reg 18	8.135	reg 31	8.138
reg 18(1)	4.54	reg 32	8.144
reg 18(2)	4.54, 8.134	regs 33–34	4.71
reg 18(3)	4.54, 8.134	reg 34	4.71
reg 18(4)	4.54, 8.134	Statutory Maternity Pay (General) Regulations 1986, SI 1986/1960	5.38
regs 18A	4.5		
reg 20	4.5		
reg 20(3)	4.58	Statutory Maternity Pay, Social Security (Maternity Allowance) and Social Security	
reg 21	4.58, 8.135, 8.137		
reg 22	4.59		
reg 23	4.59		

Statutory Maternity Pay, Social Security (Maternity Allowance) and Social Security —*continued* (Overlapping Benefits) (Amendment) Regulations 2006, SI 2006/2379	
reg 1(2)	5.38
Statutory Paternity Pay (Adoption) and Statutory Adoption Pay (Adoptions from Overseas) Regulations 2003, SI 2003/1192	5.42
Statutory Paternity Pay and Statutory Adoption Pay (General) Regulations 2002, SI 2002/2822	5.42
reg 21(5)	5.44
Statutory Paternity Pay and Statutory Adoption Pay (Weekly Rates) Regulations 2002, SI 2002/2818	
reg 3	5.44
reg 8	5.43
reg 14	5.43
Statutory Sick Pay (General) Regulations 1982, SI 1982/894	5.36
Teachers' Pensions Regulations 1997, SI 1997/3001	3.9, 5.49
reg 6(2)	3.9
reg 6(3)	3.9
reg 7(1)(b)	3.11
reg 7(2)	3.12
reg 7(3)	3.12

The School Teacher Appraisal (Wales) Regulations 2002, SI 2002/1394	4.77
The Working Time Regulations 1998, SI 1998/1833	4.26
Transfer of Undertakings (Protection of Employment) Regulations 2006, SI 2006/246	1.23, 8.9, 8.147, 9.17, 10.1
reg 2(1)	10.1
reg 3	10.1
reg 4(4)	10.6
reg 4(5)	10.6
reg 13	9.12
reg 13(1)	9.17
reg 13(2)	9.17, 9.18
reg 13(4)	9.19
reg 13(6)	9.17
reg 13(9)	9.20
reg 15(8)(b)	9.22
reg 16(4)	9.21
Unfair Dismissal and Statement of Reasons for Dismissal (Variation of Qualifying Period) Order 1999, SI 1999/1436	8.7
Working Time Regulations 1998, SI 1998/1833	5.27, 8.41
reg 4	5.27
reg 5	5.27
reg 13	5.28
reg 20	5.27

TABLE OF CASES

References are to paragraph numbers.

Abbey National plc v Formoso [1999] IRLR 222, EAT	6.85
Abbotts v Wesson-Glynwed Steels Ltd [1982] IRLR 51, EAT	7.23
Abrahams v Performing Rights Society Ltd [1995] ICR 1028, [1995] IRLR 486, (1995) *The Times*, June 5, CA	5.5
Advocate General for Scotland v Macdonald; *sub nom* Secretary of State for Defence v MacDonald; Macdonald v Ministry of Defence; Pearce v Governing Body of Mayfield Secondary School [2003] UKHL 34, [2003] ICR 937, [2003] IRLR 512, (2003) IDS Brief 737, HL; 2001 SLT 819, 2001 SCLR 795, [2001] IRLR 431, Ct of Sess	6.45
Ahmad v Inner London Education Authority [1978] QB 36, [1977] 3 WLR 396, [1978] 1 All ER 574, CA	4.81, 8.76
Ahmad v UK (1982) 4 EHRR 126, ECommHR	6.163, 8.76
Ahmed v UK (2000) 29 EHRR 1, [1999] IRLR 188, 5 BHRC 111, ECHR	6.166
Alabaster v Barclays Bank plc *sub nom* Alabaster v Barclays Bank plc (formerly Woolwich plc), [2005] EWCA Civ 508, [2005] All ER (D) 02 (May), [2005] ICR 1246, [2005] IRLR 576, (2005) Times, 27 May, 149 Sol Jo LB 579	6.15
Alexander v Bridgen Enterprises Ltd [2006] All ER (D) 224 (Apr), [2006] ICR 1277 [2006] IRLR 422	2.38, 2.46, 7.27, 8.96
Ali v Christian Salvesen Food Services Ltd *sub nom* Salvesen (Christian) Food Services Ltd v Ali [1997] 1 All ER 721, [1997] ICR 25, [1997] IRLR 17, [1996] 41 LS Gaz R 29, 140 Sol Jo LB 231	5.16
Allan v Newcastle-upon-Tyne City Council; Degnan v Redcar and Cleveland Borough Council [2005] All ER (D) 197 (Apr), [2005] ICR 1170, [2005] NLJR 619, [2005] IRLR 504	6.150
Allonby v Accrington and Rossendale College [2001] EWCA Civ 529, [2001] All ER (D) 285 (Mar), [2001] ICR 1189, [2001] CMLR 559	6.22
AM v (1) WC and (2) SPV [1999] ICR 1218, [1999] IRLR 410, EAT	6.73
Amies v Inner London Education Authority [1977] 2 All ER 100, [1977] ICR 308, [1977] 1 CMLR 336, EAT	6.81
Anya v University of Oxford [2001] EWCA Civ 405, [2001] All ER (D) 266 (Mar), [2001] ICR 847, [2001] IRLR 377	6.32
Anyanwu v South Bank Student Union (Commission for Racial Equality, interveners) [2001] UKHL 14, [2001] WLR 638, [2001]All ER (D) 272 (Mar), [2001]All ER 353, [2001] ICR 391, [2001] IRLR 305, [2001] 21 LS Gaz R 39, 151 NJL 501	6.76
Aparau v Iceland Frozen Foods plc [1996] IRLR 119, EAT	5.7
Archibald v Fife Council [2004] UKHL 32, [2004] 4 All ER 303, [2004] IRLR 651,[2004] ICR 954, 82 BMLR 185	6.147
Armstrong v Newcastle Upon Tyne NHS Hospital Trust [2005] EWCA Civ 1608, [2005] All ER (D) 341 (Dec), [2006] IRLR 124	6.22, 6.153
Arnold Clark Automobiles v Stewart (UKEATS/0052/05) (2005) (unreported) 20 December	2.10
Asda Stores Ltd v Thompson [2003] All ER (D) 434 (Nov), [2004] IRLR 598	8.89
Aspden v Webbs Poultry & Meat Group (Holdings) Ltd [1996] IRLR 521	4.35
Azmi v Kirklees Metropolitan Borough Council [2007] All ER (D) 528 (Mar), [2007] ICR 1154, [2007] IRLR 484, (2007) Times, April 17	6.103

Balgobin v Tower Hamlets London Borough Council [1987] ICR 829, [1987] IRLR 401,
 [1987] LS Gaz R 2530   6.73
Bank of Credit and Commerce International SA v Ali [1999] 4 All ER 83, [1999] ICR
 1079, [1999] IRLR 508, [1999] 30 LS Gaz R 28, ChD   5.10
Barber v RJB Mining UK Ltd [1999] ICR 679, [1999] IRLR 308, [1999] 2 CMLR 833,
 QBD   5.17, 5.29
Barratt Construction Ltd v Dalrymple [1984] IRLR 385, EAT   7.23
Bartholomew v London Borough of Hackney [1999] IRLR 246, CA   5.25
BBC v Beckett [1983] IRLR 43, EAT   5.10, 8.63
Beard v Governors of St Joseph's School [1978] ICR 1234, [1979] IRLR 144, (1978) 77
 LGR 278   8.85
Berrisford v Woodard Schools (Midland Division) Ltd [1991] ICR 564, [1991] IRLR 247,
 [1991] TLR 133, EAT   6.52
Biggs v Somerset County Council [1996] ICR 364, [1996] IRLR 203, (1996) 140 SJLB 59,
 (1996) 146 NLJ Rep 174, CA; affirming [1995] ICR 811, [1995] IRLR 452, [1995]
 TLR 413, EAT   6.16
Bilka-Kaufhaus GmbH v Weber von Hartz: 170/84 [1986] ECR 1607, [1986] 2 CMLR
 701, [1986] IRLR 317, [1987] ICR 110, ECJ   6.157
Birch v Liverpool University [1985] ICR 470, [1985] IRLR 165, (1985) 129 SJ 245, CA   8.27
Birmingham City Council v Equal Opportunities Commission *sub nom* R v Birmingham
 City Council, ex p Equal Opportunities Commission [1989] AC 1155, [1988] 3
 WLR 837, 86 LGR 741, [1988] IRLR 430, 132 Sol Jo 993, CA   6.33
BMK Ltd v Logue [1993] ICR 601, [1993] IRLR 477   8.32
BNP Paribas v Mezzotero [2004] All ER (D) 226 (Apr), [2004] IRLR 508, 148 Sol Jo LB
 666   2.49
Boorman v Allmakes Ltd [1995] ICR 842, [1995] IRLR 553, (1995) *The Times*, April 21,
 CA   8.112
Borders Regional Council v Maule [1993] IRLR 199, EAT   5.22
Briggs v North Eastern Education and Library Board [1990] IRLR 181,NICA   6.59, 6.61
British Broadcasting Corporation v Farnworth [1998] ICR 1116   8.84
British Home Stores Ltd v Burchell [1980] ICR 303; *sub nom* British Home Stores Ltd v
 Birchell [1978] IRLR 379, (1978) 13 ITR 560, EAT   8.65
Brown v London Borough of Croydon [2007] EWCA Civ 32, [2007] All ER (D) 239 (Jan),
 [2007] IRLR 259, [2007] ICR 909   6.29
Brown v Rentokil Ltd (C-394/96) [1998] All ER (EC) 791, [1998] ICR 790, [1998] 2 FLR
 649, [1998] IRLR 445, ECJ   5.58, 6.55
BUPA Care Homes (BNH) Ltd v Cann; Spillett v Tesco Stores Ltd [2006] All ER (D) 299
 (Feb), [2006] IRLR 248, [2006] ICR 643   2.30, 6.78

Cantor Fitzgerald International v Callaghan [1999] 2 All ER 411, [1999] ICR 639, [1999]
 IRLR 234, CA   5.6, 5.35, 8.23
Carry All Motors Ltd v Pennington [1980] ICR 806, [1980] IRLR 455, EAT   7.3
Cast v Croydon College [1998] ICR 500, [1998] IRLR 318, (1998) 95 (16) LSG 26, (1998)
 142 SJLB 119, CA   6.82
Catamaran Cruisers Ltd v Williams [1994] IRLR 386, EAT   8.82
Cerberus Software Ltd v Rowley [2001] ICR 376, CA   5.5
Chapman v Simon [1994] IRLR 124   6.32
Chattopadhyay v Headmaster of Holloway School [1982] ICR 132, [1981] IRLR 487,
 EAT   6.35
Chief Constable of West Yorkshire Police v Khan [2001] UKHL 48, [2001] WLR 1947,
 [2001] 4 All ER 834, [2001] All ER (D) 158 (Oct), ICR 1065, [2001] IRLR 830,
 [2001] 42 LS Gaz R 37, 145 Sol Jo LB 230   6.38
Chief Supplementary Benefit Officer v Leary [1985] 1 WLR 84, [1985] 1 All ER 1061,
 (1984) 128 SJ 852, CA   1.20
City of Bradford Metropolitan District Council v Pratt [2007] All ER (D) 19 (Jan), [2007]
 IRLR 192   2.13
City of Edinburgh Council v Brown [1999] IRLR 208, EAT   5.6
Clark v Civil Aviation Authority [1991] IRLR 412, EAT   8.92
Clark v TDG Ltd t/a Novacold [1999] ICR 951   6.140
Cole v Birmingham City District Council [1978] ICR 1004, [1978] IRLR 394; *sub nom*
 Cole v Birmingham District Council (1978) 13 ITR 505, EAT   7.14

Table of Cases

Collins (Phil) v Imtrat Handelsgesellschaft mbH: C-92/92, C-326/92 [1993] ECR I-5145, [1993] 3 CMLR 773, [1994] EMLR 108, ECJ 6.41
Commissioner of Police of the Metropolis v Hendricks [2003] ICR 530 6.80
Commotion Ltd v Rutty *sub nom* Rutty v Commotion Ltd [2006] All ER (D) 122 (Jan), [2006] IRLR 171, [2006] ICR 290 2.10
Cook v Thomas Linnell & Sons Ltd [1977] ICR 770, [1977] IRLR 132, (1977) 12 ITR 330, EAT 8.54
Cornelius v London Borough of Southwark [1998] ELR 563 8.138
Cosgrove v Caesar and Howie [2001] IRLR 653, EAT 6.148
Courage Take Home Trade Ltd v Keys [1986] ICR 874, [1986] IRLR 427, EAT 8.15
Cox v Sun Alliance Life Ltd [2001] EWCA Civ 649, [2001] IRLR 448, CA 5.25
Crossley v Faithful & Gould Holdings Ltd [2004] EWCA Civ 293, [2004] 4 All ER 447, [2004] ICR 1615, CA 5.49

Davis v New England College of Arundel [1977] ICR 6, [1976] ITR 278, EAT 8.3, 8.4
Day v T Pickles Farms Ltd [1999] IRLR 217, EAT 6.53, 6.54
De Falco v Crawley Borough Council; Silvestri v Crawley Borough Council [1980] QB 460, [1980] 2 WLR 664, [1980] 1 All ER 913, CA 8.124
Defrenne v Sabena [1976] ECR 455, [1976] ICR 547, [1976] 2 CMLR 98, [1981] 1 All ER 122, ECJ 6.6
Degnan v Redcar and Cleveland Borough Council [2005] EWCA Civ 726, [2005] All ER (D) 167 (Jun),[2005] IRLR 615 6.151
Delaney v Staples (RJ) (t/a De Montfort Recruitment) [1992] 1 AC 687, [1992] 2 WLR 451, [1992] 1 All ER 944, [1992] ICR 483, [1992] IRLR 191, HL; [1991] 2 QB 47, [1991] 2 WLR 627, [1991] 1 All ER 609, [1991] ICR 331, [1991] IRLR 112, CA 5.33
Derbyshire v St Helens Metropolitan Borough Council [2007] UKHL 16, [2007] 3 All ER 81, [2007] All ER (D) 207 (Apr), [2007] ICR 841, [2007] IRLR 540, [2007] NLJR 635, (2007) *The Times*, April 27, 151 Sol Jo LB 573 6.38
Digital Equipment Co Ltd v Clements (No 2) [1998] ICR 258, [1998] IRLR 134, (1998) 95(3) LSG 24, CA; [1997] ICR 237, [1997] IRLR 140, (1996) *The Times*, December 11, EAT 1.20
Dresdner Kleinwort Wasserstein Ltd v Adebayo [2005] IRLR 514 6.28
Duffy v Yeomans & Partners Ltd [1995] ICR 1, [1994] IRLR 642, (1994) *The Times*, July 26, CA 7.22
Dyke v Hereford & Worcester County Council [1989] ICR 800, EAT 8.94

East Lindsey District Council v Daubney [1977] ICR 566, [1977] IRLR 181, (1977) 12 ITR 359, EAT 8.57
Eastwood v Magnox Electric Plc; McCabe v Cornwall CC [2004] UKHL 35, [2005] 1 AC 503, [2004] 3 WLR 322, HL 5.9
EB v BA [2006] IRLR 471 6.30
Edebi v Canary Wharf Management Ltd [2006] All ER (D) 03 (Apr), [2006] ICR 719, [2006] IRLR 416 2.9
Egg Stores (Stamford Hill) Ltd v Leibovici [1977] ICR 260, [1976] IRLR 376, 11 ITR 289, EAT 8.30
European Commission v United Kingdom: C-484/04, [2006] All ER (D) 32 (Sep), [2007] ICR 592, [2006] 3 CMLR 1322, [2006] IRLR 888, (2006) *The Times*, September 21, ECJ 4.26
European Roma Rights Centre v Immigration Officer at Prague Airport (United Nations High Commissioner for Refugees intervening) [2004] UKHL 55, [2005] 2 AC 1, [2005] WLR 1, [2205] 1 All ER 527, [2004] All ER (D) 127 (Dec), [2005] 3 LRC 657, [2005] IRLR 115, [2004] NLJR 1893, (2004) *The Times*, December 10, 149 Sol Jo LB 27, 18 BHRC 1 6.21

Faccenda Chicken Ltd v Fowler; Fowler v Faccenda Chicken Ltd [1987] Ch 117, [1986] 3 WLR 288, [1986] ICR 297, CA; [1985] 1 All ER 724, [1984] ICR 589, [1984] IRLR 61 5.78
Farrant v The Woodroffe School [1998] ICR 184, [1998] IRLR 176, EAT 8.75, 8.83
Fay v North Yorkshire County Council [1986] ICR 133, (1987) 85 LGR 87, CA 8.84

Ford v Warwickshire County Council [1983] AC 71, [1983] 2 WLR 399, [1983] 1 All ER
   753, [1983] ICR 273, [1983] IRLR 126, HL   8.8
Francovich and Bonifaci v Italian Republic (Cases C-6/90 and C-9/90) [1995] ICR 722,
   [1992] IRLR 84, [1991] ECR 133, ECJ   6.16
Freemans plc v Flynn [1984] ICR 874, [1984] IRLR 486, EAT   8.119
French v Barclays Bank plc [1998] IRLR 646, CA   4.28, 5.9

Galaxy Showers Ltd v Wilson [2006] IRLR 83, EAT   2.10
Gilbank v Miles [2006] EWCA Civ 543, [2006] All ER (D) 160 (May), [2006] ICR 1297,
   [2006] IRLR 538   6.77, 6.84
Girls Public Day School Trust v Khanna [1987] ICR 339, [1987] LS Gaz R 189, EAT   5.74
Glasenapp v Germany (1987) 9 EHRR 25   6.164
Goold (W A) (Pearmak) Ltd v McConnell [1995] IRLR 516, EAT   5.13
Governing Body of Clifton Middle School v Askew [2000] ICR 286, [1999] ELR 425,
   [1999] Ed CR 800, CA   10.2
Governing Body of the Plume School v Langshaw [2003] ELR 97, [2002] All ER (D) 490
   (Jul), EAT   4.31
Grant v South-West Trains Ltd (Case C-249/96) [1998] ECR I-621, [1998] 1 FLR 839,
   [1998] ICR 449, [1998] All ER (EC) 193, ECJ   6.45
Greenaway Harrison Ltd v Wiles [1994] IRLR 380, EAT   8.23
Gryf-Lowczowski v Hinchingbrooke Healthcare NHS Trust [2005] EWHC 2407 (QB),
   [2005] All Er (D) 21 (Nov), [2006] ICR 425, [2006] IRLR 100, 87 BMLR 46   5.21

Haddow v Inner London Education Authority [1979] ICR 202, EAT   8.91
Halford v UK (1997) 24 EHRR 523, [1997] IRLR 471, (1997) 3 BHRC 31, ECHR   6.161
Hallam v Avery [2001] UKHL 15, [2001] 1 WLR 655, [2001] All ER (D) 273 (Mar), [2001]
   ICR 408, [2001] IRLR 312, [2001] LGR 278, [2001] 21 LS Gaz R 39, 145 Sol Jo
   LB 116   6.76
Hampson v Department of Education and Science [1990] 2 All ER 25, [1989] ICR 179,
   [1989] IRLR 69, (1989) 133 SJ 151, CA   6.61
Handels-og-Kontorfunktionaerernes Forbund I Danmark v Dansk Arbejdsgiverforening,
   sub nom Hertz v Aldi Marked K/S (C-109/88) [1991] ICR 449, [1991] IRLR 31,
   ECJ   5.58
Hardy & Hansons plc v Lax [2005] ICR 1565   6.22
Harper v Virgin Net Ltd [2004] EWCA Civ 271, [2005] ICR 921, [2004] IRLR 390, [2004]
   TLR 174, CA   8.55
Harrington v Kent County Council [1980] IRLR 353, EAT   8.29
Harris (Ipswich) Ltd v Harrison [1978] ICR 1256, [1978] IRLR 382, EAT   8.68
Harrison v Kent County Council [1995] ICR 431n, [1990] IRLR 15   9.8
Hart v English Heritage (Historic Buildings and Monuments Commission for England)
   [2006] All ER (D) 343 (Feb), [2006] IRLR 915, [2006] ICR 655   2.5
Hawkins v Ball and Barclays Bank plc [1996] IRLR 258, EAT   6.78
Hayward v Cammell Laird Shipbuilders Ltd (No 2) [1988] AC 894, [1988] 2 WLR 1134,
   [1988] 2 All ER 257, [1988] ICR 464, [1988] IRLR 257, HL; reversing [1988] QB
   12, [1987] 3 WLR 20, [1987] 2 All ER 344, [1987] ICR 682, [1987] IRLR 186, CA   6.151
Healey v Bridgend County Borough Council [2002] EWCA Civ 1996, All ER (D) 204
   (Nov), [2004] ICR 561, [2003] 04 LS Gaz R 31   4.34
Hogg v Dover College [1990] ICR 39, EAT   8.24
Hollister v NFU [1979] ICR 542, [1979] IRLR 238, CA   8.48
Hooper v British Railways Board [1988] IRLR 517, CA   8.87
Howard v Governor of Brixington Infants School [1999] ELR 191, [1999] ICR 1096   8.140,
   8.141, 8.146, 8.155
Huddersfield Parcels Ltd v Sykes [1981] IRLR 115, EAT   7.3, 7.23
Huddersfield Police Authority v Watson [1947] KB 842, [1948] LJR 182, 111 JP 463, DC   1.20
Hurley v Mustoe [1981] ICR 490, [1981] IRLR 208, EAT   6.64
Hutchings v Islington London Borough Council [1998] 1 WLR 1629, [1998] 3 All ER 445,
   [1998] ICR 1230, CA   5.49

Igen Ltd v Wong; Chamberlin Solicitors v Emokpae; Brunel University v Webster [2005]
   EWCA Civ 142, [2005] ICR 931, [2005] IRLR 259, CA   6.28, 6.30
Inner London Education Authority v Gravett [1988] IRLR 497, EAT   8.110

Table of Cases

Inner London Education Authority v Lloyd [1981] IRLR 394, EAT   8.55, 8.80
Item Software (UK) Ltd v Fassihi; *sub nom* Fassihi v Item Software (UK) Ltd [2004]
   EWCA Civ 1244, [2004] BCC 994, [2005] 2 BCLC 91, [2005] ICR 450, CA   5.80

James W Cook & Co (Wivenhoe) Ltd v Tipper [1990] ICR 716   7.18
Johnson v Unisys Ltd [2001] UKHL 13, [2003] 1 AC 518, [2001] IRLR 279   5.9
Johnstone v Bloomsbury Health Authority [1992] QB 333, [1991] 2 WLR 1362, [1991]
   ICR 269, [1991] 2 All ER 293, CA   5.14
Jones v Governing Body of Barton Court Grammar School (EAT/0920/02) [2003] All ER
   (D) 12 (Jun), EAT   4.35
Jones v Governing Body of Burdett Coutts School [1999] ICR 38, [1998] IRLR 521,
   (1998) 142 SJLB 142, CA   8.24, 8.31
Jones v Gwent County Council [1992] IRLR 521   5.20, 5.21
Jones v Lee and Guilding [1980] ICR 310, [1980] IRLR 67, (1979) 78 LGR 213, CA   5.20, 8.131
Jones v Mid-Glamorgan County Council [1997] ICR 815, [1997] IRLR 685, CA   8.25
Jones v Post Office [2001] EWCA Civ 558, [2001] All ER (D) 133 (Apr), [2001] ICR 805,
   [2001] IRLR 384   6.142

Keen v Commerzbank AG *sub nom* Commerzbank AG v Keen [2006] EWCA Civ 1536,
   [2006] All ER (D) 239 (Nov), [2007] ICR 623, [2007] IRLR 132   5.14
Kelly-Madden v Manor Surgery [2006] All ER (D) 232 (Oct), [2007] ICR 203, [2007]
   IRLR 17   8.96
Kenny v Hampshire Constabulary [1999] ICR 27, [1999] IRLR 76, [1999] Disc LR 118,
   (1998) *The Times*, October 22, EAT   6.148
Kerry Foods Ltd v Lynch [2005] All ER (D) 351 (Jun), IRLR 680, EAT   8.23
Kidd v Axa Equity & Law Life Assurance Society plc [2000] IRLR 301, QBD   5.25
King v Great Britain China Centre [1992] ICR 516, [1991] IRLR 513,   6.32
Kopel v Safeway Stores plc [2003] All ER (D) 05 (Sep), [2003] IRLR 753, EAT   1.29
Kosiek v Germany (1986) 9 EHRR 328   6.164
Kramer v South Bedfordshire Community Health Care Trust [1995] ICR 1066, (1995) *The
   Times*, October 16, ChD   8.62, 8.78

Ladbroke Racing Ltd v Arnott [1983] IRLR 154, Ct of Sess   8.66
Larsson v Dansk Handel and Service [1997] IRLR 643   5.58
Lawrence v HM Prison Service [2007] IRLR 468   2.5
Lawrence v Regent Office Care Ltd: C-320/00 [2002] ECR I-7325, [2002] All ER (D) 84,
   (Sep), [2002] IRLR 822, [2002] 3 CMLR 761, [2003] ICR 1092, (2002) *The Times*,
   October 10   6.153
Laws Stores Ltd v Oliphant [1978] IRLR 251, EAT   8.66
Lee v GEC Plessey Telecommunications Ltd [1993] IRLR 383, QBD   5.46
Lennon v Commissioner of the Police of the Metropolis [2004] ICR 1114   5.49
Lewis v Motorworld Garages Ltd [1986] ICR 157, [1985] IRLR 465, CA   1.31
Linfood Cash and Carry Ltd v Thompson [1989] ICR 518, [1989] IRLR 235, EAT   8.89
Luce v Bexley London Borough Council [1990] ICR 591, [1990] IRLR 422, 88 LGR 909,
   EAT   9.4

Madarassy v Nomura International plc [2007] EWCA Civ 33, [2007] All ER (D) 226 (Jan),
   [2007] ICR 867, [2007] IRLR 246   6.27
Mahmud v BCCI; Malik v BCCI [1998] AC 20, [1997] 3 All ER 1, [1997] 3 WLR 95, HL   5.9
Mangold v Helm (C-144/04) [2006] IRLR 143   6.12
Mark Warner Ltd v Aspland [2006] IRLR 87   2.10
Marleasing SA v La Commercial Internacional de Alimentacion SA: C-106/89 [1990] ECR
   I-4135, [1992] 1 CMLR 305, [1993] BCC 421, 135 Sol Jo 15   6.17
Marshall v Alexander Sloan & Co Ltd [1981] IRLR 264, EAT   8.77
McGowan v Scottish Water [2004] All ER (D) 130 (Nov), [2005] IRLR 167   6.162
McMenemy v Capita Business Services Ltd [2006] IRLR 761, EAT   6.92
Meikle v Nottinghamshire County Council *sub nom* Nottinghamshire County Council v
   Meikle [2004] EWCA Civ 859, [2004] 4 All ER 97, [2004] All ER (D) 123 (Jul),
   [2004] IRLR 703, [2005] ICR 1, 80 BMLR 129, (2004) *The Times*, July 15, 148 Sol
   Jo LB 908   8.21
Meridian Ltd v Gomersall [1977] ICR 597, [1977] IRLR 425, (1977) 121 TR 323, EAT   8.108

Metropolitan Borough of Solihull v National Union of Teachers [1985] IRLR 211, HC   9.10
Ministry of Defence v Jeremiah [1980] QB 87, [1979] 3 WLR 857, [1979] 3 All ER 833,
    [1980] ICR 13; sub nom Jeremiah v Ministry of Defence [1979] IRLR 436, CA   6.46, 6.66
Mitchell v Arkwood Plastics (Engineering) Ltd [1993] ICR 471, (1993) *The Times*, March
    12, EAT   8.58
Morissens v Belgium (1988) 56 DR 127, ECHR   6.165
Mugford v Midland Bank plc [1997] ICR 399, [1997] IRLR 208, EAT   7.23, 7.26, 8.94
Murray v British Rail [1976] IRLR 382   8.62, 8.78
Murray v Foyle Meats Ltd [1999] 3 WLR 356, [1999] 3 All ER 769, [1999] ICR 827, [1999]
    IRLR 562, HL   7.3
Murray v Strathclyde Regional Council [1992] IRLR 396, EAT   5.33

Nagarajan v London Regional Transport [2000] 1 AC 501, [1999] 3 WLR 425, [1999] 4 All
    ER 65, [1999] ICR 877, HL   6.37
Nandi v General Medical Council [2004] EWHC 2317 (Admin), [2004] All ER (D) 25
    (Oct)   3.42
National Union of Teachers v St Mary's Church of England (Aided) Junior School
    Governing Body; sub nom Fidge v Governing Body of St Mary's Church of
    England (Aided) Junior School; National Union of Teachers v Governing Body of
    St Mary's Church of England (Aided) Junior School [1997] 3 CMLR 630, [1997]
    Eu LR 221, [1997] ICR 334, CA   6.13
New Southern Railway Ltd v Quinn [2006] All ER (D) 367 (Nov), [2006] ICR 761, [2006]
    IRLR 266, EAT   6.54
Norfolk County Council v Bernard [1979] IRLR 220, EAT   8.69
Notcutt v Universal Equipment Co (London) Ltd [1986] 1 WLR 641, [1986] 3 All ER
    582, [1986] ICR 414, CA   8.30
Nothman v London Borough of Barnet (No 2) [1980] IRLR 65, CA   8.108
Nottinghamshire County Council v Bowly [1978] IRLR 252, EAT   8.69
Nottinghamshire County Council v Lee [1980] ICR 635, (1980) 78 LGR 568; sub nom Lee
    v Nottinghamshire County Council [1980] IRLR 284, CA   7.4, 8.84
NRG Victory Reinsurance Ltd v Alexander [1992] ICR 675, EAT   1.29, 8.15

O'Hanlon v Commissioners v HM Revenue & Customs [2006] ICR 1579   6.148
O'Neill v Governors of St Thomas More RCVA Upper School; O'Neill v Bedfordshire
    County Council [1997] ICR 33, [1996] IRLR 372, EAT   6.51, 6.52
Omilaju v Waltham Forest London Borough Council [2004] EWCA Civ 1493, [2005] 1 All
    ER 75, [2004] All ER (D) 174 (Nov), [2005] ICR 481, [2005] IRLR 35, (2004) *The
    Times*, November 26, 148 Sol Jo LB 1370   8.22

P (a minor) v National Association of Schoolmasters/Union of Women Teachers [2003]
    UKHL 8, [2003] 2 AC 663, [2003] WLR 545, [2003] ELR 357, [2003] 1 All ER 993,
    [2003] All ER (D) 384 (Feb), [2003] IRLR 307, [2003] NLJR 350, (2003) *The
    Times*, March 6   9.10
P v Nottinghamshire County Council [1992] ICR 706, [1992] IRLR 362, (1992) *The
    Times*, May 18, CA   8.72
Parkinson v March Consulting Ltd [1998] ICR 276, [1997] IRLR 308, (1997) *The Times*,
    January 9, CA   8.94
Peake v Automotive Products Ltd [1978] QB 233, [1977] 3 WLR 853, [1977] ICR 968; *sub
    nom* Automotive Products Ltd v Peake [1977] IRLR 365, CA   6.46
Polkey v AE Dayton Services Ltd [1988] AC 344, [1987] 3 WLR 1153, [1987] 3 All ER
    974, [1988] ICR 142, HL   8.95, 8.114, 8.115, 8.116
Port of London Authority v Payne [1994] ICR 555, [1994] IRLR 9, CA   8.106
Portec (UK) Ltd v Mogensen [1976] 3 All ER 565, [1976] ICR 396, [1976] IRLR 209,
    EAT   1.20
Potter v Hunt Contracts Ltd [1992] ICR 337, [1992] IRLR 108, EAT   5.34
Printers & Finishers Ltd v Holloway [1965] 1 WLR 1   5.79

Qua v John Ford Morrison Solicitors [2003] ICR 482, [2003] IRLR 184, (2003) 153 NLJ
    95, EAT   5.70
Qureshi v London Borough of Newham [1991] IRLR 264, CA   6.34

Qureshi v Victoria University of Manchester [2001] ICR 863, EAT	6.32
R (Douglas) v North Tyneside Metropolitan Borough Council [2003] EWCA Civ 1847, [2004] 1 WLR 2363, [2004] ELR 117, [2004] 1 All ER 709, CA	6.10
R (on the application of Dorling) v Sheffield City Council [2002] EWHC 2505 (Admin), [2003] ELR 486, [2002] All ER (D) 191 (Nov), [2003] ICR 424	4.34
R (on the application of Phillips) v General Medical Council [2004] EWHC 1858 (Admin), [2004] All ER (D) 49 (Jul), 82 BLMR 135	3.43
R (on the application of Redgrave) v Commissioner of Police for the Metropolis [2003] 1 WLR 1136	3.44
R (on the application of Verner) v Derby City Council [2003] EWHC 2708 (Admin), [2004] All ER (D) 203 (Nov), [2004] ICR 535, [2004] LGR 786	4.34
R v British Coal Corporation and Secretary of State, ex parte Price [1994] IRLR 72	9.13
R v Greater Manchester Coroner, ex p Tal [1985] QB 67, [1984] 3 WLR 643, [1984] 3 All ER 240, 128 Sol Jo 500	1.20
R v Liverpool City Corpn, ex p Ferguson and Ferguson [1985] IRLR 501, QBD	5.30
R v Secretary of State for Education, ex p Standish (1993) Times November 15, QBD	3.20
R v Secretary of State for Employment, ex p Seymour-Smith: C-167/97 [1999] 2 AC 554, [1999] 3 WLR 460, [1999] All ER (EC) 97, [1999] ICR 447, [1999] ECR I-623, [1999] 2 CMLR 273, [1999] IRLR 253	6.18, 6.60
Ramsey v Walkers Snack Foods Ltd; Hamblet v Walkers Snack Foods Ltd [2004] IRLR 754, EAT	8.89
Redbridge London Borough Council v Fishman [1978] ICR 569, [1978] IRLR 69, (1978) 76 LGR 408, EAT	8.74, 8.83, 8.109
Redcar & Cleveland Borough Council v Bainbridge [2007] All ER (D) 197 (Nov), [2007] IRLR 91, EAT	6.155
Richmond Precision Engineering Ltd v Pearce [1985] IRLR 179, EAT	8.82
Rigby v Ferodo Ltd [1988] ICR 29, [1987] IRLR 516, HL	5.35
Robert Cort & Son Ltd v Charman [1981] ICR 816, [1981] IRLR 437, EAT	8.32
Roger Bullivant Ltd v Ellis [1987] ICR 464, [1987] IRLR 491, [1987] FSR 172, CA	5.78
Ryan v Blackburn with Darwen Borough Council (UKEAT/0928/03/DM) (2004) (unreported), 30 September, EAT	4.11, 8.138
S v Brent London Borough Council [2002] EWCA Civ 693, [2002] ELR 556, CA	4.49
Saeed v Inner London Education Authority [1985] ICR 637, [1986] IRLR 23, (1985) 82 LS Gaz 2911	8.68
Safeway Stores plc v Burrell [1997] ICR 523, [1997] IRLR 200, 567 IRLB 8, EAT	7.3
Sainsbury's Supermarkets Ltd v Hitt; sub nom Sainsburys Supermarkets Ltd v Hitt; J Sainsbury Ltd v Hitt; J Sainsbury Plc v Hitt [2002] EWCA Civ 1588, [2003] ICR 111, [2003] IRLR 23, CA	8.65
Salveson v Simons [1994] ICR 409, [1994] IRLR 52, EAT	8.11
Sandhu v (1) Department of Education and Science and (2) London Borough of Hillingdon [1978] IRLR 208, (1978) 13 ITR 314, EAT	8.79
Sayers v Cambridgeshire County Council [2006] EWHC 2029 (QB), [2007] IRLR29	5.29
SBJ Stephenson Ltd v Maudy [2000] IRLR 233, QBD	5.79
Scally v Southern Health and Social Services Board [1992] 1 AC 294, [1991] 3 WLR 778, [1991] 4 All ER 563, [1991] ICR 771, [1991] IRLR 522, HL	5.18, 5.49
Scott-Davies v Redgate Medical Services (UKEAT/273/06) [2007] ICR 348, [2006] All ER (D) 29 (Dec), EAT	2.3
Secretary of State for Employment v Globe Elastic Thread Co Ltd [1980] AC 506, [1979] 3 WLR 143], [1979] 2 All ER 1077, [1979] ICR 706, [1979] IRLR 327, 123 Sol Jo 504	7.6
Secretary of State for Trade and Industry v Cook [1997] ICR 288, [1997] IRLR 150, EAT	1.20
Shamoon v Chief Constable of the Royal Ulster Constabulary [2003] UKHL 11, [2003] ICR 337, [2003] 2 All ER 26, HL	6.29, 6.47, 6.66
Sheffield v Oxford Controls Co Ltd [1979] ICR 396, [1979] IRLR 133, EAT	8.25, 8.26, 8.27
Shepherd v North Yorkshire County Council [2005] All ER (D) 354 (Dec), [2006] IRLR 190, EAT	6.76

Sim v Rotherham Metropolitan Borough Council; Townend v Doncaster Metropolitan Borough Council; Barnfield v Solihull Metropolitan Borough Council; Rathbone v Croydon London Borough Council [1987] Ch 216, [1986] 3 WLR 851, [1986] 3 All ER 387, [1986] ICR 897, [1986] IRLR 391   5.30, 5.76, 8.125

Sinclair Roche & Temperley v Heard [2004] All ER (D) 432 (Jul), [2004] IRLR 763, EAT   6.75

Slater v Leicester Health Authority [1989] IRLR 16, CA   8.91

Smith v Churchills Stairlifts plc [2005] EWCA Civ 1220, [2005] All ER (D) 318 (Oct), [2006] ICR 524, [2006] IRLR 41   6.142, 6.147

Society of Licensed Victuallers v Chamberlain [1989] IRLR 421, EAT   5.75

Speciality Care plc v Pachela [1996] ICR 633, [1996] IRLR 248, (1996) *The Times*, March 22, EAT   9.8

Spence v Intype Libra Ltd (UKEAT/0617/06) [2007] All ER (D) 261 (Apr), EAT   6.148

Sporrong and Lönnroth v Sweden (Applications 7151/75 and 7152/75), (1982) 5 EHRR 35   3.46

Spring v Guardian Assurance plc and Others [1995] 2 AC 296, [1994] 3 WLR 354, [1994] 3 All ER 129, HL   5.25

Stanley Cole (Wainfleet) Ltd v Sheridan; *sub nom* Sheridan v Stanley Cole (Wainfleet) Ltd [2003] EWCA Civ 1046, [2003] 4 All ER 1181, [2003] ICR 1449, CA; affirming [2003] ICR 297, [2003] IRLR 52, EAT   5.10

Stewart v Cleveland Guest (Engineering) Ltd [1996] ICR 535, [1994] IRLR 440, (1994) *The Times*, July 6, EAT   6.48, 6.49

Stewart v YMCA Training Ltd *sub nom* YMCA Training Ltd v Stewart [2006] All ER (D) 69 (Dec), [2007] IRLR 185, EAT   8.96

Stoker v Lancashire County Council [1992] IRLR 75, CA   8.87

Strathclyde Regional Council v Wallace [1998] 1 WLR 259, [1998] 1 All ER 394, [1998] ICR 205, [1998] IRLR 146, HL   6.154

Surrey County Council v Lewis [1987] ICR 982   8.8

Sybron Corporation v Rochem Ltd [1984] Ch 112, [1983] 3 WLR 713, [1983] ICR 801, CA   5.80

Tarbuck v Sainsbury's Supermarkets Ltd [2006] All ER (D) 50 (Jun), [2006] IRLR 664, EAT   6.148

Taylor v Kent County Council [1969] 2 QB 560, [1969] 3 WLR 156, [1969] 2 All ER 1080, 67 LGR 483, 113 Sol Jo 425   7.8

Taylor v OCS Group Ltd [2006] EWCA Civ 702, [2006] All ER (D) 51 (Aug), [2006] ICR 1602, [2006] IRLR 613, (2006) *The Times*, July 12, 150 Sol Jo LB 810   8.93

Telephone Information Services Ltd v Wilkinson [1991] IRLR 148, EAT   1.29

The Scotts Co (UK) Ltd v Budd [2003] ICR 299   5.7

Thomas & Betts Manufacturing Ltd v Harding [1980] IRLR 255, CA   7.22

Thompson v SCS Consulting Ltd [2001] All ER (D) 03 (Sep), [2001] IRLR 801, EAT   1.31

Thornett v Scope *sub nom* Scope v Thornett [2006] EWCA Civ 1600, [2006] All ER (D) 357 (Nov), [2007] ICR 236, [2007] IRLR 155   8.115

Treganowan v Robert Knee & Co Ltd [1975] ICR 405, [1975] IRLR 247, [1975] ITR 121, 119 SJ 490, DC   8.86

Truelove v Safeway Stores plc [2005] All ER (D) 343 (Feb), [2005] ICR 589, EAT   5.71

Turner v Vestric Ltd [1980] ICR 528, [1981] IRLR 23, EAT   8.86

Van Marle and others v Netherlands (Applications 8543/79, 8674/70, 8675.79, 8685/79), (1986) 8 EHRR 483   3.46

Vento v Chief Constable of West Yorkshire Police [2002] EWCA Civ 1871, [2002] All ER (D) 363 (Dec), [2003] ICR 318, [2003] IRLR 102, [2003] 10 LS Gaz R 28, (2002) Times December 27, 147 Sol Jo LB 181   6.84

Vogt v Germany (Application No 17851/91) (1996) 21 EHRR 205, [1996] ELR 232, ECHR   6.164

Wandsworth London Borough Council v D'Silva [1998] IRLR 193, CA   5.6

Webb v EMO Air Cargo (UK) Ltd (C-32/93) [1994] QB 718, [1994] 4 All ER 115, [1994] ICR 770, [1994] IRLR 482, ECJ   6.53

Webb v EMO Air Cargo (UK) Ltd (No 2) [1995] 1 WLR 1454, [1995] 4 All ER 577, [1995] ICR 1021, [1995] IRLR 645, HL   6.51

Webb v EMO Air Cargo (UK) Ltd [1993] 1 WLR 49, [1992] 4 All ER 929, [1993] ICR 175, [1993] IRLR 27, [1993] 1 CMLR 259, HL   6.61

Table of Cases xliii

Webley v Department for Work and Pensions [2004] EWCA Civ 1745, [2004] All ER (D) 368 (Dec), [2005] ICR 577, [2005] IRLR 288, (2005) *The Times*, 17 January.	8.84
Western Excavating (ECC) Ltd v Sharp [1978] QB 761, [1978] 2 WLR 344, [1978] 1 All ER 713, [1978] ICR 221, [1978] IRLR 27, CA	8.19
Westminster City Council v Cabaj [1996] ICR 960, [1996] IRLR 399, (1996) *The Times*, May 8, CA	8.87
Westwood v Secretary of State for Employment [1985] AC 20, [1985] ICR 209, [1984] IRLR 209, HL	5.2
White v London Transport Executive [1982] QB 489, [1982] 2 WLR 791, [1981] IRLR 261, EAT	8.55
Williams v Roffey Bros & Nicholls (Contractors) Ltd [1991] 1 QB 1, [1990] 2 WLR 1153, [1990] 1 All ER 512, CA	5.46
Williams v Watsons Luxury Coaches Ltd [1990] ICR 536, [1990] IRLR 164, EAT	8.30
Wilson v Mars UK Ltd (t/a Masterfoods) [2007] All ER (D) 35 (Dec), [2007] ICR 370, EAT	2.14
Wilson v St Helens Borough Council; *sub nom* British Fuels Ltd v Baxendale; Meade v British Fuels Ltd; Baxendale v British Fuels Ltd [1999] 2 AC 52, [1998] 3 WLR 1070, [1998] 4 All ER 609, [1998] ICR 1141, HL; [1998] ICR 387, [1997] IRLR 505, [1997] 3 CMLR 1267, CA	10.5
Wiltshire County Council v National Association of Teachers in Further and Higher Education and Guy [1980] ICR 455, [1980] IRLR 198, (1980) 78 LGR 445, CA	8.18
Wiluszynski v Tower Hamlets London Borough Council [1989] ICR 493, [1989] IRLR 259, (1989) 133 SJ 628, 88 LGR 14, CA	5.30
Winterhalter Gastronom Ltd v Webb [1973] ICR 245, [1973] IRLR 120, 8 ITR 313, NIRC	8.52
Wood Group Heavy Industrial Turbines Ltd v Crossan [1998] IRLR 680, EAT	8.107
X v Y (Employment: Sex Offender); *sub nom* X v Y (Unfair Dismissal) [2004] EWCA Civ 662, [2004] ICR 1634, [2004] IRLR 625, CA	8.69
Young & Woods Ltd v West [1980] IRLR 201, CA	8.11

Chapter 1

INTRODUCTION AND OVERVIEW

INTRODUCTION

1.1 This chapter contains an overview of the law of employment as it relates to schools. In it, the specific provisions which apply to employment in a State school are listed. The effects of those specific provisions are described elsewhere in the book. The purpose of listing the applicable provisions here is to provide an aide-memoire and a checklist for those who are familiar with the area. Those who are not familiar with the area are likely to find in particular the number of sets of regulations which affect employment in State schools surprising. It is in any event helpful to contrast the position of independent schools with that of State schools, and accordingly to highlight the relatively few provisions which apply to employment in an independent school.

1.2 Several questions of general application are also dealt with in this chapter (and only in this chapter). These are the doctrine of precedent and the manner in which disputes concerning employment are determined. Several subsidiary issues relating in the main to the determination of disputes by employment tribunals and the Employment Appeal Tribunal (EAT) are then considered. They are:

(1) the effect of the rules relating to the award of costs in employment tribunals and the EAT, and

(2) the occasions when an appeal can validly be made, in particular to the latter tribunal.

EMPLOYMENT LAW GENERALLY

The development of the law

1.3 The content of the law of employment is, as is so often the case in England and Wales, largely the result of the grafting on of statutory provisions to a situation which was originally governed in part by the common law (that is, the law resulting from decisions of the courts which are not directly based on statutes). In part, because the common law is itself a product of centuries of development, not all of it systematic, the law of employment contains a number of areas where there is a tension between different principles. That is especially so in the case of the law of employment in State schools.

Who is the employer?

1.4 The situation has been made even more difficult in the case of schools maintained by local education authorities[1] as a result of the enactment of the provisions concerning the delegation of budgets to the governing bodies of such schools (that is, the provisions giving rise to what is usually known as local management), originally contained in the Education Reform Act 1988. Those provisions were later consolidated (that is, re-enacted without major alteration) in the Education Act 1996 and then replaced by new provisions in the School Standards and Framework Act 1998, but their effect remains the same.

1.5 Indeed, where a school is entitled to a delegated budget, the split in responsibilities between the governing body of the school and the local education authority which maintains it has led to some complicated situations. In regard to some matters, employees have lost rights which they would have had if they had continued to be and to be regarded as being employed by the local education authority (LEA) for all purposes.

1.6 However, where a maintained school is entitled to a delegated budget, and the governing body of the school is the primary respondent to a claim made to an employment tribunal,[2] the governing body *is* the employer for all practical purposes. That much is clear.

Who are employees?

1.7 At present, much (but by no means all) of the law of employment applies only to people who are in fact employees. Voluntary helpers and (generally) supply teachers are not normally covered by the law of employment as far as the governing body of a school is concerned (except, in the case of a supply teacher, by the law of discrimination) because there will usually be no relevant contract of employment in existence. Voluntary helpers are unlikely to have any contract at all. In the case of supply teachers, usually the only contract is a contract between the supply teacher and the supplier of the supply teacher. The supply teacher may be either self-employed or (more likely) employed under a contract of employment by the supplier. It will only be when the supply teacher is employed continuously for a reasonably long period of time that he[3] may become an employee. The question of when a person is self-employed rather than an employee may arise on a number of occasions. It is of fundamental importance, and it is therefore considered below.[4] Regulations may be made in

---

[1] Section 162 of the Education and Inspections Act 2006 empowers the Secretary of State to repeal any reference in any statutory provision to a local authority and to replace it with a reference 'to, as the case may be, an English local authority or a Welsh local authority, or to both'. However, at the time of writing the term 'local education authority' remained current.
[2] See para **8.147** below regarding the times when this occurs.
[3] In what follows, the word 'he' is to be read as 'he or she', and cognate expressions are to be read in a similar manner. This is purely for the sake of simplicity. It is noted that the same approach is taken in legislative material except that which relates to discrimination on the ground of sex.
[4] See para **8.3** onwards.

the future, under s 23 of the Employment Relations Act 1999, equating the position of some persons who are currently self-employed with that of employees. However, there was at the time of writing no sign of such regulations on the horizon, and as a result the question whether a person who by his personal labour provides services is an employee or self-employed remains potentially crucial.

Prospective employees

1.8 The law of employment affects the situation even before a person becomes an employee. This is because of the prohibitions on discrimination in advertisements and recruitment contained in the Sex Discrimination Act 1975, the Race Relations Act 1976, the Disability Discrimination Act 1995, the Employment Equality (Religion or Belief) Regulations 2003,[5] the Employment Equality (Sexual Orientation) Regulations 2003,[6] and the Employment Equality (Age) Regulations 2006.[7]

WHAT LAW IS APPLICABLE TO EMPLOYMENT, BOTH GENERALLY AND IN SCHOOLS?

General employment law

1.9 Where a person has become an employee, the situation is governed principally by:

(1) the anti-discrimination provisions in the Sex Discrimination Act 1975, the Race Relations Act 1976 and the Disability Discrimination Act 1995, the Part-time Workers (Prevention of Less Favourable Treatment) Regulations 2000,[8] the Fixed-term Employees (Prevention of Less Favourable Treatment) Regulations 2002,[9] the Employment Equality (Religion or Belief) Regulations 2003, the Employment Equality (Sexual Orientation) Regulations 2003, and the Employment Equality (Age) Regulations 2006;

(2) the law of contract as it applies via the contract of employment;

(3) the law of tort (that is, mainly regarding negligence and defamation) in so far as it supplements the law of contract; and

---

[5] SI 2003/1660. In the case of an independent school, these regulations must be read in conjunction with the Independent Schools (Employment of Teachers in Schools with a Religious Character) Regulations 2003, SI 2003/2037. In relation to State schools, ss 58–60 of the School Standards and Framework Act apply in a similar way to mitigate the effect of the Employment Equality (Religion or Belief) Regulations 2003. See further para **4.78** onwards below.
[6] SI 2003/1661.
[7] SI 2006/1031.
[8] SI 2000/1551.
[9] SI 2002/2034.

(4) a number of provisions contained in the Employment Rights Act 1996 and the Trade Union and Labour Relations (Consolidation) Act 1992.

1.10 Furthermore, the requirements of the Health and Safety at Work etc Act 1974 and regulations made under that Act should be borne in mind by employers.

1.11 After a contract of employment has ended, both the employer and the employee continue to have some obligations towards the other, mainly in the law of contract.

Employment in a state school

1.12 The employment of (principally) teachers in State schools in England and Wales is also subject to the provisions of the following enactments, some of which apply only in England and some of which apply only in Wales (although where that is so, the regulations tend to be in similar terms):

(1) ss 142–144 of the Education Act 2002;

(2) the Education (Prohibition from Teaching or Working with Children) Regulations 2003;[10]

(3) the Education (Health Standards) (England) Regulations 2003,[11] the Education (Teachers' Qualifications and Health Standards) (Wales) Regulations 1999[12] and the Education (Health Standards) (Wales) Regulations 2004;[13]

(4) the Education (School Teachers' Qualifications) (England) Regulations 2003[14] and the Education (School Teachers' Qualifications) (Wales) Regulations 2004;[15]

(5) the Education (School Teachers' Prescribed Qualifications, etc) Order 2003;[16]

(6) the Education (Head Teachers' Qualifications) (England) Regulations 2003[17] and the Head Teachers' Qualifications and Registration (Wales) Regulations 2005;[18]

---

[10] SI 2003/1184 as amended.
[11] SI 2003/3139.
[12] SI 1999/2817 as amended.
[13] SI 2004/2733 (W 240).
[14] SI 2003/1662 as amended.
[15] SI 2004/1729 (W 173).
[16] SI 2003/1709 as amended.
[17] SI 2003/3111 as amended.
[18] SI 2005/1227 (W 85).

(7) the Education (Specified Work and Registration) (England) Regulations 2003[19] and the Education (Specified Work and Registration) (Wales) Regulations 2004;[20]

(8) the Education (Induction Arrangements for School Teachers) (Consolidation) (England) Regulations 2001[21] and the Education (Induction Arrangements for School Teachers) (Wales) Regulations 2005;[22]

(9) the Education (School Teacher Performance Management) (England) Regulations 2006[23] and the Education (School Teacher Appraisal) (Wales) Regulations 2002;[24]

(10) the School Staffing (England) Regulations 2003[25] and the Staffing of Maintained Schools (Wales) Regulations 2006;[26]

(11) the Education (Modification of Enactments Relating to Employment) (England) Order 2003[27] and the Education (Modification of Enactments Relating to Employment) (Wales) Order 2006;[28]

(12) the Education (Review of Staffing Structure) (England) Regulations 2005[29] and the Education (Review of Staffing Structure) (Wales) Regulations 2005;[30] and

(13) the Education (School Teachers' Pay and Conditions) (No 2) Order 2006,[31] and related Orders, assuming that there is no permitted derogation from the application of that Order.[32]

1.13 More generally, the employment of staff in State schools is governed in addition by:

(1) the principles of public law (including, where relevant, in so far as they may be taken to modify the effect of the law of contract); and

---

[19] SI 2003/1663 as amended.
[20] SI 2004/1744 (W 183).
[21] SI 2001/2897 as amended.
[22] SI 2005/1818 (W 146).
[23] SI 2006/2661.
[24] SI 2002/1394 as amended.
[25] SI 2003/1963 as amended.
[26] SI 2006/873 (W 61) as amended.
[27] SI 2003/1964 as amended.
[28] SI 2006/1073.
[29] SI 2005/1032.
[30] SI 2005/1910 (W 153).
[31] SI 2006/2133, as amended.
[32] See further paras **4.22** onwards below.

(2) European Community law (more often called now European Union law, but technically the term 'European Community law' is correct[33]) in so far as it has not been properly implemented in England and Wales.

Employment in an independent school

1.14 The employment of teachers (and others) in independent schools (ie not including non-maintained special schools, to which some of the regulations mentioned in the preceding paragraph above apply) is governed only by ss 142–144 of the Education Act 2002 and the Education (Prohibition from Teaching or Working with Children) Regulations 2003, which were made under s 142. However, the Education (Independent School Standards) (England) Regulations 2003[34] and the Education (Independent School Standards) (Wales) Regulations 2003[35] require independent schools to implement policies in several DfES circulars which may have an effect on the employment of staff, including that which is now DfES circular 04217-2006, entitled 'Safeguarding Children and Safer Recruitment in Education' (concerning which see further Chapter 4 below).

THE DOCTRINE OF PRECEDENT

1.15 The importance of the doctrine of precedent to the law of England and Wales cannot be over-emphasised. This is because cases where points of principle (and not just the manner in which existing principles are applied to the facts of the case) are decided by the higher courts *are* the law, unless or until they are overturned by a higher court or by legislation.

1.16 The doctrine of precedent applies in the following manner. Earlier decisions of courts and tribunals will sometimes (but not always) bind courts or tribunals when deciding subsequent cases. Furthermore, the decision of a court or tribunal is not regarded as an indivisible whole: some parts may have binding effect, but other parts may not.

1.17 Broadly speaking, where a principle of law is applied as a necessary part of its decision in a case by a court or tribunal which is higher in the hierarchy than other courts or tribunals (as described below), those other courts or tribunals are bound to apply that principle to relevant cases which subsequently come before them. Sometimes, a judgment will include comments which are not strictly necessary for the determination of the case. When that occurs, these comments will not bind any other courts or tribunals, although they may be persuasive as far as later courts or tribunals are concerned. The Latin terms used to describe these two kinds of statement are *ratio decidendi* (for binding statements) and *obiter dicta* (for ones which do not bind). The first can be

---

[33] See para **6.5**, n 4 below.
[34] SI 2003/1910 as amended.
[35] SI 2003/3234 (W 314) as amended.

translated loosely as 'reason for the decision', and the second can be translated loosely as 'something said by the way'. There may be more than one principle laid down in a case, however, and the definition of *ratio decidendi* is not entirely clear. The following definition is suggested in a leading textbook on the matter:[36]

> 'The *ratio decidendi* of a case is any rule of law expressly or impliedly treated by the judge as a necessary step in reaching his conclusion, having regard to the line of reasoning adopted by him, or a necessary part of his direction to the jury. (The adoption of one line of reasoning by the judge is not incompatible with his adopting a further line of reasoning. Allowance must always be made for the fact that a case may have more than one *ratio decidendi*.)'

1.18 The highest court in the land is the Judicial Committee of the House of Lords and the members of that committee are known as Law Lords. They are appointed as life peers, primarily to sit as members of that committee. Decisions of the Judicial Committee of the House of Lords bind all other courts or tribunals, including the next court below, which is the Court of Appeal. Below the Court of Appeal, so far as relevant, there are the High Court and the EAT. The EAT is regarded as being on the same level as the High Court. Employment tribunals are directly below the EAT. An appeal from a county court lies to the Court of Appeal, but a county court is lower in the hierarchy than the High Court.

1.19 The decisions of courts from other common law jurisdictions (such as Northern Ireland) are of persuasive, but not binding, authority.

1.20 The effect of the doctrine of precedent, both generally and on employment matters, is broadly as follows. The House of Lords may decline to follow an earlier decision of that House. The Court of Appeal is bound by decisions of the House of Lords. Principles laid down by the Court of Appeal normally bind that court, and always bind the High Court and the EAT. Principles laid down by the House of Lords, the Court of Appeal and the EAT bind an employment tribunal. A decision on a point of principle made by a judge of the High Court will not bind a judge deciding a later case in that court, but will be departed from only if the court hearing the later case is convinced that the decision was wrong.[37] Similarly, the EAT is not bound by a previous decision of that tribunal, but such a decision will only be departed from in exceptional circumstances or where there are previous inconsistent decisions.[38] Strictly speaking, a decision of the High Court will not bind the EAT,[39] although such a decision will be of great persuasive authority and the

---

[36] Sir Rupert Cross and Dr J W Harris *Precedent in English Law* 4th edn (Oxford University Press, 1991), at p 72.
[37] *Huddersfield Police Authority v Watson* [1947] KB 842, 848; *R v Greater Manchester Coroner, ex parte Tal* [1985] QB 67, 81.
[38] *Secretary of State for Trade and Industry v Cook* [1997] ICR 288, 292; *Digital Equipment Co Ltd v Clements (No 2)* [1997] ICR 237.
[39] See *Chief Supplementary Benefit Officer v Leary* [1985] 1 All ER 1061 and *Portec (UK) Ltd v Mogensen* [1976] ICR 396, 400.

EAT would not lightly depart from it.[40] However, an employment tribunal will be bound by a relevant decision of the High Court.[41]

WHO DETERMINES EMPLOYMENT DISPUTES?

1.21 Most employment disputes are determined by employment tribunals. Some disputes, however, may have to be determined by the High Court, including applications for judicial reviews of decisions which are affected by public law. It is rare for an employment matter to be affected by the principles of public law, but where relevant in this book, mention is made of the possibility of an application for judicial review.

1.22 Some employment law issues affecting schools are purely contractual, and in some cases they could be determined only by the county court or the High Court.

Employment tribunals

1.23 Employment tribunals are, to use legal jargon, creatures of statute. That means that they can decide only matters which Parliament has given them to decide. Their jurisdiction includes:

(1) claims of unfair dismissal;

(2) claims of less favourable treatment on a prohibited ground, such as that the employee has made a protected disclosure within the meaning of the Employment Rights Act 1996;

(3) claims of unlawful discrimination on the various grounds mentioned above, such as sex, race, or disability;

(4) claims regarding trade union rights conferred on individuals by the Trade Union and Labour Relations (Consolidation) Act 1992;

(5) claims of breach of contract where the claimant has been dismissed; and

(6) claims of, or in relation to, a breach of one or more obligations to consult in respect of redundancies or transfers under the Transfer of Undertakings (Protection of Employment) Regulations 2006.[42]

1.24 An employment tribunal will normally consist of two lay members, and a chairman who will be either a solicitor or a barrister. The lay members are appointed from persons nominated by employers' representatives on the one

---

[40] *Portec (UK) Ltd v Mogensen* [1976] ICR 396, 400.
[41] *Chief Supplementary Benefit Officer v Leary* [1985] 1 All ER 1061.
[42] SI 2006/246.

hand, and employees' representatives on the other hand. The EAT, which hears appeals from the tribunals, is staffed in much the same way, although the chairman is either a High Court judge or a circuit judge.

1.25 The existence of the two lay members in the employment tribunal has led to them being characterised as the 'industrial jury' (the term 'industrial' having been adopted in the days when these tribunals were known as industrial tribunals). The practical expertise in employment relations provided by the lay members is one of the reasons for a marked reluctance on the part of appellate bodies to interfere with decisions of employment tribunals.

Employment Act 2002 grievance procedures

1.26 Currently, a number of claims may not proceed unless and until the claimant has initiated the applicable grievance procedure as provided for by the Employment Act 2002. The statutory grievance procedures provided for by that Act are considered in Chapter 2 below.

A PRACTICAL FACTOR: THE RARE AWARD OF COSTS

1.27 One factor which affects the practice of the law of employment to a significant extent is the situation relating to the award of costs in the employment tribunal and the EAT. The normal practice in relation to costs in civil courts is that the successful party is awarded his costs, and the unsuccessful party pays both his own costs and those of the successful party. However, costs may only be awarded in the employment tribunal in strictly defined circumstances. Ignoring certain specific circumstances, such as where an employment tribunal hearing is adjourned on the application of a party,[43] a costs order may be made only if in the opinion of the tribunal (or a chairman, if sitting alone) a party:

> 'has in bringing the proceedings, or he or his representative has in conducting the proceedings, acted vexatiously, abusively, disruptively or otherwise unreasonably, or the bringing or conducting of the proceedings by the paying party has been misconceived.'[44]

A costs order may be made also against a party who has not complied with an order or practice direction.[45] In all of these cases, the employment tribunal (or the chairman, if sitting alone) 'may have regard to the paying party's ability to pay when considering whether it or he shall make a costs order or how much that order should be'.[46]

---

[43] See r 40(1) of the Employment Tribunals Rules of Procedure 2004, set out in Sch 1 to the Employment Tribunals (Constitution and Rules of Procedure) Regulations 2004, SI 2004/1861.
[44] Ibid, r 40(2) and (3). The term 'paying party' is technical, and means the party against whom the order is, or may be, made: see r 38(1)(a).
[45] Ibid, r 40(4).
[46] Ibid, r 41(2).

1.28 Similarly, costs may be awarded by the EAT only in certain circumstances. Ignoring also certain specific circumstances such as that a party has failed to comply with a direction of the EAT or has caused an adjournment of 'proceedings',[47] the EAT may make a costs order only where it appears to that tribunal that 'any proceedings brought by the paying party were unnecessary, improper, vexatious or misconceived or that there has been unreasonable delay or other unreasonable conduct in the bringing or conducting of the proceedings by the paying party'.[48] Accordingly, costs are only rarely awarded to successful parties in matters which are dealt with by employment tribunals. However, public funding (formerly known as 'legal aid') at the time of writing was not, and had never been, available for industrial or employment tribunal proceedings (although it is available for EAT proceedings).

1.29 Despite these rules relating to costs, it is not open to an employer to 'buy off' an employee's right to claim unfair dismissal (or breach of any other statutory employment law right) by offering the employee the maximum which could conceivably be granted by way of compensation by an employment tribunal, and arguing that the employee was acting 'vexatiously, abusively, disruptively or otherwise unreasonably' in pursuing his rights before an employment tribunal. This was expressly decided by the EAT in *Telephone Information Services Ltd v Wilkinson*.[49] Only if the employer expressly admitted the claim (and did not seek to prevent the employee from stating that the employer had done so) and offered to pay the employee the maximum which could have been ordered to be paid by an employment tribunal, would such a tribunal be likely to order the employee to pay the costs incurred by the employer in defending the claim after the making of the offer.[50] However, even then, complications could occur.[51] The only safe way to prevent an employee from continuing with most kinds of claim to an employment tribunal is to enter into a binding compromise agreement with the employee under s 203 of the Employment Rights Act 1996[52] or an equivalent provision in any other relevant employment legislation.

A FURTHER PRACTICAL FACTOR: RESTRICTIONS ON APPEALING

1.30 A further factor which affects the practice of employment law is that appeals may be brought from decisions of employment tribunals to the EAT only on a point of law. The same is true (although the wording in the Civil

---

[47] See r 34A(2)(a) and (c) of the Employment Appeal Tribunal Rules 1993, SI 1993/2854, as amended, concerning such circumstances.
[48] Ibid, r 34A(1).
[49] [1991] IRLR 148.
[50] The EAT in *Kopel v Safeway Stores plc* [2003] IRLR 753 was not referred to either *Wilkinson* or the authority referred to in the next footnote below.
[51] See *NRG Victory Reinsurance Ltd v Alexander* [1992] ICR 675.
[52] See para **8.12** onwards below.

Procedure Rules 1998 concerning appeals does not say so in terms) in respect of appeals from (a) the county court, (b) the High Court and (c) the EAT to the Court of Appeal, and from the Court of Appeal to the House of Lords.

1.31 It is not always easy to discern whether a point of law is involved in an appeal. Indeed, it is difficult to describe when a question is one of fact, law, or mixed fact and law. However, it can safely be said that if an appeal is brought merely on the basis that the employment tribunal made the wrong decision on the facts, then the appeal will involve a question of law only if it is alleged that the employment tribunal (a) failed to take into account a relevant factor or (b) took into account an irrelevant factor, or that the employment tribunal's decision was perverse in that no tribunal, having properly directed itself as to the applicable law, could reasonably have come to it.[53] Furthermore, it is also clear that if an employment tribunal is alleged in an appeal to the EAT to have applied the law incorrectly, then the appeal will be on a point of law.

1.32 It is usually difficult to show that an employment tribunal's decision was perverse in the sense just mentioned. As a result, in part in order to avoid imposing costs on the respondents to appeals in which it is alleged that a decision of an employment tribunal was perverse, the EAT has instituted a 'filter' process for appeals. Under that process, an appellant may be required to attend a preliminary hearing of the EAT if it is not clear that a point of law is involved in the appeal. The potential respondent to the appeal is not obliged to attend that hearing. If the potential respondent does attend, the potential respondent is not allowed to make any representations to the EAT. If the appellant succeeds at that stage in satisfying the EAT that the appeal is one on a point of law which is of sufficient merit to be permitted to be pursued, then the appeal will be allowed to proceed. If, however, the EAT decides that a point of law is not involved, then the appeal will be dismissed.

THE AIM OF THIS BOOK

1.33 This book is intended as a practical rather than a definitive or academic guide to the law of employment as it applies in schools. It is hoped that this book contains an indication of all the factors which a court or tribunal would be likely to regard as relevant when determining the kinds of dispute which arise most commonly between employees in schools and their employers. The areas which have accordingly been concentrated on most are the law of unfair dismissal, statutory provisions applying directly to employment in schools, the law of discrimination (including European Community law), and various aspects of the employer/employee relationship. It is also hoped that the guidance within the book will avoid unnecessary disputes or, at least, their referral to a court or tribunal.

---

[53] The most clear and helpful indication of the applicability of the first two of these three tests – which are in truth public law tests – is in the EAT's judgment in *Thompson v SCS Consulting Ltd* [2001] IRLR 801, at para 37(5). However, Glidewell LJ said something very similar in *Lewis v Motorworld Garages Ltd* [1986] ICR 157, at 171F.

1.34 Examples, taken from real cases, have been given wherever possible in order to illustrate what is said in the text.

Chapter 2

DISPUTE RESOLUTION PROCEDURES IN THE EMPLOYMENT ACT 2002

INTRODUCTION AND OVERVIEW

New statutory procedures

2.1 As from 1 October 2004 a series of new procedural requirements applicable to most claims made to employment tribunals were introduced by the Employment Act 2002 (which is referred to in the rest of this chapter as 'the Act') and the Employment Act 2002 (Dispute Resolution) Regulations 2004[1] (which are referred to below as 'the Dispute Resolution Regulations'). The procedures are of two sorts: (1) grievance procedures and (2) dismissal and disciplinary procedures.

2.2 The procedures themselves are relatively simple. However, they have proved to be unattractive in some respects (at least to the EAT) and otherwise problematic in practice, with the result that already by the time of writing there was a considerable body of case law concerning them. The grievance procedures and their impact are described below first. The dismissal and discipline procedures and their impact are then described. Certain parts of the Act apply to both the grievance procedures and the dismissal and discipline procedures, and for convenience they are set out or their effects are described below only in relation to the grievance procedures. A word of warning is necessary, however, and it is this: at the time of writing, the Government had started a review of the manner in which the procedures and sanctions introduced by the Act had been working. There was therefore a possibility that those procedures and sanctions would be either modified or repealed. Accordingly, the usual caveat concerning the currency of the law as at the time of writing applies here even more acutely than in relation to the other aspects of the law which are described in this book.

Sanctions for non-compliance

2.3 The sanctions for failing to follow the procedures differ as between employers and employees. As far as employers are concerned, a failure to follow the applicable procedure (whether in whole or in part) is likely to lead to increased compensation for the employee to whose complaint the procedure should have been applied, if the employee makes a successful claim to an

---

[1] SI 2004/752.

employment tribunal in respect of the subject-matter of that complaint. If the procedure which was not followed was the statutory dismissal and discipline procedure and the employee is dismissed, then the employer will have dismissed the employee unfairly as a result of the failure to follow the procedure. However, there is no free-standing right to claim unfair dismissal where the employer has failed to follow the statutory dismissal procedure: it will be of value only to an employee who has more than a year's continuous employment or the claim is not one to which the requirement of a year's continuous employment applies.[2]

2.4 As far as employees are concerned, the sanction for a failure to follow the applicable procedure will depend on the circumstances. A failure to follow the employer's grievance procedure (whether in whole or in part) may lead to the employee being barred from making a claim to an employment tribunal in relation to the matter in question. A failure to follow the employer's dismissal and discipline procedure (for example by failing to appeal against dismissal) on the other hand may lead only to a diminution in the compensation payable to the employee if the employee makes a successful claim of unfair dismissal.

THE STATUTORY GRIEVANCE PROCEDURES

Introduction

2.5 The grievance procedures are set out in Sch 2 to the Act. They apply 'in relation to any grievance about action by the employer that could form the basis of a complaint by an employee to an employment tribunal under a jurisdiction listed in Schedule 3 or 4 [of the Act], or could do so if the action took place'.[3] However, they do not apply to a claim about a dismissal, whether actual or contemplated (unless it is a 'constructive' dismissal).[4] Nor do they apply to disciplinary action short of dismissal taken or proposed to be taken in relation to what the employer describes as an employee's conduct or capability, unless the employee's grievance is either (1) that the action amounted to, or, if it has yet to take place, would amount to, unlawful discrimination, or (2) 'that the grounds on which the employer took the action or is contemplating taking it were or are unrelated to the grounds on which he asserted that he took the action or is asserting that he is contemplating taking it'.[5]

2.6 The grievance procedures themselves are relatively straightforward. The most complicated aspect of the Act in so far as it applies to grievance procedures (and, in fact, dismissal and discipline procedures) is its effect (read

---

[2] *Scott-Davies v Redgate Medical Services* [2006] UKEAT/273/06.
[3] Dispute Resolution Regulations 2004 (DRR 2004), reg 6(1).
[4] See DRR 2004, reg 6(5), read with the definition of 'dismissed' in reg 2(1). The grievance procedures therefore do not apply to a complaint that the employer has discriminated against the employee by dismissing him expressly: see *Hart v English Heritage* [2006] IRLR 915, para 16, and *Lawrence v HM Prison Service* [2007] IRLR 468.
[5] DRR 2004, regs 6(6) and 7(1) read with the definition of 'relevant disciplinary action' in reg 2(1). See further paras **2.23** and **2.24** below concerning this situation.

as it is necessary to do so in conjunction with the Dispute Resolution Regulations) where the employee fails to follow the applicable procedure.

The grievance procedures

2.7 There are two grievance procedures in Pt 2 of Sch 2 to the Act: the 'standard' procedure and the 'modified' procedure. There is no substitute for the wording of the Act. The two procedures are as follows:

'**Chapter 1**

Standard procedure

Step 1: statement of grievance

6 The employee must set out the grievance in writing and send the statement or a copy of it to the employer.

Step 2: meeting

7 (1) The employer must invite the employee to attend a meeting to discuss the grievance.
 (2) The meeting must not take place unless –
  (a) the employee has informed the employer what the basis for the grievance was when he made the statement under paragraph 6, and
  (b) the employer has had a reasonable opportunity to consider his response to that information.
 (3) The employee must take all reasonable steps to attend the meeting.
 (4) After the meeting, the employer must inform the employee of his decision as to his response to the grievance and notify him of the right to appeal against the decision if he is not satisfied with it.

Step 3: appeal

8 (1) If the employee does wish to appeal, he must inform the employer.
 (2) If the employee informs the employer of his wish to appeal, the employer must invite him to attend a further meeting.
 (3) The employee must take all reasonable steps to attend the meeting.
 (4) After the appeal meeting, the employer must inform the employee of his final decision.

Chapter 2

Modified procedure

Step 1: statement of grievance

9 The employee must –

(a) set out in writing –
  (i) the grievance, and

   (ii) the basis for it, and
(b) send the statement or a copy of it to the employer.

Step 2: response

10 The employer must set out his response in writing and send the statement or a copy of it to the employee.'

General requirements of the procedures in Schedule 2

2.8 There are some general requirements which apply to both the grievance procedures and the discipline and dismissal procedures in Sch 2 to the Act. They are set out in Pt 3 of Sch 2, and are in the following terms:

'*Timetable*

12 Each step and action under the procedure must be taken without unreasonable delay.

Meetings

13(1) Timing and location of meetings must be reasonable.
(2) Meetings must be conducted in a manner that enables both employer and employee to explain their cases.
(3) In the case of appeal meetings which are not the first meeting, the employer should, as far as is reasonably practicable, be represented by a more senior manager than attended the first meeting (unless the most senior manager attended that meeting).'

What is a grievance for the purposes of Schedule 2 to the Act?

2.9 The procedures set out in Part 2 of Sch 2 are only applicable to matters raised by an employee with his employer as a grievance.[6] An employee is required to 'set out the grievance in writing and send the statement or a copy of it to the employer'.[7] The EAT has given a liberal interpretation to the word 'grievance' in this context. It has decided that the proper approach to take when deciding whether or not an employee has raised a grievance about the subject-matter of a claim is to see whether or not the employee has referred in any way to the subject-matter of the claim in any kind of written complaint. Thus, if the employer, on a fair reading of the statement and having regard to the particular context in which it was made, could be expected to appreciate that a relevant grievance is being raised, then the employee will have satisfied the requirement to state his grievance for the purposes of the standard grievance procedure.[8]

---

[6] Paragraph 15(1) of Sch 2 to the Act.
[7] Ibid, Sch 2, para 6.
[8] See eg *Canary Wharf Management Ltd v Edebi* [2006] ICR 719, para 25.

2.10 Similarly, a grievance does not need to be raised under the employer's grievance procedure, or to state that it is raised as a grievance under the applicable statutory procedure. Even a letter of resignation can be a grievance for the purposes of the statutory grievance procedures,[9] as can be a letter from the employee's solicitor.[10] So can be a formal request to work a three-day week after an informal request has been refused.[11]

2.11 However, certain statements of complaint are specifically not to be taken to be grievances for the purposes of the statutory grievance procedures. These are[12] formal questions asked under certain statutory prohibitions on discrimination, namely s 7B of the Equal Pay Act 1970, s 74 of the Sex Discrimination Act 1975, s 65 of the Race Relations Act 1976, s 56 of the Disability Discrimination Act 1995, reg 33 of the Employment Equality (Religion or Belief) Regulations 2003[13] and reg 33 of the Employment Equality (Sexual Orientation) Regulations 2003.[14]

2.12 Further, a complaint of a protected disclosure (within the meaning of s 43A of the Employment Rights Act 1996 (ERA 1996)) probably must state that it relates to that matter. This is the result of para 15 of Sch 2 to the Act, which provides:

> '15(1) The procedures set out in Part 2 are only applicable to matters raised by an employee with his employer as a grievance.
> (2) Accordingly, those procedures are only applicable to the kind of disclosure dealt with in Part 4A of the Employment Rights Act 1996 (c 18) (protected disclosures of information) if information is disclosed by an employee to his employer in circumstances where –
>   (a) the information relates to a matter which the employee could raise as a grievance with his employer, and
>   (b) it is the intention of the employee that the disclosure should constitute the raising of the matter with his employer as a grievance.'

2.13 It will be noted that the modified procedure requires the employee to do more than merely state the grievance in writing. In addition, the employee must state 'the basis for it'. It was held by the EAT in *City of Bradford Metropolitan District Council v Pratt*[15] that merely stating 'I have been subjected to unlawful sex discrimination in relation to pay and conditions' was not enough to satisfy that requirement. In order to satisfy the requirement of the modified procedure, a grievance must set out 'not only the grievance he holds but the

---

[9] *Galaxy Showers Ltd v Wilson* [2006] IRLR 83.
[10] *Mark Warner Ltd v Aspland* [2006] IRLR 87. In *Arnold Clark Automobiles v Stewart* UKEATS/0052/05, the EAT specifically held (in para 29) that 'the "Without prejudice" formula did not prevent' a solicitors' letter from being properly viewed as a statement of grievance at step 1.
[11] *Commotion Ltd v Rutty* [2006] IRLR 171.
[12] See DRR 2004, reg 14.
[13] SI 2003/1660.
[14] SI 2003/1661.
[15] [2007] IRLR 192.

essential reasons why he holds his grievance, in sufficient detail to enable the employer to respond'.[16] The EAT also said this:[17]

> 'The amount of detail the employee will be able to give is likely to depend on the nature of the grievance. There will be some grievances where the employee will know as much as or more than the employer, if for example the grievance relates to discriminatory harassment or bullying. Then the employee, who (it must be remembered) has opted for or at least agreed to the [modified grievance procedure], will be expected to set out his account in reasonable detail, not necessarily mentioning every detail but certainly informing the employer of the important matters which the employer should investigate and consider. There will be other grievances where, in the nature of things, an employee may not have full access to the facts, but has formed a grievance based on a suspicion or set of suspicions that certain facts exist. Then it will suffice that the written statement identifies not only his grievance but, in reasonable detail, why he holds the suspicions he does. Detailed evidence (in the sense of the prepared statements which would be appropriate for a tribunal hearing) is not required.'

What is required from an employee who appeals?

2.14 An employee need not state any reasons for appealing against a decision of his employer, in order to comply with the relevant requirement of the applicable statutory grievance procedure. He needs merely to 'inform the employer' that he wishes to appeal.[18]

When does the modified procedure apply?

2.15 The Act says nothing about the circumstances in which the standard grievance procedure is not to apply, and the modified procedure is to do so. The Dispute Resolution Regulations state the circumstances in which both procedures will apply. The standard procedure applies unless specific circumstances exist, in which case the modified procedure will apply. The modified procedure will apply when the employee has ceased to be employed by the employer and the employer was:

(1) unaware of the grievance before the employment had ceased,

(2) was so aware but the standard grievance procedure was not commenced before the last day of the employee's employment, or

(3) if it was so commenced, was not completed before the last day of the employee's employment,

and (in all of these cases) the employer and the employee have agreed that the modified procedure should be used.[19]

---

[16] [2007] IRLR 192, para 44.
[17] Ibid.
[18] *Masterfoods (a division of Mars UK Ltd) v Wilson* [2007] ICR 370.
[19] DRR 2004, reg 6(3).

What amounts to non-compliance with a grievance procedure in Schedule 2 to the Act?

2.16 In some situations, it may not be entirely clear whether a requirement of the applicable grievance procedure is to be regarded as not having been complied with. For example, is there such non-compliance if a meeting which is intended to comply with that procedure is held at an unreasonable time or location? The Dispute Resolution Regulations provide for a number of situations. There are regulations which apply generally, and regulations which apply to particular situations. In some situations, the parties are to be treated as having complied with the requirements of the applicable grievance procedure.

General circumstances affecting the application of the statutory grievance procedures

2.17 Regulation 12 of the Dispute Resolution Regulations provides some clarification of the general question when there will be non-compliance with a grievance procedure in Sch 2 to the Act. Its terms are these:

> **'Failure to comply with the statutory procedures**
>
> (1) If either party fails to comply with a requirement of an applicable statutory procedure, including a general requirement contained in Part 3 of Schedule 2, then, subject to paragraph (2), the non-completion of the procedure shall be attributable to that party and neither party shall be under any obligation to comply with any further requirement of the procedure.'

2.18 The rest of reg 12 is complicated, and has to be read together with regs 11 and 13. Regulation 11 stipulates some 'general circumstances in which the statutory procedures do not apply or are treated as being complied with'. Regulation 13 applies where there is a failure to attend a meeting. Regulation 12(2) is relatively uncomplicated, because it links reg 11 to reg 12(1) in that it provides that 'where the parties are to be treated as complying with the applicable statutory procedure, or any requirement of it, there is no failure to comply with the procedure or requirement'. However, this is stated to be subject to reg 12(4). The effect of these interlinking parts of the Dispute Resolution Regulations is as follows.

2.19 If a party has reasonable grounds for believing that starting the applicable grievance procedure or complying with a requirement of that procedure once it has been started 'would result in a significant threat to himself, his property, any other person or the property of any other person', then the procedure will not apply, unless the behaviour of one of the parties has had that result, in which case the applicable procedure will be regarded as having applied and that party's behaviour will be treated as having caused a failure to comply with the relevant requirement of that procedure.[20]

---

[20] DRR 2004, regs 11(1), (2) and (3)(a) and 12(3) and (4).

2.20 In addition, the applicable grievance procedure will not apply if a party 'has been subjected to harassment and has reasonable grounds to believe that commencing the procedure or [if it has already been commenced] complying with [a requirement of it] would result in his being subjected to further harassment'.[21] Harassment for this purpose is defined as it is throughout the current law of discrimination, namely 'conduct which has the purpose or effect of . . . (a) violating the person's dignity, or (b) creating an intimidating, hostile, degrading, humiliating or offensive environment for him', with the caveat that 'conduct shall only be regarded as having that purpose or effect if, having regard to all the circumstances, including in particular the perception of the person who was the subject of the conduct, it should reasonably be considered as having that purpose or effect'.[22] In this situation also, if the harassment was the result of the behaviour of one of the parties, then the applicable procedure will be regarded as having applied and that party will be treated as having caused the failure to comply with the relevant requirement of the procedure.[23]

2.21 The applicable grievance procedure will not apply also if it is 'not practicable for the party to commence the procedure or comply with the subsequent requirement within a reasonable period'.[24] It is of note that it must be 'not practicable', and not 'not reasonably practicable'.

2.22 In the case of meetings which are part of the grievance procedure, if it is 'not reasonably practicable' for either:

(a) the employee or, if he is exercising his right to be accompanied under s 10 of the Employment Relations Act 1999, his companion, or

(b) the employer,

to attend a meeting which was 'organised in accordance with the applicable statutory procedure for a reason which was not foreseeable when the meeting was arranged', then the party in question will 'not be treated as having failed to comply with that requirement of the procedure'.[25] The employer will in that situation nevertheless be under a continuing duty to invite the employee to attend a meeting and, where the employee wishes to be accompanied by a representative pursuant to s 10 of the Employment Relations Act 1999 and the employee proposes an alternative time under s 10(4), to invite the employee to attend the meeting at that time.[26] If, however, the employer invites the employee to attend a further meeting and it is again not reasonably practicable for:

(a) the employee or (if appropriate) his companion, or

---

[21] DRR 2004, reg 11(1), (2) and (3)(b).
[22] Ibid, reg 11(4).
[23] See ibid, reg 12(3) and (4).
[24] Ibid, reg 11(1) and (3)(c).
[25] Ibid, reg 13(1). It will be noted that the reason must have been not foreseeable, as opposed to not reasonably foreseeable.
[26] Ibid, reg 13(2).

(b) the employer,

to attend the meeting 'for a reason which was not foreseeable when the meeting was arranged', then the employer will be under no further such duty and the parties will be treated as having complied with the applicable grievance procedure.[27]

Particular circumstances affecting the application of the statutory grievance procedures

2.23 Where an employer has taken, or is contemplating taking, 'relevant disciplinary action' (meaning 'action, short of dismissal, which the employer asserts to be based wholly or mainly on the employee's conduct or capability, other than suspension on full pay or the issuing of warnings (whether oral or written)',[28] and an employee is aggrieved on the basis that the relevant disciplinary action amounted to, or, if it took place, would amount to, unlawful discrimination,[29] then the standard or (as the case may be) the modified grievance procedure will apply, but the parties will be treated as having complied with it if the employee sets out the grievance in a written statement and sends the statement, or a copy of it, to his employer before the meeting referred to in para 3 or para 5 of Sch 2 to the Act (which are the appeal meetings for the standard and modified dismissal and discipline procedures).[30] The parties will also be treated as having complied with the applicable grievance procedure if neither the standard nor the modified dismissal and discipline procedure is being followed but the employee has set out the grievance in a written statement and sent it, or a copy of it, to his employer 'before presenting any complaint arising out of the grievance to an employment tribunal'.[31]

2.24 Similarly, where an employee's grievance is that the employer has taken, or is contemplating taking, relevant disciplinary action against the employee and one of the reasons for the grievance is that 'the grounds on which the employer took the action or is contemplating taking it were or are unrelated to the grounds on which he asserted that he took the action or is asserting that he is contemplating taking it,' then the standard or (as the case may be) modified grievance procedure will apply but the parties will be treated as having complied with it if the employee takes either of the two steps referred to in the preceding paragraph above.[32] Thus the parties will be treated as having

---

[27] DRR 2004, reg 13(3) and (4).
[28] Ibid, reg 2(1).
[29] 'Unlawful discrimination' is discrimination contrary to the Equal Pay Act 1970, the Sex Discrimination Act 1975, the Race Relations Act 1976, the Disability Discrimination Act 1995, the Employment Equality (Religion or Belief) Regulations 2003, SI 2003/1660, the Employment Equality (Sexual Orientation) Regulations 2003, SI 2003/1661, or the Employment Equality (Age) Regulations 2006, SI 2006/1031: see DRR 2004, reg 7(3), as amended.
[30] DRR 2004, reg 7(1)(a) and (2)(a).
[31] Ibid, reg 7(1)(a) and (2)(b).
[32] Ibid, reg 7(1)(b) and (2).

complied with the applicable grievance procedure if the employee sends to the employer a written statement setting out the grievance, or a copy of that statement, either (1) before the appeal meeting referred to in para 3 or para 5 of Sch 2 to the Act, or (2) if neither the standard nor the modified dismissal and discipline procedure is being followed, before presenting any complaint arising out of the grievance to an employment tribunal.[33]

2.25 Where the standard grievance procedure is applicable, the employee has ceased to be employed by the employer, the employee has set out the grievance in writing and sent the statement or a copy of it to the employer, and since the end of the employment it has ceased to be reasonably practicable for the employee or the employer to comply with the requirements in para 7 or para 8 of Sch 2 to the Act (which concern the initial meeting and the appeal meeting), then, with one exception, the parties will be treated as having complied with such requirement(s) of Sch 2 as have not been complied with.[34] That exception is that the requirements of paras 7(1) to (3) of Sch 2 have been complied with but the requirement in para 7(4) has not.[35] In that situation, the employer will be treated as having failed to comply with para 7(4) unless he 'informs the employee in writing of his decision as to his response to the grievance'.[36] Accordingly, the employer will only be absolved from his responsibility in those circumstances for informing the employee of his right of appeal.

2.26 The final two situations in which the statutory grievance procedures do not apply are the simplest to state but probably of greatest application. One is that 'a person who is an appropriate representative of the employee having a grievance' has 'written to the employer setting out the grievance' on behalf not only of the employee but also at least one other employee.[37] Thus the statutory grievance procedures do not apply where a collective grievance is raised by an 'appropriate representative'. An 'appropriate representative' is the same for these purposes as for the purposes of collective employment rights, concerning which see Chapter 9 below.[38]

2.27 Similarly, if there is 'a procedure in operation, under a collective agreement made between two or more employers or an employers' association and one or more independent trade unions, that provides for employees of the employer to raise grievances about the behaviour of the employer and have them considered,' and the employee is entitled to raise his grievance under that procedure, and does so, then the parties will be treated as having complied with the applicable grievance procedure.[39]

---

[33] DRR 2004, reg 7(2).
[34] Ibid, reg 8(1).
[35] Ibid, reg 8(2).
[36] Ibid.
[37] Ibid, reg 9(1).
[38] Ibid, reg 9(2) and (3).
[39] Ibid, reg 10.

The effect of a failure to follow the applicable grievance procedure

2.28 An employee who has a grievance to which the procedures in the Act apply may be wise to follow the applicable grievance procedure. The effect of a failure to follow the applicable procedure depends on the matter which is the subject of the grievance. An employer will also in most cases benefit from following the applicable procedure, but for different reasons.

Effect on the employee

2.29 A failure to start the applicable grievance procedure will mean that the employee will not be able to make a claim to an employment tribunal about the subject of the complaint if the claim is one of those which are set out in Sch 4 to the Act, as amended.[40] A claim for damages for breach of contract which arises or is subsisting on the ending of the contract of employment (which is the only kind of claim for damages for breach of contract which may be made to an employment tribunal[41]) is not included in Sch 4. This is probably because a claim for damages for breach of contract could be made in, for example, a county court even if access to an employment tribunal were precluded by the failure to follow the applicable grievance procedure. In any event, whatever the reason, a claim for damages for breach of contract of the relevant kind may be pursued in employment tribunal proceedings even though the employee has not followed either of the grievance procedures set out in Pt 2 of Sch 2 to the Act.

2.30 If, however, the employee has started the applicable grievance procedure but has not started to do so until after the expiry of the time limit for making a claim to an employment tribunal, then the claim will still be barred unless the time limit is extended by the tribunal. Even then, the claim cannot be made more than one month after the expiry of what the Act refers to as 'the original time limit',[42] but which has been interpreted (by the EAT in *Bupa Care Homes (BNH) Ltd v Cann*[43]) where the time limit has been extended by the tribunal to mean the time limit as so extended.

2.31 Further, and separately, an employee must wait at least 28 days after initiating the relevant grievance procedure before making a claim to an employment tribunal.[44] If he attempts to make the claim before that 28-day period has expired, then the claim will be rejected.[45] The employee will therefore have to make a fresh claim which is within the applicable time limit if his claim is to be permitted to proceed. This is a trap for the unwary employee.

---

[40] See s 32(1) and (2) of the Act.
[41] See the Industrial Tribunals Extension of Jurisdiction (England and Wales) Order 1994, SI 1994/1623, read with s 3(2) of the Employment Tribunals Act 1996.
[42] See s 32(4) of the Act.
[43] [2006] ICR 643.
[44] See s 32(3) of the Act.
[45] See rule 3 of the Employment Tribunals Rules of Procedure 2004, as set out in Sch 1 to the Employment Tribunals (Constitution and Rules of Procedure) Regulations 2004, SI 2004/1861.

2.32 A failure by an employee to follow the applicable grievance procedure may also mean that the compensation awarded to the employee in respect of the subject-matter of the complaint is reduced. This is the result of s 31(2) and (4) of the Act. The claims to which s 31 applies are set out in Sch 3 to the Act. It is of note that a claim for damages for breach of contract on the ending of the contract of employment is included in Sch 3.

2.33 Section 31(2) of the Act provides this:

> '(2) If, in the case of proceedings to which this section applies, it appears to the employment tribunal that –
>
> (a) the claim to which the proceedings relate concerns a matter to which one of the statutory procedures applies,
>
> (b) the statutory procedure was not completed before the proceedings were begun, and
>
> (c) the non-completion of the statutory procedure was wholly or mainly attributable to failure by the employee –
>
> (i) to comply with a requirement of the procedure, or
>
> (ii) to exercise a right of appeal under it,
>
> it must, subject to subsection (4), reduce any award which it makes to the employee by 10 per cent and may, if it considers it just and equitable in all the circumstances to do so, reduce it by a further amount, but not so as to make a total reduction of more than 50 per cent.'

2.34 Section 31(4) of the Act provides this:

> '(4) The duty under subsection (2) or (3) to make a reduction or increase of 10 per cent does not apply if there are exceptional circumstances which would make a reduction or increase of that percentage unjust or inequitable, in which case the tribunal may make no reduction or increase or a reduction or increase of such lesser percentage as it considers just and equitable in all the circumstances.'

Effect on the employer

2.35 An employer who fails to follow the applicable statutory grievance procedure may need to pay more compensation to the employee in question than would otherwise have been the case. This is the effect of s 31(3) and (4) of the Act. Section 31(3) provides this:

> '(3) If, in the case of proceedings to which this section applies, it appears to the employment tribunal that –
>
> (a) the claim to which the proceedings relate concerns a matter to which one of the statutory procedures applies,
>
> (b) the statutory procedure was not completed before the proceedings were begun, and
>
> (c) the non-completion of the statutory procedure was wholly or mainly attributable to failure by the employer to comply with a requirement of the procedure,
>
> it must, subject to subsection (4), increase any award which it makes to the employee by 10 per cent and may, if it considers it just and equitable in all

the circumstances to do so, increase it by a further amount, but not so as to make a total increase of more than 50 per cent.'[46]

Extension of time where employee complies with statutory grievance procedure within primary time limit

2.36 There is one aspect of the statutory grievance procedure legislation which is helpful to an employee. That is that the time limit for making any claim to which the procedures apply is automatically extended where the employee starts one of the two grievance procedures in Sch 2 to the Act within the primary time limit. It is then extended by three months.[47]

THE STATUTORY DISMISSAL AND DISCIPLINE PROCEDURES

Introduction

2.37 The statutory dismissal and discipline procedures (DDPs) are set out in Pt 1 of Sch 2 to the Act, and are in similar terms to those of the statutory grievance procedures in that Schedule. The roles are, of course, reversed. Thus, instead of the employee being obliged to set out his grievance in writing, the employer is obliged to state the basis for the proposed action. Otherwise, however, the principles are the same. For example, an employee who has reasonable grounds for believing that a dismissal or disciplinary procedure, whether statutory or otherwise, was being followed in respect of matters which consisted of or included the substance of a tribunal complaint at the expiry of the normal time limit for making that complaint, will have an extra three months to make the complaint.[48]

In what circumstances will the statutory dismissal and discipline procedures apply?

2.38 The DDPs apply whenever an employer 'contemplates dismissing' an employee, and for whatever reason.[49] Thus they apply where the employer is proposing to dismiss the employee for redundancy.[50] However, they do not apply in a number of circumstances, set out in reg 4 of the Dispute Resolution Regulations. These include that 'the employer's business suddenly ceases to function, because of an event unforeseen by the employer, with the result that it is impractical for him to employ any employees'.[51] They also include that 'the dismissal is one of a number of dismissals in respect of which the duty in s 188

---

[46] See para **2.34** above for s 31(4).
[47] DRR 2004, reg 15(1)(b).
[48] Ibid, reg 15(1)(a) and (2).
[49] Ibid, reg 3(1). As noted above, the DDPs do not apply to a 'constructive' dismissal. This is because reg 2(1) defines 'dismissed' as having 'the meaning given to it in section 95(1)(a) and (b) of the [ERA 1996]'.
[50] *Alexander v Brigden Enterprises Ltd* [2006] ICR 1277.
[51] DRR 2004, reg 4(1)(e).

of the 1992 Act (duty of employer to consult representatives when proposing to dismiss as redundant a certain number of employees) applies'.[52] Similarly, the DDPs do not apply where an employer dismisses 'all the employees of a description or in a category to which the employee belongs . . . provided that the employer offers to re-engage all the employees so dismissed either before or upon the termination of their contracts'.[53]

2.39 The DDPs also do not apply where an employer is proposing to dismiss an employee on retirement.[54] Nor do they apply where the employer could not continue to employ the employee without contravening a statutory restriction or prohibition.[55] As far as schools are concerned, this latter exception is most likely to apply where a teacher has failed his induction period.[56]

2.40 The DDPs apply whenever an employer 'contemplates' taking 'relevant disciplinary action' against an employee.[57] The term 'disciplinary action' is not defined by the Act. The term 'relevant disciplinary action' is defined as stated in para **2.23** above, namely as 'action, short of dismissal, which the employer asserts to be based wholly or mainly on the employee's conduct or capability, other than suspension on full pay or the issuing of warnings (whether oral or written)'.[58] Accordingly, the DDPs do not apply where the employer is proposing to give an employee even a final written warning.

What are the statutory dismissal and discipline procedures?

2.41 As with the statutory grievance procedures, there is a standard statutory DDP and a modified statutory DDP. Their terms need to be stated in full.

> '**Chapter 1**
>
> **Standard procedure**
>
> *Step 1: statement of grounds for action and invitation to meeting*
>
> 1 (1) The employer must set out in writing the employee's alleged conduct or characteristics, or other circumstances, which lead him to contemplate dismissing or taking disciplinary action against the employee.
> (2) The employer must send the statement or a copy of it to the employee and invite the employee to attend a meeting to discuss the matter.

---

[52] DRR 2004, reg 4(1)(b); see para **9.14** onwards below concerning the duty in s 188.
[53] Ibid, reg 4(1)(a).
[54] Ibid, reg 4(1)(h). See para **6.107** onwards below for the details of the procedure which must be followed where an employer is proposing to retire an employee.
[55] Ibid, reg 4(1)(f).
[56] See para **3.50** below for the prohibition.
[57] DRR 2004, reg 3(1).
[58] Ibid, reg 2(1).

Step 2: meeting

2 (1) The meeting must take place before action is taken, except in the case where the disciplinary action consists of suspension.
(2) The meeting must not take place unless –
   (a) the employer has informed the employee what the basis was for including in the statement under paragraph 1(1) the ground or grounds given in it, and
   (b) the employee has had a reasonable opportunity to consider his response to that information.
(3) The employee must take all reasonable steps to attend the meeting.
(4) After the meeting, the employer must inform the employee of his decision and notify him of the right to appeal against the decision if he is not satisfied with it.

Step 3: appeal

3 (1) If the employee does wish to appeal, he must inform the employer.
(2) If the employee informs the employer of his wish to appeal, the employer must invite him to attend a further meeting.
(3) The employee must take all reasonable steps to attend the meeting.
(4) The appeal meeting need not take place before the dismissal or disciplinary action takes effect.
(5) After the appeal meeting, the employer must inform the employee of his final decision.

Chapter 2

Modified procedure

Step 1: statement of grounds for action

4 The employer must –

(a) set out in writing –
   (i) the employee's alleged misconduct which has led to the dismissal,
   (ii) what the basis was for thinking at the time of the dismissal that the employee was guilty of the alleged misconduct, and
   (iii) the employee's right to appeal against dismissal, and
(b) send the statement or a copy of it to the employee.

Step 2: appeal

5 (1) If the employee does wish to appeal, he must inform the employer.
(2) If the employee informs the employer of his wish to appeal, the employer must invite him to attend a meeting.
(3) The employee must take all reasonable steps to attend the meeting.
(4) After the appeal meeting, the employer must inform the employee of his final decision.'

When does the modified procedure apply?

2.42 As with the statutory grievance procedures, the standard DDP applies unless the modified procedure is stated by the Dispute Resolution Regulations to apply. The modified procedure applies in relation to a dismissal where the circumstances set out in reg 3(2) apply. Those circumstances are that:

'(a) the employer dismissed the employee by reason of his conduct without notice,
(b) the dismissal occurred at the time the employer became aware of the conduct or immediately thereafter,
(c) the employer was entitled, in the circumstances, to dismiss the employee by reason of his conduct without notice or any payment in lieu of notice [that is, to dismiss the employee summarily because of a repudiation or fundamental breach by the employee of his contract of employment], and
(d) it was reasonable for the employer, in the circumstances, to dismiss the employee before enquiring into the circumstances in which the conduct took place,'

unless the employee presents a claim to an employment tribunal in respect of the dismissal before the employer has complied with the requirements of para 4 of Sch 2 to the Act.[59]

Circumstances in which the parties are treated as having complied with the dismissal and discipline procedures

2.43 In two circumstances, the appeal procedure in the applicable DDP is treated by the legislation as having been complied with. These are set out in reg 5 of the Dispute Resolution Regulations. One is that the employee has applied to an employment tribunal for what is called 'interim relief' under s 128 of the ERA 1996 (which is applicable in only some situations, perhaps the most notable of which is that the employee is dismissed and claims that he was dismissed for making a protected disclosure), and the applicable DDP has been started but there has not yet been an appeal meeting. The other situation where the appeal procedure in the applicable DDP is treated as having been complied with is where there is in existence an appeal procedure which 'operates by virtue of a collective agreement made between two or more employers or an employers' association and one or more independent trade unions' which 'gives the employee an effective right of appeal against dismissal or disciplinary action taken against him', and the employee has appealed under that procedure.

Effect of a failure to follow all or part of the statutory dismissal and discipline procedures

2.44 The primary effect of a failure by an employer to follow the applicable dismissal procedure is that the dismissal of the employee in question will be

---

[59] See para **2.41** above for Sch 2, para 4.

automatically unfair as a result of s 98A(1) of the ERA 1996. A further effect is that unless in the opinion of the employment tribunal it would result in 'injustice to the employer', the employee's basic award[60] must be a minimum of four weeks' pay (capped at the current maximum provided for by s 227 of the ERA 1996, which at the time of writing was £310 per week).[61]

2.45 The effects as far as an employee is concerned of a failure by him to comply with the requirements of the applicable DDP are stated in s 31(2) and (4) of the Act, and those subsections are set out in paras **2.33** and **2.34** above.

What is required for compliance by the employer with the dismissal and discipline procedures?

2.46 The DDPs 'are concerned only with establishing the basic statutory minimum standard'.[62] Thus:

> 'It is plainly not the intention of Parliament that all procedural defects should render the dismissal automatically unfair with the increased compensation that such a finding attracts. They are intended to apply to all employers, large and small, sophisticated and unsophisticated. They are not intended to impose all the requirements breach of which might, depending on the circumstances, render a dismissal unfair.'[63]

2.47 Accordingly:

> '**38** ... At the first step the employer merely has to set out in writing the grounds which lead him to contemplate dismissing the employee, together with an invitation to attend a meeting. At that stage, in our view, the statement need do no more than state the issue in broad terms. We agree with [counsel for the employer] that at step one the employee simply needs to be told that he is at risk of dismissal and why. In a conduct case this will be identifying the nature of the misconduct in issue, such as fighting, insubordination or dishonesty. In other cases it may require no more than specifying, for example, that it is lack of capability or redundancy. ...
>
> **39** It is at the second step that the employer must inform the employee of the basis for the ground or grounds given in the statement. This information need not be reduced into writing; it can be given orally. The basis for the grounds are simply the matters which have led the employer to contemplate dismissing for the stated ground or grounds. In the classic case of alleged misconduct this will mean putting the case against the employee; the detailed evidence need not be provided for compliance with this procedure, but the employee must be given sufficient detail of the case against him to enable him properly to put his side of the story. The fundamental elements of fairness must be met.'[64]

---

[60] Within the meaning of s 119 of the ERA 1996. See para **8.111** below concerning basic awards.
[61] See s 120(1A) of the ERA 1996.
[62] *Alexander v Brigden Enterprises Ltd* [2006] ICR 1277, para 35.
[63] Ibid.
[64] Ibid.

2.48 The similarity of the requirements in the final two sentences of this extract with the 'ordinary' law of unfair dismissal[65] may be noticed. This may explain why s 98A(2) of the ERA 1996 has provided protection in the law of unfair dismissal for an employer who has failed to comply with some other procedural requirement and who shows that he would have dismissed the employee even if he had complied with that requirement.[66]

WITHOUT PREJUDICE NEGOTIATIONS

2.49 Finally, it is worth noting that the initiation by the employer of negotiations which are described as 'without prejudice' negotiations before the ending of the statutory procedures described above, could be problematic. This is the result of *BNP Paribas v Mezzotero*.[67] Only if there is a genuine dispute which the employer and the employee are genuinely attempting to resolve by negotiation would the 'without prejudice' privilege apply. The act of raising a grievance does not by itself mean that the parties to an employment relationship are necessarily in dispute.[68] Caution is therefore advisable in this situation.

---

[65] See in particular para **8.92** below.
[66] See paras **8.95–8.96** below for the impact of s 98A(2).
[67] [2004] IRLR 508.
[68] Ibid, para 28.

Chapter 3

THE REGULATION OF EMPLOYMENT IN SCHOOLS

INTRODUCTION

3.1 The subject-matter of this chapter is the regulation of the employment of persons to work in schools. There are separate sets of regulations concerning Wales in many instances, but they are in most cases in similar terms. Where they differ, that is stated below. The initial focus in this chapter is on the English regulations. This is because it would unduly complicate the text if the regulations which apply in Wales were always described in the same detail.

3.2 A person may not teach in a maintained school or in a non-maintained special school unless he satisfies certain qualification requirements and certain health requirements. A person may also not teach in any school (including an independent school) if he has been barred or suspended from doing so by the Secretary of State, the General Teaching Council for England (GTCE), or the General Teaching Council for Wales (GTCW). A person who is not a teacher may also be barred or suspended from working in a school by reason of his conduct.

PROHIBITION ON THE DOING OF SPECIFIED WORK IN A MAINTAINED SCHOOL OR A NON-MAINTAINED SPECIAL SCHOOL

3.3 Certain kinds of work, called 'specified work' may not be carried out by persons in a maintained school or a non-maintained special school in England except by a 'qualified teacher' or a person who is not a qualified teacher but satisfies certain requirements.[1] This 'specified work' is essentially the core work of a teacher, namely (1) planning and preparing lessons and courses for pupils, (2) delivering lessons to pupils, (3) assessing the development, progress and attainment of pupils, and (4) reporting on the development, progress and attainment of pupils.[2] The manner in which a person becomes a qualified

---

[1] See reg 5 of the Education (Specified Work and Registration) (England) Regulations 2003, SI 2003/1663, read with s 133(6) of the Education Act 2002. See the Education (Specified Work and Registration) (Wales) Regulations 2004, SI 2004/1744 (W 183) for the equivalent provisions in Wales.
[2] See reg 6 of those regulations.

teacher is mentioned below.[3] The persons who are not qualified teachers but who may nevertheless carry out such specified work are:[4]

(1) certain existing unqualified teachers in nursery classes or nursery schools who were in post before 1 September 1989;

(2) certain student or other trainee teachers;

(3) instructors with special qualifications or experience; and

(4) overseas trained teachers within the first four years of their teaching in the UK.

3.4 A person who is neither a qualified teacher nor able to satisfy these requirements may nevertheless carry out such specified work in a maintained school or a non-maintained special school 'in order to assist or support the work of a qualified teacher or a nominated teacher in the school', but only if the head teacher is satisfied that the person has the skills, expertise and experience required to carry out such work.[5] Furthermore, the person must be subject to the direction and supervision of a qualified or nominated teacher in accordance with arrangements made by the head teacher of the school.[6] In determining whether a person has such skills, expertise and experience, the head teacher may (not must) have regard to 'such standards for higher-level teaching assistants, or guidance concerning school support staff as may be published from time to time by the Secretary of State', and to 'such guidance as to contractual matters relating to school support staff as may be published from time to time by any local education authority or other employer'.[7]

QUALIFIED TEACHER STATUS

3.5 In order to be a 'qualified teacher' for this purpose (and any other purpose of the Education Acts), a person must satisfy the requirements of the Education (School Teachers' Qualifications) (England) Regulations 2003[8] and the Education (School Teachers' Qualifications) (Wales) Regulations 2004.[9] Qualified teacher status under those regulations is awarded by the GTCE or (as the case may be) the GTCW or the National Assembly, although that appears simply to be a formality as long as the teacher satisfies the requirements in one of (in England) paras 4–13 of Sch 2 to the regulations relating to England or

---

[3] See para **3.5** below.
[4] See Sch 2 to both sets of regulations (SI 2003/1663 and SI 2004/1744).
[5] See para 10(2)(a) and (c) of Sch 2 to the Education (Specified Work and Registration) (England) Regulations 2003. The parallel provisions in the regulations relating to Wales are in para 8 of Sch 2 to the Education (Specified Work and Registration) (Wales) Regulations 2004.
[6] Education (Specified Work and Registration) (England) Regulations 2003, Sch 2, para 10(2)(b); see Sch 2, para 10(3) for the definition of a 'nominated teacher' for this purpose.
[7] Education (Specified Work and Registration) (England) Regulations 2003, Sch 2, para 10(4).
[8] SI 2003/1662.
[9] SI 2004/1729 (W 173).

(in Wales) paras 5–14 of Sch 2 to the regulations relating to Wales.[10] The GTCE does so by 'written notification'.[11] The regulations apply not only to what one might call 'ordinary' teachers, but also to mandatory additional qualifications for teachers of (1) hearing impaired pupils,[12] (2) visually impaired pupils,[13] and (3) pupils who are both hearing and visually impaired.[14] There are also provisions in the regulations relating to teachers of art, handicraft, music, needlecraft and domestic subjects, science subjects, speech and drama, and to certain 'other qualifications'.[15]

REQUIREMENT (SUBJECT TO EXCEPTIONS) TO BE REGISTERED AS A TEACHER

3.6 As the titles to the Education (Specified Work and Registration) (England) Regulations and their Welsh counterpart suggest, not only must a person be a qualified teacher in order lawfully to do the work specified in those regulations (concerning which see para **3.3** above), but in order lawfully to be able to do that work, he or she must (subject to exceptions) be registered as a teacher in the register kept under s 3 of the Teaching and Higher Education Act 1998.[16]

3.7 In the case of a teacher in England, for these purposes, the teacher must be fully registered, in the register kept under the General Teaching Council for England (Registration of Teachers) Regulations 2000,[17] unless either of the limited exceptions in Sch 3 to the Education (Specified Work and Registration) (England) Regulations 2003 applies. Those exceptions apply to

(1) teachers who have failed to complete their induction period in accordance with the applicable regulations (concerning which, see para **3.50** onwards below) but who have appealed against the decision that they have failed to complete that period, and

(2) teachers who are eligible for registration and are taking up their first post as a teacher or are resuming their careers as a teacher and have applied to be registered.

They are then exempted from the requirement to be registered for the first four weeks of their employment as a teacher.

---

[10] See reg 10 of SI 2003/1662 and reg 6 of SI 2004/1729 (W 173).
[11] SI 2003/1662, reg 10(1). See reg 6 of SI 2004/1729 (W 173) for the equivalent provision in Wales.
[12] See regs 6, 8 and 9 of SI 2003/1662; see in relation to Wales regs 11, 13 and 14 of the Education (Teachers' Qualifications and Health Standards) (Wales) Regulations 1999, SI 1999/2817.
[13] See regs 7, 8 and 9 of SI 2003/1662; see in relation to Wales regs 12, 13 and 14 of SI 1999/2817.
[14] See regs 8 and 9 of SI 2003/1662; see in relation to Wales regs 13 and 14 of SI 1999/2817.
[15] See SI 2003/1662, Sch 2, Pt 2; see in relation to Wales SI 2004/1729, Sch 2, Pt 2.
[16] See reg 7 of both SI 2003/1663 and SI 2004/1744. See further para **3.36** below in relation to the keeping of the register.
[17] SI 2000/2176, as amended.

3.8 In the case of a teacher in Wales, reg 7 of the Education (Specified Work and Registration) (Wales) Regulations merely provides that the teacher must for these purposes be registered in the register kept under the General Teaching Council for Wales (Functions) Regulations 2000.[18] In contrast to the position under the regulations concerning England, a teacher who has not satisfactorily completed his induction period and who has appealed against the decision that he has failed to do so, is eligible to be registered in the register applicable to Wales pending the outcome of the appeal.[19] There is no equivalent in the Welsh regulations of the exemption for the first four weeks of employment of a new, or returning, teacher.

CONDITIONS AS TO HEALTH AND PHYSICAL CAPACITY

3.9 A 'person' (ie any person, and not just a teacher) may be employed in a maintained or non-maintained special school (or, in fact, a further education institution) in carrying out certain specified activities 'only . . . if, having regard to any duty of his employer under Part II of the Disability Discrimination Act 1995, he has the health and physical capacity to carry out that activity'.[20] In addition, any person who is in receipt of a pension (which was granted on the ground of ill-health) under reg E4(4) of the Teachers' Pensions Regulations 1997[21] 'is not to be regarded as having the health or physical capacity for teaching' unless he was granted such a pension before 1 April 1997.[22] In the latter case, the person may be appointed on a part-time basis to carry out the relevant activity.[23]

3.10 The relevant activities to which both sets of regulations apply are stated in reg 5. They are:

(1) planning and preparing lessons and courses for children;

(2) delivering lessons to children (including via distance learning or computer-aided techniques);

(3) assessing the development, progress and attainment of children;

(4) reporting on the development, progress and attainment of children;

---

[18] SI 2000/1979 (W 140), as amended.
[19] See reg 3A of SI 2000/1979 (W 140).
[20] See reg 6(1) of both the Education (Health Standards) (England) Regulations 2003, SI 2003/3139 and the Education (Health Standards) (Wales) Regulations 2004, SI 2004/2733, read with s 141(5) of the EA 2002. The word 'or' is used after the word 'health' in reg 6(1) of the regulations relating to Wales, whereas in reg 6(1) of the regulations relating to England, the word 'and' is used after the word 'health'. It is unlikely that any difference in effect is intended.
[21] SI 1997/3001, as amended.
[22] See reg 6(2) of both sets of regulations.
[23] See reg 6(3) of both sets of regulations.

(5) an activity which assists or supports teaching;

(6) supervising, assisting and supporting a child;

(7) an administrative or organisational activity which supports the provision of education; and

(8) an activity which is ancillary to the provision of education.

3.11 If an employer is satisfied that an existing employee may no longer have the health or physical capacity to carry out a relevant activity, then the employer must follow the procedure required by reg 7 of both sets of regulations. The employer must afford the employee an opportunity to submit medical evidence and make representations to the employer. The employer must consider that evidence and those representations, and may require the employee to submit to a medical examination. If the employee 'without good reason' fails to attend the medical examination or 'refuses to make available medical evidence or information sought by the medical practitioner', then the employer may reach a conclusion in the matter on the available evidence 'notwithstanding that further medical evidence may be desirable'.[24] The employer must in any event take into account '[medical] evidence which has been furnished in confidence on the ground that it would not be in the best interests of the person concerned to see it'.[25]

3.12 An employee has the right to require the employer to arrange a medical examination by a qualified medical practitioner appointed by the employer.[26] Either the employer or the employee may 'at any time before' a medical examination arranged under reg 7 takes place 'submit to the appointed medical practitioner a statement containing evidence or other matter relevant to the examination'.[27] The medical examination 'may be attended by a qualified medical practitioner appointed by the person being examined'.[28] It is not stated in either set of regulations whether this provision confers a right on an employee to insist on the attendance of his chosen medical practitioner, so that if the latter is unavailable for several months then the medical examination cannot proceed. It is possible that (1) the use of the word 'may' and (2) the failure by the regulations to state that the employee has a right to insist on the attendance of his chosen medical practitioner, have the effect that the employer would not contravene the regulations if it insisted on the examination going ahead without the employee's chosen doctor being present if such presence would unduly delay the examination. However, the situation is probably best

---

[24] The wording of the regulation applicable to Wales is slightly different from that of the regulation which applies in England. It appears that there will in practice be no difference in the effect of the two regulations.
[25] See reg 7(1)(b) of both sets of regulations. The wording of the provision relating to Wales is different, but to the same effect.
[26] See reg 7(1)(c) of SI 2003/3139 and reg 7(1)(d) of SI 2004/2733.
[27] See reg 7(2) of both sets of regulations.
[28] See reg 7(2) of the regulations relating to England. The wording of the equivalent provision relating to Wales (reg 7(3)) is slightly different, but is to the same effect.

regarded as governed in part by the implied term of trust and confidence, to which reference is made in paras **5.9** and **5.10** below. Thus, if it would be conduct which would be likely to damage seriously or destroy the relationship of trust and confidence for which there was no reasonable and proper cause, then it would be a 'constructive' dismissal to go ahead with the examination without the employee's chosen medical practitioner present. Alternatively, it could be said if the medical condition was a disability within the meaning of the Disability Discrimination Act 1995, that the failure to allow the employee's chosen medical practitioner to be present was less favourable treatment for a reason related to the disability (see further para **6.138** onwards below). However, for the reasons stated below, that might not be the correct conclusion.

THE BARRING OF PERSONS FROM TEACHING OR OTHERWISE WORKING WITH CHILDREN IN RELATION TO THE PROVISION OF EDUCATION

Introduction; Secretary of State's guidance

3.13 The regime governing the barring of persons from teaching or otherwise working with children in schools on the ground of their conduct is now quite complex, with interlocking responsibilities and powers. The Secretary of State has issued guidance in relation to barring unsuitable people from working with children and young persons. The current guidance was issued in September 2005 and is available on the internet.[29]

3.14 The Secretary of State has also issued guidance in relation to preventing unsuitable people from working with children and young persons in the education service. It is available on the same website, and has the number DFES-04217-2006.

The statutory framework

3.15 Section 142(1) of the Education Act 2002 (EA 2002) empowers the Secretary of State in relation to England, and the Secretary of State acting concurrently with the National Assembly for Wales in relation to Wales,[30] to direct that a person may not carry out work to which s 142 applies, or may do so only in certain circumstances or subject to specific conditions. Section 142 applies to:

(1) providing education (which for the purposes of s 142 includes vocational, social, physical and recreational training[31]) at:

---

[29] At http://www.teachernet.gov.uk.
[30] References below in this section to the Secretary of State should be read as applying also to the National Assembly for Wales on this basis.
[31] See EA 2002, s 142(9).

(a) a school[32] (including an independent school[33]) or

(b) an institution within the further education sector or an institution which is maintained by a local education authority (an LEA) and provides further education,

(2) providing education as an employee or under a contract for services where the other party to the contract is a local education authority or a person exercising a function relating to the provision of education on behalf of the local education authority, and

(3) taking part in the management of an independent school.[34]

It also applies[35] to work of a kind which brings a person regularly into contact with children[36] and which is carried out (whether or not under a contract) at the request or with the consent of a 'relevant employer', namely:

(1) an LEA,

(2) a person exercising a function relating to the provision of education on behalf of an LEA,

(3) the proprietor of a school,[37] which means the governing body in relation to a community, foundation or voluntary or community or foundation special school,[38] or

(4) the governing body of a further education institution.[39]

Grounds for giving a direction

3.16 A direction may be given under s 142(1) only on the grounds set out in s 142(4). These are:

(1) that the person to whom the direction relates is included (otherwise than provisionally) in the list kept under s 1 of the Protection of Children Act 1999 (POCA 1999),

(2) that the person is 'unsuitable to work with children',

(3) grounds relating to the person's misconduct,

---

[32] The term 'school' for these purposes is defined by EA 2002, ss 142(9), 212(2) and 212(3)(f), and EA 1996, s 4.
[33] See EA 2002, s 142(9).
[34] Ibid, s 142(2) and (9) and s 140(3).
[35] See ibid, s 142(3).
[36] That is, persons below the age of 18: ibid, s 142(9).
[37] Including an independent school: ibid, s 142(9).
[38] See EA 2002 s 212(2)–(4) and EA 1996, s 579(1).
[39] See EA 2002, s 142(9), which also defines (by reference to s 140) the meaning of the term 'further education institution'.

(4) grounds relating to the person's health, or

(5) only in relation to the management of an independent school, grounds relating to the person's professional incompetence.

Procedure for giving a direction

3.17 Section 142(5) of the EA 2002 empowers the making of regulations relating to the procedure to be followed in the giving of a direction under s 142(1), and the current regulations are the Education (Prohibition from Teaching or Working with Children) Regulations 2003.[40] They apply in both England and Wales except in one respect, which is stated below.[41] They afford a person in relation to whom the Secretary of State is considering making a direction (other than where the Secretary of State is required to give a direction, concerning which see the next paragraph below) an opportunity to make representations to him and, where appropriate, to submit medical evidence or other evidence to him within two months of the date of notification of the opportunity to do so (unless the Secretary of State does not know the whereabouts of the person).[42] Regulation 5 requires the Secretary of State to consult the employer of the person to whom the direction would relate, unless the Secretary of State is obliged by reg 8 to give a direction under s 142 (ie a direction barring a person from carrying out work to which s 142 applies). If the person is employed under arrangements made by an agent, the Secretary of State is obliged by reg 5 to consult that agent.

Circumstances in which a direction must be given

3.18 The Secretary of State is required to give a direction under s 142(1)(a) in a number of circumstances where certain criminal offences have been committed. The circumstances are stated in reg 8 of, and Sch 2 to, the Education (Prohibition from Teaching or Working with Children) Regulations 2003.[43] These include:

(1) that the person concerned pleads guilty to, or is convicted of, committing certain offences;[44]

---

[40] SI 2003/1184, as amended.
[41] See para **3.32** onwards below.
[42] See regs 6(1) and (3) and 8A of the Education (Prohibition from Teaching or Working with Children) Regulations 2003. The time limit may be extended by the Secretary of State if he considers that the person had good reason for not complying with the time-limit: regs 6(1) and 8A(2). A notice is deemed to be served 48 hours after the date on which it was sent: reg 6(2).
[43] SI 2003/1184, as amended, most recently by SI 2007/195. There is no substitute for a consideration of the complicated provisions of reg 8 and Sch 2 in any particular case.
[44] The offences are set out in Sch 2 to the Education (Prohibition from Teaching or Working with Children) Regulations 2003, as substituted by SI 2007/195.

(2) that the person concerned is the subject of a 'risk of sexual harm order within the meaning of section 123 of the Sexual Offences Act 2003';[45]

(3) in some cases that before or at the time of committing or being convicted of the offence, the person was carrying out work to which s 142 of the EA 2002 applies; and

(4) in most cases that at the time when the offence was committed, the person was aged 18 or over.

3.19 The Secretary of State is also required to give a direction under s 142(1)(a) of the EA 2002 in relation to a person where he is included (otherwise than provisionally) in the list kept by the Secretary of State under s 1 of the POCA 1999.[46] The Secretary of State is in addition required to give a direction under s 142(1)(a) where, on or after 1 June 2003, a person is made subject to a 'disqualification order' (meaning[47] an order made under s 30 of the Criminal Justice and Court Services Act 2000 (CJCSA 2000)).[48]

Appeals, revocations and power to vary directions

3.20 A person in respect of whom a direction has been given under s 142 may (subject to certain exceptions, concerning which see para **3.23** below) appeal 'to the Tribunal established under s 9 of the Protection of Children Act 1999' (known as, and referred to below as, the Care Standards Tribunal) against the decision to give the direction or against a decision not to vary or revoke the direction.[49] The procedure of the tribunal is governed by the Protection of Children and Vulnerable Adults and Care Standards Tribunal Regulations 2002.[50] It was held in *R v Secretary of State for Education, ex parte Standish*[51] that the Secretary of State must, when barring a teacher, make express findings of fact and give reasons for his decision. However, the subsequently-conferred right of appeal to the Care Standards Tribunal has probably superseded this ruling, since a finding on the facts as to the suitability of the person concerned to teach or otherwise come into contact with children will have to be made by that tribunal, under the Education (Prohibition from Teaching or Working with Children) Regulations 2003.[52] This is because under reg 13(1) of those regulations, if the tribunal considers that the direction 'is not

---

[45] See para 9 of Sch 2 to the Education (Prohibition from Teaching or Working with Children) Regulations 2003.
[46] See reg 8(1) and (2) of the Education (Prohibition from Teaching or Working with Children) Regulations 2003.
[47] See ibid, reg 2 as amended by SI 2007/195.
[48] See reg 8 and para 2 of Sch 2 of to the Education (Prohibition from Teaching or Working with Children) Regulations 2003; if the disqualification order occurred before 28 February 2007, then the person concerned must have been carrying out work to which s 142 of the EA 2002 applies before he was convicted of the offence to which the disqualification order relates.
[49] EA 2002, s 144.
[50] SI 2002/816, as amended.
[51] (1993) *The Times*, November 15.
[52] SI 2003/1184.

appropriate', then it may (not must) order the Secretary of State to revoke or vary the direction. It is difficult to envisage circumstances where, having arrived at such a conclusion, it would be lawful not to make such an order.

3.21 Only the Care Standards Tribunal has the power to revoke a direction that a person is unsuitable to work with children.[53] Such a revocation may occur only if the person in question makes an application to review the direction, and the application to review must be made in accordance with regs 10, 10A and 11 of the Education (Prohibition from Teaching or Working with Children) Regulations 2003.[54] The Care Standards Tribunal's permission is required for the making of such an application,[55] and certain conditions must be satisfied before such an application can be made.[56] For example, no such application may be made in the case of an adult until 10 years have elapsed since the direction was made.[57]

3.22 The Secretary of State may revoke or vary a direction given under s 142 which he has power to revoke[58] if he is 'in possession of information relevant to the decision to give the earlier direction which he did not have at the time that the decision was made' *and* he 'is in possession of evidence of a material change of circumstances of the person concerned occurring since the earlier direction was given'.[59] The Secretary of State must revoke a direction under s 142 given in relation to a person because he is included in the list kept by the Secretary of State under s 1 of the POCA 1999 where he is removed from that list.[60] Similarly, the Secretary of State must revoke a direction given under s 142 in relation to a person who is subject to a disqualification order where the order ceases to have effect.[61]

3.23 Appeals to the Care Standards Tribunal other than applications to review are governed by reg 12 of the Education (Prohibition from Teaching or Working with Children) Regulations 2003. No such appeal may be made against a direction under s 142 imposed pursuant to reg 8 of those regulations.[62] Nor may such an appeal be made on the ground of information of the sort referred to in the preceding paragraph above 'unless that information or evidence has first been brought to the attention of the Secretary

---

[53] See ss 142(6), 144(2) and 144(3) of the EA 2002.
[54] SI 2003/1184.
[55] See ibid, regs 10A(2) and 11(1).
[56] See ibid, regs 10A(1) and 11(2)–(4).
[57] See ibid, reg 11(4). In the case of a person who was a child when the barring order was made, the period is 5 years: reg 11(3).
[58] See ibid, reg 9(1) for the circumstances in which the Secretary of State may not revoke a direction. They are that either condition A or condition B stated in paras 1 and 2 of Sch 2 respectively is satisfied, or that a direction has been given 'on the grounds that a person is unsuitable to work with children and the person claims that he is no longer unsuitable to work with children'.
[59] See ibid, reg 9(2).
[60] Ibid, reg 9(3).
[61] Ibid, reg 9(4).
[62] See ibid, reg 12(1). See paras **3.18** and **3.19** above for the circumstances in which a direction must be given under reg 8.

of State under regulation 9'.[63] Furthermore, a finding of fact on which a conviction 'of any offence involving misconduct' must be taken to have been based may not be challenged on an appeal under the regulations.[64]

3.24 The Care Standards Tribunal may order the Secretary of State to revoke or vary a direction given under s 142 (other than, of course, an automatic prohibition imposed under reg 8 of the Education (Prohibition from Teaching or Working with Children) Regulations 2003) if it 'considers that the direction is not appropriate'.[65] However, it is precluded by reg 13(2) from considering 'any information relevant to the decision to give a direction or not to revoke or vary a direction which the Secretary of State did not have at the time the decision was made' or 'any evidence of a material change of circumstances of the person concerned occurring since the decision to give a direction or not to revoke or vary a direction was given'. The apparent purpose of this prohibition is to ensure that such information must first be put before the Secretary of State under reg 12(2).

Effect of a barring direction under section 142

3.25 One effect of a direction given under s 142(1) in relation to a person is that a relevant employer may not lawfully use that person to carry out work in contravention of the direction.[66] Another – perhaps more stark – consequence of a direction given under s 142(1) in relation to a person is that it is a criminal offence to employ such a person in a position known as a 'regulated position' within the meaning of s 36(1) of the CJCSA 2000, knowing that such a direction has been made in relation to him. This is the effect of s 35(2) of that Act, which makes it an offence for an individual – not a person, so the offence applies only to a natural person – knowingly to offer work in a regulated position to an individual who is disqualified from working with children, or to fail to remove an individual from such work. Such disqualification occurs:

(1) after an order has been made by a court under s 28, 29 or 29A of that Act in relation to a person,

(2) if the person in question is included (otherwise than provisionally) in a list kept under s 1 of the POCA 1999,

(3) he is included, 'on the grounds that he is unsuitable to work with children' in any list kept by the Secretary of State or the National Assembly for Wales under s 165 or 166 of the EA 2002,[67] or

---

[63] See ibid, reg 12(2). See the preceding para above concerning reg 9.
[64] See SI 2003/1184, reg 12(3).
[65] Ibid, reg 13(1).
[66] EA 2002, s 142(8). See para **3.15** above for the meaning of the term 'relevant employer'.
[67] The reference in s 35(4) of the CJCSA 2000 is to ss 470 and 471 of the Education Act 1996. However, those sections have been repealed and replaced by ss 165 and 166 of the EA 2002, and therefore, by virtue of s 17(2)(a) of the Interpretation Act 1978, the references to ss 470 and 471 must be read as references to ss 165 and 166.

(4) he is 'subject to a direction under' s 142 of the EA 2002 'given on the grounds that he is unsuitable to work with children'.[68]

3.26 In addition, it is an offence, contrary to s 35(1) of the CJCSA 2000, for a person who is disqualified from working with children for the purposes of that Act knowingly to apply for, or offer to do, or accept or do any work in a regulated position (unless the person proves on the balance of probabilities that 'he did not know, and could not reasonably be expected to know, that he was disqualified from working with children'[69]). Both that offence and the offence referred to in the preceding paragraph above are triable either way (ie either in a Magistrates' Court or the Crown Court) and the maximum penalty (if the case is tried on indictment, ie in the Crown Court) is imprisonment for 5 years and an unlimited fine.[70] If the case is tried in a Magistrates' Court, then the maximum penalties are a six-month prison term and a fine of £5,000.[71]

3.27 A 'regulated position' for these purposes is defined by s 36 of the CJCSA in the following manner. So far as relevant, it is:

(1) 'a position whose normal duties include work in an establishment mentioned in subsection (2)', which include 'an educational institution';

(2) 'a position whose normal duties include caring for, training, supervising or being in sole charge of children'[72];

(3) 'a position whose normal duties involve unsupervised contact with children under arrangements made by a responsible person';

(4) 'a position whose normal duties include supervising or managing an individual in his work in a regulated position'; and

(5) being 'a member of the governing body of an educational institution'.

3.28 A 'responsible person' for these purposes means so far as relevant a 'member of the governing body of an educational institution', the 'chief education officer of a local education authority', or 'the person in charge of any establishment mentioned in subsection (2) in which the child is accommodated . . . or receives education, and any person acting on behalf of such a person'.[73] An 'educational institution' is defined for these purposes by s 42(1) of the CJCSA 2000, and it is 'an institution which is exclusively or mainly for the provision of full-time education to' persons under the age of 18.

---

[68] CJCSA 2000, s 35(4), read with ss 42(1) and 30(5)(a).
[69] Ibid, s 35(3).
[70] See ibid, s 35(6).
[71] See ibid, s 35(6), read with Sch 1 to the Interpretation Act 1978, as amended, and s 32 of the Magistrates' Courts Act 1980, as amended.
[72] The word 'child' is defined for the purposes of ss 35 and 36 of the CJCSA 2000 by s 42(1) of that Act to mean 'a person under the age of 18'.
[73] See ibid, s 36(13)(b) and (d) read together with s 36(6).

Information to be given when an employee is dismissed or might have been dismissed from employment at a school

3.29 Regulation 4 of the Education (Prohibition from Teaching or Working with Children) Regulations 2003 applies only in relation to England (ie and not Wales, as to which, see below[74]). It requires the giving to the Secretary of State of specific information (stated in para **3.31** below) where a relevant employer[75] has ceased to use a person's services on a ground (not *the* ground):

'(i) that the person is unsuitable to work with children;
(ii) relating to the person's misconduct; or
(iii) relating to the person's health where a relevant issue is raised',

or where the employer 'might have ceased to use a person's services on such a ground had the person not ceased to provide those services'. Agents are also required by reg 4 to report similar information to the Secretary of State in analogous circumstances.

3.30 A 'relevant issue' for these purposes is defined by reg 2 of the Education (Prohibition from Teaching or Working with Children) Regulations 2003 to be:

'an issue which arises where the circumstances of the case, including occasions of conduct other than that in question, are such as to raise an issue concerning the safety and welfare of children.'

3.31 The information which is required by reg 4 to be given to the Secretary of State by a relevant employer is any of the following information or documents:[76]

(1) a 'statement of reasons for ceasing to use the person's services';

(2) 'Employer's records relating to the cessation of the use of the person's services or any contemplated cessation, including notes and minutes of meetings, interview notes and evidence supplied to or obtained by the employer';

---

[74] See reg 1(4) of SI 2003/1184.
[75] This is defined by reg 2 of SI 2003/1184 to have the meaning given by s 142(9) of the EA 2002 (concerning which, see para **3.15** above). A little oddly, since the term 'relevant employer' includes the proprietor of an independent school, there is a separate obligation to inform the Secretary of State imposed on such a proprietor by reg 8 of the Education (Provision of Information by Independent Schools) (England) Regulations 2003, SI 2003/1934. The obligation is equivalent to that which is provided for by reg 4 of SI 2003/1184, except that reg 8 of SI 2003/1934 imposes a time limit of a month for compliance. In addition reg 8 imposes an obligation to provide the Secretary of State 'such further information as may be requested by the Secretary of State which he considers relevant to the exercise of his functions under section 142 of the 2002 Act'. The situation in Wales is more straightforward in this respect: see para **3.32** below.
[76] See Pt 1 of Sch 1 to SI 2003/1184.

(3) 'Employer's records relating to conduct which eventually led to the cessation of the use of the person's services or might, but for the person having ceased to provide those services, have led the employer to cease to use his services, including notes and minutes of meetings, interview notes and evidence supplied to or obtained by the employer';

(4) 'Employer's letters, warnings or notices issued to a person in relation to the cessation of the use of his services or contemplated cessation, or the conduct which eventually led to the cessation of the use of the person's services or might, but for the person having ceased to provide those services, have led the employer to cease to use his services and the person's replies or representations in relation thereto';

(5) 'Any other statements, representations and evidence submitted by a person to the employer in relation to the cessation of his services or contemplated cessation, or the conduct which eventually led to the cessation of the use of the person's services or might, but for the person having ceased to provide those services, have led the employer to cease to use his services';

(6) 'Letter advising a person's intention to cease to provide services'; and, finally,

(7) 'Any other document or information which the employer considers is relevant to the exercise of the Secretary of State's functions under section 142 of the 2002 Act.'[77]

3.32 In relation to Wales, the Education (Supply of Information) (Wales) Regulations 2003[78] provide for an equivalent obligation, although in this case the obligation is to provide the relevant information to the National Assembly rather than to the Secretary of State. The obligation is imposed by regs 4 and 6 (reg 4 applying to employers and reg 6 applying to agents). The information which is to be conveyed is stated in the Schedule to those regulations in terms which are nearly identical to those of Sch 1 to the Education (Prohibition from Teaching or Working with Children) Regulations 2003. The only possibly material difference is that the word 'the' is inserted before 'conduct' in para 3 of Pts 1 and 2 of the Schedule to the Welsh regulations. The obligation imposed by the Education Supply of Information) (Wales) Regulations 2003 in relation to a teacher who was employed at an independent school is supplemented by reg 6 of the Independent Schools (Provision of Information) (Wales) Regulations 2003,[79] which provides:

> 'The proprietor of a registered school must, within 15 days of a request, provide the National Assembly for Wales with such information as may be requested by it which it considers is relevant to the exercise of its functions or the Secretary of

---

[77] See Pt 2 of Sch 1 to SI 2003/1184 for the equivalent information which is required to be given by an agent to the Secretary of State.
[78] SI 2003/542.
[79] SI 2003/3230.

State's functions under section 142 of the 2002 Act, and which has not already been provided under the Education (Supply of Information) (Wales) Regulations 2003.'

3.33 As described in the following paragraphs below, the GTCE and the GTCW now have disciplinary functions in relation to teachers, but they are precluded from considering cases where a relevant issue defined as stated in para **3.30** above arises and the Secretary of State (or, as the case may be, the National Assembly for Wales) wishes to consider the case with a view to exercising his (or its) powers under s 142.[80]

THE GENERAL TEACHING COUNCILS

Introduction

3.34 The functions of the GTCE and the GTCW (referred to where relevant below as 'the GTCs') are as provided for by the Teaching and Higher Education Act 1998 (THEA 1998) and regulations made under that Act. By far the most important of the functions of the GTCs as far as the employment of staff is concerned, are their disciplinary functions. Before those are described, however, it is helpful to refer to certain other functions of the GTCs.

Advice

3.35 The functions of the GTCs are in part advisory, in that they must, when they think fit, advise the Secretary of State or (as the case may be) the National Assembly for Wales, and such other bodies as he (or it) may designate on a number of matters.[81] Those matters are:

(1) standards of teaching,

(2) standards of conduct for teachers,

(3) the role of the teaching profession,

(4) the training, career development and performance management of teachers,

(5) recruitment to the teaching profession,

(6) the supply of teachers,

(7) the retention of teachers within the teaching profession,

---

[80] See reg 9 of the General Teaching Council for England (Disciplinary Functions) Regulations 2001, SI 2001/1268, as amended, and reg 9 of the General Teaching Council for Wales (Disciplinary Functions) Regulations 2001, SI 2001/1424 (W 99), as amended.
[81] THEA 1998, ss 2, 8(1) and 9.

(8) the standing of the teaching profession, and

(9) medical fitness to teach.[82]

If the Secretary of State or the National Assembly asks it to do so, the relevant GTC must advise (but only in a general way[83]) him (or it):

(1) on any of these matters,

(2) on any other matter which he (or it) requires relating to teaching, or

(3) as to whether any power of his (or it) under s 142 of the EA 2002 to prohibit or restrict the employment of a teacher should or should not be exercised in any particular case.[84]

The relevant GTC may publish any advice given on any of these matters except the last one.[85]

Register of teachers

3.36 The GTCs must establish and maintain a register of teachers under s 3 of the THEA 1998 containing the name of every person who is eligible for registration and who applies to be registered in the register in accordance with regulations made under s 4 of that Act.[86] The GTCs have the related duty of keeping records of:

(1) persons whose names have been removed from the register unless such removal was at their own request or it was because they had died, and

(2) various other persons, including qualified teachers who are not registered teachers.[87]

3.37 As stated in para **3.6** onwards above, in order to be eligible to teach in a maintained school or a non-maintained special school, it is necessary to be registered (or, in England, fully registered) in the register. A person is eligible for registration (or, in England, full registration) in the register kept pursuant to s 3 if:

---

[82] THEA 1998, s 2(2), as amended.
[83] Ibid, s 2(6).
[84] Ibid, s 2(3) and (4).
[85] Ibid, s 2(7).
[86] The current regulations are the General Teaching Council for England (Registration of Teachers) Regulations 2000, SI 2000/2176, as amended, and the General Teaching Council for Wales (Functions) Regulations 2000, SI 2000/1979 (W 140), as amended.
[87] See the General Teaching Council for England (Additional Functions) Order 2000, SI 2000/2175, as amended, and the General Teaching Council for Wales (Additional Functions) Order 2000, SI 2000/1941, as amended.

(1) he is a qualified teacher within the meaning of s 132 of the EA 2002 (concerning which, see para **3.5** above), and

(2) he is not:
   (a) the subject of a direction under s 142(1)(a) of that Act (concerning which see para **3.15** onwards above),
   (b) subject to a disciplinary order made by the GTCE or the GTCW under Sch 2 to the THEA 1998 (concerning which, see para **3.40** onwards below) by virtue of which he is not eligible for registration (or full registration), or
   (c) ineligible for registration as a teacher, or disqualified from being a teacher in any school, by virtue of any prescribed provision of the Law of Scotland or Northern Ireland.[88]

A person is not normally[89] eligible for registration (or, in England, full or provisional registration) if, having served an induction period in accordance with regulations made under s 19 of the THEA 1998,[90] he has failed to complete it satisfactorily for the purposes of those regulations.[91] In England, a person is not eligible for full or provisional registration unless at the time of intended registration the GTCE is or was 'satisfied as to his suitability to be a teacher'.[92]

3.38 Fees may be charged by the GTCs for applications for registration or for the registration, restoration, or retention of entries on the register.[93] The deduction of such fees from teachers' salaries and their remission to the relevant GTC is required by the General Teaching Council for England (Deduction of Fees) Regulations 2001,[94] and the General Teaching Council for Wales (Fees) Regulations 2002,[95] which were made under s 12 of the THEA 1998. The amount of the fees must be approved by the Secretary of State.[96]

3.39 There is a right of appeal to the High Court against a refusal to include a person in the register kept under s 3 where the refusal is on the ground that the relevant GTC was at the relevant time 'not satisfied as to [the relevant

---

[88] THEA 1998, s 3(3). The prescribed provisions are set out in reg 3 of the General Teaching Council for England (Registration of Teachers) Regulations 2000, SI 2000/2176 and reg 3 of the General Teaching Council for Wales (Functions) Regulations 2000, SI 2000/1979 (W 140).
[89] That is, except in circumstances prescribed by regulations; in relation to England the exceptions are set out in Sch 3 to the Education (Specified Work and Registration) (England) Regulations 2003, SI 2003/1663. The position in this regard is slightly different in Wales: see paras **3.7**–**3.8** above.
[90] See para **3.50** onwards below regarding induction periods.
[91] THEA 1998, s 3(4).
[92] See ibid, s 3(3B).
[93] See ibid, s 4(2)(g) and (4), reg 9 of the General Teaching Council for England (Registration of Teachers) Regulations 2000, SI 2000/2176, and reg 9 of the General Teaching Council for Wales (Functions) Regulations 2000, SI 2000/1979 (W 140).
[94] SI 2001/3993, as amended.
[95] SI 2002/326, as amended.
[96] THEA 1998, s 4(4).

person's] suitability to be a teacher.'[97] It is of interest that the right of appeal is not stated to be a right of appeal on a point of law. This, taken with the facts that (1) on the appeal, the High Court may make 'any order which appears appropriate',[98] and (2) the appeal is final,[99] suggests that the appeal could be on the facts (ie and not only on a point of law).[100]

The GTCS' disciplinary powers in relation to teachers

3.40 The GTCs have the power to issue:

(a) a reprimand,

(b) a conditional registration order,

(c) a suspension order (suspending a person's registration as a teacher), and

(d) a prohibition order.[101]

However, a suspension order may not last for more than 2 years,[102] although conditions may be placed by the GTC on the ability of the person concerned again to become registered.[103]

3.41 The regulations concerning the disciplinary functions of the GTC are the General Teaching Council for England (Disciplinary Functions) Regulations 2001.[104] In relation to Wales the current regulations are the General Teaching Council for Wales (Disciplinary Functions) Regulations 2001.[105]

3.42 Salient features of those regulations include that there is provision for an Investigating Committee, established under reg 3 of both sets of regulations.[106] Regulation 3 provides that that committee has the function of deciding whether there is a case to answer in relation to (i) 'unacceptable professional conduct[107]

---

[97] See THEA 1998, s 4A. The time limit for appealing is 28 days from service of the notice of the decision on the person concerned: see s 4A(1) and for example in relation to Wales reg 4C of the General Teaching Council for Wales (Functions) Regulations 2000, SI 2000/1979.
[98] See THEA 1998, s 4A(3).
[99] See ibid, s 4A(4).
[100] See further para **3.42** below concerning the manner in which the High Court would approach the appeal.
[101] THEA 1998, Sch 2, paras 2(3) and 4 (the latter as substituted by the EA 2002).
[102] Ibid, Sch 2, para 4(1).
[103] Ibid, para 4(2).
[104] SI 2001/1268, as amended.
[105] SI 2001/1424, as amended. There are few material differences between the two sets of regulations so, for the sake of simplicity, except where necessary, reference is made below only to those concerning England.
[106] Unless indicated otherwise below, where reference is made to a regulation concerning the disciplinary functions of the GTCs, it is to the same regulation in both SI 2001/1268 and SI 2001/1424.
[107] The term 'unacceptable professional conduct' means 'conduct which falls short of the standard expected of a registered teacher': THEA 1998, Sch 2, para 8(1).

or conviction of a relevant offence', (ii) 'serious professional incompetence', or (iii) any of those matters, *and*, in all cases, that 'the case should be referred for determination by' a Professional Conduct Committee or a Professional Competence Committee as the case may be. The latter two types of committee may require the attendance of witnesses,[108] who may be required to give evidence on oath or affirmation[109] or to 'produce documents or other material evidence' at the hearing.[110] Furthermore, the hearing of either of those two kinds of committee must normally be in public.[111] There is a right of appeal to the High Court within 28 days against a disciplinary order made under the regulations.[112] This right of appeal is not stated to lie only on a point of law. It is therefore clear that the right is to appeal on a factual ground. However, by analogy with the case law concerning appeals from disciplinary decisions made by the General Medical Council (GMC), it is clear that the High Court would exercise considerable restraint. A clear statement of the manner in which the High Court will approach an appeal on the facts from a decision of the GMC is to be found in para 29 of the judgment of Collins J in *Nandi v General Medical Council*,[113] where he said this:

> 'This court has taken over from the Privy Council the consideration of appeals from decisions of, among others, the General Medical Council. The Privy Council would rarely, if ever, hear evidence on an appeal. There would be no need because there is kept a full transcript of the evidence and that is put before the court if it is said that the findings were not supported by the evidence or were wrong in the light of the evidence which was given. So it seems to me that practice direction 22.32 should be reconsidered because it is, in my view, clearly inappropriate for appeals such as this. However, Mr De La Rosa did not submit, and in my view rightly did not submit, that there was any need for there to be a hearing of evidence. He accepted I could properly, and generally this court will, deal with the matter on the basis of the transcript of the material heard before the Committee. Indeed, I cannot think of circumstances in which this court would hear fresh evidence, although one must always be careful in this jurisdiction not to say never because then there comes a case when one realises that exceptionally it is appropriate to take a particular course, but it is very difficult to conceive of any circumstances in which it would be appropriate for this court to hear evidence and, whatever is meant by a re-hearing, it does not involve a reconsideration of evidence such as, for example, takes place in the Crown Court on an appeal against a decision of the magistrates' court. This is a case where the normal rules of the Court of Appeal will apply in the way that I have indicated.'

---

[108] See regs 2(4) and 13 of SI 2001/1268 and regs 2(3) and 13 of SI 2001/1424.
[109] See regs 2(4) and 15 of SI 2001/1268 and regs 2(3) and 15 of SI 2001/1424.
[110] See reg 13.
[111] See regs 2(4) and 14 of SI 2001/1268 and regs 2(3) and 14 of SI 2001/1424.
[112] See reg 24. Time starts to run from the date of service of the notice of the relevant order: ibid. See reg 26 for the permitted ways in which service may be effected for the purposes of reg 18(5) (which provides that a disciplinary order takes effect on the date on which notice of it is served on the person to whom it relates) and the times when such notice is to be regarded as having been served. In the case of what is clearly intended to include first class post, service of such a notice is deemed to occur 'on the second day after the day on which [the notice] was sent': see reg 26(2)(b). There is no equivalent provision affecting the service of a notice under reg 24.
[113] [2004] EWHC 2317 (Admin).

3.43 It seems clear by analogy with the case law concerning the disciplinary functions of the GMC that it would not be possible for a GTC lawfully to consider charges of unacceptable professional misconduct where it would be an abuse of process to do so. This is the effect of para 37 of the judgment of Newman J in *R (Phillips) v General Medical Council*,[114] paras 40 and 68 of which make it clear also that the decision as to whether or not the inquiry is to any extent an abuse of process is to be made by the relevant GTC and not the High Court. This does not mean that the decision cannot be taken by an Investigating Committee. As Collins J said in *Dixon*:[115]

> 'Of course there may be cases where it is plain that on any view the case will have to be stopped because it would be an abuse of process. In such a case the PPC [ie the Preliminary Proceedings Committee, which is the GMC's equivalent of the GTCs' Investigating Committees] should itself decide.'

3.44 The test for determining whether or not it would be an abuse of process for a Professional Conduct Committee to hear allegations concerning an employee's conduct where there have been previous criminal proceedings concerning that same conduct was stated most clearly by Simon Browne LJ in *R (Redgrave) v Commissioner of the Metropolis*:[116]

> 'I would end this judgment by commending to disciplinary boards generally two particular paragraphs included in the 1999 Home Office Guidance on Police Unsatisfactory Performance, Complaints and Misconduct Procedures:
>
>> "3.70 In deciding matters of fact the burden of proof lies with the presenting officer, and the tribunal must apply the standard of proof required in civil cases, that is, the balance of probabilities. The straightforward legal definition of the civil standard of proof is that the adjudicator is convinced by the evidence that it is more likely or probable that something occurred than that it did not occur. Relevant case law makes it clear that the degree of proof required increases with the gravity of what is alleged and its potential consequences. It therefore follows that, where an allegation is likely to ruin an officer's reputation, deprive them of their livelihood or seriously damage their career prospects, a tribunal should be satisfied to a high degree of probability that what is alleged has been proved."
>>
>> "3.31 Where criminal proceedings have taken place for an offence arising out of the matter under investigation and those proceedings have resulted in the acquittal of an officer, that determination will be relevant to a decision on whether to discipline an officer: (a) where the conduct under investigation is in substance the same as the criminal charge so determined, and where the alleged failure is so serious and the likely sanction serious such that it would be reasonable to look for proof to a high degree of probability (see paragraph 3.70), it will normally be unfair to institute disciplinary proceedings; or (b) where the conduct under investigation is not in substance the same as the criminal charge so determined, it may nevertheless be unfair

---

[114] [2004] EWHC 1858 (Admin).
[115] [2001] EWHC 645.
[116] [2003] 1 WLR 1136, 1147–1148, para 46.

to proceed where a matter essential to the proof of the misconduct was in issue in criminal proceedings and had been resolved in the officer's favour.'"

3.45 If there has been a finding of an employment tribunal on a particular issue of fact, then ignoring that finding is more likely to constitute an abuse of process than ignoring an acquittal of a criminal offence. This is because:

(1) no reason is usually given for an acquittal,

(2) the acquittal may have been for a number of reasons, none of which were to do with the factual basis of the charge, and

(3) an acquittal will at best (for present purposes) have been based on a finding that the prosecution have not proved a particular factual matter beyond reasonable doubt, whereas an employment tribunal's finding on a particular factual matter will have been made on the balance of probabilities.

3.46 The European Convention on Human Rights is relevant in this context also. According to the case law concerning Art 1 of the First Protocol to the Convention, it is necessary for a body exercising disciplinary functions in relation to a group of professional persons such as teachers to act proportionately. This is not least because:

(1) such a body is in a position to deprive a person of that which is properly to be regarded as a property right and accordingly which falls within Art 1 of the First Protocol to the European Convention on Human Rights;[117] and

(2) it has repeatedly been said by the European Court of Human Rights since *Sporrong v Sweden*[118] that any interference with property rights protected by Art 1 of the First Protocol must be proportionate.

3.47 The GTCs are empowered to issue, and from time to time to revise, a code 'laying down standards of professional conduct and practice expected of registered teachers'.[119] It must make this code available free of charge to each registered teacher at least once.[120] A failure by a teacher to comply with the code may be taken into account by a disciplinary committee of the GTC in any disciplinary proceedings against the teacher.[121]

---

[117] See *Van Marle v Netherlands* (1986) 8 EHRR 483.
[118] (1982) 5 EHRR 35.
[119] See THEA 1998, s 5(1) and reg 13 of the General Teaching Council for England (Registration of Teachers) Regulations 2000, SI 2000/2176 and reg 13 of the General Teaching Council for Wales (Functions) Regulations 2000, SI 2000/1979.
[120] See reg 14(1) of both SI 2000/1979 and SI 2000/2176.
[121] See reg 7 of SI 2001/1268 and reg 7 of SI 2001/1424.

Supply of information relating to teachers

3.48 The Education (Restriction of Employment) (Amendment) Regulations 2001[122] inserted a reg 5A into the Education (Restriction of Employment) Regulations 2000,[123] requiring the Secretary of State to refer an allegation of:

(1) 'unacceptable professional conduct' on the part of a registered teacher, or

(2) that the teacher had been convicted of a 'relevant offence', to the relevant GTC unless the Secretary of State was of the view that a 'relevant issue' arose.

There is no such requirement in the Education (Prohibition from Teaching or Working with Children) Regulations 2003[124] (although one may imagine that the Secretary of State would not hesitate to refer such an allegation to the GTC). In contrast, there is a duty imposed on a relevant employer by reg 29 of the General Teaching Council for England (Disciplinary Functions) Regulations 2001[125] and reg 5 of the Education (Supply of Information) (Wales) Regulations 2003[126] to inform the relevant GTC only of the ending by the employer of a teacher's employment on a ground relating to the teacher's professional incompetence or because the teacher left the employment in circumstances where the employer might have so ended that employment and (in both cases) the circumstances which led to the ending of the employment.[127]

3.49 This may be because s 14 of the THEA 1998 requires the provision by the Secretary of State and/or the National Assembly for Wales to the two GTCs of such information relating to individual teachers as he (or it) considers it to be necessary or desirable for either of them to have for the purpose of carrying out any of the functions conferred on them by or under Ch I of Pt I of that Act. Section 14 of the THEA 1998 also requires each GTC to supply certain information to the Secretary of State, any information prescribed in regulations to any other person or body so prescribed, and to supply the other GTC with information which it is either necessary or desirable for that council to have for the purpose of carrying out any of the functions conferred on them by or under Chapter I of Part I of the THEA 1998.[128]

---

[122] SI 2001/1269.
[123] SI 2000/2419.
[124] SI 2003/1184, as amended.
[125] SI 2001/1268, as amended. The definition of an employer for this purpose is in reg 2 of SI 2001/1268. It is similar to, but not the same as, the meaning of the term 'relevant employer' for the purposes of s 142, as to which see para **3.15** above.
[126] SI 2003/542.
[127] Agents are also so obliged: see reg 29(2) of SI 2001/1268 and reg 7 of SI 2003/542.
[128] The relevant obligations are imposed by the General Teaching Council for Wales (Functions) Regulations 2000, SI 2000/1979, as amended, and the General Teaching Council for England (Registration of Teachers) Regulations 2000, SI 2000/2176, as amended.

INDUCTION PERIOD TO BE SERVED SATISFACTORILY BY A SCHOOL TEACHER

3.50 A person may not (subject to certain defined exceptions) work as a teacher in a school which is maintained by a local education authority or a non-maintained special school[129] unless he has served an induction period of not less than three school terms in:

(1) such a school,

(2) an independent school, or

(3) in circumstances prescribed by the regulations, a further education institution.

This is the effect of:

(a) s 19 of the THEA 1998,

(b) the Education (Induction Arrangements for School Teachers) (Consolidation) (England) Regulations 2001[130] (the English Induction Regulations), and

(c) the Education (Induction Arrangements for School Teachers) (Wales) Regulations 2005[131] (the Welsh Induction Regulations).

For the sake of simplicity, the situation as provided for by the English Induction Regulations is described more fully below.

3.51 Subject to certain exceptions (which include that the person in question has served an induction period in Wales[132]), reg 7 of the English Induction Regulations prohibits a person from being employed as a teacher at a school maintained by a local education authority or a non-maintained special school unless he has satisfactorily completed an induction period of not less than three school terms in:

(a) a school which is maintained by a local education authority;

(b) an independent school which (by and large) follows the National Curriculum in relation to the pupils taught by the person in question; or

---

[129] See THEA 1998, s 19(10)(b), as substituted by EA 2002, Sch 21, para 85.
[130] SI 2001/2897, as amended.
[131] SI 2005/1818 (W 146).
[132] See SI 2001/2897, Sch 2, para 6. It is of note that a person who is employed as a supply teacher 'for a period of less than one term . . . during the period of a school year and one term commencing on the date that he is first employed as a supply teacher (by that or any other employer)', need not have served an induction period under the regulations: ibid, para 4. The other exceptions are set out in the rest of Sch 2 to SI 2001/2897.

(c) a sixth-form college (that is, a further education institution principally concerned with the provision of full-time education suitable to the requirements of persons who have not attained the age of 19 years[133]).[134]

3.52 The situation is similar in Wales.[135] However, the Welsh Induction Regulations permit an induction period to be served not only in a sixth-form college but also a further education college.

3.53 An induction period may not be served in a pupil referral unit.[136] Nor (subject to two exceptions) may such a period be served in a school which has been inspected under the Education Act 2005 in relation to which the inspector has given a notice to the National Assembly for Wales under s 37(2) of that Act that special measures are required to be taken in relation to the school.[137] The exceptions to this prohibition are that:

(a) the person in question began his induction period or was employed as a graduate teacher, a registered teacher or a teacher on the employment-based teacher training scheme at the school at a time when the school was not subject to such a report, or

(b) one of Her Majesty's Inspectors of Education, Childrens' Services and Skills in England (or as the case may be one of Her Majesty's Inspectors of Education and Training in Wales) has certified in writing that he is satisfied that the school is fit for the purpose of providing induction supervision and training.[138]

Length of induction period

3.54 A person's employment during an induction period of the sort required by s 19 of the THEA 1998 must be as a qualified teacher.[139] Where a person is employed full-time, the induction period must in England (and in Wales must normally) be of a year, or, in certain cases, such number of terms at the relevant institution which amount to a school year.[140] The Welsh Induction Regulations are rather less prescriptive than the English Induction Regulations. For example, reg 8(3) of the Welsh Induction Regulations provides that 'The length of the induction period where the three term rule does not apply is such length as the appropriate body determines'. The appropriate body for the purposes of

---

[133] See reg 3(1) of the English Induction Regulations.
[134] See regs 7 and 8 of the English Induction Regulations, read with reg 3(1).
[135] See regs 3(1), 6 and 7 of the Welsh Induction Regulations, which are subject to the exceptions stated in Sch 1 to those regulations.
[136] See reg 8(2)(b) of the English Induction Regulations, and reg 7(2)(b) of the Welsh Induction Regulations. In what follows, where appropriate the English provision is stated first, and the Welsh provision is stated second, with no further attribution.
[137] See reg 8(2)(a) and reg 7(2)(a) respectively.
[138] See also reg 8(2)(a) and reg 7(2)(a) respectively. The wording of the latter is slightly different from that of the former, but the effect is the same.
[139] See reg 10(1) and reg 9(1) respectively.
[140] Regulations 9 and 8 respectively.

the Welsh Induction Regulations is defined by reg 5 of the Welsh Induction Regulations and is usually an LEA. No period as a supply teacher counts for the purposes of the English Induction Regulations unless the head teacher of the school or sixth form college agrees before the start of the period that it is to do so.[141] A person may not serve an induction period in a further education college in Wales unless before the start of the induction period the governing body of the college and an LEA have agreed that the LEA are to act as the appropriate body in relation to the college.[142] Where the relevant person works part-time, or in two or more relevant schools, the period under the English Induction Regulations must be 'the period of time it would take in accordance with his contract of employment or the terms of his engagement for him to complete 378 school sessions'.[143] Where the person works either wholly or partly in a sixth-form college, the period under the English Induction Regulations is that which 'it would take in accordance with his contract of employment or the terms of his engagement for him to complete 189 working days falling in term time'.[144]

3.55 If the person undergoing an induction period is absent from work for an aggregate period of more than 30 working days falling in term time, then the induction period in England must (and in Wales may) be extended by that aggregate period,[145] unless (in England) the absence is 'by reason of the maternity leave period specified in reg 7(1) of the Maternity and Parental Leave etc Regulations 1999',[146] in which case the employee may choose whether it should be so extended.[147] Regulation 11(3) of the English Induction Regulations (of which there is no equivalent in the Welsh Induction Regulations) permits the extension (subject to limits) of the induction period before its end by agreement between the relevant person and the appropriate body within the meaning of the English Induction Regulations. (The appropriate body for the purposes of the English Induction Regulations is defined by reg 5 of those regulations, and, as is the case in Wales, is usually an LEA.) Regulation 11(3) permits such an extension in the following two situations. The first is where 5 years or more have passed since a teacher in full-time service started his induction period but he has not completed that period. In that situation, the teacher may with the agreement of the appropriate body choose to extend the induction period by a maximum of one school year. Similarly, a teacher in part-time service whose induction period started 5 or more years ago and has not been completed may with the agreement of the appropriate body extend the period by such time as it will take in accordance

---

[141] See reg 10(3).
[142] See reg 7(4), read with reg 3(1), of the Welsh Induction Regulations.
[143] Regulation 9(2).
[144] Regulation 9(3).
[145] See reg 11(1) and reg 10(1) respectively.
[146] SI 1999/3312.
[147] See reg 11(2) of the English Induction Regulations, of which there is no equivalent in the Welsh Induction Regulations, probably in part because of the use of the word 'may' in reg 10(1) of the latter rather than the use of the word 'shall' in reg 11(1) of the former. Regulation 10(1) of the Welsh Induction Regulations also permits the appropriate body to extend the period 'by any lesser period as it considers appropriate'.

with his contract of employment or terms of engagement to complete a maximum of 378 school sessions or (in relation to an induction period spent in a sixth-form college) 189 working days falling within term time. Otherwise, the induction period may be extended only in certain circumstances.[148] Subject to the possibility of such an extension, only one induction period may be served.[149]

Supervision and training during the induction period

3.56 A person who is undergoing an induction period under the induction period regulations is not explicitly entitled by the English Induction Regulations to supervision and training during that period. However, it is apparent from reg 13 that supervision and training is to be given to that person during that period. Regulation 13(2) provides that the 'duties assigned to a person serving an induction period, his supervision and the conditions under which he works shall be such as to facilitate a fair and effective assessment of his conduct and efficiency as a teacher'. Regulation 13(1) is to the effect that the head teacher of the school or sixth form college at which a person is undergoing his induction period *and* the appropriate body in relation to the school or college[150] are responsible for the supervision and training of that person during that period. The situation in relation to Wales is slightly simpler, but is to much the same effect: reg 12 of the Welsh Induction Regulations provides merely that:

> 'The head teacher of an institution in Wales in which a person serves an induction period and the appropriate body in relation to that institution is [sic] responsible for that person's supervision and training during the induction period.'

3.57 A teacher who is serving an induction period under the regulations is not required to be appraised under regulations made under s 131 of the EA 2002.[151]

Completion of an induction period

3.58 Regulation 15 of the English Induction Regulations gives the Secretary of State power to decide what are the standards against which a person who has completed an induction period is to be assessed for the purpose of deciding whether he has satisfactorily completed an induction period.[152] Regulation 13

---

[148] See regs 16(3)(b), 16A, 17 and 19 of the English Induction Regulations and regs 14(2)(b), 15 and 17 of the Welsh Induction Regulations. Note also reg 18A of the English Induction Regulations in relation to certain teachers who have not passed the numeracy skills test after 31 August 2002.
[149] See reg 12 and reg 11 respectively.
[150] Defined, as stated in the preceding para above, by reg 5.
[151] THEA 1998, s 19(7). The current regulations are the Education (School Teacher Performance Management) (England) Regulations 2006, SI 2006/2661 and the Education (School Teacher Appraisal) (Wales) Regulations 2002, SI 2002/1394.
[152] These are set out in the TDA booklet entitled 'Induction Standards – TDA Guidance for newly qualified teachers', which is available at http://www.tda.gov.uk.

of the Welsh Induction Regulations gives the same power to the National Assembly for Wales.[153] Where a person's induction period has been completed, the head teacher of the school or sixth form college at which he is employed (or, if there is more than one such institution, the lead head teacher[154]) must make a written recommendation to the appropriate body as to whether the person has achieved those standards.[155] That recommendation must be made within the period of 10 working days from the date when the period was completed, and the head teacher must at the same time send a copy of the recommendation to the person in question.[156]

Effect of failure satisfactorily to complete induction period

3.59 If a person who is employed at a maintained school or a non-maintained special school has failed satisfactorily to complete an induction period within the meaning of s 19 of the THEA 1998, his employer must secure the termination of his employment as a teacher unless the person appeals to the GTCE under reg 19 of the English Induction Regulations, or (as the case may be) to the GTCW under reg 17 of the Welsh Induction Regulations, against the decision of the appropriate body and the appeal is allowed.[157] The procedure to be followed in relation to the appeal is governed by Sch 3 to the English Induction Regulations and Sch 2 to the Welsh Induction Regulations. Salient features of the procedure include that if an appeal is withdrawn then no further appeal may be instigated in relation to the decision in question.[158] Furthermore:

(1) an appeal may be decided without an oral hearing if neither party wants such a hearing and the relevant GTC agrees,[159] and

(2) an appeal hearing must be in public unless the appeal body determines that it is 'fair and reasonable for the hearing or any part of it to be in private'.[160]

3.60 If the person appeals under reg 19 of the English Induction Regulations or reg 17 of the Welsh Induction Regulations, his employer may allow his employment to continue pending the outcome of that appeal, but only if the

---

[153] The standards are published on the National Assembly's website at http://www.learning.wales.gov.uk.
[154] See reg 16(1) of the English Induction Regulations and see reg 14 concerning employment in two or more institutions simultaneously. The equivalent (in fact rather simpler) provisions in the Welsh Induction Regulations are regs 14(1) and 7(5) respectively.
[155] See reg 16(2)(a) of the English Induction Regulations and reg 14(2)(a) of the Welsh Induction Regulations.
[156] See reg 16 of the English Induction Regulations and reg 14 of the Welsh Induction Regulations generally regarding the completion of an induction period. The relevant person has a right to make written representations to the appropriate body within 10 working days of that body's receipt of the head teacher's recommendation: reg 16(4) and reg 14(4) respectively.
[157] See reg 18(2) (read with reg 6) and reg 16(2) (read with reg 3(1)) respectively.
[158] Schedule 3, para 4(3) and Sch 2, para 4(3) respectively.
[159] Schedule 3, para 11(1); Sch 2, para 11(1) respectively.
[160] Schedule 3, para 16(2); Sch 2, para 16(2) respectively.

employer secures that the person undertakes only such 'limited teaching duties' as (in relation to England) the Secretary of State or (in relation to Wales) the National Assembly may decide.[161] In any event, the employer must take whatever steps are necessary to secure the termination of the person's employment by no later than 10 working days from:

(a) the date when the employer received written notification from the person that he did not intend to appeal against the relevant decision of the appropriate body,

(b) the expiry of the time-limit for so appealing (which is 20 working days from the date of receipt by the person of notification of the decision[162]), or

(c) the date when the employer received notice that the person's appeal was unsuccessful.[163]

Charges for independent schools and sixth form colleges

3.61 The appropriate body in relation to an independent school or sixth form college (or, in Wales, a further education college) may charge the governing body of the school or college a reasonable sum (not exceeding the cost of the provision) for the service provided to the governing body under the English Induction Regulations or (as the case may be) the Welsh Induction Regulations.[164] This is a little obscure. It appears that it was intended that the appropriate body would be able to impose such a charge on the proprietor of an independent school (which at least under the Education Act 1996 may be the governing body of the school, but may be a private individual or a company[165]). However, the wording is not apt to do this.

Secretary of State's and National Assembly's Guidance

3.52 Any person or body exercising a function under the English Induction Regulations must 'have regard' to any guidance given by the Secretary of State from time to time as to the exercise of that function.[166] A person or body exercising a function under the Welsh Induction Regulations must 'have regard' to any guidance given by the National Assembly for Wales from time to time as to the exercise of that function.[167]

---

[161] See reg 18(5) and reg 16(5) respectively.
[162] See Sch 3, para 2(1) and Sch 2, para 2(1) respectively.
[163] See reg 18(3) and (4) and reg 16(3) and (4) respectively.
[164] See reg 21 and reg 19 respectively.
[165] See EA 1996, s 579(1).
[166] See reg 22. Such guidance is published on the teachernet website at http://www.teachernet.gov.uk.
[167] See reg 20. Such guidance is published on the National Assembly's website at http://www.learning.wales.gov.uk.

QUALIFICATION TO BE A HEAD TEACHER

3.63 As a result of regs 3 and 4 of the Education (Head Teachers' Qualifications) (England) Regulations 2003,[168] in order to become a head teacher (for the first time) of a school which is maintained by an LEA[169] or a non-maintained special school in England, after 1 April 2004, a person must (subject to two exceptions) have acquired either:

(1) the 'National Professional Qualification for Headship' which is awarded by the Secretary of State to a person if he is satisfied that the person has successfully completed a course of training for that qualification which is approved by the National College for School Leadership Limited;

(2) the National Professional Qualification for Headship in Wales;

(3) the Scottish Standard for Headship;

(4) the Professional Qualification for Headship in Northern Ireland; or

(5) a comparable qualification obtained in Switzerland or any European Economic Area country, other than the United Kingdom.

3.64 The Education (Head Teachers' Qualifications) (England) Regulations 2003 do not apply to a person who before 1 April 2004 had been appointed as the head teacher of:

(1) a school maintained by a local education authority,

(2) an independent school, or

(3) a 'similar educational institution outside England and Wales'.[170]

One of the two exceptions to the requirement imposed by regs 3 and 4 is that if:

(a) the person is appointed to such a post before 1 April 2009 and at the time of his appointment he has successfully applied for a training course for the purpose of gaining the National Professional Qualification for Headship, and

(b) the period of four years from the date of appointment has not expired,

---

[168] SI 2003/3111, as amended, made under s 135 of the EA 2002.
[169] This means a maintained school within the meaning of s 20 of the School Standards and Framework Act 1998 (SSFA 1998): see EA 2002, s 212(2)–(4) and SSFA 1998, 142(8). It therefore includes a nursery school which is a special school, but not (a) a nursery school which is not a special school, or (b) a pupil referral unit. Regulation 4(2) of SI 2003/3111 specifically provides that it does not apply in relation to a pupil referral unit.
[170] See SI 2003/3111, reg 2(2).

then he may serve as such a head teacher without that qualification.[171] The other of the two exceptions applies only to maintained nursery schools, and is that a person may serve as a head teacher of such a school without a relevant qualification if he holds, or has successfully applied for a training course for the purpose of gaining, the National Professional Qualification in Integrated Centre Leadership.[172] Acting head teachers are not affected by the requirements of regs 3 and 4 of the Education (Head Teachers' Qualifications) (England) Regulations 2003.[173]

3.65 The situation in relation to Wales is similar. There, the Head Teachers' Qualifications and Registration (Wales) Regulations 2005[174] make similar provision from 1 September 2005 onwards, although they provide in addition that a person may not serve as a head teacher in a school maintained by a local education authority or a special school which is not so maintained unless he or she:

(1) is a qualified teacher (or has a qualification which has equivalent effect by virtue of the European Communities (Recognition of Professional Qualifications) (First General System) Regulations 2005), and

(2) is registered under s 3 of the THEA 1998.[175]

---

[171] SI 2003/3111, reg 5(1). The four-year period is extended by the amount of any maternity, parental, paternity or adoption leave which the employee has taken (in the case of the last three only if the leave is taken pursuant to the right to do so granted by the Employment Rights Act 1996; in relation to maternity the leave must have been taken pursuant to the right to take it either under the employee's contract of employment or that Act, or 'because of her pregnancy', and the employee must have a right to return to work): see SI 2003/3111, reg 5(2). See Chapter 5 below for the right to those various periods of leave.
[172] See SI 2003/3111, regs 3 and 5(3) concerning this exception.
[173] See ibid, reg 6.
[174] SI 2005/1227 (W 85).
[175] See regs 2, 4 and 5.

Chapter 4

RECRUITMENT AND STAFFING OF SCHOOLS

INTRODUCTION

4.1 This chapter concerns the legal issues which can arise in relation to the recruitment and employment of staff in schools. Reference is made in the chapter to the standard statutory provisions which apply, such as those concerning the need to give a statement of the main terms and conditions of the employment and the potential sanctions for failing to do so (although the law of discrimination is not considered in this chapter; it is considered in Chapter 6 below). Certain aspects of the effect in general terms of the common law on the employment relationship are described in this chapter, such as when a contract of employment comes into existence (although the terms implied by the common law are described in Chapter 5 below, where a number of common law and statutory obligations which apply to all employment relationships are described). The main focus of this chapter is the effects of the statutory provisions which apply exclusively to the employment relationship in maintained schools, apart from those which apply to the dismissal of staff, since those are dealt with in Chapter 8 below. The continuing effects of the Burgundy Book are also considered. However, before turning to the legal issues which can arise generally in the recruitment process, it is necessary to refer to some current guidance given by the DfES in relation to the recruitment of persons to work with children in schools and the statutory provisions which have only recently been enacted requiring the obtaining of detailed checks on the past of applicants for employment in schools.

THE NEED FOR CAUTION IN RELATION TO RECRUITMENT

4.2 The process for the recruitment of staff for schools currently has a rather high profile, following the case of the murders carried out by Ian Huntley in Soham, Cambridgeshire, and the subsequent report of the Bichard Inquiry into the 'effectiveness of relevant intelligence-based record keeping, vetting practices since 1995 and information sharing with other agencies'.[1] It is helpful to bear in mind that the recommendations of that report included these:

---

[1] See The Bichard Inquiry Report, a copy of which is on the Home Office website, at www.homeoffice.gov.uk/pdf/bichard_report.pdf.

'16 Head teachers and school governors should receive training on how to ensure that interviews to appoint staff reflect the importance of safeguarding children.
17 From a date to be agreed, no interview panel to appoint staff working in schools should be convened without at least one member being properly trained.
18 The relevant inspection bodies should, as part of their inspection, review the existence and effectiveness of a school's selection and recruitment arrangements.'

4.3 In addition, it is necessary to bear in mind the guidance issued by the Secretary of State in November 2006, entitled 'Safeguarding Children and Safer Recruitment in Education'.[2] That guidance refers to the making of checks with the Criminal Records Bureau (CRB) before employing a member of staff. It is of interest that until recently there was no statutory basis for the involvement of the CRB in the recruitment of persons to work in schools.[3] The role of the CRB was helpfully stated in para 19 of DfES/0278/2002 (which is now superseded by the guidance mentioned above), in the following manner:

'The CRB aims to help employers and voluntary organisations make safer recruitment decisions by identifying candidates who may be unsuitable for certain work, especially work which involves children or vulnerable adults, through a service called Disclosure.'

4.4 In addition, seeking the assistance of the CRB will maximise the chances of avoiding breaching s 142(8) of the EA 2002, which makes it unlawful to use a person to carry out work in contravention of a direction given under s 142. However, seeking the assistance of the CRB is not required in order to avoid committing the offence in s 35(2) of the Criminal Justice and Court Services Act 2000. This is because an individual commits such an offence only if he *knowingly* (1) offers work in a regulated position to an individual who is disqualified from working with children, or (2) fails to remove an individual from such work.[4]

Criminal Records Bureau and other checks

4.5 There has, since 12 May 2006, been in England a statutory obligation to obtain an 'enhanced criminal record certificate issued pursuant to Part V of the Police Act 1997' in respect of any person appointed under reg 11 or reg 20 of the School Staffing (England) Regulations 2003,[5] or in respect of 'any person appointed by a local education authority for the purpose of working at a [maintained school] in the temporary absence of a member of staff of the school'.[6] Further, checks of the same sort must have been carried out in

---

[2] DFES-04217-2006, of which a copy is available on the DCFS website.
[3] The current position is stated in paras **4.5-4.7** and **4.47** below.
[4] See para **3.25** above.
[5] SI 2003/1963.
[6] See ibid, regs 11(3) (which is subject to reg 11(4) and (6)), 11A and 20, as amended.

relation to supply staff who work in maintained schools,[7] and in relation to any member of the staff of a school who was appointed before 12 May 2006 and who after 1 January 2007 moves from a post which does not bring him regularly into contact with children or young persons into a post which does.[8] In Wales, equivalent obligations have existed since 29 March 2007.[9] Some aspects of these obligations are described in more detail below, where the effects of the current regulations governing the recruitment of staff to a maintained school are described.[10] The application of these obligations to the proprietors of independent schools and non-maintained special schools in England as from 1 May 2007 (via amendments made to the Education (Independent School Standards) (England) Regulations 2003[11] and the Education (Non-Maintained Special Schools) (England) Regulations 1999[12]), should be noted.[13] In Wales, the Independent Schools (Miscellaneous Amendments) (Wales) Regulations 1007[14] amended the Independent School Standards (Wales) Regulations 2003[15] to a similar effect.

Obligation to keep a register of checks made

4.6 As from 1 January 2007, there has been an obligation to keep a register in relation to each member of staff who was appointed to work at a maintained school in England, showing various things.[16] These are whether:

(a) his identity was checked,

(b) a check was made to establish whether he is subject to any direction made under s 142 of the Education Act 2002[17] or any prohibition, restriction or order having effect as such a direction,

(c) checks were 'undertaken to ensure that he met the requirements with respect to qualifications or registration mentioned in regulation 3(3)(a)',[18]

---

[7] See regs 15A and 24A of SI 2003/1963, as inserted by SI 2006/3197.
[8] SI 2003/1963, regs 18A and 26A, as so inserted.
[9] See regs 9A, 9B, 15A, 18A, 20A, 24A and 26A of the Staffing of Maintained Schools (Wales) Regulations 2006, SI 2006/873 (W 81), as inserted by SI 2007/944.
[10] See para **4.47** below.
[11] SI 2003/1910.
[12] SI 1999/2257.
[13] The amendments were made by the Education (Independent School Standards) (England) (Amendment) Regulations 2007, SI 2007/1087, and the Education (Non-Maintained Special Schools) (England) (Amendment) Regulations 2007, SI 2007/1088.
[14] SI 2007/947.
[15] SI 2003/3234 (W 314).
[16] See reg 11(7) of SI 2003/1963, as inserted by SI 2006/3197. The register may be kept in electronic form, as long as the information recorded 'is capable of being reproduced in legible form': reg 11(14). There was at the time of writing no obligation in Wales to keep such a register. On 25 May 2007, the obligations in England were applied to federations and federated schools: see reg 32 of, and Sch 9 to, SI 2007/960.
[17] See para **3.15** above onwards concerning s 142.
[18] The registration and qualification requirements) referred to in reg 3(3)(a) are considered in Ch 3 above.

(d) 'an enhanced criminal record certificate was obtained in respect of him',

(e) checks were made pursuant to reg 11(4) of the School Staffing (England) Regulations 2003,[19] and

(f) 'a check of his right to work in the United Kingdom was made'.[20]

As from 1 April 2007, subject to an exception, the register has had to show in relation to any person who was appointed to work at the school in question at any time before 1 January 2007 'whether each [such] check . . . was made and whether an enhanced criminal record certificate was obtained, together with the date on which any check was completed or certificate obtained'.[21] The exception is that there is no need to show those things in the register in the case of a person appointed before 12 May 2006 if his post does not 'bring him regularly into contact with children and young persons'.[22]

4.7 In relation to persons who have been supplied by 'an employment business to work at the school' (that is, supply staff), the register must show whether written notification has been received from the employment business that:

(a) it has made checks of the sort described in the preceding paragraph above,

(b) it or another employment business has 'applied, with a children's suitability statement, for an enhanced criminal record certificate', and

(c) 'it has obtained such a certificate in response to an application made by that or another employment business'.[23]

The date of such notification must also be recorded in the register.[24] If the employment business has notified the employer in accordance with arrangements for the supply of staff to the school that the business has in its possession relevant information concerning a supply member of staff obtained from an enhanced criminal record certificate or provided to the business 'in accordance with section 113B(6) of the Police Act 1997',[25] then the register must also show whether the business supplied a copy of the certificate to the school.[26]

---

[19] See para **4.47** below regarding reg 11(4).
[20] See reg 11(8) of SI 2003/1963, as inserted by SI 2006/3197. The check need not have been made, and the certificate need not have been obtained, pursuant to a legal obligation: reg 11(13).
[21] SI 2003/1963, reg 11(9), as so inserted.
[22] Ibid, reg 11(10), as so inserted.
[23] Ibid, reg 11(11), as so inserted.
[24] Ibid.
[25] Section 113B(6)(b) concerns information which '(a) might be relevant . . ., (b) ought not to be included in the certificate, in the interests of the prevention or detection of crime, and (c) can, without harming those interests, be disclosed to the registered person'.
[26] SI 2003/1963, reg 11(12), as inserted by SI 2006/3197.

THE LEGAL ISSUES WHICH CAN ARISE WHEN RECRUITING STAFF

4.8 There are several stages of the recruitment process at which legal issues may arise. The first is when a post is advertised, the second is the interview stage, and the third is when the parties seek to reach agreement about the terms of the contract of employment. At each of these stages, the law relating to discrimination on the ground of (1) sex, (2) race, (3) disability, (4) religion or belief, (5) sexual orientation and (6) age, must be given special attention. Discrimination is considered in detail in Chapter 5, but it is important to note that in order to minimise the risk of discriminating unlawfully it is helpful to:

(1) draw up a list of criteria for the selection of a person to a post;

(2) determine the order of importance of those criteria;

(3) apply those criteria when interviewing;

(4) record thoughts about the interviewees at the time of, or shortly after, the interview; and

(5) keep records of recruitment interviews for some time after the interviews.

4.9 Furthermore, if a claim of unlawful discrimination is made by an unsuccessful applicant for a post, then these records should be kept safe from destruction.

4.10 The question whether, and if so, when, a contract of employment has come into existence may arise when recruiting staff. (It should be noted that there is no need for any formality about the formation of a contract, and a letter of appointment often contains the best evidence of the initial terms of a contract of employment.) For example, an employer and a potential employee may plan to enter into a contract of employment and draft terms may accordingly be drawn up, but one of the parties may then decide not to sign the document. However, the potential employee may nevertheless start to work for the employer.

4.11 The question when a contract of employment comes into existence is determined by the case-law and principles in the ordinary law of contract. Those principles are relatively easy to state, but on occasion difficult to apply. A contract may come into existence despite the fact that there are still some terms which have yet to be agreed. However, an alleged agreement must be sufficiently certain to be enforceable as a contract. Furthermore, the written terms may be overridden by an express assurance or representation made by one party to the other to induce the other to enter into the agreement. In addition (and this is of potentially great significance for employment in schools), a contract may be entered into subject to a condition subsequent, such as the obtaining of a satisfactory CRB check. In that event, the contract can be terminated 'forthwith' in the event that the check is unsatisfactory.[27]

4.12 It is wise to be as clear as possible about the following matters when drawing up a contract of employment:

(1) the employee's pay and the intervals at which it is to be paid;

(2) the employee's duties/responsibilities;

(3) the employee's entitlement to sick pay;

(4) the employee's entitlement to participate in a pension scheme (in State schools that will be the Teachers' Pension Scheme or the Local Government Pension Scheme, both of which are referred to in para **5.49** below);

(5) the employee's holiday entitlement (including in relation to public holidays) and the manner in which
 (a) the employee's accrued holiday pay is to be paid on the termination of the employment, or
 (b) an amount is to be deducted from the employee's final pay if the employee has, at the termination of his employment, taken more than his pro-rata holiday entitlement;

(6) the notice period required to be given by the employee and by the employer to terminate the contract;

(7) whether the employer may terminate the contract of employment by giving pay in lieu of notice;

(8) the grievance procedure applicable to the employee;

(9) the disciplinary procedure applicable to the employee; and

(10) whether any collective agreements apply to the employment.

4.13 Most of this information is required to be given to employees by s 1 of the ERA 1996, to which further reference is made in the following paragraph below. It is in any event normally sensible to give as much information about these matters as possible. It should be borne in mind, though, that the more elaborate the procedures which apply to the employment (such as the procedures which apply in the event of redundancy), the more likely it is that the employer will inadvertently breach the contract of employment or at least act unfairly if the employee is dismissed. Accordingly, it is usually best to

---

[27] See *Ryan v Blackburn with Darwen Borough Council* UKEAT/0928/03/DM, which is curiously unreported.

ensure that any disciplinary or capability procedures, or any procedures which apply in the event of dismissal by reason of redundancy, are as straightforward and easy to understand and apply as possible.

STATEMENT OF TERMS AND CONDITIONS

4.14 An employer is obliged by s 1 of the ERA 1996 to give an employee a statement (a s 1 statement) of a number of the contractual terms applicable to his employment. The s 1 statement may be given before the employment starts,[28] and a letter or written contract of employment may contain the necessary information.[29] An employer is obliged by s 4 of that Act to give a further statement when any of those terms is changed. The employer is obliged to give a s 1 statement no later than two months after the beginning of the employment, and a statement under s 4 within one month of the change. Most of the information which is required to be given in a s 1 statement is referred to in para **4.12** above. The relevant additional information (ignoring that which is clearly inapplicable) is this:

(1) the names of the employer and the employee;

(2) the date when the employment began;

(3) the date when the employee's continuous employment began (which may be the same date);[30]

(4) any terms and conditions relating to hours of work (including any terms and conditions relating to normal hours);

(5) the title of the job;

(6) if the employment is not intended to be permanent, the period for which it is expected to continue, or, if it is for a fixed term, the date when it is to end;

(7) either the place of work or, where the employee is required or permitted to work at various places, an indication of that and of the address of the employer; and

(8) where a collective agreement to which the employer is not a party directly affects the terms and conditions of the employment, the parties by whom the agreement was made.

---

[28] ERA 1996, s 7B.
[29] Ibid, s 7A.
[30] See para **8.7** below regarding continuity of employment.

4.15 If there are no particulars to be given in any case, then the s 1 statement must state that fact.

4.16 A failure to comply with the obligations imposed by ss 1 and 4 of the ERA 1996 has two consequences. One is that the employee in question may ask an employment tribunal to determine the relevant term(s) of his employment, under s 11 of the ERA 1996. There is no sanction for a failure properly to specify the relevant terms in the event of such a referral: the tribunal merely has the duty of determining what information should have been included in the statement in question.

4.17 However, a failure either to give an employee a statement under s 1 or s 4 of the ERA 1996, or fully to comply with either of those sections, may lead to an award by an employment tribunal of between two and four weeks' pay (calculated by reference to the maximum stated in s 227 of the ERA 1996, which at the time of writing was £310). This is the effect of s 38 of the Employment Act 2002, which applies where almost any claim is made to an employment tribunal of a breach of an employee's individual rights.[31] Only if the tribunal concludes that there are 'exceptional circumstances which would make [such] an award . . . unjust or inequitable' will no such award be made.[32]

REHABILITATION OF OFFENDERS ACT 1974

4.18 The Rehabilitation of Offenders Act 1974 precludes an employer from discriminating against an employee because of a conviction which is 'spent'. However, since 'any work . . . in a regulated position' (within the meaning of Pt I of the Criminal Justice and Court Services Act 2000, which includes employment in a school[33]) is specifically excluded from the prohibitions in that Act,[34] this is highly unlikely to affect schools.

PAY AND CONDITIONS

Introduction

4.19 Under the Teachers' Pay and Conditions Act 1987 (the TPCA 1987), the Secretary of State was given power to determine the pay and conditions of teachers in State schools. Since pay and conditions of employment are in the vast majority of situations determined contractually, this took away the

---

[31] The rights are those which are listed in Sch 5 to the Employment Act 2002 and include a claim of discrimination on any relevant ground, of unfair dismissal, and of a breach of contract which is outstanding on, or arises from, the termination of an employee's contract of employment.
[32] See s 38(5) of the Employment Act 2002.
[33] See para **3.27** above for the definition of a 'regulated position'.
[34] See art 4(b) of the Rehabilitation of Offenders Act 1974 (Exceptions) Order 1975, SI 1975/1023, read with para 14 of Pt II of Sch 1 to that Order, and the definition of a regulated position in Pt IV of that Schedule.

freedom of the employers of teachers in State schools to negotiate terms and conditions of staff. The TPCA 1987 was replaced by the School Teachers' Pay and Conditions Act 1991 (the STPCA 1991). That Act was in turn repealed and replaced by ss 119–130 of the EA 2002.

To which teachers do the pay and conditions documents apply?

4.20 Sections 119–130 of the EA 2002 apply to the employment of school teachers as defined by s 122(3) to (5) of the EA 2002 (unless they are in an Education Action Zone and the Secretary of State has ordered under s 128(2) of the EA 2002 that s 122(2) does not apply to the school[35]). This means:

(1) qualified teachers providing primary or secondary education under a contract of employment or for services where the other party to the contract is an LEA or the governing body of a foundation, voluntary aided or foundation special school, and the contract requires the teacher to carry out work specified in regulations made under s 133(1) of the EA 2002;[36]

(2) head teachers of schools maintained by LEAs;[37] and

(3) persons who fall within one of five categories (including that they are undertaking training).[38]

4.21 Where a school is a member of an education action zone, the governing body of the school may apply to the Secretary of State for an order (which, although made by statutory instrument, need not be approved in any way by Parliament[39]) made under s 128(2) 'that section 122(2) shall not apply to any school teacher at the school'. The governing body must have consulted all of the school teachers at the school before making such an application,[40] and the application must not state a date for its commencement earlier than three months after the date of the application.[41] Once an order made under s 128(2) is in force in relation to a school, the terms and conditions of the teachers at the school relating to remuneration and other conditions of employment at the school will be either as they have been determined by the governing body or, where the governing body has made no such determination, those terms which had effect under the latest school teachers' pay and conditions order before the order made under s 128(2) came into effect.[42] The Secretary of State may under s 128(6) make regulations about the application of s 122(2) where an order

---

[35] Such an order needs to be made by statutory instrument: see EA 2002, s 210. See the next para below concerning the making of such an order.
[36] See EA 2002, s 122(3); see para **3.3** above for the current regulations made under s 133(1).
[37] Ibid, s 122(4).
[38] See ibid, s 122(5) and the Education (School Teachers' Prescribed Qualifications, etc) Order 2003, SI 2003/1709.
[39] See s 210(5)(c) of the EA 2002.
[40] Ibid, s 128(4).
[41] Ibid, s 128(5)(a).
[42] Ibid, s 128(3).

made under s 128(2) either (a) is revoked, or (b) lapses (in whole or in part) because one or more schools to which the order relates ceases to form part of an EAZ. No such regulations had been made at the time of writing.

The school teachers' pay and conditions documents

4.22 Sections 119–121 of the EA 2002 concern the School Teachers' Review Body, which was established under s 1 of the STPCA 1991. Section 122 is the central provision of the EA 2002 concerning the pay of school teachers. It confers on the Secretary of State power:

> 'by order [to] make provision for the determination of –
>
> (a) the remuneration of school teachers;
> (b) other conditions of employment of school teachers which relate to their professional duties or working time.'

4.23 The effect of such an order is that the remuneration of the school teacher 'shall be determined and paid in accordance with any provision of the order which applies to him',[43] and any provision of the order 'which relates to a condition of employment other than remuneration and which applies to him shall have effect as a term of his contract of employment'.[44] Thus, a provision of the current order made under s 122 concerning pay must be complied with, but not as a matter of the law of contract. In contrast, other provisions of that order which apply to an individual teacher do take effect as a term of that teacher's contract of employment.

4.24 Another effect of an order made under s 122 of the EA 2002 is that 'a term of [the] contract [of employment of a teacher to whom the order relates] shall have no effect in so far as it makes provision which is prohibited by the order or which is otherwise inconsistent with a provision of the order'.[45] Thus the nationally agreed terms of employment of teachers are ousted in so far as they are inconsistent with the order. This does not normally give rise to difficulty in practice, since pay and conditions documents made under the relevant Acts have not contained all the terms and conditions which one would expect in a contract of employment. So, for example, there is no provision in those documents concerning the rights and obligations of the parties in relation to notice periods and therefore pay in relation to such periods. Accordingly, in the event of a need to give notice, it would be necessary to consider the terms of the booklet known as the Burgundy Book (because of its colour) containing the terms agreed collectively at a national level. Those terms are in some respects not entirely straightforward, however, and several issues of interpretation of those terms, and related matters, have been the subject of judicial consideration. Similarly, the part of the school teachers' pay and conditions documents issued since 2001 which relates to threshold payments

---

[43] EA 2002, s 122(2)(a).
[44] Ibid, s 122(2)(b).
[45] Ibid, s 122(2)(c).

has given rise to some difficulty in practice, and some of the issues which have arisen in both of these contexts are considered below.

4.25 Before turning to those issues, however, reference can usefully be made here to the Secretary of State's power to give guidance under s 127 'about the procedure to be followed in applying provision of an order under section 122' [sic]. The governing body of a school and the LEA must have regard to such guidance, and a failure to 'follow' the guidance may be taken into account in any proceedings in a court or tribunal.[46]

4.26 In addition, it is likely to be helpful to mention that all of the provisions of the school teachers' pay and conditions document which was current at the time of writing, the School Teachers' Pay and Conditions Document 2006[47] (the STPCD 2006) relating to working hours are expressly stated to be subject to European Community directive 93/104/EC, which gave rise to the Working Time Regulations 1998.[48] It should be noted that an employer is under an obligation to ensure that employees are able to take the rests to which they are entitled under those regulations.[49]

Issues concerning the application of the school teachers' pay and conditions documents

Reviews of determinations concerning performance thresholds, advanced skills teacher standards, the excellent teacher standards and the fast track teacher standards

4.27 One matter which may give rise to difficulty concerns the manner in which payments come to be made to teachers who pass a 'performance threshold', as provided for by paras 19 to 21 and Annex 1 of the STPCD 2006. There is now no provision for a review of the determination, made under para 21, of whether a teacher 'has or has not met all the performance threshold standards throughout the relevant period'.[50] The question how a dissatisfied teacher could challenge a determination that he has not met such standards throughout the relevant period therefore arises. Since it is a matter relating to the pay of the teacher concerned, and since a provision relating to pay in the STPCD 2006 (as with all teachers' pay and conditions documents) does not take effect as a term of the contract of employment,[51] the teacher would not be able to make a claim of breach of contract in relation to the application of para 21. It is possible that a challenge to a determination that a teacher 'has not met all the performance threshold standards throughout the relevant period'

---

[46] EA 2002, s 127(2) and (3). Such guidance has been issued. It is available at http://www.teachernet.gov.uk.
[47] The 2006 document has its effect by virtue of the Education (School Teachers' Pay and Conditions) (No 2) Order 2006, SI 2006/2133.
[48] SI 1998/1833. See para 59.4 of the 2006 document, which provides that nothing in that document 'shall be taken to conflict with Council Directive 93/104/EC'.
[49] *European Commission v United Kingdom*, Case C-484/04, [2007] ICR 592.
[50] See para **21.5**.
[51] See para **4.23** above.

could be made by seeking, under s 23 of the ERA 1996, payment of the relevant additional pay, on the basis that the teacher had indeed so met such standards.[52] However, it is difficult to see how an employment tribunal could properly make a decision of that sort, bearing in mind the fact that the decision will involve almost exclusively an exercise of professional judgment, applying expertise which the members of the tribunal will in the vast majority of cases not have. It is possible that the tribunal could properly decide the matter only by reference to procedural issues, and that it would not be able to decide for example that the teacher had indeed met all the performance threshold standards throughout the relevant period. However, even if there had been a procedural flaw, that would not entitle the tribunal to conclude that the teacher should be regarded as a post-threshold teacher.

4.28 A teacher could, however, make a claim of a breach of the implied term of trust and confidence arising from the manner in which such an assessment was carried out. This is because the assessment under para 21 falls to be carried out by the head teacher of the school or (where the teacher is an 'unattached teacher') 'a person with management responsibility for the applicant'.[53] A claim of a breach of that term could be made without the employee needing to resign.[54] If the employee did not resign, then the claim could be made in the local county court. If the employee resigned and claimed that he had been 'constructively' dismissed, then the claim could be made in the employment tribunal.[55]

4.29 Similar issues arise in relation to the assessment of teachers 'against the advanced skills teacher standards, the excellent teacher standards and the Fast Track teacher standards', under paras 32–34 of the STPCD 2006. Paragraph 33.1 of the STPCD 2006 requires the Secretary of State to make arrangements for the appointment of assessors for the latter purposes. An assessor appointed under para 33 must 'exercise his functions without unlawful discrimination'.[56] The assessment is carried out under para 34. A teacher can ask under para 35.1 for an 'independent review' of the assessment on the (essentially public law) grounds in para 35.2. The manner in which the independent reviewer is to be appointed is not stated in the STPCD 2006. The person conducting the review must 'take such steps as he thinks fit'.[57] However, assuming that the reviewer was in no way connected to the teacher's employer, the review could not be challenged in the law of contract. (If the reviewer could be said to have acted on behalf of the employer, then the manner in which the review was carried out could theoretically give rise to a claim of a breach of the implied term of trust and confidence.[58]) However, as with a claim of a wrongful

---

[52] See para **5.32** below for the right not to have unlawful deductions made.
[53] See para **21.3**.
[54] See for example *French v Barclays Bank plc* [1998] IRLR 646.
[55] See the Employment Tribunals Extension of Jurisdiction (England and Wales) Order 1994, SI 1994/1623.
[56] STPCD 2006, para 33.3.
[57] Ibid, para 35.3.
[58] See the preceding para above.

determination that a teacher has not met all of the 'performance threshold standards throughout the relevant period', a teacher could theoretically make a claim under s 23 of the ERA 1996 of an alleged wrongful failure to award the payment which is payable to a teacher who has attained, for example, the advanced teacher standards. Again, however, the question arises how such a claim could be determined by an employment tribunal, bearing it in mind that the determination that the employee has not met the relevant standards involves almost exclusively the exercise of judgment. Presumably, there would in theory be the possibility of an application for judicial review. However, the High Court could at best (from the point of view of the teacher) decide no more than that the decision should be retaken. Thus claiming under s 23 of the ERA 1996 would probably be the only way in which an assessment could realistically be challenged, and even that might well be fruitless.

4.30 In addition, teachers may be 'recognised' as 'Fast Track' teachers, by a 'recognising body' appointed by the Secretary of State under para 36.1 of the STPCD 2006. That body may also cease to recognise a teacher as a Fast Track teacher.[59] The Secretary of State is also empowered by para 36.1 to 'make arrangements . . . for the independent review of such decisions'. Where no appointment of a recognising body has been made, the Secretary of State is the recognising body.[60] The question arises how a determination by for example the recognising body could be challenged. Theoretically the decision made on behalf of the Secretary of State could be judicially reviewed. However, again, the High Court could at best (from the point of view of the teacher) decide no more than that the decision should be retaken. Again, therefore, the matter would probably be best dealt with under s 23 of the ERA 1996, with the caveat that the employment tribunal might properly conclude that it could not determine the claim in favour of the teacher.

Is temporary safeguarding of pay lawful?

4.31 Another issue which has given rise to difficulty is whether it is open to an employer to award an employee only temporary safeguarding under what is now para 49.1.2 of the STPCD 2006. Paragraph 49.1.2 of the STPCD 2006 applies to teachers who took up a new post on or before 31 December 2005 as a result (broadly) of something other than a reorganisation, or the closure, of a school or other relevant educational 'establishment'. The employing LEA where para 49.1.2 applies may pay a teacher who would otherwise have suffered a diminution in pay that which he would have been paid before the proposed diminution. There is no mention in para 49 of a power to do so only temporarily (although in certain defined circumstances the safeguarding may cease[61]). In *Governing Body of the Plume School v Langshaw*,[62] the EAT decided that it was not open to an employer to grant a temporal limitation on the effect of such a determination.

---

[59] STPCD 2006, para 37.
[60] Ibid, para 36.1.
[61] See ibid, para 49.8.
[62] [2003] ELR 97.

4.32 In contrast, in relation to the appointment of a teacher to a new post as a result of a reorganisation or closure of an educational 'establishment or service' which occurred on or after 1 January 2006, any safeguarding will be for no more than three years.[63] Similarly, the safeguarding of the pay of a member of the leadership group, an advanced skills teacher or an 'excellent teacher' in the circumstances described in para 51.1 of the STPCD 2006 will necessarily be for a fixed period only.[64]

Issues relating to the Burgundy Book

Dorling v Sheffield City Council

4.33 Under para 6.1 of section 4 of the Burgundy Book:

> 'In the event of a teacher exhausting in part or full his/her entitlements under paragraph 2.1 above [which confer a right to sick pay] and being given notice of the termination of his/her contract without returning to work on the ground of permanent incapacity or for some other reason related to the sickness absence, he/she shall be paid full salary for the notice period with normal deductions only.'

4.34 In *R (Dorling) v Sheffield City Council*,[65] the High Court held that reg 7 of the Education (Teachers' Qualifications and Health Standards) (England) Regulations 1999,[66] imposed an obligation not to employ a person who did not have the requisite capacity (in terms of health) to teach, with the result that such person's employer was obliged to dismiss him. This then meant, bearing in mind para 6.1 of section 4 of the Burgundy Book, that the employer was obliged to pay a teacher employed under the terms of that book his full pay for his notice period, even though the teacher was sick and even though the teacher might now be in receipt of an early retirement pension, granted on the basis that he was permanently incapacitated. The Court of Appeal reached a different conclusion in the subsequent case of *Healey v Bridgend County Borough Council*,[67] but the case was not argued as fully as it might have been. The matter was then considered fully by Lindsay J in *R (Verner) v Derby City Council*.[68] His determination was that the teacher is not entitled to notice pay in the circumstances.

---

[63] See STPCD 2006, para 50.4.
[64] See ibid, paras 51.5(c) and 51.6(a) read with para 5.3.
[65] [2003] ICR 424.
[66] SI 1999/2166. There is no equivalent provision in the Education (Health Standards) (England) Regulations 2003, SI 2003/3139, possibly because of the difficulties caused by the *Dorling* case. Regulation 6 of the latter regulations (which are considerably more simple than the regulations which they replace) merely provides that 'A relevant activity may only be carried out by a person if, having regard to [the employer's duty to the employee under the DDA 1995], he has the health and physical capacity to carry out that activity' and that a person in receipt of a pension granted under the Teachers' Pension Scheme by reason of the person's ill health will (subject to one exception) not be regarded as having the health or physical capacity for teaching.
[67] [2002] EWCA Civ 1996, [2004] ICR 561.
[68] [2003] EWHC 278 (Admin), [2004] ICR 535.

Is an employee entitled to the full amount of sick pay under the Burgundy Book before he is dismissed because of the incapacity?

4.35 In *Jones v Governing Body of Barton Court Grammar School*,[69] the EAT ruled that the fact that para 6.1 of section 4 of the Burgundy Book refers to the termination of a teacher's contract of employment in the event that the teacher's entitlement to sick pay is only partly exhausted, means that an employer can lawfully terminate the contract of employment before the teacher's full sick pay entitlement has expired. This was despite the line of cases including *Aspden v Webbs Poultry & Meat Group (Holdings) Ltd*,[70] according to which in certain circumstances where an employee has the right to sickness benefits (in all the relevant cases, they were payable by insurers), an employer's express power to terminate the contract of employment will be restricted.

The required notice period

4.36 However, in the same case, the EAT concluded that a failure to give sufficient notice to ensure that a relevant teacher's contract of employment is terminated on or before the end of the period of notice to which he is entitled by reason of s 86 of the ERA 1996[71] means that the teacher will be entitled to notice to the end of the following, and not just the current, term. This is a situation which can occur only in relation to the autumn or spring terms, since under the Burgundy Book an employer must give at least three months' notice before 31 August if the teacher's employment is terminated during the summer term. The Burgundy Book, however, requires the giving of only two months' notice to terminate on 31 December or 30 April (as the case may be).[72] The problem in issue arises if a teacher has nine or more years of continuous employment by the time that notice needs to be given: this is because he will then be entitled to more than two calendar months' notice.

4.37 Arguably, the EAT erred in its finding on this issue: why, after all, should not the parties be taken to have agreed that if the employer gives at least two months' notice, but less than (say) 11 weeks' notice, then the teacher will receive additional pay only for the part of the notice period which exceeds two months (that is, between two and three weeks' pay)?

APPOINTMENT OF A MEMBER OF THE STAFF OF A MAINTAINED SCHOOL

Introduction and overview

4.38 The primary legislation relating to the appointment and dismissal of staff in a maintained school is now much simpler than it used to be. This is the

---

[69] EAT/0920/02.
[70] [1996] IRLR 521.
[71] See para **5.2** below for the effect of s 86.
[72] See para 4 of section 3.

result of the enactment of ss 35 and 36 of, and Sch 2 to, the EA 2002 and the replacement by those (short) provisions of the detailed provisions of Schs 16 and 17 to the SSFA 1998 with regulatory powers. Section 35 applies to community, voluntary controlled, community special and maintained nursery schools. A teacher in such a school is employed by the LEA.[73] If the school does not have a delegated budget, then the LEA has all of the relevant employment powers, fettered only by s 58 of the SSFA 1998 in relation to a voluntary controlled school.[74] Section 36 applies to foundation, voluntary aided and foundation special schools. A teacher or other employee appointed to work under a contract of employment at such a school must (unless regulations made under s 36(4) otherwise provide) be employed under a contract of employment the other party to which is the governing body of the school.[75] If the school does not have a delegated budget, the LEA has extensive (but not unfettered) powers in relation to the staffing of the school.[76]

4.39 The School Staffing (England) Regulations 2003[77] and the Staffing of Maintained Schools (Wales) Regulations 2006[78] were made under ss 35 and 36 of the EA 2002. Those regulations apply to all schools with delegated budgets.[79] They apply in addition to new schools.[80] The regulations relating to England also apply to situations in which the governing bodies of two or more schools act jointly.[81] Sections 35(8) and 36(8) of the EA 2002 empower the Secretary of State and the National Assembly for Wales to issue guidance in relation to the exercise of functions under regulations made under those sections. Governing bodies, local education authorities and head teachers have to 'have regard' to such guidance.

4.40 The School Staffing (England) Regulations make similar provision to that which was contained in Schs 16 and 17 to the SSFA 1998 (for example in that the regulations give to the governing body of a community, voluntary controlled, community special, and maintained nursery school the power to control the staff[82]), although the regulations make rather simpler provision than Schs 16 and 17.[83]

4.41 The Staffing of Maintained Schools (Wales) Regulations 2006 make provision in relation to appointments which is similar to that of the School

---

[73] EA 2002, s 35(2).
[74] See ibid, s 35(7) and Sch 2, paras 1–4. See para **4.78** onwards below for the effects of s 58 of the SSFA 1998.
[75] EA 2002, s 36(2).
[76] See ibid, s 36(7) and Sch 2, paras 5–10.
[77] SI 2003/1963.
[78] SI 2006/873 (W 81).
[79] See EA 2002, ss 35(7) and 36(7).
[80] See regs 33–37 of SI 2003/1963 and regs 35–39 of SI 2006/873.
[81] See regs 28–32 of SI 2003/1963.
[82] See ibid, regs 6, 7, 16 and 17; see further below.
[83] For example, there is no provision relating to foundation, voluntary aided and foundation special schools which is equivalent to regs 6, 7, 16 and 17. This is in contrast to Sch 17, which included, in paras 21, 23 and 24, similar provision to that which is now in regs 6, 7, 16 and 17.

Staffing (England) Regulations 2003, although the wording is in some respects different, and there are several additional provisions in the regulations relating to Wales. The position in England is stated first below.

The staffing situation in a maintained school in England with a delegated budget

Local Education Authority concerns about the head teacher

4.42 Where the LEA 'has any serious concerns about the performance of the head teacher of' any kind of school which it maintains, then it must 'make a written report of its concerns to the chair of the governing body of the school, at the same time sending a copy to the head teacher'.[84] The chair of the governing body must then 'notify the authority in writing of the action he proposes to take in the light of the report'.[85]

Conduct, discipline and capability of staff

4.43 The governing body of any kind of maintained school must 'establish procedures' (a) 'for the regulation of the conduct and discipline of staff at the school' and (b) 'by which staff may seek redress for any grievance relating to their work at the school'.[86] The governing body must also 'establish procedures for dealing with lack of capability on the part of the staff at the school'.[87]

4.44 Although it is not stated specifically in the School Staffing (England) Regulations 2003, or elsewhere in the applicable legislation, the effect of these requirements is that the governing body of a maintained school which has a delegated budget, and not the LEA, has power to control the staff of the school.

Appointment of staff

4.45 The manner in which school staff may be appointed differs according to whether the school in question is:

(1) a community, voluntary controlled, community special or maintained nursery school, or

(2) a foundation, voluntary aided or foundation special school.

---

[84] SI 2003/1963, reg 5(a).
[85] Ibid, reg 5(b).
[86] Ibid, reg 6(1).
[87] Ibid, reg 7.

Appointment of staff in a community, voluntary controlled, community special or maintained nursery school where there is a delegated budget

4.46 *General requirements concerning the appointment of staff.* Any person who is appointed to work at a community, voluntary controlled, community special or maintained nursery school (or a federated such school) must meet 'all relevant staff qualification requirements'.[88]

4.47 It is for the governing body to decide whether a person whom it has selected to work at the school is to be appointed:

(a) under a contract of employment with the LEA,

(b) by the LEA to work otherwise than under a contract of employment, or

(c) by the governing body otherwise than under a contract of employment.[89]

Before that person can lawfully be appointed, however, his identity must be checked and a check must be made of his right to work in the United Kingdom.[90] An 'enhanced criminal record certificate issued pursuant to Part V of the Police Act 1997' must also be obtained in respect of any person who is so appointed 'before or as soon as practicable after his appointment', unless one of two exceptions applies. One is that that person has, during a period which ended not more than three months before his appointment:

(1) worked in a school in England in a post:
    (a) which brought him regularly into contact with children or young persons, or
    (b) to which he was appointed on or after 12 May 2006 and which did not bring him regularly into contact with children or young persons, or

(2) worked in an institution within the further education sector in England in a post which involved the provision of education which brought him regularly into contact with children or young persons.[91]

The other exception is that the person has lived outside the United Kingdom with the result that obtaining an enhanced criminal record certificate 'is not sufficient to establish his suitability to work in a school' (or, as the case may be,

---

[88] SI 2003/1963, reg 11(2), read with reg 32 of, and para 4 of Sch 9 to, the School Governance (Federations) (England) Regulations 2007, SI 2007/960. Regulation 32 and Sch 9 modify the School Staffing (England) Regulations 2003 so that they apply generally with appropriate modifications to the staffing of federations. The following paragraphs below should be read accordingly.
[89] SI 2003/1963, reg 11(1).
[90] Ibid, reg 11(2) and (5).
[91] Ibid, reg 11(3).

federation or federated school).[92] Where that second exception applies, the LEA must subject the person to 'such checks as the authority considers appropriate, having regard to any guidance issued by the Secretary of State'.[93]

4.48 A representative of the LEA may 'attend and offer advice at all proceedings relating to the selection . . . of any teacher',[94] which must include a head teacher or deputy head teacher. Any such advice must be 'considered' by the governing body or person(s) with delegated authority to appoint the teacher.[95]

4.49 *Appointment of head teacher and deputy head teacher.* The governing body must notify the LEA of 'any vacancy for the head teacher', and, where it 'identifies the post of deputy head teacher as one to be filled, that post'.[96] It must 'advertise any such vacancy or post in such manner as it considers appropriate', unless it has 'good reason not to advertise and conduct a selection process to fill the vacancy or post'.[97] Such 'good reason' may not be taken to override the need for the person appointed to 'meet all relevant staff qualification requirements'.[98]

4.50 The governing body must appoint a selection panel with at least three members.[99] The panel must select for interview 'such applicants for the post as it thinks fit and, where the post is that of head teacher, notify the authority in writing of the names of the applicants so selected'.[100] The panel must then interview the applicants who attend for the purpose and, 'where they consider it appropriate, recommend to the governing body for approval one of the applicants interviewed by them'.[101] If the LEA within seven days of receiving notification of the names of the applicants makes written representations to the selection panel 'that any applicant is not a suitable person for the appointment', then the panel must consider those representations and, if it decides nevertheless to recommend that person for the appointment in question, notify both the governing body and the LEA in writing of its reasons for doing so.[102]

---

[92] SI 2003/1963, reg 11(4), read with reg 32 of, and para 5 of Sch 9 to, SI 2007/960.
[93] Ibid.
[94] Ibid, reg 12(1).
[95] Ibid, reg 12(2).
[96] Ibid, reg 13(1).
[97] Ibid, reg 13((2) and (7). The Secretary of State has issued guidance under ss 35(8) and 36(8) of the EA 2002 as to the circumstances in which a governing body may decide that there is 'good reason' not to advertise a relevant post. This is available at http://www.governornet.co.uk/linkAttachments/ACF3B38.doc. The relevant part of that document is paras 2.15 to 2.21. That guidance appears to be unduly restrictive, since it purports to prescribe the only times when a governing body can properly decide that there is such 'good reason'. This is surely unlawful, since the governing body has a discretion in that regard, which cannot properly be removed by the Secretary of State's guidance even though (see para **4.39** above) there is a duty to have regard to that guidance: see for example *S v Brent London Borough Council* [2002] ELR 556.
[98] See SI 2003/1963, reg 13(7).
[99] Ibid, reg 13(3).
[100] Ibid, reg 13(3)(a).
[101] Ibid, reg 13(3)(b) and (c).
[102] SI 2003/1963, reg 13(4).

4.51 If the selection panel's recommendation for appointment is approved by the governing body, then the LEA must appoint the recommended person unless the governing body itself is going to do so under reg 11(1)(c), or unless the person does not meet all the relevant staff qualification requirements.[103] If:

(a) the selection panel does not recommend any applicant for the relevant vacancy or post,

(b) the governing body declines to approve the person recommended by the selection panel, or

(c) the LEA declines to appoint the applicant approved by the governing body (presumably because the applicant does not meet all of the relevant staff qualification requirements),

then the panel may select another person for recommendation, including in the case of (b) or (c) from among the existing applicants.[104]

4.52 *Appointment of other teachers.* There are no specific requirements in the School Staffing (England) Regulations 2003 concerning the appointment for a period of no more than four months of a teacher other than a head teacher or a deputy head teacher. Thus, a teacher may be appointed for an ordinary school term without having to follow any particular process.

4.53 Where the governing body proposes to appoint a teacher (ie in this context a teacher other than a head teacher or deputy head teacher) for a period of more than four months, it must send a specification for the post to the LEA.[105] The LEA must then appoint the person who is selected by the governing body for the post, unless either the person does not meet the relevant staff qualification requirements or the governing body is to appoint the person otherwise than under a contract of employment.[106]

4.54 *Appointment of support staff.* Where the LEA is responsible for the provision of school meals in a maintained school, the LEA is responsible for the appointment of school meals staff.[107] Where, however, the governing body has responsibility for the provision of school meals in its school (and that will occur only where the school has a delegated budget and an order transferring the LEA's responsibility to governing bodies has been made by the Secretary of State under s 512A(1) of the EA 1996[108]), the governing body is responsible for the appointment of any staff for that purpose.[109] The governing body may, however, have entered into an agreement with the LEA that the LEA will

---

[103] Ibid, reg 13(5).
[104] See ibid, reg 13(6).
[105] Ibid, reg 14(1) and (2).
[106] Ibid, reg 14(3).
[107] Ibid, reg 18(1).
[108] See EA 1996, s 512A(6).
[109] See SI 2003/1963, reg 18(2) and (4).

provide lunches at the school. If it has done so, then the governing body may require any member of staff who is employed by the LEA for that purpose at the school to cease to work at the school.[110]

4.55 Generally, where the governing body 'identifies a support staff post to be filled', then it 'may' recommend a person to the LEA for appointment to that post.[111] The recommendation must be accompanied by a 'job specification for the post', which must include the governing body's recommendations as to:

'(a) the duties to be performed,
(b) the hours of work (where the post is part-time),
(c) the duration of appointment,
(d) the grade [on the scale of grades applicable in relation to employment with the LEA; the grade must be 'such as the governing body considers appropriate'], and
(e) the remuneration.'[112]

4.56 If, within seven days of receiving the job specification, the LEA makes written representations to the governing body relating to the grade or remuneration to be paid, then the governing body must consider those representations and, if it decides not to change the grade or remuneration to be paid, notify the LEA in writing of its reasons for doing so.[113] Subject to this, where the LEA has any discretion with respect to remuneration, it must exercise that discretion in accordance with the governing body's recommendation.[114] The LEA must also appoint the person who is selected by the governing body for the post, unless either the person does not meet the relevant staff qualification requirements or the governing body is to appoint the person otherwise than under a contract of employment.[115]

Appointment of staff in a foundation, voluntary aided or foundation special school

4.57 As one would expect, since the governing body of a foundation, voluntary aided or foundation special school is the employer in the law of contract of its staff,[116] the provisions in the School Staffing (England) Regulations 2003 concerning those schools are in some respects more straightforward than those which apply to the staffing of a community, voluntary controlled, community special or maintained nursery school. However, there are provisions of sorts which do not apply to the latter kinds of school but which apply to foundation, voluntary aided and foundation special schools.

---

[110] Ibid, reg 18(3).
[111] Ibid, reg 15(1).
[112] Ibid, reg 15(2) and (3).
[113] Ibid, reg 15(5).
[114] See ibid, reg 15(4), which also states (uncontroversially) in what circumstances the LEA is to be regarded as having a discretion for this purpose.
[115] Ibid, reg 15(6).
[116] See EA 2002, s 36(2).

4.58 The requirement to obtain an enhanced criminal record certificate is the same for a foundation, voluntary aided or foundation special school as that which applies in relation for example to a community school.[117] There is in relation, for example, to a foundation school no direct equivalent of the power of an LEA to provide advice to the governing body of a community school in relation to appointments to its staff,[118] but the LEA may nevertheless provide such advice if:

(1) there is in existence an agreement between it and the governing body to the effect that it may do so, or

(2) the Secretary of State has determined that the LEA may do so (and has not withdrawn that determination).[119]

4.59 The appointment of a head teacher or deputy head teacher in a foundation, voluntary aided or foundation special school is dealt with in the School Staffing (England) Regulations 2003 in a similar manner to such appointments in for example a community school,[120] unless the school is a voluntary aided school and the trustees under a trust deed relating to the school 'are also trustees of a Roman Catholic religious order'.[121] However, in relation to the appointment of other teachers who are to be employed for more than four months, those regulations merely require the governing body to 'send a specification of the post to' the LEA.[122] The appointment of support staff is subject to no restrictions, but the appointment may be by the LEA if it and the governing body agree that the appointment should be made by the LEA.[123]

Collaborating governing bodies

4.60 Where two or more governing bodies decide to collaborate on any function relating to individual members of the schools' staff, the School Staffing (England) Regulations 2003 apply with appropriate modifications.[124] Thus, for example, a selection panel for the appointment of a head teacher or a deputy head teacher must 'consist of at least three governors taken from any of the collaborating governing bodies', and the selection panel must 'make their recommendation to the governing body of the relevant school'.[125] As for the

---

[117] See SI 2003/1963, reg 20(3)–(5); see para **4.47** above concerning the requirement as it applies to a community, voluntary controlled, community special or maintained nursery school.
[118] Concerning which, see para **4.48** above.
[119] See SI 2003/1963, reg 21.
[120] See ibid, reg 22.
[121] See ibid, reg 27 in relation to the appointment of a head teacher in such a school. The Major Superior of the order may propose one or more candidates for the post who are members of the order and the governing body must interview those persons and appoint one of them unless the governing body has 'good reason for not making any such appointment'.
[122] Ibid, reg 23.
[123] Ibid, reg 24.
[124] See SI 2003/1963, reg 28.
[125] See ibid, reg 29.

appointment of other teachers and support staff, the collaborating governing bodies may delegate the appointment to:

(a) the head teacher of one or more of the collaborating schools,

(b) one or more governors from any of the collaborating schools, or

(c) one or more head teachers with one or more governors from any of the collaborating schools.[126]

However, the decision relating to the appointment of a member of staff must be unanimous.[127] If the head teacher of the school at which the member of staff is to be employed does not make the decision, then he is 'entitled to attend and offer advice', which must be considered by the person or persons to whom the delegation has been made.[128] Where the LEA has a right to offer advice to any individual governing body which is collaborating, the LEA has the same entitlement to offer advice to the other collaborating governing bodies.[129]

Delegation of powers

4.61 The School Staffing (England) Regulations 2003 empower the governing body to delegate to a single member of the governing body, or two or more such members, or to the head teacher (or to one or more governors and the head teacher), its powers of appointment of staff other than the head teacher or deputy head teacher.[130] The question of delegation is complicated by the fact that there is in the School Governance (Procedures) (England) Regulations 2003[131] a separate power to delegate to a committee of the governing body any function, including any function which it has by virtue of the School Staffing (England) Regulations 2003 except the function of appointing a head teacher or a deputy head teacher.[132]

The staffing situation in a maintained school in Wales with a delegated budget

4.62 The Staffing of Maintained Schools (Wales) Regulations 2006[133] make similar provision to that which is in the School Staffing (England) Regulations 2003, but there are several significant additional provisions. The additional provisions are described in the following paragraphs. The provisions in the regulations relating to Wales which are similar to or the same as those concerning England are then stated.

---

[126] Ibid, reg 30(1).
[127] Ibid, reg 30(2).
[128] Ibid, reg 30(3).
[129] Ibid, reg 32.
[130] Ibid, reg 4.
[131] SI 2003/1377.
[132] See ibid, reg 16, as amended by SI 2003/1963.
[133] SI 2006/873 (W 81), as amended by SI 2007/944 (W 80).

Significant additional powers and duties

Sufficiency of staff

4.63 The Staffing of Maintained Schools (Wales) Regulations 2006 repeat the provision which was formerly in reg 4 of the Education (Teachers' Qualifications and Health Standards) (Wales) Regulations 1999[134] concerning the sufficiency of staff in a maintained school. The new provision is reg 4(1) of the 2006 Regulations, and it is in the following terms:

> 'A governing body and a local education authority must exercise their respective functions under these Regulations and any other enactment with a view to ensuring that there is employed, or engaged otherwise than under contracts of employment, a staff suitable and sufficient in numbers for the purpose of securing the provision of education appropriate to the ages, abilities, aptitudes and needs of the pupils having regard to any arrangements for the utilisation of the services of staff employed or engaged otherwise than at the school in question.'

Independent investigation of child protection matter

4.64 In addition, there is a new obligation imposed on a governing body when 'allegations are made against a member of the school's staff that involve issues of child protection'. The obligation is to 'appoint an independent investigator to investigate the allegations prior to the hearing of any proceedings relating to those allegations'.[135]

Acting head teachers and deputy head teachers

4.65 In Wales, a selection panel for a head teacher or a deputy head teacher of a maintained school may recommend a person to be an acting head teacher or acting deputy head teacher if it appears before the date on which the post falls vacant that it will not be filled.[136] Similarly, the governing body of a maintained school 'may, in connection with any absence of the person for the time being holding the post of head teacher or deputy head teacher of the school', appoint an acting head teacher or (as the case may be) deputy head teacher.[137]

Selection panels

4.66 Selection panels in Wales may include persons who are not governors, as long as there is a majority of governors.[138] The panel must elect a chair from among its members who are neither paid to work at the school nor a pupil at the school, but the governing body may remove that chair from office at any

---

[134] SI 1999/2817.
[135] SI 2006/873, reg 7(3). See reg 7(4) for the circumstances in which a person appointed as an independent investigator is to be regarded as independent. See further para **8.138** below.
[136] See ibid, regs 10(2)–(4) and 24(2)–(4).
[137] See SI 2006/873, regs 11(1) and 25(1).
[138] Ibid, regs 10(13) and (14) and 24(12) and (13).

time.[139] Where there is an equal number of votes on a matter, the chair, if a governor, has a second or casting vote.[140] Any decision of the selection panel must be 'taken by a vote representing an absolute majority of all the members of the panel (whether or not taking part in the vote)'.[141]

Requirement to advertise post of head teacher or deputy head teacher

4.67 The governing body of a maintained school in Wales is obliged to advertise any vacancy in the post of head teacher or deputy head teacher 'in such publications circulating throughout England and Wales as it considers appropriate';[142] there is no power to decide not to do so for good reason.

Right to give advice in relation to appointments

4.68 The chief education officer of the LEA, or his representative, has an absolute right to attend 'for the purpose of giving advice . . . all proceedings (including interviews)' of the governing body or any other persons relating to appointments or engagements of teachers (including head teachers, deputy head teachers, acting head teachers and acting deputy head teachers) to be employed at a foundation, voluntary aided or foundation special school.[143] The chief education officer or his representative may also give advice with respect to the appointment or engagement of a head teacher, a deputy head teacher, an acting head teacher or an acting deputy head teacher, or 'any matter arising in connection with any such appointment or engagement'.[144]

4.69 In addition, the 'appropriate diocesan officer' (nominated by the appropriate diocesan authority) in relation to a voluntary aided Church of England, Church in Wales or Roman Catholic Church school, has the same advisory rights as the chief education officer.[145] The governing body of a foundation school of the same denominations may agree with the appropriate diocesan authority to accord to the appropriate diocesan officer the same advisory rights with respect to some or all of the teachers at the school.[146] The agreement must be in writing, and may be withdrawn by notice in writing to the appropriate diocesan authority.[147]

4.70 The head teacher may also give advice to the governing body or any person acting with delegated power in relation to the appointment of a teacher at a maintained school of any sort in Wales.[148]

---

[139] Ibid, regs 10(10)–(12) and 24(9)–(11).
[140] Ibid, regs 10(15) and 24(14).
[141] Ibid, regs 10(16) and 24(15).
[142] Ibid, regs 10(8) and 24(7).
[143] See ibid, reg 21(1)–(3).
[144] Ibid, reg 21(2).
[145] See ibid, reg 23(1), (2) and (6).
[146] SI 2006/873, reg 23(3).
[147] Ibid, reg 23(4).
[148] See ibid, regs 14 and 22.

The framework of the regulations relating to the staffing of maintained schools in Wales

4.71 Otherwise, as stated above, the regulations relating to the staffing of maintained schools in Wales are similar to those relating to the staffing of maintained schools in England. Part 2 of the regulations relating to Wales applies to community, voluntary controlled, community special and ('once they have established governing bodies') maintained nursery schools,[149] and Part 3 applies to foundation, voluntary aided and foundation special schools.[150] Minor differences between the regulations relating to Wales and those relating to England include that the governing body of a maintained school in Wales may choose not to use a selection committee in connection with the appointment of a head teacher or deputy head teacher, and, instead, may make the selection itself.[151]

REQUIREMENT TO REVIEW STAFFING STRUCTURE

4.72 The Education (Review of Staffing Structure) (England) Regulations 2005[152] and the Education (Review of Staffing Structure) (Wales) Regulations 2005[153] required the 'relevant body' (ie the governing body of a maintained school which has a delegated budget and the LEA in the case of such a school which does not have a delegated budget[154]) to 'review the school's staffing structure in accordance with' reg 3 of those regulations. Regulation 3 required the relevant body to conduct the review 'with a view to ensuring that' (a) 'the management and deployment of all staff, and (b) the allocation of responsibilities and duties to all staff, make effective use of its resources'. In conducting the review, the relevant body had to consult (1) all staff, (2) representatives of recognised trade unions, and (3) 'such other persons as the relevant body considers appropriate'.[155] In England, the review had to be carried out by 31 December 2005, and in Wales it had to be carried out by 31 March 2006.[156] In both cases, an implementation plan had to be made by that date,[157] and the date by which any changes to the school's staffing structure will be fully implemented under that plan must be no later than 31 December 2008.[158]

4.73 Both sets of regulations require the relevant body in managing the head teacher to 'have regard to the desirability of the head teacher being able to

---

[149] Ibid, regs 9 to 15A inclusive concern appointments.
[150] Ibid, regs 20–27 and 33–34 concern appointments.
[151] See ibid, reg 34.
[152] SI 2005/1032.
[153] SI 2005/1910 (W 153).
[154] See reg 2(1) of both sets of regulations. All references below in this paragraph are to the same regulation in both sets of regulations.
[155] Regulation 3(5).
[156] Regulation 3(6)(a).
[157] Regulation 3(6)(b).
[158] See reg 3(7).

achieve a satisfactory balance between the time required to discharge his [or her] professional duties and the time required to pursue personal interests outside work'.[159] This duty is not time-limited.

STAFFING FOR NON-SCHOOL ACTIVITIES

4.74 Section 27(1) of the EA 2002 empowers the governing body of a maintained school to provide 'community facilities', namely:

> 'any facilities or services whose provision furthers any charitable purpose for the benefit of –
>
> (a) pupils at the school or their families, or
> (b) people who live or work in the locality in which the school is situated'.

4.75 This power includes a power to 'provide staff, goods, services and accommodation to any person'.[160] It is subject to s 28 of the EA 2002, which among other things empowers the making of regulations which restrict the exercise of the power. No such regulations had been made at the time of writing.

4.76 The reason for mentioning the power in s 27 of the EA 2002 here is that s 51A of the SSFA 1998 has two effects which need to be borne in mind when deciding how to deploy the staff of a maintained school. Section 51A(1) provides that as against third parties, expenditure incurred by a governing body in the exercise of the power conferred by s 27 is to be treated as part of the expenses of maintaining the school under s 22 of the SSFA 1998, but that if it is met by the LEA then it may be recovered by the LEA from the governing body. Section 51A(2) of the SSFA 1998 provides that except as provided by regulations made under s 50(3)(b) of that Act, no expenditure incurred by the governing body in the exercise of the power conferred by s 27 of the EA 2002 to provide community facilities may be met from the school's budget share for any (in Wales) 'financial year' or (in England) 'funding period'. The only regulations made so far of that nature apply only to maintained nursery schools.[161]

SCHOOL TEACHER APPRAISAL

4.77 The appraisal of teachers in England is also subject to specific regulation. In England, the Education (School Teacher Performance

---

[159] See reg 5 of both sets of regulations. The regulations relating to Wales use the words 'his or her', and therefore do not take advantage of s 6(a) of the Interpretation Act 1978, according to which 'words importing the masculine gender include the feminine'.
[160] EA 2002, s 27(2)(d).
[161] See SI 2004/444, amending SI 2002/378.

Management) (England) Regulations 2006[162] apply. In Wales, the School Teacher Appraisal (Wales) Regulations 2002[163] apply. Both sets of regulations were empowered by s 131 of the EA 2002.

TEACHERS, RELIGIOUS EDUCATION AND RELIGIOUS OPINIONS

4.78 Section 58(2) of the SSFA 1998[164] provides that where the number of teachers at a foundation or voluntary controlled school which has a religious character (and such a school 'has a religious character' if it is designated as a school having such a character by an order made by the Secretary of State under s 69(4) of the SSFA 1998[165]) is more than two, the teachers must include persons who are selected for their fitness and competence to give religious education in accordance with arrangements made under para 3(3) of Sch 19 to the SSFA 1998 and are specifically appointed to do so. That subparagraph requires the governing body of such a school in some circumstances to arrange for religious education to be given in accordance with the trust deed for the school or, where provision of that sort is not made by the trust deed, in accordance with the tenets of the religion or religious denomination specified in relation to the school under s 69(4) of the SSFA 1998. Such staff are called 'reserved teachers'.[166] They must not number more than a fifth of the total number of teachers (including the head teacher) at the school.[167] For this purpose, where the total number of teachers is not a multiple of five, then it is to be treated as if it were the next higher multiple of five. The head teacher of a foundation or voluntary controlled school with a religious character is not to be regarded as a reserved teacher while he holds the post of head teacher.[168]

4.79 The LEA must consult the foundation governors[169] before appointing a person to be a reserved teacher in a voluntary controlled school with a religious

---

[162] SI 2006/2661, which came into force on 1 September 2007. They replaced the Education (School Teacher Appraisal) (England) Regulations 2001, SI 2001/2855, but only prospectively.

[163] SI 2002/1394.

[164] It should be noted that it is expressly provided by reg 39 of the Employment Equality (Religion or Belief) Regulations 2003, SI 2003/1660, that those regulations do not affect ss 58–60 and 124A of the SSFA 1998.

[165] See SSFA 1998, s 58(1).

[166] See ibid, s 58(9).

[167] Ibid, s 58(3).

[168] Ibid, s 58(4).

[169] A 'foundation governor' is a person appointed as such a governor under regulations made under s 19 of the EA 2002: see SSFA 1998, s 142(1) as amended by the EA 2002. Regulation 8 of the School Governance (Constitution) (England) Regulations 2007, SI 2007/957 applies in this regard. Such a governor is one who is appointed otherwise than by the LEA for the purpose of securing that the character of the school (including, where it has a particular religious character, that character) is preserved and developed: reg 8(1)(a). Where the school has a foundation within the meaning of s 21 of the SSFA 1998, a foundation governor will also be appointed 'for the purpose of securing that the school is conducted in accordance with the foundation's governing documents, including, where appropriate, any trust deed relating to the school': reg 8(1)(b).

character, and may not appoint the person to be such a teacher unless the foundation governors are satisfied as to his fitness and competence to give religious education in accordance with arrangements made under para 3(3) of Sch 19 to the SSFA 1998.[170] The governing body of a foundation school with a religious character is bound in the same way: it must consult the foundation governors before appointing a person to be a reserved teacher in the school, and may not appoint the person to be such a teacher unless the foundation governors are satisfied as to his fitness and competence to give religious education in accordance with arrangements made under para 3(3) of Sch 19.[171] If the foundation governors of a relevant voluntary controlled school consider that a reserved teacher has failed to give religious education in accordance with arrangements made under para 3(3) of Sch 19 efficiently and suitably, then they may require the LEA to dismiss him from employment as a reserved teacher in the school or, in the case of a teacher who is engaged otherwise than under a contract of employment, require the governing body to terminate his engagement.[172] If the foundation governors of a relevant foundation school consider the same thing, then they may require the governing body of the school to dismiss the reserved teacher in question from employment as a reserved teacher at the school, or, in the case of a teacher who is engaged otherwise than under a contract of employment, require the governing body to terminate his engagement.[173] Of course, none of these provisions ousts in any way the law of unfair dismissal in so far as it applies to dismissals for perceived incapability (concerning which, see Chapter 8 below).

4.80 Section 58(7) of the SSFA 1998 applies to a voluntary aided school which has a religious character[174] and is to the following effect. If a teacher appointed to give religious education in such a school (except in accordance with an agreed syllabus as defined by s 375(2) of the Education Act 1996) fails to give such education 'efficiently and suitably', then he may be dismissed on that ground by the governing body without the consent of the LEA. It is provided by s 58(8) (presumably for the avoidance of doubt) that where such a school has a delegated budget, s 58(7) does not apply. Again, the law of unfair dismissal should of course nevertheless be borne in mind.

Protection of staff in certain maintained schools regarding religious opinions, and permitted positive discrimination in voluntary aided and foundation schools with a religious character

4.81 Sections 59 and 60 of the SSFA 1998 protect staff against discrimination on the ground of their religious opinions and related matters and permit some positive discrimination in those respects. Section 59 applies to schools which do not have a religious character: (1) community schools, community and foundation special schools, and (2) foundation and voluntary schools which do

---

[170] SSFA 1998, s 58(5) and (9).
[171] Ibid.
[172] Ibid, s 58(6) and (9).
[173] Ibid.
[174] See ibid, s 58(1)(b).

not have a religious character. Section 59(2) has the effect that no person may be disqualified from being a teacher at such a school or from being employed or engaged for the purposes of the school otherwise than as a teacher 'by reason of his religious opinions, or of his attending or omitting to attend religious worship'. According to s 59(3), no teacher at such a school may be required to give religious education. Section 59(4) has the effect that no teacher at such a school may be paid less or be deprived of, or disqualified for, any promotion or 'other advantage' (a) because he does or does not give religious education, (b) because of his religious opinions, or (c) because he attends or omits to attend religious worship. These provisions would, however, not entitle a teacher to take time off in breach of contract to attend a religious service.[175]

4.82 Section 60 of the SSFA 1998 applies to foundation and voluntary schools which have a religious character (and such a school 'has a religious character' if it is designated as a school having such a character by an order made by the Secretary of State under s 69(4) of the SSFA 1998[176]). The members of the staff of a foundation or voluntary controlled school which has a religious character are, unless they are reserved teachers or the head teacher, protected in the same way as are all the staff of a maintained school which does not have a religious character, since s 59(2)–(4) are specifically applied to them.[177] Section 60(4) and (5) permit some positive discrimination. In connection with the appointment of a person to be the head teacher of a foundation or voluntary controlled school which has a religious character, s 60(4) allows regard to be had to that person's 'ability and fitness to preserve and develop the religious character of the school'. Section 60(5) permits preference to be given, in connection with the appointment, remuneration or promotion of teachers at a voluntary aided school which has a religious character or reserved teachers in a foundation or voluntary controlled school which has a religious character,[178] to persons of three sorts. These are:

(a) persons whose religious opinions are in accordance with the tenets of the religion or religious denomination specified in relation to the school under s 69(4) of the SSFA 1998,

(b) persons who attend religious worship in accordance with those tenets, or

(c) persons who give, or are willing to give, religious education at the school in accordance with those tenets.[179]

---

[175] *Ahmad v Inner London Education Authority* [1978] QB 36, CA. The European Commission of Human Rights dismissed the employee's complaint under the European Convention on Human Rights: see (1982) 4 EHRR 126. The facts of the case are described in para **8.76** below.
[176] See SSFA 1998, s 58(1).
[177] Ibid, s 60(2).
[178] Section 60(5) is applied to reserved teachers at a foundation or voluntary controlled school with a religious character by s 60(3).
[179] Since no distinction is drawn in SSFA 1998, s 60(5) between head teachers, deputy head teachers and other teachers, s 60(5) applies to all such teachers.

4.83 In connection with the termination of the employment or engagement of any teacher at a voluntary aided school which has a religious character or the termination of the employment or engagement of a reserved teacher at a foundation or voluntary controlled school which has a religious character, regard may be had to 'any conduct on his part which is incompatible with the precepts, or with the upholding of the tenets, of the religion or religious denomination' specified in relation to the school under s 69(4) of the SSFA 1998.[180] However, no person may be disqualified because of his religious opinions, or because he attends or omits to attend religious worship, from being employed or engaged otherwise than as a teacher for the purposes of a voluntary aided school which has a religious character.[181]

Discrimination in certain independent schools in favour of persons whose religious opinions are in accordance with the tenets of a particular religion or religious denomination

4.84 Given the enactment of the Employment Equality (Religion or Belief) Regulations 2003,[182] it was necessary to protect independent schools which have a religious character against claims, made by employees or applicants for employment, of unlawful discrimination contrary to those regulations. New ss 124A and 124B were accordingly inserted into the SSFA 1998. Section 124A(2) permits the giving of preference 'in connection with the appointment, promotion or remuneration of teachers at the school' to persons '(a) whose religious opinions are in accordance with the tenets of the religion or religious denomination specified in relation to the school under section 124B(2), (b) who attend religious worship in accordance with those tenets, or (c) who give, or are willing to give, religious education at the school in accordance with those tenets'. Section 124A(2) permits having regard 'in connection with the termination of the employment or engagement of any teacher at the school, to any conduct on his part which is incompatible with the precepts, or with the upholding of the tenets, of the religion or religious denomination so specified'.

4.85 Section 124B of the SSFA 1998 permits the making of orders under s 69(3) of the SSFA 1998 in relation to independent schools. Thus independent schools may be made the subject of an order made by the Secretary of State or the National Assembly designating them as having a religious character. Such schools may then benefit from the limited exemption granted by s 124A of the SSFA 1998 from the application of the Employment Equality (Religion or Belief) Regulations 2003.

---

[180] Ibid, s 60(5).
[181] Ibid, s 60(6).
[182] SI 2003/1660, concerning which, see para **6.102** below.

Chapter 5

EMPLOYMENT RIGHTS AND DUTIES

PERMANENT OR TEMPORARY EMPLOYEES?

5.1 One question which is likely on occasion to arise in the mind of an employer is whether an employer is under any greater obligation towards an employee who is 'permanent' than towards one who is 'temporary'. The answer is that the employer may owe fewer obligations towards the temporary employee, but that this will be primarily because the employee may not have the right to claim unfair dismissal because of insufficient continuous service. The only other area in respect of which a temporary employee is at a disadvantage is that of the right to pay during a notice period before the termination of the employment.

THE OBLIGATION TO GIVE NOTICE

5.2 The obligation to give a certain period of notice is placed on an employer by either the contract of employment, or statute, or both. The statutory right (which is to a period of notice which is not less than one week's notice in certain circumstances, and up to a maximum of 12 weeks' notice in others[1]) takes effect as a term of the contract.[2] A failure to give proper notice under the contract of employment will, if there is no term providing for pay to be given in lieu of notice, normally give rise to a right only to damages for breach of contract.

5.3 A teacher or other employee on a fixed-term contract is not entitled to notice at the end of the term. The term simply expires.

5.4 Where there is an obligation to pay damages because of a failure to give an employee his proper notice, the employee will be under an obligation to mitigate his loss during the period in respect of which damages are claimed. This is an obligation to take reasonable steps to obtain alternative employment. This does not necessarily include accepting a job which has a lower status, and it is clear that an employee is allowed a certain amount of time to try to find a job of the same status.

---

[1] ERA 1996, s 86.
[2] *Westwood v Secretary of State for Employment* [1985] ICR 209.

5.5 However, if the contract of employment contains a right to pay in lieu of notice rather than a power on the part of the employer to give pay in lieu of notice, then the employee may be entitled to a sum representing the amount payable in lieu of notice, and is not obliged to take steps to mitigate his loss.[3]

THE OBLIGATION TO COMPLY WITH THE CONTRACT OF EMPLOYMENT

5.6 An employer cannot unilaterally alter the terms of a contract of employment (in other words do so without the agreement of the employee) unless such alteration is allowed by a term in a contract.[4] Even if such a term exists, however, a court or tribunal would be slow to decide that it allows the employer to impose a major alteration in the terms of the contract of employment.[5]

5.7 If an employer sought to impose a new term or set of terms on an employee, and the employee did not object to those terms but simply carried on working, the employer would be unlikely to be able to rely on the new term or terms if the changes which they purported to introduce did not have an immediate effect.[6] However, if the change consisted of a reduction in pay, then that would have an immediate effect, and the employee would be likely to be decided by a court or tribunal to have consented to the reduction if he neither:

(1) objected to it; nor

(2) took action to enforce the original terms,

in each case within a reasonable period of time (which might be several months).

FULL-TIME OR PART-TIME EMPLOYEES?

5.8 One question which might arise is whether there are any differences between the rights of full-time and part-time employees. Part-time employment simply involves employment for fewer hours than the number of hours which the employer would normally require full-time employees to work. Part-time employees have the same rights as their full-time colleagues except, of course, in

---

[3] *Abrahams v Performing Rights Society Ltd* [1995] ICR 1028; *Cerberus Software Ltd v Rowley* [2001] ICR 376.
[4] *Cantor Fitzgerald International v Callaghan* [1999] ICR 639; *City of Edinburgh Council v Brown* [1999] IRLR 208. It is unusual for a teacher's or head teacher's contract to include such a term.
[5] *Wandsworth London Borough Council v D'Silva* [1998] IRLR 193, para 31.
[6] *Aparau v Iceland Frozen Foods plc* [1996] IRLR 119; *The Scotts Co (UK) Ltd v Budd* [2003] ICR 299.

regard to pay. They are, however, in addition protected against being discriminated against unjustifiably on the ground of their part-time status.[7]

IMPLIED TERMS IN THE CONTRACT OF EMPLOYMENT

Trust and confidence

5.9 There are several implied terms in the contract of employment which have grown in importance during the years since employees have been given the statutory right not to be unfairly dismissed. The most important of these is the implied term of 'trust and confidence': applied to the employer, it is that the employer will not, without reasonable and proper cause, conduct himself in a manner which is likely to destroy or seriously damage the relationship of confidence and trust existing between employer and employee. That term was recognised by the House of Lords in the case of *Malik v BCCI*.[8] Their lordships made it clear not only that the term exists, but also that damages for a breach of the term may be awarded for a breach during the currency of the employment relationship.[9] The term is also of great significance in the law of unfair dismissal.[10]

5.10 The implied term of trust and confidence applies not only to behaviour of a general sort, but also to the manner in which express terms (conditions) are acted upon by an employer. So, for example, if an employer imposes a disciplinary penalty, it must not be out of proportion to the 'offence', even if there is a general power in the contract to impose the penalty.[11] However, the implied term of trust and confidence does not require an employer to reveal its own misdeeds.[12]

Good faith

5.11 In addition, there is an implied obligation of 'good faith' under the contract of employment, which is likely to be relevant in much the same way as the implied term of trust and confidence.

---

[7] See further para **6.91** onwards below.
[8] [1998] AC 20.
[9] An example of a case where damages were awarded for breach of the implied term of trust and confidence where the contract continued, is *French v Barclays Bank plc* [1998] IRLR 646. There are, however, limits on the extent to which the implied term of trust and confidence can have effect in areas in which Parliament has made statutory provision, such as in relation to dismissal: see *Johnson v Unisys Ltd* [2003] 1 AC 518 and *Eastwood v Magnox Electric plc* [2005] 1 AC 503.
[10] See further paras **8.19–8.22** below.
[11] See for example *BBC v Beckett* [1983] IRLR 43 and *Stanley Cole (Wainfleet) Ltd v Sheridan* [2003] ICR 297.
[12] *Bank of Credit and Commerce International SA v Ali* [1999] ICR 1079; [1999] IRLR 226.

Safe place and system of work

5.12 An employer has an implied obligation to provide a safe place of work and a safe system of work. It is clear that a breach of that duty could be relevant also to a claim of unfair ('constructive') dismissal.[13] This might impose an obligation, for example, to provide security measures to protect staff from intruders.

Grievances

5.13 An employer is under an obligation to afford an employee a reasonable opportunity of obtaining redress of grievances reasonably and promptly.[14]

HOURS

5.14 An employer cannot safely argue that merely because the employee has contractually agreed to work a large number of hours, the employee cannot sue the employer in respect of illness caused by stress from long working hours. This is because the contractual term in question may be regarded as unreasonable and so contravene the Unfair Contract Terms Act 1977.[15]

ANNUALISED HOURS

5.15 An employee may be employed to work annualised hours; that is the contract may specify the number of hours to be worked per year, rather than per day or per week. A teacher employed under the terms of the School Teachers' Pay and Conditions Documents may be required to work in addition to his basic hours 'such reasonable hours as may be needed to enable him effectively to discharge his professional duties' subject, of course, to the right not to be required to work excessive hours (see paras 59.3, 59.4 and 78.7 of the 2006 Document).[16]

5.16 If an employee who is employed under annualised hours leaves his employment before the end of the year having worked more hours than would have been required if the contract had required regular hours, he will have no implied right to be paid for the extra hours worked.[17]

---

[13] See further paras **8.19–8.21** below.
[14] *Goold (W A) (Pearmak) Ltd v McConnell* [1995] IRLR 516.
[15] *Johnstone v Bloomsbury Health Authority* [1992] QB 333. The decision of the Court of Appeal in *Keen v Commerzbank AG* [2007] ICR 623 does not affect this issue.
[16] See para **4.26** above for the impact of para 59.4.
[17] *Ali v Christian Salvesen Ltd* [1997] ICR 25.

MAXIMUM HOURS

5.17 It was decided by the High Court in *Barber v RJB Mining UK Ltd*[18] that the right to decline to work for more than 48 hours a week[19] takes effect not only as a prohibition enforceable as a health and safety obligation,[20] but also as a term of an employee's contract of employment.

PENSION ARRANGEMENTS

5.18 An employer is under an obligation, in certain circumstances, to notify an employee of a right contained in complex pension provisions which has been collectively negotiated between representative bodies, where the right is contingent on the employee taking certain action.[21]

PROBATIONERS

5.19 An employer is under an obligation to give guidance to a probationer employee.[22] In this connection it is necessary to be aware that reg 13(2) of the Education (Induction Arrangements for School Teachers) (Consolidation) (England) Regulations 2001[23] provides that the 'duties assigned to a person serving an induction period, his supervision and the conditions under which he works shall be such as to facilitate a fair and effective assessment of his conduct and efficiency as a teacher'. It is of interest that there is no equivalent provision in the Education (Induction Arrangements for School Teachers) (Wales) Regulations 2005.[24]

CONTRACTUAL DISCIPLINARY PROCEDURES

5.20 An employee's employment will often be governed by a disciplinary procedure and this procedure may take effect as a term of the contract. Where it does so, the employee may be able to claim damages for a failure by the employer to comply with the terms of the procedure. An injunction may be granted where damages would not be an appropriate remedy and where there is

---

[18] [1999] ICR 679.
[19] Conferred by reg 4 of the Working Time Regulations 1998, regarding which, see para **5.27** below.
[20] Regarding which, see para **5.26** below.
[21] *Scally v Southern Health and Social Services Board* [1992] 1 AC 294.
[22] See para **8.55** below.
[23] SI 2001/2897. See further para **3.50** onwards above regarding those regulations.
[24] SI 2005/1818 (W 146).

a clear failure to adhere to the provisions of the contractual disciplinary procedure. Examples of cases where this occurred are *Jones v Lee*[25] and *Jones v Gwent County Council*.[26]

Jones v Lee

The headteacher of a Roman Catholic voluntary aided primary school was appointed by the school's managers (who would now constitute the governing body) on terms set out in a letter from the chief education officer of the LEA. The letter stated that the employment would be in accordance with the conditions of tenure for teaching staff in schools maintained by the LEA. A copy of those conditions was attached to the letter. The conditions relating to dismissal included that:

(1) before any decision relating to dismissal was taken, the teacher should have the right to be heard and to be represented before the 'local education authority whose consent is required to his . . . dismissal'; and

(2) before any decision was taken to give consent to the dismissal of a teacher, the LEA would at his request give the teacher a hearing.

Subsequent to his appointment as the head teacher of the school, his marriage was dissolved, and he then re-married a divorced woman in a register office. Following this, he was summarily dismissed from his post. He issued proceedings claiming an injunction to restrain the school's managers from:

(1) dismissing him from the post of headteacher of the school without the consent of the local education authority given after a hearing in accordance with the LEA's conditions of tenure; or

(2) acting on any purported dismissal.

Decision of the Court of Appeal

The Court of Appeal decided that by sending the conditions of tenure to the head teacher when notifying him of his appointment, the LEA as agents for the managers of the school had incorporated the conditions, and in particular the conditions relating to dismissal, into his contract of employment. It decided that the head teacher therefore had had a right to be heard and represented before the LEA before any decision relating to his dismissal was taken, and that the managers had acted wrongly in purporting to dismiss him without the consent of the authority.

5.21 Thus an employee may be able to obtain an injunction preventing dismissal despite a breakdown in mutual trust and confidence between him and his employer.[27] The facts of *Jones v Gwent County Council*[28] are illustrative of the type of circumstances in which this might occur.

---

[25] [1980] ICR 310.
[26] [1992] IRLR 521.
[27] See for a recent example of a case where an injunction was granted despite such a breakdown, *Gryf-Lowczowksi v Hinchingbrooke Healthcare NHS Trust* [2006] ICR 425. However, in that case the employee was not seeking to return to the employer's workplace, at least for the time being.
[28] [1992] IRLR 521.

Jones v Gwent County Council

Mrs Jones was employed as a lecturer in catering. The college was maintained by the County Council as the LEA, and had an instrument and articles of government. It had a governing body, and was similar in constitution to a maintained school. Delegated budgets had not yet been introduced, and the lecturer was employed by the LEA. However, her employment was subject to a contractual disciplinary procedure which provided for a right to a hearing before a disciplinary sub-committee of the governing body of the college if consideration was to be given to the possibility of her dismissal for misconduct. It also provided that if consideration was to be given to her dismissal, then 10 days' notice in writing had to be given to her, informing her that the question of dismissal was to be considered and specifying in full any charge. If notice was to be given, then a different provision in the lecturer's contract of employment had to be relied upon, and the employee would have a right of appeal.

In 1987 the lecturer made an unsuccessful claim of sex discrimination. She was suspended and disciplinary proceedings were brought against her by the LEA in June 1988 on the ground that in pursuit of her claims she had provided false information regarding:

(1)   her academic qualifications; and

(2)   the examination results achieved by her students.

In accordance with the contractual disciplinary procedure, the complaint was heard by a disciplinary sub-committee established by the college governors. Their report made no finding of misconduct. However, the sub-committee felt that because of the publicity surrounding the case and the feelings it had engendered, the lecturer should not return to her employment at the college, and recommended to the LEA that it should seek to redeploy the lecturer. The LEA subsequently informed the governors that no alternative employment was available. A second disciplinary sub-committee then recommended that a further effort should be made to redeploy the lecturer, but that if this was unsuccessful then she should be reinstated at the college.

The governors decided to reject this decision and to ask the LEA to take steps to terminate the lecturer's employment. The LEA took no action. The governors then wrote to the lecturer, asking her to attend a third disciplinary hearing which, they informed her, 'may result in serious disciplinary action being taken against you'. The letter did not, in terms, inform the lecturer that her dismissal was to be considered at the hearing.

The lecturer objected to the proposed hearing, contending to the LEA that there were no grounds for further disciplinary action and that the charges had not been adequately particularised. The hearing went ahead without the lecturer's attendance, and it was decided that she should be dismissed. The LEA issued a letter of dismissal. The lecturer sought an injunction restraining the LEA from dismissing her unless, in accordance with her contract of employment, proper grounds existed and a proper procedure had been followed.

Decision of the High Court

The High Court granted an injunction in the terms sought. The court decided that the letter from the LEA purporting to dismiss the lecturer after she had been cleared of misconduct by two disciplinary hearings was not valid because it did not comply with her contract of employment. The letter received by the lecturer asking her to attend a disciplinary hearing was not a sufficient notice for the purposes of her conditions of service, in that it did not state that the question of her dismissal was to be considered at that hearing. Nor did the charge against her that her return to the college 'would cause an irrevocable breakdown in relationships between management and staff based on your past behavour' satisfy the requirement of her conditions of service that full particulars of the charge be given. Furthermore, the governors' belief that the claimant's return to the college would cause an irrevocable breakdown in relationships could not justify dismissal for misconduct. In any event, the elements on which the governors' expression of belief were said to be based were either charges which had been adjudicated by an earlier disciplinary committee and could not be revived, or else were wholly unparticularised.

TIME OFF FOR PUBLIC DUTIES

5.22 Employers are obliged to allow employees a reasonable amount of time off during working hours to perform public duties.[29] An employer is not obliged to pay an employee for the time taken off work for those purposes. The public duties to which this obligation applies include acting as a member of the governing body of a maintained school. They also include acting as a member of a health authority, a local authority or a police authority, or as a magistrate. If the employee holds a number of such public offices, the employer is not obliged to permit the employee to take what would be a reasonable amount of time off for one activity in connection with each activity. This is clear from the case of *Borders Regional Council v Maule*.[30]

> *Borders Regional Council v Maule*
>
> A primary school teacher held a number of public appointments including as a member of the Borders Social Security Appeals Tribunal (the SSAT). During 1990 and 1991, respectively, she had 24 and 22 days off work for those purposes. There was some discussion about the amount of time off to be allowed and an arrangement was made to try to restrict the teacher's absences to an average of two days per month. In April 1991, parents expressed concern that she was away from school too often.
>
> In October, the teacher was notified of a training day to be held on 14 November for members of the SSAT. Accordingly, she requested leave of absence on that day. Her request was refused. In refusing the request, the employer took account of the fact that the teacher had already been absent from work on account of her public duties on 6 and 7 November. The teacher complained to an industrial tribunal that her employer had breached the requirement to allow her a reasonable amount of time off for public duties. The tribunal concluded that the complainant should have been allowed time off to attend the training session. According to the tribunal, in granting her permission to serve on a public body, her employer had taken on concomitant responsibilities. Those were not carried out, and the claimant was disadvantaged as a result. The employer appealed to the EAT.

---

[29] ERA 1996, s 50.
[30] [1993] IRLR 199.

Decision of the Employment Appeal Tribunal

The EAT allowed the appeal. It said that the industrial tribunal was wrong simply to say that the employer was under concomitant responsibilities as a result of granting the claimant permission to sit on a tribunal and it had failed to take all proper considerations into account. In deciding whether an employer is in breach of what is now s 50 by refusing to permit an employee to take time off for public duties, the tribunal must consider the whole circumstances, including the number and frequency of similar absences which have been permitted. The industrial tribunal had failed to make it clear that it did take all relevant considerations into account, or to explain how these considerations were balanced. Nor did the industrial tribunal make reference to the needs of the school, or the concerns of parents. The EAT commented that it would normally be expected that where an employee is undertaking duties of this kind, there would be discussion between the employer and the employee in order to establish, by agreement, a pattern for the absences from work required by the duties.

5.23 The potential penalty for a breach of s 50 is that the affected employee may make a claim to an employment tribunal, which may make an award of compensation to the employee. There is no limit to the amount of compensation which the tribunal could order the employer to pay, but it seems clear that any award would be compensatory only, and not penal. So, for example, if the employee has been permitted to take time off with full pay, then no compensation should be payable.

TIME OFF FOR TRADE UNION DUTIES AND ACTIVITIES

5.24 An employer is obliged to allow an employee a reasonable amount of time off for trade union duties and activities. That obligation is considered in **Chapter 9** below.

EMPLOYER'S COMMON LAW OBLIGATIONS AFTER THE CONTRACT HAS ENDED[31]

5.25 An employer has an obligation after the contract of employment has ended not to act negligently in relation to the provision of a reference for the employee. This duty was clearly imposed by the House of Lords in *Spring v Guardian Assurance plc*,[32] and was clarified by the Court of Appeal in *Bartholomew v London Borough of Hackney*[33] and *Cox v Sun Alliance Life Ltd*.[34] *Bartholomew* made it clear that a reference must not only be true,

---

[31] An employer also has continuing duties to an employee after the ending of his employment in the law of discrimination: see further **Chapter 6** below.
[32] [1995] 2 AC 296.
[33] [1999] IRLR 246.
[34] [2001] IRLR 448.

but it must also be accurate and fair 'taken in the round and in context'.[35] In *Cox*, Mummery LJ said that 'there is a duty to take reasonable care to provide an accurate and fair reference', and that 'Discharge of that duty will usually involve making reasonable inquiry into the factual basis of the statements in the reference'.[36] He also said this:[37]

> 'The essential point about a reference is that it will normally satisfy the requirements of a duty to take reasonable care if it is accurate and fair. Although it must not contain misleading information or create a misleading impression, a reference does not, as a general rule, have to provide a full and comprehensive report on all the material facts concerning the subject: *Bartholomew v London Borough of Hackney* [1999] IRLR 246 and *Kidd v AXA Equity & Law Life Assurance Society plc* [2000] IRLR 301.'

HEALTH AND SAFETY LAW

5.26 The details of an employer's duties under the law of health and safety are outside the scope of this book. However, it is important to mention that under s 2 of the Health and Safety at Work etc Act 1974, an employer must 'ensure, so far as is reasonably practicable, the health, safety and welfare at work of all his employees'. It is also important to note that under s 3 of that Act, an employer must conduct his undertaking in such a way as to ensure, so far as is reasonably practicable, that persons not in his employment who may be affected are not thereby exposed to risks to their health and safety. A breach of either of these and other related requirements under that Act may give rise to criminal proceedings. Certain persons acting on behalf of the employer who are personally at fault may also be charged and convicted in the same way.

THE WORKING TIME REGULATIONS 1998

5.27 The Working Time Regulations 1998[38] preclude an employer from requiring an employee to work for more than 48 hours a week, subject to exceptions.[39] The main exception is that the employee has agreed to do so under reg 5. This prohibition does not apply to certain types of employee, including 'managing executives or other persons with autonomous decision-taking powers',[40] for example, a head teacher.

5.28 Another important provision is that which affords an employee a right to a certain amount of paid holiday per year.[41] This provision is most likely to

---

[35] [1999] IRLR 246, para 18.
[36] [2001] IRLR 448, para 97.
[37] Ibid, para 104.
[38] SI 1998/1833.
[39] Ibid, reg 4.
[40] See ibid, reg 20.
[41] Ibid, reg 13.

affect the position of sessional teachers (that is, teachers who are employed under fixed-term contracts of employment of, for example, one term at a time).

5.29 The Working Time Regulations 1998 may be enforced in the same way as obligations under the Health and Safety At Work etc Act 1974. Employees may also enforce some of their rights under the Working Time Regulations 1998 by making a complaint to an employment tribunal. Although the limit on weekly working hours is not enforceable by an employee in this manner, as noted in para **5.16** above, the High Court decided in *Barber v RJB Mining UK Ltd*[42] that this limit confers a contractual right on employees. It is possible that this decision will not be followed.[43]

PAY AND OTHER BENEFITS

The right to be paid

5.30 The right of an employee to be paid arises only under the contract of employment. If an employee is ready, willing and able to work then he is entitled to be paid, even if he is unable to do so because of a strike by his fellow employees.[44] The striking employees will not be entitled to be paid (see for example *Sim v Rotherham MBC*[45] and *Wiluszynski v Tower Hamlets London Borough Council*[46]).

National minimum wage

5.31 Under the National Minimum Wage Act 1998, an employee's contractual right to be paid is to be treated as including a right to be paid no less than the relevant national minimum wage. That Act applies not only to employees but also workers supplied by agencies. The National Minimum Wage Regulations 1999[47] set out the current minima. There is no minimum wage for a person below the age of 18, and the standard minimum wage for an adult is £5.35 per hour.[48] There is much more detail in the National Minimum Wage Regulations 1999, for example regarding the calculation of the pay period, which is outside the scope of this book.

---

[42] [1999] ICR 679.
[43] See *Sayers v Cambridgeshire County Council* [2007] IRLR 29, para 263; the House of Lords has given permission to appeal in the case of *Inland Revenue v Ainsworth* to which reference is there made.
[44] *R v Liverpool City Corporation, ex parte Ferguson* [1985] IRLR 501.
[45] [1986] ICR 897.
[46] [1989] ICR 493.
[47] SI 1999/584.
[48] See ibid, reg 11, as amended by SI 2006/2001. The rate has in the past been increased annually as from 1 October.

Deductions

5.32 In addition to a right to be paid in accordance with his contract of employment, an employee has a right not to have money deducted from wages due under the contract, except in certain circumstances.[49] Normally, a deduction may be made only if:

(1) it has been authorised by a term in the contract of employment; or

(2) the employee has previously signified in writing his agreement or consent to the making of the deduction.

5.33 However, the deduction of an overpayment of wages or an overpayment in respect of expenses incurred by the employee in carrying out his employment is permitted.[50] Nevertheless, the employee is entitled to make a claim to the employment tribunal if a purported overpayment is deducted from his wages, and the tribunal is then obliged to consider whether the deduction was justified.[51] A deduction from wages made by an employer where the employee has taken part in a strike or other industrial action is not unlawful.[52] There are further exceptions, but these are the ones most likely to be important in practice. Despite some initial uncertainty, it is now clear that a complete failure to pay an employee amounts to a deduction from wages for these purposes.[53]

5.34 Where a claim by an employee is successful, the employer is ordered to pay the employee the amount in question, and is precluded from recovering the amount from the employee by any other means.[54] So, for example, if an employer deducted from an employee's pay a certain amount in respect of a loan, and the employee had not agreed to that deduction from his pay, then the employee would be able to claim that amount from the employer and the employer would no longer have any right to recover the amount deducted. Among other things, this emphasises that these employees' rights are additional to those arising under the common law.

5.35 Where an employee is not undertaking industrial action, a deliberate refusal by his employer to honour the employee's right to pay (whether outright or partial) will usually be a repudiation of the employee's contract of employment.[55] An employee is not obliged to accept a reduction in pay, but may sue to enforce the right to be paid in full, either by way of an action for breach of contract or under s 13 of the ERA 1996.[56]

---

[49] ERA 1996, s 13. The right is enforced by making an application to an employment tribunal under s 23 of that Act.
[50] ERA 1996, s 14(1).
[51] See *Murray v Strathclyde Regional Council* [1992] IRLR 396.
[52] ERA 1996, s 14(5).
[53] *Delaney v Staples* [1991] 2 QB 47, CA. This aspect of the decision of the Court of Appeal was not appealed against on appeal to the House of Lords ([1992] AC 687).
[54] ERA 1996, s 25(4); *Potter v Hunt Contracts Ltd* [1992] ICR 337.
[55] See *Cantor Fitzgerald International v Callaghan* [1999] ICR 639.
[56] See for example *Rigby v Ferodo Ltd* [1998] ICR 29.

Statutory sick pay

5.36 Employees have the right to be paid sick pay.[57] Such statutory sick pay is not payable for the first three days of sickness in any period of entitlement.[58]

Right to be suspended with pay on medical grounds

5.37 Employees who can satisfy certain conditions have a right to pay if they are suspended from work on certain medical grounds.[59] In order to benefit from this right, an employee must have more than one month's continuous employment and must have been suspended from work in consequence of a requirement imposed by or under a provision of certain enactments.[60] An employee who has been so suspended is entitled (subject to several exceptions) to be paid remuneration for up to 26 weeks while suspended. The exceptions include that the employee has unreasonably refused to perform suitable alternative employment. Furthermore, the employee must not be incapable of work by reason of illness or disablement.

Maternity pay

5.38 Women are entitled to be paid statutory maternity pay (SMP) for (currently) a maximum of 39 weeks.[61] The right arises (subject to exceptions, contained in the Statutory Maternity Pay (General) Regulations 1986) when:[62]

(1) a woman has been employed for a continuous period of at least 26 weeks ending with the week immediately preceding the fourteenth week before the expected week of confinement but has ceased to work for the employer;

(2) her normal weekly earnings for the period of eight weeks ending with the week immediately preceding the fourteenth week before the expected week of confinement are not less than the lower earnings limit in force at the relevant time; and

---

[57] In accordance with ss 151 to 157 of the Social Security Contributions and Benefits Act 1992 and the Statutory Sick Pay (General) Regulations 1982, SI 1982/894 as amended. At the time of writing, the rate was £72.55 per week.
[58] Social Security Contributions and Benefits Act 1992, s 155(1).
[59] ERA 1996, ss 64 and 65.
[60] The relevant enactments are reg 10 of the Control of Lead at Work Regulations 2002, SI 2002/2676, reg 24 of the Ionising Radiations Regulations 1999, SI 1999/3232, and reg 11 of the Control of Substances Hazardous to Health Regulations 2002, SI 2002/2677.
[61] See ss 164 and 165 of the Social Security Contributions and Benefits Act 1992 and the Statutory Maternity Pay (General) Regulations 1986, SI 1986/1960, as amended. Regulation 2 of the latter, read with reg 1(2) of SI 2006/2379, provides for a maximum of 39 weeks of SMP for women whose expected week of confinement commenced on or after 1 April 2007. Section 165(1) of the Social Security Contributions and Benefits Act 1992 as amended provides that regulations may prescribe up to 52 weeks as the 'maternity pay period'.
[62] See s 164(2) of the Social Security Contributions and Benefits Act 1992.

(3) she has become pregnant and has reached, or been confined before reaching, the commencement of the eleventh week before the expected week of confinement.

5.39 However, the employee must also have given at least 28 days' notice before her entitlement to SMP is due to begin (or, if that is not reasonably practicable, as soon as is reasonably practicable).[63] The notice must be given to 'the person who will be liable to pay' the SMP.[64] An employee is entitled, when she has a right to SMP, to be paid for 6 weeks at the 'higher rate', which is nine-tenths of her normal weekly earnings, and for the rest of the period at the 'lower rate'.[65]

5.40 Where a woman is not entitled to SMP, she may be entitled to State maternity allowance.[66] However, since this is paid by the State rather than the employer, it is outside the scope of this book.

5.41 A woman has the right to suspension with pay on maternity grounds in certain circumstances, as provided for by ss 66-68 of the ERA 1996.[67]

Statutory paternity pay

5.42 An employee is entitled to two weeks' statutory paternity pay in certain circumstances.[68] Statutory paternity pay is payable not only to fathers but also to the partner (who may be a woman) of the person who adopts a child. The employee must, in order to qualify for the right to such pay, have been employed continuously by the employer for at least 26 weeks before the fifteenth week before the expected week of confinement or (if the child is adopted) by the week in which an approved match is made with the child who is placed for adoption. The employee must also have continuous employment from that week up to the date of the child's birth or placement. Statutory paternity pay is not payable to a person who elects to receive statutory adoption pay.[69]

5.43 In addition, the employee must normally give his employer at least 28 days' notice before the date when the entitlement to pay is to commence. The right to paternity pay must normally be exercised within 56 days of the birth or

---

[63] Social Security Contributions and Benefits Act 1992, s 164(4).
[64] Ibid.
[65] Which at the time of writing was £108.85.
[66] See s 35 of the Social Security Contributions and Benefits Act 1992.
[67] See further para **5.51** below.
[68] See primarily ss 171ZA–171ZE of the Social Security Contributions and Benefits Act 1992 and the Statutory Paternity Pay and Statutory Adoption Pay (General) Regulations 2002, SI 2002/2822. In relation to adoption from overseas, see the Statutory Paternity Pay (Adoption) and Statutory Adoption Pay (Adoptions from Overseas) Regulations 2003, SI 2003/1192.
[69] See s 171ZB(4) of the Social Security Contributions and Benefits Act 1992.

(as the case may be) placement of the child.[70] The amount of the pay is either £112.75 or 90% of the employee's pay, whichever is less.[71]

Statutory adoption pay

5.44 Statutory adoption pay is payable currently for a maximum of 39 weeks.[72] It is not payable to employees who have elected to receive statutory paternity pay.[73] It is payable only to one member of a couple with whom the relevant child is placed for adoption.[74] It is payable to employees who were continuously employed by their employer for at least 26 weeks ending with the week in which they were matched by an adoption agency with a child or children for adoption, and who were earning above the lower earnings limit for the period of 8 weeks ending with the relevant week.[75] The amount of the pay is £112.75 or, if less, 90% of the normal weekly earnings of the employee.[76]

PROMOTIONS AND OTHER CONTRACTUAL VARIATIONS

5.45 In England and Wales, it is necessary for there to be what is called 'consideration' (normally a sum of money) for a contract to come into existence. The consideration does not need to be substantial or fair – it simply needs to be of economic value. Consideration may, however, be executory; in other words, to be performed in the future. In order to be enforceable, a variation of a contract must also be supported by consideration.

5.46 From this, it can be seen that if an employer merely agrees to pay an employee a pay rise as from a certain date, it may look as if there is no consideration for the increase. However, since an employee is not bound to continue to work for the employer and could terminate the contract of employment by giving notice, the employer has a factual benefit in this promise to pay more, in that the employee is more likely to remain in the employment. Indeed, as long as there is no duress involved, it is now safe to say that there is indeed consideration for the increase.[77] In some cases, an employee may have an

---

[70] See regs 8 and 14 of the Statutory Paternity Pay and Statutory Adoption Pay (General) Regulations 2002.
[71] See reg 2 of the Statutory Paternity Pay and Statutory Adoption Pay (Weekly Rates) Regulations 2002, SI 2002/2818, as amended by SI 2007/688.
[72] See s 171ZN(2) of the Social Security Contributions and Benefits Act 1992 and reg 21(5) of the Statutory Paternity Pay and Statutory Adoption Pay (General) Regulations 2002, SI 2002/2822. Section 271ZN(2) provides that the maximum period which may be prescribed for this purpose by regulations is 52 weeks.
[73] See s 171ZL(4)(a) of the Social Security Contributions and Benefits Act 1992.
[74] See ibid, s 171ZL(4)(b) and (4A).
[75] See ibid, s 171ZL(2)(b) and (d).
[76] See reg 3 of the Statutory Paternity Pay and Statutory Adoption Pay (Weekly Rates) Regulations 2002, SI 2002/2818.
[77] See *Williams v Roffey Bros & Nicholls (Contractors) Ltd* [1991] 1 QB 1; *Lee v GEC Plessey Telecommunications Ltd* [1993] IRLR 383.

express or implied right under the contract to be paid an increase every year. If so, then there will be a right under the contract to such increased pay.

5.47 Where an employee is promoted, the situation is different, in that there will then clearly be contractual consideration for an entitlement to greater contractual benefits such as pay. The question of when the right to higher pay takes effect may arise. The new appointment will usually take effect on some date in the future. Usually, once the offer of a new post is made and accepted, there is a binding agreement in relation to the new post. The employee will not have carried out any duties in relation to the post, but there will then be a contractual right to the relevant level of pay for the new post as from the commencement date for that post. Accordingly, if the employer subsequently refuses to promote the employee, then the employee will nevertheless normally have the right to be paid as if he had started the new job as from the commencement date, and after that date he will have a right to claim unfair ('constructive') dismissal (as to which, see para **8.19** onwards below) if the employer refuses to recognise the employee's new status.

5.48 From a legal point of view, the employee and the employer have mutually agreed to terminate the old contract and enter into a new one, or, alternatively, the employer and the employee have agreed a variation to the original contract of employment.

PENSIONS

5.49 Teachers and other employees in State schools are entitled to participate in the Teachers' Pension Scheme[78] and the Local Government Pension Scheme[79] respectively. The details of the two schemes are outside the scope of this book, but it is worth saying that the right to a pension under the schemes is not contractual but statutory. An employee can enforce his rights under the relevant scheme by an ordinary court action (rather than only in a public law action).[80] The employee will, in addition, have the right to sue in the law of negligence if the employer or (if different) the body which administers the pension scheme does so negligently and the employee suffers loss as a result (although it is not often that liability will arise in the law of negligence in this context[81]). Furthermore, if the employer fails to notify the employee of a valuable right under the pension scheme in circumstances where the employee could not reasonably be expected to know about it and needs to take certain action in order to be able to exercise it, then the employee could theoretically sue the employer (on the basis of *Scally v Southern Health and Social Services Board*[82]).

---

[78] See SI 1997/3001.
[79] See SI 1997/1612.
[80] *Hutchings v Islington London Borough Council* [1998] ICR 1230.
[81] See in particular *Crossley v Faithful & Gould Holdings Ltd* [2004] ICR 1615, but note *Lennon v Commissioner of the Police of the Metropolis* [2004] ICR 1114.
[82] [1992] 1 AC 294; see para **5.17** above.

MATERNITY RIGHTS

Time off for ante-natal care

5.50 A pregnant employee who has, on the advice of a registered medical practitioner, registered midwife or registered nurse, made an appointment to attend at any place for the purpose of receiving ante-natal care, is entitled to be permitted by her employer to take time off (with pay) during her working hours in order to be able to keep the appointment.[83] After the first such appointment, an employer is entitled to require the employee to produce a certificate from such a medical practitioner, midwife or health visitor stating that the employee is pregnant and an appointment card or other document showing that the appointment has been made.

Suspension with pay or suitable alternative work

5.51 An employee has the right in certain circumstances to be suspended with pay on the ground that she is pregnant, has recently given birth, or is breastfeeding a child.[84] The employee must not have unreasonably refused suitable alternative work. The employee also has a right to be offered suitable alternative work which is both suitable in relation to her and appropriate for her to do in the circumstances, and the terms and conditions of which are not substantially less favourable than those of the work she normally performs.

Right to maternity leave

5.52 An employee who is pregnant or has given birth to a child has the right to unpaid leave, where she complies with certain provisions. This period is of up to 52 weeks in total.[85] It consists of two periods: an 'ordinary' maternity leave period and an 'additional' maternity leave period. The ordinary maternity leave period is of 26 weeks from the beginning of the period, as determined in accordance with reg 6 of the Maternity and Parental Leave etc Regulations 1999, or until the end of the compulsory period of maternity leave provided for by reg 8 of those regulations (which starts at the birth of the child and ends two weeks later), if this ends later than the 26-week period would have ended.[86] This ordinary maternity leave period may be extended where any statutory requirement (apart from one which gives rise to the right to be suspended with pay on maternity grounds) prohibits the employee, by reason of her having recently given birth, from working for any period after the ending of the initial period. The period of ordinary maternity leave may also be curtailed

---

[83] ERA 1996, ss 55–57.
[84] See ss 66–70 of the ERA 1996. This right arises only if the employee is suspended in consequence of a requirement imposed under certain enactments or of a recommendation in a specified provision of a code of practice issued or approved under s 16 of the Health and Safety at Work etc Act 1974.
[85] See reg 7 of the Maternity and Parental Leave etc Regulations 1999, SI 1999/3312, as amended.
[86] See ibid, reg 7(1).

by the dismissal of the employee.[87] The additional period of maternity leave is also of 26 weeks. It commences on the ending of the ordinary maternity leave period.[88]

5.53 The employee (within certain time limits) must notify the employer of her pregnancy and of the date when she intends her maternity leave period to commence. She must also (within certain time limits) inform her employer of the date of her intended return to work. (Curiously, there is now a requirement to give 8 weeks' notice of an intention to return earlier than the end of the additional maternity leave period, but no requirement to give any notice of an intention to return before the end of the ordinary maternity leave period.[89])

5.54 Although the leave is (subject to what is said above[90]) unpaid, the employee has the right to the benefit of all other terms and conditions of her employment during the leave period.[91] The employee may be made redundant during that period, but the dismissal will be automatically unfair unless it is not practicable because of redundancy for the employer to continue to employ her, and a suitable alternative vacancy does not occur.[92]

5.55 An employee may carry out up to 10 days' work for her employer during her statutory maternity leave period (that is, either her ordinary or her additional maternity leave period) otherwise than in the two weeks after the birth of her child, and not lose her right to maternity leave.[93]

5.56 If an employee has a contractual right which is more generous than any corresponding statutory right relating to maternity leave, then the employee may benefit only from the contractual right. However, the employee has the best of both worlds, in that she may take the benefit of the most advantageous provisions of each set of rights, and may therefore have a selection of contractual and statutory rights relating to maternity leave.[94]

5.57 If an employee fails to comply with a procedural requirement regarding maternity leave and her employer fails to take her back, then she may nevertheless have been dismissed and therefore have the right to claim unfair dismissal. Whether she has such a right will depend on the circumstances.

---

[87] See Maternity and Parental Leave etc Regulations 1999, reg 7(5); but see para **5.58** below.
[88] See ibid, reg 6(3).
[89] See reg 11 of the Maternity and Parental Leave etc Regulations 1999, as amended by SI 2006/2014.
[90] In paras **5.38–5.40**.
[91] See reg 9 of the Maternity and Parental Leave etc Regulations 1999.
[92] See ibid, regs 10 and 20. The absence of the word 'reasonably' before the word 'practicable' should be noted. See further para **5.58** below regarding automatically unfair dismissal for pregnancy or a related reason.
[93] See ibid, reg 12A.
[94] See ibid, reg 21.

Dismissal on maternity grounds

5.58 If an employee is dismissed because she is pregnant or for any other reason connected with pregnancy, then she will normally have been dismissed unfairly, and she will have the right to claim unfair dismissal.[95] The same is true in a number of related circumstances, such as where an employee is dismissed, her maternity leave period is ended by the dismissal, and the reason is that she has given birth to a child, or any other reason connected with her having given birth to a child. It is possible that an employee will not, however, be entitled to the benefit of this protection if she has returned to work and has then been dismissed because of an illness, even if the illness would not have happened but for the pregnancy.[96]

PARENTAL LEAVE

5.59 Employees who have continuous employment of one year or more may take parental leave in certain circumstances.[97] This right arises only in relation to a child for whom the parent is responsible or for whom the parent expects to be responsible, and is a right to take leave for the purpose of caring for the child. The child must be aged no more than five, unless several exceptions apply.[98] These include that the child is entitled to a disability living allowance, in which case the employee may take parental leave in respect of the child at any time before the child is aged 18. The maximum period of parental leave is 13 weeks unless the child is entitled to disability living allowance, in which case the maximum period is 18 weeks.[99] A period of parental leave may be taken by a woman in addition to a period of maternity leave.

5.60 There is no obligation on the employer to pay the employee during the period of parental leave, but certain other contractual obligations of the employer continue, as do certain contractual obligations of the employee.[100]

5.61 No more than four weeks' leave may be taken in any one year per child (but if for example there are twins, then up to eight weeks' leave per year may be taken – four weeks per child), unless the employee's contract of employment

---

[95] ERA 1996, s 99 and Maternity and Parental Leave etc Regulations 1999, SI 1999/3312, reg 20.
[96] The effect of the ECJ case law of *Hertz v Aldi Marked K/S* [1991] IRLR 31, *Larsson v Dansk Handel and Service* [1997] IRLR 643, and *Brown v Rentokil Ltd* [1998] ICR 790 is that an employee's protection against detrimental treatment on the ground of her pregnancy does not extend to detrimental treatment as a result of an illness which arises after her maternity leave period has ended even if that illness would not have occurred if she had not been pregnant. However, s 3A(3)(b) of the SDA 1975, read literally, gives an employee protection against detrimental treatment in respect of a pregnancy-related illness which arises at any time. See para **5.54** above regarding dismissal for redundancy where the employee has been on maternity leave.
[97] Maternity and Parental Leave etc Regulations 1999, SI 1999/3312, reg 13.
[98] See ibid, reg 15.
[99] Ibid, reg 14.
[100] See ibid, reg 17.

provides for a greater entitlement.[101] Normally, no less than a week's leave may be taken at a time.[102] The employee must give notice to the employer of his intention to take the leave for the entitlement to arise.[103] Unless the leave is requested to commence on the birth of the child or the placement of the child for adoption with the employee, the employer can postpone the period of leave if it considers that the operation of the business would be unduly disrupted by the employee taking the leave as requested. However, the period of postponement may not be greater than six months.[104]

PATERNITY AND ADOPTION LEAVE

5.62 The Employment Act 2002 introduced a power to make regulations conferring additional rights on parents (additional, that is, to the right to parental leave). The additional rights were to paternity and adoption leave. The Paternity and Adoption Leave Regulations 2002[105] conferred the new rights. The Work and Families Act 2006 will, when it is fully in force, add to these rights.

Paternity leave

5.63 Paternity leave is available to both men and women who have been continuously employed for not less than 26 weeks ending with the week immediately preceding the fourteenth week before the expected week of confinement or (in the case of adoption) ending with the week in which the child's adopter is notified of having been matched with the child.[106] The entitlement is to leave 'for the purpose of caring for a child or supporting the child's mother' or adopter, as the case may be. The employee must be the partner (which term includes the spouse or civil partner) of the mother or adopter, and if the employee is not the child's father, the employee must have, or expect to have, the main responsibility (apart from that of the mother or adopter) for the upbringing of the child. If the employee is the father of the child then the employee must have or expect to have responsibility for the upbringing of the child. The period of the leave is two weeks, although it may be taken in two separate periods of one week.[107] It must be taken within 56 days of the date of the child's birth or adoption.[108] The employee taking paternity leave may be required to sign a declaration of entitlement to the leave and as to the purpose of the leave.[109]

---

[101] See Maternity and Parental Leave etc Regulations 1999, Sch 2, para 8.
[102] Ibid, Sch 2, para 7.
[103] See ibid, Sch 2, paras 1(b) and 3–5.
[104] See ibid, Sch 2, para 6.
[105] SI 2002/2788.
[106] See regs 4 and 8 of the Paternity and Adoption Leave Regulations 2002.
[107] See ibid, regs 5(1) and 9(1).
[108] Ibid, regs 5(2) and 9(2).
[109] See ibid, regs 6(3) and 10(3).

5.64 During the period of paternity leave, the employee is entitled to the benefit of his terms and conditions of employment other than the right to remuneration,[110] and is bound by the terms of his contract of employment except the obligation to work.[111] The employee has the right to return to work after the period of leave of the same sort as that which applies to periods of maternity leave.[112]

Adoption leave

5.65 An employee will be entitled to adoption leave where the other parent or partner takes paternity leave. Adoption leave is more extensive than paternity leave. The right is to a period of ordinary adoption leave and a period of additional adoption leave, of the same sort as the periods of maternity leave (and therefore the maximum period of adoption leave is 52 weeks).[113] For the sake of brevity, most of the details of the law relating to adoption leave are accordingly not included in this book.[114] It is noted, however, that reg 22 of the Paternity and Adoption Leave Regulations 2002 applies where an expected adoption placement does not occur, the child is returned to the adoption agency, or the child dies. The adoption leave period then normally ends eight weeks after that event. One exception arises where the employee is taking additional adoption leave and there are fewer than eight weeks to the end of the additional adoption leave period. The adoption leave then ends at the end of that period.[115]

TIME OFF FOR DEPENDANTS

5.66 Employees have a qualified (rather than an absolute) right to be permitted by their employers to take time off during working hours in order to take action which is necessary:

(a) to provide assistance on an occasion when a dependant falls ill, gives birth or is injured or assaulted,

(b) to make arrangements for the provision of care for a dependant who is ill or injured,

(c) in consequence of the death of a dependant,

---

[110] But see paras **5.42–5.43** above concerning the right to statutory paternity pay.
[111] See reg 12 of the Paternity and Adoption Leave Regulations 2002, read with ss 80C(1)(b) and 80C(5)(b) of the ERA 1996.
[112] See regs 13 and 14 of the Paternity and Adoption Leave Regulations 2002.
[113] See ibid, regs 15–30.
[114] See paras **5.52–5.57** above concerning maternity leave periods and related matters.
[115] See reg 22(2) of the Paternity and Adoption Leave Regulations 2002, which also provides for one other uncontroversial exception, which arises where there are fewer than eight weeks to the end of the ordinary adoption leave period.

(d) because of the unexpected disruption or termination of arrangements for the care of a dependant, or

(e) to deal with an incident which involves a child of the employee and which occurs unexpectedly in a period during which an educational establishment which the child attends is responsible for him.[116]

5.67 The right arises only if the employee tells his employer the reason for the absence as soon as is reasonably practicable, and, if possible, for how long he expects to be absent.[117]

5.68 A 'dependant' means, for these purposes,[118] primarily either a spouse, a child, a parent, or a person who lives in the same household as the employee otherwise than by reason of being the employee's employee, tenant, lodger, or boarder. However, where time off is sought to assist or look after a dependant who is ill, has been injured or assaulted, or has given birth, a dependant includes in addition a person who reasonably relies on the employee for assistance on an occasion when the person falls ill or is injured or assaulted or to make arrangements for the provision of care in the event of illness or injury. Further, where time off is sought because of the unexpected disruption or termination of arrangements for the care of a dependant, a dependant includes in addition any person who reasonably relies on the employee to make such arrangements.

5.69 The right to time off under s 57A is not absolute because the employee can complain about a refusal to give him time off only by way of a complaint to an employment tribunal, and the tribunal can award him compensation only if the refusal of time off was unreasonable.[119] The right to time off is therefore a right to take time off without pay for one or more relevant purposes when it is reasonable to do so.

5.70 Several decisions of the EAT have clarified the extent of the rights conferred by s 57A of the ERA 1996. In *Qua v John Ford Morrison Solicitors*,[120] it was said that 'the disruption caused to the employer's business by the employee's time off is not relevant to the question of whether a reasonable amount of time was taken'.[121] It was also said that:

> 'The right to time off to "provide assistance", etc, in subsection (1)(a) does not in our view enable employees to take time off in order themselves to provide care for a sick child, beyond the reasonable amount necessary to enable them to deal with the immediate crisis.'[122]

---

[116] ERA 1996, s 57A(1).
[117] Ibid, s 57A(2).
[118] See ibid, s 57A(3)–(6).
[119] See ibid, s 57B.
[120] [2003] ICR 482.
[121] Ibid, para 29.
[122] Ibid, para 16.

5.71 That which needs to be communicated by the employee to the employer in order to cause the right to time off under s 57A to arise was stated in *Truelove v Safeway Stores plc*,[123] where it was said that 'There must be a communication which imparts an understanding into the mind of the employers that something has happened to cause the breakdown of what would otherwise be a stable arrangement affecting in this case a child and making it necessary urgently for the employee to leave work.' However, since the 'legislation is designed for operation by parents who are facing a sudden and difficult situation affecting their child', they 'cannot be expected to communicate in the language of the statute'.[124]

PROTECTION FROM DETRIMENT

5.72 Employees are protected from being subjected by their employers to detrimental treatment because they have taken, or sought to take, time off in the manner described above. The protection is conferred by reg 19 of the Maternity and Parental Leave etc Regulations 1999[125] and reg 28 of the Paternity and Adoption Leave Regulations 2002.[126]

EMPLOYEES' OBLIGATIONS

Express terms of a teacher's contract of employment

5.73 An employee's express obligations are to be found in the terms of the contract of employment (which may be contained in the letter of appointment, for example), and, in the case of a teacher in a State school, in the current School Teachers' Pay and Conditions Document, made under s 122 of the Education Act 2002. Since some of the salient features of that document are mentioned above[127] and the document should be readily available in State schools, no further reference to its terms is made here, except to say that the cases below concern matters which are now dealt with by that document. Accordingly, those cases are likely to be relevant only to teachers who are not employed under the terms of that document. However, the employment of all teachers is affected by the implied obligations of an employee referred to in para **5.78** onwards below.

5.74 *Girls Public Day School Trust v Khanna*[128] concerned a question which would not now recur, which is whether or not an employee had sufficient hours of employment per week in order to be able to claim unfair dismissal (there being now no minimum number of hours per week required for a week of

---

[123] [2005] ICR 589, para 17.
[124] [2005] ICR 589, para 17.
[125] SI 1999/3312.
[126] SI 2002/2788.
[127] See para **4.22** onwards above.
[128] [1987] ICR 339.

employment to count for that purpose). However, the rulings made in it provide a good indication of a teacher's contractual duties, especially in an independent school. They concern the manner in which the express terms of a teacher's contract of employment are to be interpreted.

Girls Public Day School Trust v Khanna

An employee was employed as a part-time teacher. Her letter of appointment required her not only to teach but also to share in supervisory duties and assist the head teacher in providing a proper educational and pastoral programme. She was dismissed and claimed unfair dismissal. She needed to be able to satisfy the industrial tribunal that she was employed for 16 or more hours per week in order to do so. She taught and supervised for an undisputed 14 hours and 50 minutes per week. She claimed that in addition to that time, she was employed:

- doing three hours' preparation work at home;
- during two 20-minute morning breaks;
- for periods of 10 minutes before morning assembly and before afternoon lessons; and
- for a 30-minute discussion period with her head of department which took place in most weeks.

The industrial tribunal made no ruling on whether preparation work at home or time before assembly and afternoon lessons should be included, but it decided that both the mid-morning breaks and the discussions with the head of department were 'specific, regular and necessary' and normally took place once a week. Accordingly, the industrial tribunal included these times in the claimant's normal weekly hours of employment, and decided that she was therefore normally employed for 16 hours a week and thus had the right to make a complaint of unfair dismissal. Her employer appealed to the EAT.

Decision of the Employment Appeal Tribunal

The EAT dismissed the appeal. It decided that the claimant was not obliged to do preparatory work outside school hours in order to fulfil her contractual duties. It decided also that sufficient time was allocated for preparatory work within the 14 hours 50 minutes of undisputed weekly employment, and that it was to be presumed that the industrial tribunal had considered that the claimant was not entitled to include additional hours for preparation. The EAT also decided that it was not part of the claimant's contractual duties to be present before morning assembly and afternoon lessons and that she was not entitled to include that time in calculating her weekly employment. However, the EAT decided that the necessary test to be applied to the 20-minute break periods was whether the claimant was contractually obliged to perform any duties, and that although a break between teaching periods would not ordinarily be treated as a period on duty, the commitment to duties outside class time included in the claimant's letter of appointment meant that she could have been required to perform supervisory or pastoral duties during the break periods. Accordingly, it was correct to include those periods in her weekly hours of employment. Furthermore, the industrial tribunal's decision that the 30-minute meetings with the head of department were regular and necessary, and normally took place weekly, and should therefore be included in the claimant's total weekly employment, was correct.

5.75 *Society of Licensed Victuallers v Chamberlain*[129] is to a similar effect. There, a teacher was employed for 15 hours 40 minutes a week, consisting of 21 teaching periods of 40 minutes each, plus a morning break of duty of 25 minutes and one period of lunch supervision of 1 hour 15 minutes. In addition, the teacher had three free periods per week. For the most part, although not exclusively, he used those free periods for preparing lessons and marking work, both of which were contractual requirements. He needed to prove that he had 16 hours' employment a week in order to claim unfair dismissal. An industrial tribunal decided that he did have such employment, because he was to be regarded as employed during the time which he spent during his free periods preparing lessons and marking work. The employer appealed, but the appeal was dismissed. The EAT said that the requirement that the claimant properly prepare his lessons created an implication of additional work over and above the hours spent teaching or on duty. The claimant would require at least 20 minutes in the course of a week to fulfil that contractual requirement, and the obvious place to locate those 20 plus minutes was during his free periods.

IMPLIED OBLIGATIONS OF TEACHERS

5.76 *Sim v Rotherham Metropolitan Borough Council*[130] is a helpful case concerning the implied obligations of a teacher.

>*Sim v Rotherham Metropolitan Borough Council*
>
>Four secondary school teachers were employed under contracts of employment which contained no express provision regarding covering for fellow teachers who were absent from work on account of sickness. However, as a matter of practice, the four teachers, like other secondary school teachers, provided such cover for no extra pay during non-timetable periods which were assigned to them for:
>
>- marking papers;
>- preparing for classes; or
>- undertaking special duties.
>
>Their union instructed them to discontinue that practice. They complied with that instruction, and as a result their employers deducted from their salaries a small sum based on a percentage of their monthly salaries. The teachers issued writs in the High Court against their employers, contending that:
>
>- the cover arrangements operated by secondary school teachers were operated entirely as a matter of goodwill;
>- the cover arrangements did not form part of the teachers' contractual obligations; and
>- their employers were not entitled to make any deductions from their monthly salaries in respect of their refusal to teach, supervise or otherwise cover the classes of absent fellow teachers.

---

[129] [1989] IRLR 421.
[130] [1986] ICR 897.

Decision of the High Court

The High Court dismissed the teachers' claims. It decided that although their contracts of employment contained no express provision as to whether they owed any contractual duty to provide cover for absent colleagues when asked to do so, teachers were members of a profession and it was their contractual duty to discharge the professional obligations of teachers. The High Court stated that those obligations were not limited to imparting knowledge to pupils during periods assigned by the timetable for teaching but included, among other things, co-operating in the proper running of the school. Accordingly, teachers had a contractual obligation to comply with the head teacher's reasonable directions for the proper administration of the school. The court concluded that since the school timetable, together with arrangements for cover for absent teachers by utilisation of the non-teaching periods on the timetable, were necessary for that proper administration, the teachers had been in breach of their contracts in refusing to cover for absent members of the staff.

5.77 One question which is likely to arise relatively frequently in a modern school is whether a teacher could be required to administer medicines to a pupil or otherwise provide medical assistance to a pupil. It seems clear that there is no implied obligation on a member of staff to do that.[131] Thus, there would have to be an express term in the employee's contract of employment empowering the employer to require the employee to give a pupil medical assistance of any sort before an employee could be in breach of contract for refusing to give such assistance.

IMPLIED OBLIGATIONS OF ALL EMPLOYEES

5.78 An employee is subject to the implied term of trust and confidence, just as much as the employer.[132] In addition, an employee is under the implied obligations:

– not to misuse confidential information (distinguishing for this purpose confidential information which is in the nature of a trade secret, or similar information);

– not to compete with the employer while the relationship subsists;

– not to use trade secrets and confidential information akin to a trade secret (such as a list of customers[133]) either while the relationship exists or (to a lesser extent[134]) after the relationship has ended; and

---

[131] It is of interest to note that that is the Secretary of State's view also: see para 16 of 'Managing Medicines in Schools and Early Years Settings', 1448-2005DCL-EN, issued by the Department of Health and the Department for Education and Skills in March 2005.
[132] See paras **5.9–5.10** above regarding this term.
[133] *Roger Bullivant Ltd v Ellis* [1987] ICR 464.
[134] See *Faccenda Chicken Ltd v Fowler* [1987] Ch 117.

– not to seek to entice customers away from the employer while the contract subsists.

5.79 However, an employee may use with impunity his 'individual skill and experience' acquired in the course of his employment.[135]

5.80 Finally, an employee is not obliged to disclose his own wrongdoings to his employer, although an employee might be obliged to disclose the wrongdoings of other employees, even if as a result of such disclosure the employee's own misdeeds would be revealed.[136]

---

[135] *Printers & Finishers Ltd v Holloway* [1965] 1 WLR 1; as explained in *SBJ Stephenson Ltd v Maudy* [2000] IRLR 233.
[136] *Sybron Corporation v Rochem Ltd* [1983] ICR 801; *Item Software (UK) Ltd v Fassihi* [2005] ICR 450, paras 15 and 60.

Chapter 6

DISCRIMINATION AND HUMAN RIGHTS

INTRODUCTION

6.1 The law concerning discrimination in employment is complex. Only certain kinds of discrimination are unlawful, of course. For example, there is normally nothing wrong with discriminating in favour of a person who is better able to do a job than another person (as long as the discrimination is not also on the ground of the other person's race, sex, age, sexual orientation, part-time status, religion, or disability[1]). If, however, for example, the other person is a woman who has responsibilities in regard to the care of children, then the discrimination may constitute indirect discrimination on the ground of sex, contrary to the Sex Discrimination Act 1975 (SDA 1975).[2] However, even then, the discrimination will not contravene that Act if it is objectively justified. Similarly, age discrimination can be justified, as may at least some disability discrimination.

6.2 It is usually very helpful to draw up and then implement an equal opportunities policy. Not only does it concentrate the mind, but it may also be of assistance if a claim of unlawful discrimination is subsequently made.[3] It might be helpful to include an overview of the way in which the law of discrimination now takes effect. In any event, some principles are applicable in the same way in each area of the law. Accordingly, in this chapter, an overview of the manner in which the law of discrimination 'bites', or takes effect, is first given. The specific provisions which apply in each area are then stated.

6.3 A detailed explanation of the effects of the SDA 1975 is given first below, if only because that was chronologically the first of the enactments prohibiting discrimination in employment. In fact, some aspects of the SDA 1975 are more complex than the later enactments, in part because of the complexities of the subject-matter (including that the SDA 1975 prohibits discrimination on the ground of marital status as well as discrimination on the ground of sex). Appellate decisions on parallel provisions in other legislation concerning discrimination are referred to in that explanation, and those parallel provisions are not themselves described in this chapter, although the provisions themselves are mentioned. Certain aspects of the legislation concerning other types of discrimination are different. Those different aspects are described

---

[1] It is of interest that the list of prohibitions has lengthened considerably since the first edition of this book was published.
[2] See para **6.58** onwards below.
[3] See para **6.73** below.

rather than merely mentioned. An obvious example of an area which merits detailed exposition is the law of disability discrimination, which is necessarily somewhat different from what one might now call 'ordinary' discrimination law provisions.

6.4 The final section of this chapter consists of a brief description of the parts of the European Convention on Human Rights (the Convention) which do not themselves relate to discrimination.

THE MANNER IN WHICH DISCRIMINATION LAW PROTECTS EMPLOYEES

The relationship between national and international prohibitions on discrimination

Introduction

6.5 United Kingdom (UK) legislation concerning discrimination against employees used to consist only of certain prohibitions against discrimination on the ground of sex (imposed by the Equal Pay Act 1970 (EPA 1970) and the SDA 1975) or race (imposed by the Race Relations Act 1976 (RRA 1976)). Those prohibitions largely preceded any protection which was afforded by European Community (EC) law.[4] However, the UK was a signatory of the Convention, and decisions of the European Court of Human Rights (ECHR) were usually given effect (at least eventually) in UK legislation.

6.6 In addition, in 1976, Directive 76/207/EEC, which was known as the Equal Treatment Directive, was made by the then European Economic Community legislature. Further, in 1976 the European Court of Justice (ECJ)[5] ruled in *Defrenne v Sabena*[6] that what was then Art 119 of the EC Treaty had direct effect.[7] Furthermore, it had already by then been decided by the ECJ that EC Directives could in certain circumstances have direct effect. The doctrine of direct effect is of particular importance in relation to maintained schools, and it is described below.[8]

Human rights

6.7 Before turning to that doctrine, however, it is necessary to finish this short overview of the interlocking of the various prohibitions on discrimination by referring to the manner in which the Human Rights Act 1998

---

[4] European Community law is referred to below as 'Community law' rather than 'European Union law', because the European Union consists of the European Communities, and the rights which arise in relation to matters which are the subject of the European Union do so under the Community treaties.
[5] It will be noted that the ECJ is not to be confused with the ECHR.
[6] [1976] ICR 547.
[7] Article 119 has since been replaced by Art 141 of the EC Treaty in its current form.
[8] See paras **6.12–6.15** below.

(HRA 1998) has affected the law of discrimination. That Act incorporated in UK law many of the provisions of the Convention. Each right which is so incorporated is called a 'Convention right'.[9] However, only public bodies within the meaning of the HRA 1998 are directly bound by the incorporated provisions of the Convention. Maintained schools are clearly public bodies for this purpose. Academies probably are public bodies for this purpose also. Bodies which are not public bodies for the purposes of the HRA 1998 are bound by the incorporated provisions of the Convention only in so far as those provisions are given effect by being applied by courts or tribunals in particular cases. The HRA 1998 requires courts and tribunals, so far as it is possible to do so, to interpret and give effect to legislation in a way which is compatible with the Convention rights.[10] However, if the legislation is incompatible with a Convention right or rights, then it will not be possible to give effect to it by interpretation.

6.8 A public body may not lawfully act in a manner which is incompatible with a Convention right unless:

(1) as the result of one or more provisions of primary legislation, the body could not have acted differently; or

(2) the body was acting under and in accordance with legislation which could not be read or given effect to in a way which was compatible with the Convention right.[11]

6.9 However, compensation for an employer's acting unlawfully as a result of the contravention of a Convention right could not be sought in employment tribunal proceedings. A claim for such compensation would have to be made in a county court or the High Court, and the damages might well be relatively low.

6.10 The Convention rights include a right not to be discriminated against on the ground of 'sex, race, colour, language, religion, political or other opinion, national or social origin, association with a national minority, property, birth or other status' (Art 14 of the Convention). This right may not be relied upon on its own. Rather, Art 14 must be joined with another Convention right in that although it is not necessary to be able to prove a breach of that other Convention right, it is necessary to show that there was discrimination contrary to Art 14 in relation to the exercise by the individual of that other Convention right.[12] There is no substantive right to be employed, so Art 14 can be relied upon in relation to employment only in conjunction with for example the right to respect for private life conferred by Art 8(1).

---

[9] See para **6.159** below for the relevant Convention rights. Reference is also made to Art 14 in para **6.10** below.
[10] HRA 1998, s 3.
[11] Ibid, s 6.
[12] See for example *R (Douglas) v North Tyneside Metropolitan Borough Council* [2004] 1 WLR 2363.

6.11 There are several principles or approaches which have been adopted by the ECHR in relation to the application of the Convention rights in practice. They include the following.

(1) The ECHR takes an overall view of the situation and seeks to give a practical and effective interpretation to the rights.

(2) Any limitation of the rights (such as in Arts 8 to 11) is interpreted narrowly.

(3) The Convention is a 'living instrument', which must be interpreted in the light of present-day conditions. Societies and values change and the ECHR takes account of these changes in interpreting the Convention. In doing so, it looks to see whether there are common European standards.

(4) Any interference with a Convention right must be proportionate to the intended objective. Thus, any interference with a Convention right should be carefully designed to meet the objective in question and must not be arbitrary or unfair.

(5) There is nevertheless a margin of appreciation (or room for manoeuvre) in relation to some Convention rights. This is more likely to be applicable to Convention rights which are qualified rather than absolute.

Direct effect of European Community law

6.12 The principles governing the direct effect of Community law are by no means straightforward. Community legislation takes the form of treaty provisions, regulations, directives and decisions. Regulations and decisions have direct effect. In other words, they will have effect in the courts of the UK, despite there being no UK legislative provision implementing them in the UK. In contrast, treaty provisions and directives were not originally intended to have direct effect. However, over the years the ECJ has decided that treaty provisions and directives can have direct effect where they have not been implemented, or not implemented properly, by national legislation. The ECJ even decided in *Mangold v Helm*[13] that a general principle of Community law (in that case it was non-discrimination on grounds of age) may be applicable even before the expiry of the period for implementing a Community directive giving effect to it.

6.13 The provisions of a directive can be relied upon only by a person suing the State or an 'emanation of the State'. Since the governing body of a maintained school clearly is an 'emanation of the State' for this purpose,[14] their employees may be able to rely directly on a provision of a directive if the provision is itself clear and unambiguous, was intended to confer rights on

---

[13] [2006] IRLR 143.
[14] *National Union of Teachers v Governing Body of St Mary's Church of England (Aided) Junior School* [1997] ICR 334.

persons, and contains an obligation which is sufficiently complete to be capable of being relied upon without something more occurring.

6.14 However, even if these conditions are satisfied, certain procedural difficulties will be encountered in seeking to enforce the Community right in question. This is because the need to rely upon the relevant Community law provision will have arisen only because it has not been implemented, or not implemented properly, in UK law. Accordingly, there will be no procedural mechanism by which to enforce it.

6.15 In a number of cases in the ECJ, it has been determined that in such a situation, the national court has to allow the claimant to use a procedure which is used in analogous proceedings within the national judicial system. Furthermore, the ECJ has stated, procedural rules such as time limits must not be less favourable than those which apply to similar actions of a domestic nature and must not render the exercise of the Community law right in question impossible in practice. A recent example of the application in the UK of these principles is the decision of the Court of Appeal in *Alabaster v Barclays Bank plc*.[15]

6.16 One would have thought, therefore, that a Community right would be capable of being enforced, as a free-standing right, via analogous national proceedings. However, the Court of Appeal decided in *Biggs v Somerset County Council*[16] that that is not so: the court decided that there is no such thing as a free-standing right in Community law, and thus the Community right can only be enforced if some national provision can be 'disapplied' so as to allow the enforcement of the right. This seems to be wrong, since:

(1) the ECJ has decided (in a line of cases beginning with *Francovich and Bonifaci v Italian Republic*[17]) that an individual may in certain circumstances make a claim against a national government for compensation for failing to implement a Community law; and

(2) this cannot be anything but a free-standing right.

Indirect effect of European Community Law

6.17 Even if it is not possible to rely upon Community legislation directly, that legislation may still have an effect. This is because Community law (that is not only legislation but also decisions of the ECJ) must always be applied when interpreting national legislation which implements Community legislation or which concerns a matter which has been affected by Community legislation.[18] However, if applying Community law would involve a distortion of the language of the relevant national legislation, then the national law must be

---

[15] [2005] ICR 1246.
[16] [1996] ICR 364.
[17] [1995] ICR 722.
[18] *Marleasing SA v La Commercial International de Alimentacion SA* [1990] ECR I-4135.

applied as it stands.[19] Where this occurs, it will only be possible for a claimant to rely upon the Community law in question if it is directly effective or it gives rise to a right to claim compensation under the *Francovich* line of cases.[20]

6.18 Finally, it is of note that the ECJ decided in *R v Secretary of State for Employment, ex parte Seymour-Smith*[21] that the duty of a Member State to comply with Community law is not to be determined only at the time when legislation which allegedly contravenes Community law was enacted, but, rather, throughout the period when that legislation is in force.

Direct and indirect discrimination

6.19 Throughout UK discrimination legislation, and in the case law of both the ECJ and the ECHR, a distinction is drawn between direct unlawful discrimination and indirect unlawful discrimination.

Direct discrimination

6.20 Essentially, direct discrimination is doing something detrimental to a person purely because of that person's status, whether it be race, sex, disability, or some other prohibited ground for detrimental treatment. The rationale for the prohibition of discrimination of that sort is obvious: less favourable treatment of a person purely because of that person's status as, for example, a member of a different race, is irrational.

6.21 In *R (European Roma Rights Centre) v Immigration Officer at Prague Airport*,[22] the House of Lords held that the aim of the RRA 1976 is to prevent discrimination by stereotyping, by ensuring that an individual is not to be assumed to hold the characteristics which might be associated with the racial group to which he or she belongs irrespective of whether most members of the group in fact have such characteristics.

Indirect discrimination

6.22 Indirect discrimination might best be described as unintended discrimination on the ground of, for example, sex or race. It usually arises in relation to employment where a condition or requirement, or a provision, criterion or practice, is imposed by an employer on employees, and the members of a particular group of employees are disproportionately affected by it. For example, the requirement for full-time employment at least in the past has had (and at least in some circumstances today still has) an indirectly discriminatory effect on women. This is because women tend to bear the

---

[19] This is because the duty to apply Community legislation applies only 'so far as possible': *Marleasing* (above) at 4159, para 8.
[20] Concerning which, see para **6.16** above.
[21] [1999] ICR 447.
[22] [2005] 2 AC 1.

primary burden of looking after children at home.[23] However, it is necessary nevertheless for an employee to satisfy the employment tribunal which hears her case that there has been what might be called a disproportionate impact on women.[24] Where there is such a disproportionate impact on women, however, it may be justified objectively, and if it is so justified then it will be lawful. Further, and in any event, the claimant might not be disadvantaged by the relevant provision, criterion or practice. If he or she is not so disadvantaged, then there will also be no indirect discrimination.

Proving direct discrimination

Introduction

6.23 Those who have discriminated against employees directly on a prohibited ground will almost always refuse to admit, usually even to themselves, that they have, or may have, committed direct discrimination against a particular employee on a prohibited ground. Further, unlawful direct discrimination is purely in the mind of the person who commits it. This person will sometimes be the employer (and it is possible for a corporate body such as a governing body itself to make a discriminatory decision), but is more usually another employee of the employer for whose acts or omissions the employer will be vicariously liable under the relevant legislation. (All of the relevant legislation imposes liability on employers for the unlawfully discriminatory acts of employees unless the employer has taken such steps as were reasonably practicable to prevent the employee from doing the prohibited act or acts of that description.)

Burden of proof directive

6.24 The difficulty of proving unlawful direct discrimination led to the inclusion in several Community directives of provisions which required national governments to include in their legislation concerning discrimination a provision helping employees make claims of unlawful direct discrimination. The first such directive[25] concerned discrimination on the ground of sex. It came to be known as the Burden of Proof Directive. All subsequent Community directives incorporated provision to the like effect.[26]

---

[23] For a recent example of a case in which that proposition was specifically accepted as correct by the employer with the result that the employer's requirement for full-time working had a disproportionate impact on women, see *Hardy & Hansons plc v Lax* [2005] ICR 1565, para 13.

[24] See for example *Armstrong v Newcastle Upon Tyne NHS Hospital Trust* [2006] IRLR 124, especially at para 37. Although the decision of the Court of Appeal in that case is open to criticism in some respects, it is valuable as a reminder of the need for some rigour in the analysis of the situation. The need for logic in choosing the pool for comparison was emphasised by Sedley LJ in *Allonby v Accrington and Rossendale College* [2001] ICR 1189, para 18.

[25] 97/80/EC. It was supplemented by Council Directive 98/52/EC. It will be repealed and replaced with effect from 15 August 2009 by Directive 2006/54/EC.

[26] See most notably Council Directive 2000/78/EC, the so-called 'Framework Directive', which concerns discrimination on the grounds of religion or belief, disability, age, or sexual orientation.

6.25 The essence of the protection given by these Community directives is that it shifts the burden of proof in certain circumstances. The Burden of Proof Directive's operative provision was Art 4, which was in these terms:

> 'Member States shall take such measures as are necessary, in accordance with their national judicial systems, to ensure that, when persons who consider themselves wronged because the principle of equal treatment has not been applied to them establish, before a court or other competent authority, facts from which it may be presumed that there has been direct or indirect discrimination, it shall be for the respondent to prove that there has been no breach of the principle of equal treatment.'[27]

6.26 This was incorporated into the SDA 1975 and all of the other legislation in areas which are affected by Community directives in the same way. The precise formulation (taking the wording from s 63A(2) of the SDA 1975 as it currently stands) is this:

> 'Where, on the hearing of the complaint, the complainant proves facts from which the tribunal could, apart from this section, conclude in the absence of an adequate explanation that the respondent–
>
> (a) has committed an act of discrimination or harassment against the complainant which is unlawful by virtue of Part 2 . . . or
> (b) is by virtue of section 41 or 42 to be treated as having committed such an act of discrimination or harassment against the complainant,
>
> the tribunal shall uphold the complaint unless the respondent proves that he did not commit, or, as the case may be, is not to be treated as having committed, that act.'

6.27 The precise effect of this wording has already been the subject of a considerable amount of case law, culminating perhaps most notably in the decision of the Court of Appeal in *Madarassy v Nomura International plc*.[28] Since the House of Lords refused permission to appeal to it against the Court of Appeal's decision in that case,[29] the following statements can safely be made about the applicable principles (at least as they stood at the time of writing).

6.28 The effects of the Court of Appeal's decisions in *Igen Ltd v Wong*[30] and *Madarassy* are these.

(1) The mere fact that a claimant proves a difference of status and a difference in treatment (that is, in the case of *Madarassy* that she, being a woman who had had children, was treated differently from men) does not make the burden of proof shift. That merely indicates the possibility of discrimination and will not, without more, enable an employment tribunal

---

[27] Precisely the same terms are used for example in Art 10 of Council Directive 2000/78/EC.
[28] [2007] ICR 867.
[29] See [2007] ICR 1175.
[30] [2005] ICR 931.

to conclude on the balance of probabilities that the employer has committed an unlawful act of discrimination.[31]

(2) The words 'could conclude' in s 63A(2) mean that a reasonable tribunal could properly so conclude from all the evidence before it (coming from whichever party).[32]

(3) That evidence will include any (a) evasive or equivocal answers to legitimate queries in a questionnaire served under the relevant legislation, or (b) failure to follow a recommendation in a relevant code of practice.[33]

(4) The absence of an adequate explanation will only became relevant if a prima facie case is shown by the complainant. The consideration of the tribunal will then move to the second stage, at which the burden will be on the respondent.[34]

(5) The expression 'in the absence of an adequate explanation' does not mean that it must be presumed at the first stage that the respondent has no adequate explanation. Section 63A(2) does not expressly or impliedly prevent the tribunal at the first stage from hearing, accepting or drawing inferences from evidence adduced by the respondent disputing and rebutting the complainant's evidence of discrimination. However, at the first stage, the tribunal does not take into account the absence of an adequate explanation from the respondent employer.[35]

(6) Where there is no actual, but only a hypothetical, comparator, then the above approach remains appropriate.[36]

6.29 However, it will not necessarily be an error of law for an employment tribunal to fail to follow the two-stage approach required by s 63A(2) of the SDA 1975.[37] Failing to follow the two-stage procedure may well be appropriate where 'the identity of the relevant comparator is a matter of dispute'.[38] Further, if the tribunal moves straight to the second stage, then the employee

---

[31] *Madarassy*, para 56.
[32] *Madarassy*, para 57.
[33] See *Igen Ltd v Wong* at 956–7. Similarly, a failure to call as a witness a person who was involved in the event(s) or decision(s) about which complaint is made would be a factor which could lawfully be taken into account by an employment tribunal when deciding whether or not the burden of proof has shifted, and whether or not the employee was in fact the subject of unlawful discrimination: *Dresdner Kleinwort Wasserstein Ltd v Adebayo* [2005] IRLR 514.
[34] *Madarassy*, para 58.
[35] *Madarassy*, paras 58 and 77.
[36] *Madarassy*, para 83.
[37] See *Brown v Croydon London Borough Council* [2007] ICR 909, paras 35–39.
[38] *Shamoon v Chief Constable of Royal Ulster Constabulary* [2003] ICR 337, para 8, per Lord Nicholls, whose approach stated in paras 10–12 of his speech in that case was applied by the Court of Appeal in *Madarassy*, paras 80–84 and *Brown v Croydon London Borough Council*, paras 33–39.

will in fact be helped rather than hindered, since the employee will be relieved of the obligation to establish a prima facie case.[39]

6.30 As the Court of Appeal said in *Igen Ltd v Wong*,[40] where the burden of proof has shifted, it is for the employer to prove 'that the treatment was in no sense whatsoever on the grounds of sex, since [only] "no discrimination whatsoever" is compatible with the Burden of Proof Directive'.[41] In addition, as the Court of Appeal said in *EB v BA*,[42] an employer's explanation for apparently discriminatory treatment cannot merely be asserted: it must be proved.

6.31 There is no need for the hearing of the claim to be split into two stages; all of the evidence can be heard by the employment tribunal before it applies the two-stage test.[43]

6.32 A number of decisions by the appellate courts in the UK which were made before the Burden of Proof Directive was implemented in UK law remain helpful and relevant when an employment tribunal is determining whether or not there has been unlawful discrimination. One case which contains guidance which remains of considerable assistance is that of *Anya v University of Oxford*.[44] There, Sedley LJ, speaking on behalf of the court, set out the following guidance of Mummery J, sitting in the Employment Appeal Tribunal in the case of *Qureshi v University of Manchester*,[45] to which Sedley LJ referred as valuable amplification of the previous authorities:

> 'On the basis of (a) those authorities, (b) the experience of the members of this appeal tribunal and (c) the experience of the parties, the advisers and the industrial tribunal in this case, we tentatively add the following observations and thoughts to the guidance in Neill LJ's judgment in *King v Great Britain-China Centre* [1992] ICR 516.
>
> . . .
>
> (2) *The issues* As the industrial tribunal has to resolve disputes of fact about what happened and why it happened, it is always important to identify clearly and arrange in proper order the main issues for decision for example: (a) Did the act complained of actually occur? In some cases there will be a conflict of direct oral evidence. The tribunal will have to decide who to believe. If it does not believe the applicant and his witnesses, the applicant[46] has failed to discharge the burden of proving the act complained of and the case will fail at that point. If the applicant is believed, has he brought his application in time and, if not, is it just and equitable to extend the time? (b) If the act complained of occurred in time, was

---

[39] *Brown v Croydon London Borough Council*, para 37.
[40] [2005] ICR 931.
[41] Ibid, at 957, where the Court of Appeal set out some clear guidelines.
[42] [2006] IRLR 471.
[43] *Madarassy*, para 70.
[44] [2001] ICR 847.
[45] [2001] ICR 863.
[46] That is, now, the claimant employee.

there a difference in race involving the applicant? (c) If a difference in race was involved, was the applicant treated less favourably than the alleged discriminator treated or would treat other persons of a different racial group in the same, or not materially different, relevant circumstances? (d) If there was difference in treatment involving persons of a different race, was that treatment 'on racial grounds'? Were racial grounds an effective cause of the difference in treatment? What explanation of the less favourable treatment is given by the respondent? In answer to each of those questions the tribunal must make findings of primary fact, either on the basis of direct (or positive) evidence or by inference from circumstantial evidence.

(3) *The evidence* As frequently observed in race discrimination cases, the applicant is often faced with the difficulty of discharging the burden of proof in the absence of direct evidence on the issue of racial grounds for the alleged discriminatory actions and decisions. The applicant faces special difficulties in a case of alleged institutional discrimination which, if it exists, may be inadvertent and unintentional. The tribunal must consider the direct oral and documentary evidence available, including the answers to the statutory questionnaire. It must also consider what inferences may be drawn from all the primary facts. Those primary facts may include not only the acts which form the subject matter of the complaint but also other acts alleged by the applicant to constitute evidence pointing to a racial ground for the alleged discriminatory act or decision. . . .

(4) *Inferences* The process of making inferences or deductions from primary facts is itself a demanding task, often more difficult than deciding a conflict of direct oral evidence. In *Chapman v Simon* [1994] IRLR 124, 129, para 43 Peter Gibson LJ gave a timely reminder of the importance of having a factual basis for making inferences. He said:

> "Racial discrimination may be established as a matter of direct primary fact. For example, if the allegation made by Ms Simon of racially abusive language by the headteacher had been accepted, there would have been such a fact. But that allegation was unanimously rejected by the tribunal. More often racial discrimination will have to be established, if at all, as a matter of inference. It is of the greatest importance that the primary facts from which such inference is drawn are set out with clarity by the tribunal in its fact-finding role, so that the validity of the inference can be examined. Either the facts justifying such inference exist or they do not, but only the tribunal can say what those facts are. A mere intuitive hunch, for example, that there has been unlawful discrimination is insufficient without facts being found to support that conclusion." (See also Balcombe LJ at p 128, para 33(3).)

In the present case, it was necessary for the tribunal to examine all the allegations made by Dr Qureshi of other incidents relied upon by him as evidentiary facts of race discrimination in the matters complained of. There is a tendency, however, where many evidentiary incidents or items are introduced, to be carried away by them and to treat each of the allegations, incidents or items as if they were themselves the subject of a complaint. In the present case it was necessary for the tribunal to find the primary facts about those allegations. It was not, however, necessary for the tribunal to ask itself, in relation to each such incident or item, whether it was itself explicable on 'racial grounds' or on other grounds. That is a misapprehension about the nature and purpose of evidentiary facts. The function of the tribunal is to find the primary facts from which they will be asked to draw inferences and then for the tribunal to look at the totality of those facts (including the respondent's explanations) in order to see whether it is legitimate to infer that the acts or decisions complained of in the originating applications were on 'racial grounds'. The fragmented approach adopted by the tribunal in this case would inevitably have the effect of diminishing any eloquence that the cumulative effect of the primary facts might have on the issue of racial grounds. The process of inference is itself a matter of applying common sense and judgment to the facts, and assessing the probabilities on the issue whether racial grounds were an effective cause of the acts complained of or were not. The assessment of the parties and their witnesses when they give evidence also forms an important part of the process of inference. The tribunal may find that the force of the primary facts is insufficient to justify an inference of racial grounds. It may find that any inference that it might have made is negated by a satisfactory explanation from the respondent of non-racial grounds of action or decision.

Conclusion The additional comments are intended to provide some assistance to the tribunal to whom this case is remitted (and to other tribunals) in deciding what are, in our view, the most difficult kind of case which industrial tribunals have to decide. The legal and evidential difficulties are increased by the emotional content of the cases. Feelings run high. The applicant alleges that he has been unfairly and unlawfully treated in an important respect affecting his employment, his livelihood, his integrity as a person. The person against whom an accusation of discrimination is made feels that his acts and decisions have been misunderstood, that he has been unfairly, even falsely, accused of serious wrongdoing. The accusations may not only be hurtful to him as a person but may also be damaging to his employment, his prospects and his relationships with others. In our experience, the industrial tribunals discharge this delicate, difficult function conscientiously and carefully.'

Employer's intention

6.33 It is not necessary to show that an employer intended to discriminate on the ground of (for example) sex.[47]

Is unreasonable behaviour always discrimination?

6.34 The mere fact that an employer has acted unreasonably towards, for example, a woman employee will not mean that the employer has discriminated against her. This is illustrated by the facts of *Qureshi v London Borough of Newham* (which was a race discrimination case).[48]

> *Qureshi v London Borough of Newham*
>
> An employee, Mr Qureshi, who was of Asian origin, was head of his school's physics department. At the end of 1987, he applied for the post of head of the science department. There were 12 applicants of whom four, including the employee, were short-listed. The others interviewed were of UK and Irish origin.

---

[47] *R v Birmingham City Council, ex parte Equal Opportunities Commission* [1989] AC 1155.
[48] [1991] IRLR 264.

Several days prior to the interviews, the science adviser met the head teacher to discuss what should be put in the employee's reference. Although under the employer's equal opportunities policy the employee should have been permitted to see any reference and given the opportunity to challenge it, in this case the reference was not produced until the last moment. In addition, the employer's equal opportunities policy was not complied with in several other respects:

(1) the full job specification and a person specification was not provided for the panel;

(2) the interviewers failed to keep adequate records at the interview;

(3) there was a failure to provide the necessary monitoring statistics; and

(4) the members of the interviewing panel had not been trained.

In the event, the employee was not appointed. He complained to an industrial tribunal that he had been unlawfully discriminated against on the ground of his race. The tribunal rejected the complaint that he had been discriminated against by not being offered the post, deciding that the claimant's reference played 'no part' in the authority's decision and that the claimant had therefore not been discriminated against by not being offered the post. However, the tribunal upheld the employee's assertion that he had been discriminated against contrary to s 4(2)(b) of the RRA 1976. That provision renders it unlawful for a person to discriminate against an employee 'in the way he affords him access to opportunities for promotion'. The industrial tribunal considered that it was entitled to draw an inference of discrimination in connection with access to promotion opportunities. It commented that:

> 'There is an equal opportunities policy which presumably is intended to be applied to everyone irrespective of race or colour. It can therefore be assumed that a person who was an internal candidate for a job and who was of a different racial origin than Mr Qureshi, would be dealt with in accordance with the requirements of that policy.'

Moreover, the tribunal said,

> 'The way the reference in respect of Mr Qureshi was brought into existence and the (as it seems to us) unjustifiably negative comments . . . and the failure to give him an opportunity to challenge these comments, falls so far short of what a fair and open reference policy requires as to justify an assumption that they would not have been generally applied, and therefore would not have been applied to a person of a different racial group.'

The employer appealed to the EAT. The claimant cross-appealed against the decision of the industrial tribunal that he had not been discriminated against by not being offered the post in question. The EAT allowed the LEA's appeal from the decision that it had discriminated against the claimant in its promotion arrangements and dismissed the claimant's cross-appeal that he had been discriminated against by the failure to offer him the post. The claimant appealed to the Court of Appeal.

Decision of the Court of Appeal

The Court of Appeal decided that the EAT had correctly decided that the industrial tribunal had erred in drawing the inference that the employer had unlawfully discriminated against the claimant on the ground of his race in the way in which it afforded him access to opportunities for promotion. The court further decided that the industrial tribunal had erred in reasoning that as:

(1) the authority's equal opportunities policy (including the reference policy) was intended to apply generally and equally;

(2) it was to be assumed that it would have been applied properly to a person of different racial origin from the claimant; and

(3) the policy was not applied properly to the claimant,

the claimant had been discriminated against. The defect in that reasoning was the assumption that the policy would have been applied properly to persons of different racial origin from the claimant. As the industrial tribunal found that the failure by the employers was not deliberate, there was no justification for assuming that because the policy was not applied to the claimant, the failure must have been due to discrimination. In the absence of any hint of prejudice on racial grounds, the more natural inference from a failure in relation to one person is that there would have been failure in relation to others, if not to all. The Court of Appeal stated that 'Incompetence does not, without more, become discrimination merely because the person affected by it is from an ethnic minority.'[49]

APPROACH TO BE TAKEN BY EMPLOYMENT TRIBUNALS

6.35 In determining whether there has been direct discrimination on the ground of sex, an employment tribunal is likely to be willing to consider evidence relating to the employer's general attitude towards discrimination. So, for example, the tribunal will usually be willing to hear evidence as to whether the employer had an equal opportunities policy, and whether that policy had been misapplied or ignored in the past. The concept of a 'culture of discrimination' has been referred to on behalf of claimants in employment tribunals. Indeed, the EAT decided in the case of *Chattopadhyay v Headmaster of Holloway School*[50] that acts which are discriminatory and which take place both before and after an alleged incident of discrimination may be taken into account in deciding whether the act which is the subject of the claim was discriminatory.

Chattopadhyay v Headmaster of Holloway School

An employee who was Indian in origin, was employed at Holloway School as a history teacher. In 1978 the position of head of history fell vacant and was advertised. The employee applied and was short-listed for the post. The post was offered to another member of the history staff with fewer qualifications and less experience than the employee. The employee complained to an industrial tribunal that he had been discriminated against on the ground of his race. At the hearing, he sought to give evidence of events which had happened after the decision not to offer him the post had been taken. The industrial tribunal refused to permit the

---

[49] [1991] IRLR 264, para 27.
[50] [1982] ICR 132.

evidence to be given on the ground that it did not of itself establish that the failure to appoint the complainant to the post of head of history was because of his race.

Decision of the Employment Appeal Tribunal

The EAT allowed the claimant's appeal deciding that, since it was rare for a person who complained of discrimination to have evidence of overtly racial discriminatory words or actions, he had to rely on facts which, if unexplained, were consistent with him having been treated less favourably than others on racial grounds. The EAT also decided that evidence of hostile acts other than the alleged discriminatory act was admissible if it was logically probative and showed that the person involved was treating the claimant differently from other people. As the EAT put it:

> '. . . the question is not whether the evidence, if admitted, would be decisive but whether it may tend to prove the case. If the applicant could establish (a) that a relevant person had behaved in a hostile way and (b) that such hostility was racialist, this would have a probative value in establishing that that person had racialist motives . . . Both '(a)' and '(b)' are relevant facts in making the case sought to be made. It is not in our judgment legitimate to exclude fact '(a)', if it is a fact of a kind which calls for an explanation, in the absence of proof of fact '(b)', racialist intent, if fact '(a)' is such that from it the intent could be inferred.'

The EAT commented, however, that there is a very heavy burden on legal advisers to ensure that evidence of subsequent events is not introduced into a case except where they are satisfied that there is a real probability that the evidence will affect the outcome.

HARASSMENT

6.36 Harassment on a prohibited ground is necessarily discrimination. However, wherever relevant, harassment is specifically dealt with by the legislative provisions. The most complex provisions concerning harassment are in the SDA 1975 as amended, and their effects are described below.[51]

VICTIMISATION

6.37 All of the statutory prohibitions on discrimination protect employees against detrimental treatment, including dismissal, as a result of having asserted in good faith the right not to be discriminated against contrary to the legislative provisions in question. In all cases, it is irrelevant that the prohibition is found not to have been contravened, unless the assertion of the statutory right in question was not made in good faith. At the time of writing the law of discrimination by way of victimisation had been the subject of three decisions

---

[51] See paras **6.67–6.70** below.

of the House of Lords in the previous decade. The first, that of *Nagarajan v London Regional Transport*,[52] contains the following illuminating passage from the speech of Lord Nicholls:[53]

> 'Although victimisation has a ring of conscious targeting, this is an insufficient basis for excluding cases of unrecognised prejudice from the scope of section 2 [of the RRA 1976]. Such an exclusion would partially undermine the protection section 2 seeks to give those who have sought to rely on the Act or been involved in the operation of the Act in other ways.
>
> Decisions are frequently reached for more than one reason. Discrimination may be on racial grounds even though it is not the sole ground for the decision. A variety of phrases, with different shades of meaning, have been used to explain how the legislation applies in such cases: discrimination requires that racial grounds were a cause, the activating cause, a substantial and effective cause, a substantial reason, an important factor. No one phrase is obviously preferable to all others, although in the application of this legislation legalistic phrases, as well as subtle distinctions, are better avoided so far as possible. If racial grounds or protected acts had a significant influence on the outcome, discrimination is made out.'

6.38 The second House of Lords case on the matter was that of *Chief of the West Yorkshire Police v Khan*.[54] The speeches in that case were in some respects less than straightforward to apply in practice, and the most recent of the three decisions of the House of Lords, that in *Derbyshire v St Helens Borough Council*,[55] clarified the effect of *Khan*. In *Khan*, the Chief Constable declined to give the claimant a reference in connection with the claimant's appointment to another police force and did so pending the determination of the claimant's claim of discrimination on the ground of race. The reason why that was decided not to be victimisation was because the refusal to give a reference was 'not because [the Chief Constable] wished to obstruct the conduct of those proceedings but because he believed, on advice, that any reference he gave would weaken his defence in those proceedings or aggravate the damages recoverable against him.'[56] In *Derbyshire v St Helens Borough Council*, the employer wrote letters to employees who had claimed equal pay, and, as Lord Bingham said, 'the object of sending the letters was to put pressure on the [employees] to drop their claims'.[57] The letters were held by the House of Lords to have constituted unlawful discrimination by way of victimisation.

6.39 It is important to bear it in mind that it is not necessary for an employee to prove that he was victimised on (for example) racial grounds. So, an employer who is in fact strongly opposed to discrimination on the relevant ground and whose challenged acts in no way contravened the relevant prohibition of discrimination, may nevertheless contravene the relevant

---

[52] [1999] ICR 877.
[53] At 886.
[54] [2001] ICR 1065.
[55] [2007] ICR 841.
[56] *Derbyshire v St Helens Borough Council*, para 9, per Lord Bingham.
[57] Ibid.

prohibition of victimisation. However, it is of note that in the passage set out in para **6.37** above from the speech of Lord Nicholls in *Nagarajan*, it is recognised that there may in other cases be 'unrecognised prejudice' resulting in victimisation.

6.40 All of the prohibitions of victimisation now apply where the relationship of employment has ended.

CURRENT PROHIBITIONS OF EUROPEAN COMMUNITY LAW

6.41 Before turning to the specific statutory prohibitions in UK legislation concerning discrimination in employment, the subject-matter of the current EC legislation concerning such discrimination can usefully be mentioned. There is EC legislation concerning discrimination on the ground of sex (including for this purpose discrimination in relation to pay),[58] part-time status,[59] fixed-term status,[60] racial or ethnic origin,[61] religion or belief,[62] disability,[63] age,[64] and sexual orientation.[65]

UK LEGISLATION CONCERNING DISCRIMINATION IN EMPLOYMENT

The legislation: an overview

6.42 United Kingdom legislation concerning discrimination in relation to employment now consists of the EPA 1970 and related legislation such as the Occupational Pension Schemes (Equal Treatment) Regulations 1995,[66] the SDA 1975, the RRA 1976, the Disability Discrimination Act 1995 (DDA 1995), the Part-time Workers (Prevention of Less Favourable Treatment) Regulations 2000,[67] the Fixed-term Employees (Prevention of Less Favourable Treatment) Regulations 2002,[68] the Employment Equality (Religion or Belief)

---

[58] See Art 141 of the EC Treaty, Directive 75/117/EEC, Directive 76/207/EEC as amended, both of which directives which will be replaced with effect from 15 August 2009 by Directive 2006/54/EC, and Recommendation and Code of Practice No 92/131/EEC.
[59] Directives 97/81/EC and 98/23/EC.
[60] Directive 1999/70/EC.
[61] Directive 2000/43/EC, which does not apply to discrimination on the ground of nationality. However, Art 12 of the EC Treaty prohibits discrimination against a national of a Member State of the European Union on the ground of his nationality. In *Collins v Imtrat Handelsgesellschaft mbH* [1993] ECR I-5145, the ECJ held, in para 34, that what is now Art 12 is directly effective.
[62] Directive 2000/78/EC.
[63] Ibid.
[64] Ibid.
[65] Ibid.
[66] SI 1995/3183.
[67] SI 2000/1551.
[68] SI 2002/2034.

Regulations 2003,[69] the Employment Equality (Sexual Orientation) Regulations 2003,[70] and the Employment Equality (Age) Regulations 2006.[71]

6.43 In addition, it is realistic to include in the category of legislation concerning discrimination in relation to employment, the Flexible Working (Procedural Requirements) Regulations 2002[72] and the Flexible Working (Eligibility, Complaints and Remedies) Regulations 2002.[73] Further, it is necessary to mention also the subordinate legislation concerning questions and answers to potential respondents to employment tribunal claims, such as the Equal Pay (Questions and Replies) Order 2003.[74]

The Sex Discrimination Act 1975

6.44 The SDA 1975 has been amended in many ways since it was first enacted. Its current effects are described in the following paragraphs.

Direct discrimination[75]

6.45 Direct discrimination is discrimination contrary to s 1(1)(a) of the 1975 Act. An employer contravenes that section if the employer treats a person less favourably because of ('on the ground of') that person's sex than he treats or would treat a person of the opposite sex. From now on, for the purpose of simplicity, those who are subject to discrimination on the ground of sex are referred to as female. Treating a person less favourably on the ground that he or she intends to undergo, is undergoing, or has undergone gender reassignment is discrimination against a man/woman (as appropriate).[76] Discrimination against a person on the ground of sexuality, however, is not discrimination on the ground of sex.[77]

What is 'less favourable treatment'?

6.46 A trivial difference in treatment will not contravene the 1975 Act.[78]

---

[69] SI 2003/1660.
[70] SI 2003/1661.
[71] SI 2006/1031.
[72] SI 2002/3207.
[73] SI 2002/3236.
[74] SI 2003/722.
[75] The manner in which direct discrimination is proved is the subject of extensive discussion in paras **6.23–6.35** above.
[76] SDA 1975, s 2A. Note in particular s 2A(3) in relation to absences from work or vocational training (which will of course include training to be a teacher) 'due to . . . undergoing gender reassignment'.
[77] *Grant v South-West Trains Ltd* [1998] ICR 449; *Macdonald v Ministry of Defence* [2003] ICR 937. See now para **6.104** below concerning the Employment Equality (Sexual Orientation) Regulations 2003, SI 2003/1661.
[78] *Peake v Automotive Products Ltd* [1977] ICR 968 and *Ministry of Defence v Jeremiah* [1980] ICR 13, both of which were decisions of the Court of Appeal. In the latter, Lord Denning MR said (at 25) that the only ground for the decision in *Peake* which was sound was that the alleged discrimination in that case was 'de minimis'.

How should the comparison be made?

6.47 When considering whether there has been direct discrimination, it is necessary to make a comparison of the claimant's situation with that of another employee. The comparison must be such that the circumstances of the one case are the same as, or not materially different from, those in the other.[79] Sometimes it will be impossible to decide whether there was less favourable treatment without deciding why the treatment in question occurred (and therefore on what ground).[80] Thus it may on occasion be necessary to decide for what reason the employee was treated differently before deciding whether the employee was treated less favourably on the ground of her sex. This is particularly likely to be the case where the comparison is with a hypothetical comparator.

6.48 The case of *Stewart v Cleveland Guest (Engineering) Ltd*[81] illustrates the importance of making an appropriate comparison. The decision of the employment tribunal was surprising, and the reluctance of the EAT to overturn that decision incidentally also shows how difficult it is to appeal successfully on the ground that the employment tribunal's decision was perverse (that is, irrational in the public law sense). The employee in that case had claimed that her colleagues had created an environment hostile to women. The EAT dismissed the employee's appeal against the finding by the employment tribunal that the placing of nude pictures on the walls of the factory in which she worked as an inspector, was not discriminatory on the ground of sex. The employment tribunal's basis for this finding was that a hypothetical man 'might well find this sort of display as offensive as the [claimant] did'.[82]

Handling complaints appropriately

6.49 A second element of the employee's claim in *Stewart v Cleveland Guest (Engineering) Ltd* was that the employer had discriminated against her by failing to investigate her complaint about the nude pictures on the walls either properly or within a reasonable time, and by failing to deal with the hostility to which she was subjected by fellow employees when they knew about her complaint. The EAT rejected the appeal against this finding also, but nevertheless said this at the end of its judgment:

> 'A lesson to be learnt from this case is that it is crucial that complaints of the kind made by the employee are not treated as trivial. They should be taken up, investigated and dealt with in a sympathetic and sensible fashion. In most cases, if not all, it should be possible, by a combination of sensitivity and common sense, so to arrange matters that the reasonable wishes of all those concerned are accommodated. If they cannot be and the result is proceedings of this kind, it is for the tribunal, as the "industrial jury", to hear all the evidence and decide the

---

[79] SDA 1975, s 5(3).
[80] *Shamoon v Chief Constable of the Royal Ulster Constabulary* [2003] ICR 337, paras 7–12.
[81] [1996] ICR 535.
[82] Ibid, at 539.

case. This tribunal only has jurisdiction to determine an appeal against the decision of the tribunal if there is an error of law. If the error of law relied upon is the argument that the industrial tribunal reached a decision which no reasonable tribunal, on a proper appreciation of the facts and law, would have reached, an overwhelming case to that effect must be made out. That case has not been made out here.'

6.50 *Questionnaires.* An employee may serve a questionnaire under s 74 of the SDA 1975. A failure by an employer to reply to the questionnaire within the period of 8 weeks may justify the drawing by an employment tribunal of the inference that the employer committed an unlawful act.[83] An evasive or equivocal reply may lead to the drawing of the same inference.[84]

Discrimination on the ground of pregnancy

6.51 If an employer discriminates against a woman because she is pregnant, then that will amount to discrimination on the ground of her sex. This is now provided for expressly by s 3A of the SDA 1975,[85] but was before then the clear result of the case law. That case law serves to illustrate the manner in which the law protects a woman employee who is pregnant. One illustrative case is that of *O'Neill v Governors of St Thomas More Roman Catholic Voluntary Aided Upper School*.[86]

> *O'Neill v Governors of St Thomas More Roman Catholic Voluntary Aided Upper School*
>
> A teacher of religious education and personal relationships at a Roman Catholic school became pregnant as a result of a relationship with a Roman Catholic priest. She was not allowed to return to the school after the birth of her child. She consequently complained of unfair dismissal and unlawful discrimination on the ground of her sex. The school conceded that she had been constructively dismissed and that the dismissal was unfair. However, an industrial tribunal dismissed her claim of sex discrimination on the ground that she had not been dismissed because she was pregnant but because the pregnancy was by a Roman Catholic priest. This had become public knowledge, making her position as a teacher of religious education untenable. The teacher appealed against this ruling.
>
> *Decision of the Employment Appeal Tribunal*
>
> The EAT allowed her appeal. It decided, on the basis of the House of Lords case of *Webb v Emo Air Cargo (UK) Ltd (No 2)*,[87] that a dismissal on the ground of pregnancy was a dismissal on the ground of sex for the purposes of the SDA 1975. The EAT said that the question of whether the claimant's dismissal was on account of her pregnancy was not to be answered by having regard to the subjective motives of the school governors, but by asking whether, on an objective consideration of all the surrounding circumstances, the dismissal or other

---

[83] See SDA 1975, s 74(2) and (2A).
[84] Ibid.
[85] Section 3A was inserted by SI 2005/2467 as from 1 October 2005.
[86] [1997] ICR 33.
[87] [1995] ICR 1021.

treatment complained of was on the ground of pregnancy. Pregnancy need not be the only, or even the main ground, it said. The EAT decided that the factors in the circumstances surrounding the pregnancy relied on by the industrial tribunal as the reason for the claimant's dismissal were causally related to the fact that she was pregnant, and that the ground for her dismissal was her pregnancy. Accordingly, the EAT decided that by dismissing the claimant, the governing body of the school had unlawfully discriminated against her on the ground of her sex. The EAT stressed, though, that its decision did not mean that any dismissal of a woman who is pregnant will constitute discrimination on the ground of sex. Rather, only a dismissal where the pregnancy was a reason for the dismissal will constitute such discrimination.

6.52 *Berrisford v Woodard Schools (Midland Division) Ltd*[88] can be contrasted with *O'Neill v Governors of St Thomas More Roman Catholic Voluntary Aided Upper School.*

Berrisford v Woodard Schools (Midland Division) Ltd

An unmarried assistant matron at a Church of England girls' boarding school became pregnant. The assistant matron told the head teacher of the school that she was pregnant but that she did not intend to marry the father of the child. The head teacher told her she should either marry the father of the child, or leave her employment with the school. The employee did not wish to get married, so she was dismissed. She complained to an industrial tribunal that she had been discriminated against on the ground of her sex. The tribunal accepted the evidence of the school's governors that she could not continue to be employed at the school unmarried while becoming increasingly obviously pregnant, and that a male teacher known to have been engaging in extra-marital sex would have been dismissed. The tribunal therefore dismissed her complaint. The claimant appealed to the EAT.

Decision of the Employment Appeal Tribunal

The EAT dismissed her appeal. It decided that the reason for her dismissal was not the pregnancy itself, but the poor moral example which her conduct gave the school's pupils. The EAT also decided that there was evidence to support the industrial tribunal's finding that a male teacher who had engaged in extra-marital sexual activities would also have been dismissed. Accordingly, the employee had not been discriminated against on the ground of her sex.

6.53 It may be thought that this case would not have been decided in the same way after the decision of the European Court of Justice in *Webb v Emo Air Cargo (UK) Ltd*,[89] but the reasoning of the decision in *Berrisford* is difficult to criticise. A further case concerning a pregnant woman which is worth mentioning here is that of *Day v T Pickles Farms Ltd.*[90]

---

[88] [1991] ICR 564.
[89] [1994] ICR 770.
[90] [1999] IRLR 217.

Day v Pickles Farms Ltd

An employee, Mrs Day, was employed as a counter assistant in a sandwich shop. She became pregnant and found that the constant smell of food made her feel nauseous while at work. She consulted her doctor and he certified her as unfit for work. She left work and received statutory sick pay from her employer for a further five months. The employee made a complaint to an employment tribunal claiming, among other things, sex discrimination. Among other things, the employee claimed that the employer was in breach of its obligation under the Management of Health and Safety at Work Regulations 1992 (the 1992 Regulations) to carry out a risk assessment, taking into account the risk to the health and safety of a new or expectant mother or to that of her baby, and that if such an assessment had been carried out then she would have been suspended on full pay. Accordingly, she claimed that she had suffered a detriment contrary to the SDA 1975.

The employment tribunal rejected the complaint that the failure to carry out a risk assessment had caused the employee a detriment contrary to the SDA 1975, on the basis that:

(1) the employer was under no obligation to carry out a risk assessment in accordance with the 1992 Regulations until the employee was pregnant, and

(2) the employee had not given written notice of her pregnancy to her employer as required under the 1992 Regulations, with the result that the employer did not need to consider whether, for example, to suspend the employee on full pay.

The employee appealed against the decision.

Decision of the Employment Appeal Tribunal

The EAT allowed the appeal. It decided that the employment tribunal had misdirected itself (and therefore erred in law) in finding that the employee had not suffered a detriment contrary to the SDA 1975 by reason of the employer's having failed to carry out a risk assessment in accordance with the 1992 Regulations. The tribunal had erred in law in finding that the obligation to carry out a risk assessment in accordance with the regulations only applies when an employer has a pregnant employee. The employment of a woman of child-bearing age suffices to trigger the need for a risk assessment under the regulations. In the present case, therefore, the employer should have carried out a risk assessment at the start of the employee's employment, before she became pregnant. As it was not clear what a risk assessment would have disclosed, the case was remitted to the employment tribunal to decide whether the fact that there had been no assessment at that stage subjected the employee to a detriment.

The EAT decided that the employment tribunal had also erred in finding that there was no obligation on the employer to consider whether to alter the employee's working conditions or hours of work in accordance with the 1992 Regulations, or to suspend her with pay in accordance with those regulations, because she had failed to discharge the burden of proving that she had notified her employer in writing that she was pregnant. The employee had given her employer a series of doctor's sick notes which indicated that she was pregnant. That passed the burden to her employer to show that the certificates did not amount to an indication of pregnancy. On remission, therefore, the employment tribunal should also reconsider whether notification for the purposes of the 1992 Regulations had been given and, if so, whether there had been a failure to act under those regulations which had caused detriment to the employee contrary to the SDA 1975.

6.54 With *Day v Pickles Farms Ltd* can be contrasted the decision in *New Southern Railway v Quinn*.[91] The claimant in *Quinn*, who was a duty station manager, was required by her employer to work as a support clerk while she was pregnant. The employer had carried out a risk assessment when the employee became pregnant, and the assessment was that there were high risks to the employee's health if she continued to work in that role while she was pregnant, but that the risks could be reduced to an acceptable level if her working conditions and hours were changed. However, the employer subsequently, without carrying out a further risk assessment and without consulting the employee, decided that the employee should work as a support clerk while she was pregnant. The employer claimed that the reason for the requirement to work as a support clerk was the risk to the employee's health if she continued in the role of duty station manager. The employment tribunal concluded that the real reason for this requirement was the personal feelings of certain of the employer's managers to which the employer attached a health and safety label and that it had not been necessary to demote the employee or reduce her salary in order to avoid a risk to her health. Thus it concluded that the employee had been discriminated against on the ground of her sex. The EAT dismissed the employer's appeal against this conclusion.

6.55 It is necessary to note that the dismissal of an employee for a pregnancy-related reason will be discrimination on the ground of sex.[92] However, if a woman is treated detrimentally because of an illness which is caused by her pregnancy but the illness occurs or arises after the period of maternity leave has ended, then it is possible that such detrimental treatment will not be unlawfully discriminatory on the ground of sex. This is for the following reasons. Before the enactment of s 3A(3)(b) of the SDA 1975, the position was that whether such detrimental treatment was discriminatory depended on the circumstances and how a man with a comparable illness would have been treated.[93] Now, however, s 3A(3)(b) appears to preclude an argument of such a sort being advanced, even though the ECJ's case law would permit it to be advanced. Section 3A(3)(b) provides that:

> 'where a person's treatment of a woman is on grounds of illness suffered by the woman as a consequence of a pregnancy of hers, that treatment is to be taken to be on the ground of the pregnancy'.

---

[91] [2006] ICR 761.
[92] *Brown v Rentokil Ltd* [1998] ICR 790, ECJ; SDA 1975, s 3A(3)(b).
[93] See *Brown v Rentokil Ltd*.

Victimisation[94]

6.56 Discriminating against an employee on the ground that the employee has brought proceedings under the 1975 Act is deemed to be discrimination for the purposes of that Act.[95] The same is true of:

(1) giving evidence or information in connection with proceedings brought by any person against the discriminator or any other person under the SDA 1975, the EPA 1970, or several related enactments including ss 62–65 of the Pensions Act 1995;

(2) alleging that the discriminator or any other person has committed an act which (whether or not the allegation so states) would amount to a contravention of the SDA 1975 or give rise to a claim under the EPA Act 1970 or the related enactments;

(3) otherwise doing anything under or by reference to any of those statutory provisions; or

(4) intending to do any of the things referred to above.

However, any allegation which leads to any such treatment must, if false, have been made in good faith. Discrimination of the sorts described here is referred to in s 4 of the SDA 1975 as 'discrimination by way of victimisation'.

6.57 Section 20A of the SDA 1975 contains that Act's protection of former employees (or workers engaged personally to execute any work or labour) against victimisation. Section 20A(3) protects a former employee against discrimination in the form of 'subjecting her to a detriment where the discrimination arises out of and is closely connected to the' employment (using that word in a broad sense). Section 20A(4) protects a woman in relation to 'harassment where that treatment arises out of or is closely connected' to her former employment.

Indirect discrimination

Definition of 'indirect discrimination'

6.58 Indirect discrimination involves applying a 'provision, criterion or practice' which the employer 'applies or would apply equally to a man' but '(i) which puts or would put women at a particular disadvantage when compared with men, (ii) which puts her at that disadvantage, and (iii) which [the employer] cannot show to be a proportionate means of achieving a legitimate aim'.[96] This formulation was inserted into s 1 of the SDA 1975 with effect from

---

[94] The manner in which a claim of victimisation should be approached generally is discussed in paras **6.37–6.40** above.
[95] SDA 1975, s 4.
[96] SDA 1975, s 1(2)(b).

1 October 2005. Under s 1(1)(b) of the SDA 1975, which used to apply to discrimination in relation to employment and vocational training, and which still applies to discrimination other than in relation to employment or vocational training, it was necessary to show that there was a 'requirement or condition' which was not 'justifiable irrespective of the sex of the person to whom it [was] applied' which was to the detriment of the woman because she could not comply with it, rather than a 'provision, criterion or practice' which the employer 'cannot show to be a proportionate means of achieving a legitimate aim' and which puts a woman 'at a particular disadvantage when compared with men'. The new wording is not very different from the former in effect, and some of the case law concerning the old wording is likely still to be relevant.

6.59 *What is a 'provision, criterion or practice'?* One case concerning the old wording which is likely still to be relevant, and which illustrates the difficulties which can arise in deciding whether or not a 'provision, criterion or practice' has been applied, is that of *Briggs v North Eastern Education and Library Board*.[97]

Briggs v North Eastern Education and Library Board

Mrs Briggs was an assistant science teacher. In 1982 she was promoted from a scale 1 post to a scale 2 post, conditional upon her written agreement to carry out additional duties, which included 'to assist with extra-curricular school games'. She had previously been coaching badminton on a voluntary basis in the afternoon after school hours, and it was understood by both parties that this coaching would now be a contractual obligation.

Mrs Briggs and her husband adopted a baby daughter in February 1984. When Mrs Briggs returned from leave, she discontinued coaching badminton after school hours and began to coach at lunchtime, stating that she intended to do this until her daughter reached school age. This was regarded by the head teacher of the school as unsatisfactory, and Mrs Briggs was asked to re-introduce after-school badminton coaching one day a week for a reasonable length of time. In response, she agreed to coach on one day a week after school hours.

A disciplinary meeting was held by the Board. Mrs Briggs confirmed that because of the adoption of her daughter, she could not make a regular after-school commitment for the future. As a result, the disciplinary authority informed Mrs Briggs that her post was to revert to scale 1.

Mrs Briggs claimed that she had been unlawfully discriminated against on the grounds of sex and marital status. A Northern Ireland industrial tribunal, by a majority decision, upheld her complaint and concluded that she had established a prima facie case of indirect discrimination by showing that a requirement – that she should hold a badminton practice after school – had been applied to her, that the requirement was such that the proportion of women who could comply with it was considerably smaller than the proportion of men who could comply with it, and that she had suffered a detriment because she could not comply with the requirement. The tribunal went on to find that the employers had not shown that the requirement was 'justifiable'.

---

[97] [1990] IRLR 181.

The employer appealed to the Northern Ireland Court of Appeal. For the purpose of the appeal, the case was considered as one of sex discrimination rather than as one of discrimination on the ground of marital status.

Decision of the Northern Ireland Court of Appeal

The Northern Ireland Court of Appeal decided that the industrial tribunal had not erred in finding that the employer was 'applying' a 'requirement or condition' to Mrs Briggs within the meaning of art 3(1)(b) of the Sex Discrimination (Northern Ireland) Order (the equivalent of s 1(1)(b) of the 1975 Act) by requiring her to supervise badminton after the end of afternoon classes. The mere fact that the nature of a job requires full-time attendance does not prevent there being a 'requirement' within the meaning of art 3(1)(b) or the identical wording of s 1(1)(b) of the 1975 Act, said the court. Nor does the fact that the employer merely requires the employee to carry out the job she is employed to do mean that the employer does not 'apply' a requirement to her.

6.60 *Putting at a disadvantage.* In *R v Secretary of State for Employment, ex parte Seymour-Smith and Perez*,[98] in a ruling relating to the application of the original Art 119 of the Treaty of Rome,[99] the ECJ stated that a difference between the number of women who could comply with the requirement which was in issue in that case and the number of men who could do so, of 8.5%, did 'not appear, on the face of it, to show that a considerably smaller percentage of women than men is able to fulfil the requirement imposed by the disputed rule'. The ECJ stated also that the question whether in the circumstances there was such a considerably smaller percentage was to be determined by the national court on the facts. Accordingly, the ECJ did not come to a positive ruling. However, the ECJ also said that 'if the statistical evidence revealed a lesser but persistent and relatively constant disparity over a long period between men and women who satisfy the [relevant] requirement', then there might also be indirect discrimination for the purposes of Art 119.[100] Since national laws have to be interpreted as far as possible in such a manner as to give effect to Community law,[101] the same approach should be adopted in applying s 1(2)(b) of the SDA 1975.

6.61 *What would constitute a 'proportionate means of achieving a legitimate aim'?* The question whether an employer had, in imposing a requirement or condition on an employee which was on its face discriminatory, contravened s 1(1)(b) of the SDA 1975, often turned on whether the imposition was justified. Similarly, the question whether a 'provision, criterion or practice' is a 'proportionate means of achieving a legitimate aim' within the meaning of s 1(2)(b) of the SDA 1975 will often be determinative of a claim of indirect sex discrimination in employment. In *Hampson v Department of Education and Science*,[102] Balcombe LJ said that in order for a requirement or condition to be

---

[98] [1999] ICR 447, 491, paras 63–64.
[99] Now renumbered as Art 141.
[100] [1999] ICR 447, 490, para 61.
[101] See para **6.17** above.
[102] [1989] ICR 179, approved in this regard by the House of Lords in *Webb v Emo Air Cargo (UK) Ltd* [1993] ICR 175, 182–183.

'justifiable', there had to be 'an objective balance between the discriminatory effect of the condition and the reasonable needs of the party who applies the condition'. It is of interest that in *Briggs v North Eastern Education and Library Board*,[103] the Northern Ireland Court of Appeal decided that the employer was justified in reducing the employee's pay in the manner described above. As the court said:[104]

> 'we consider, applying the test stated by the Court of Appeal in *Hampson*'s case, that the reasonable needs of the [employer] that badminton practice should be conducted in the interest of the school and for the benefit of the girls clearly necessitated that the badminton practice should not be carried out in the lunch break but should be carried out in the afternoon after school, and that the discriminatory effect of the requirement applied to the [employee] was clearly objectively justified by those needs. We further consider that in deciding to the contrary the majority of the Tribunal came to a decision to which no reasonable tribunal, properly directing themselves as to the law, could have come.'

6.62 It is likely that the outcome in *Briggs* would have been the same if the current wording had been applied.

Discrimination on the ground of marital status or civil partnership

6.63 As a result of s 3 of the SDA 1975, an employer discriminates for the purposes of the SDA 1975 if, on the ground that a person is married or is a civil partner within the meaning of the Civil Partnership Act 2004, he does anything which amounts to direct or indirect discrimination against that person.[105] It is of note that discrimination against a person on the ground that the person is *not* married or is *not* a civil partner is not discrimination within the meaning of this section. However, if a person of either sex is treated disadvantageously because the person is not married and a person of the other sex would not have been treated in the same way, there may well be discrimination on the ground of sex.

6.64 There are few reported cases concerning the application of s 3 of the SDA 1975, but one which is of note is *Hurley v Mustoe*.[106] There, an employer's policy not to employ women with young children was decided by the EAT to have been indirectly discriminatory towards married women, and therefore discrimination on the ground of marital status.

The application of the definition of discrimination to employment

6.65 It is unlawful for an employer to discriminate within the meaning of the SDA 1975 against a woman in the arrangements made by him for the purpose

---

[103] [1990] IRLR 181, for the facts of which, see para **6.59** above.
[104] Ibid, para 51.
[105] See SDA 1975, s 3, as substituted by the Civil Partnerships Act 2004, with effect from 5 December 2005, read with the definition of 'civil partnership' in Sch 1 to the Interpretation Act 1978.
[106] [1981] ICR 490.

of determining who should be offered employment.[107] It is also unlawful for an employer to discriminate by refusing or deliberately omitting to offer employment, or in relation to the terms on which the employment is offered.[108] It is necessary to note that once a person's employment has commenced, the possibility of making a claim of discrimination in relation to the terms of the employment themselves is governed only by the terms of the EPA 1970[109] and European Community law.[110]

6.66 It is also unlawful to discriminate against a person within the meaning of the SDA 1975 by restricting access to opportunities for promotion, transfer or training or any other benefits, facilities or services or by dismissing an employee, or by 'subjecting her to any other detriment'.[111] In *Ministry of Defence v Jeremiah*,[112] Brandon LJ stated that he regarded this as meaning no more than 'putting [her] under a disadvantage'. In *Shamoon v Chief Constable of the Royal Ulster Constabulary*,[113] the test was said by Lord Hope to be whether or not the treatment was 'of such a kind that a reasonable worker would or might take the view that in all the circumstances it was to his detriment', and that an unjustified sense of grievance cannot amount to a detriment. However, Lord Hope went on to say, 'it is not necessary to demonstrate some physical or economic consequence'.[114]

Harassment including sexual harassment

6.67 Harassment, including sexual harassment, within the meaning of s 4A of the SDA 1975 of an employee, or of an applicant for employment, is unlawful by virtue of s 6(2A) of the SDA 1975. Harassment includes engaging in unwanted conduct that has the purpose or effect of violating a woman's dignity or of creating an intimidating, hostile, degrading, humiliating or offensive environment for her.[115] It also includes engaging in 'any form of unwanted verbal, non-verbal or physical conduct of a sexual nature that has the purpose or effect' of doing the same things.[116] It is also harassment for the purposes of the SDA 1975 to treat a woman less favourably 'on the ground of her rejection of or submission to unwanted conduct' of either of those kinds.[117]

6.68 Conduct may be regarded as having the effect of violating a woman's dignity or of creating an intimidating, hostile, degrading, humiliating or

---

[107] SDA 1975, s 6(1).
[108] Ibid.
[109] See ibid, s 8.
[110] See paras **6.6** and **6.12–6.18** above concerning Community law.
[111] SDA 1975, s 6(2).
[112] [1980] ICR 13, 26.
[113] [2003] ICR 337, para 35.
[114] Ibid.
[115] SDA 1975, s 4A(1)(a).
[116] Ibid, s 4A(1)(b).
[117] Ibid, s 4A(1)(c).

offensive environment for her 'only if, having regard to all the circumstances, including in particular the perception of the woman, it should reasonably be considered as having that effect'.[118]

6.69 Men are protected against harassment including sexual harassment in the same way as are women.[119]

6.70 Harassment of a person on the ground that that person 'intends to undergo, is undergoing or has undergone gender reassignment' is protected in the same way as harassment on the ground of sex.[120]

Agency workers and certain self-employed workers

6.71 The employers of staff in schools should also be aware that discrimination and sexual harassment is also unlawful in relation to contract workers, for example those supplied by an agency providing supply teachers.[121] It is also unlawful to discriminate against or sexually harass apprentices and people who are employed under contracts 'personally to execute any work or labour'.[122]

Genuine occupational qualifications

6.72 There are certain exceptions to the obligation not to discriminate on the ground of sex. The main exception is that sex is a genuine occupational qualification.[123] One example of a genuine occupational qualification is where a person is sought to model clothes for one sex only. Another example is where one sex is needed for authenticity in entertainment. It is difficult to see circumstances in schools in which a person's sex could properly be said to be a genuine occupational qualification.

Liability of employer for employees and agents; liability of secondary parties

6.73 An employer is liable for the acts of its employees which contravene the SDA 1975 and which are carried out in the course of the employees' employment.[124] That is so whether or not any such act was done with the employer's knowledge or approval.[125] However, if the employer satisfies an employment tribunal that he took such steps as were reasonably practicable to prevent the employee from doing that act, then this will act as a defence to the claim.[126] If an employer has an adequate system for the supervision of staff, is

---

[118] Ibid, s 4A(2).
[119] See ibid, s 4A(5) and (6).
[120] See ibid, s 4A(3), (4) and (6).
[121] Ibid, s 9.
[122] See the definition of 'employment' in ibid, s 82(1).
[123] Ibid, ss 7, 7A, 7B and 9(3).
[124] SDA 1975, s 41(1).
[125] Ibid.
[126] Ibid, s 41(3).

unaware of a particular discriminatory act or acts, and has published an equal opportunities policy, this may be sufficient.[127] However, this will not absolve an employee from responsibility for his own acts. Even where an employer is not vicariously liable for a relevant act, the relevant employee will be personally liable.[128]

6.74 Similarly, anything done by a person as agent for another person with the authority (whether express or implied, and whether given before or after the act in question) of that other person, is treated as done also by that other person.[129] Furthermore, the agent is liable in the same manner as the principal.[130]

6.75 Finally, as a result of s 42(1) of the SDA 1975, a person who knowingly aids another person to do an act which is contrary to the SDA 1975 is to be treated as himself doing an act of the same sort. The importance of proving knowledge of the relevant sort on the part of the alleged aider needs to be stressed here.[131]

6.76 If an employer or other person who is alleged to have committed the discrimination could have acted in a number of ways in response to that which was done by the alleged aider, then there will have been no aiding within the meaning of s 42.[132] Further, 'It is one thing to take advantage of a failure, another altogether to aid it.'[133] As Lord Bingham said in *Anyanwu v South Bank Student Union*:[134]

> 'The expression "aids" in s.33(1) [of the RRA 1976, which is in the same terms as s 42(1) of the SDA 1975] is a familiar word in everyday use and it bears no technical or special meaning in this context. A person aids another if he helps or assists him. He does so whether his help is substantial and productive or whether it is not, provided the help is not so insignificant as to be negligible. While any gloss on the clear statutory language is better avoided, the subsection points towards a relationship of cooperation or collaboration; it does not matter who instigates or initiates the relationship. It is plain that, depending on the facts, a party who aids another to do an unlawful act may also procure or induce that other to do it. But the expressions "procure" and "induce" are found in sections 30 and 31, not section 33, and are differently enforced; they mean something different from "aids" and there is no warrant to interpreting "aids" as comprising these other expressions. By section 12 of the Race Relations Act 1968, the predecessor of the 1976 Act, those who deliberately aided, induced or incited another person to do an act made unlawful by Part I of that Act were to be treated as themselves doing that act, but they could not be subjected to proceedings at the direct suit of the

---

[127] See for example *Balgobin v London Borough of Tower Hamlets* [1987] ICR 829.
[128] SDA 1975, s 42(2). This was confirmed by the EAT in *AM v (1) WC and (2) SPV* [1999] IRLR 410.
[129] SDA 1975, s 41(2).
[130] Ibid, s 42(2).
[131] See *Sinclair Roche & Temperley v Heard* [2004] IRLR 763, paras 52–54.
[132] See *Hallam v Avery* [2001] ICR 408.
[133] *Shepherd v North Yorkshire County Council* [2006] IRLR 190, para 37.
[134] [2001] ICR 391, para 5.

injured party and the 1976 Act adopted a different legislative approach. It is plain that a party who causes another to do an unlawful act does not necessarily aid him to do it. A farmer who starves his sheepdog, with the result that the ravening dog savages a new-born lamb, may reasonably be said to have caused the death of the lamb, but he could not be said to have aided the dog to kill the lamb.'

6.77 Merely creating an environment in which discrimination can occur will not in itself amount to aiding within the meaning of s 42(1) of the SDA 1975.[135] However, fostering and encouraging a discriminatory culture which is targeted at the claimant will do so.[136]

Time limit for claiming compensation for discrimination contrary to the Sex Discrimination Act 1975

6.78 There is a three-month time limit for making a claim of discrimination on the ground of sex.[137] This may be extended to six months when the statutory grievance procedure in Sch 2 to the Employment Act 2002 is followed.[138] However, in any event the basic three-month time limit can be extended (and thus the period of six months can be extended to the same extent[139]). The test for an employment tribunal to apply in deciding whether the basic three-month time limit should be extended, is whether it is just and equitable in all the circumstances to do so.[140] This is a wider and more generous test as far as the employee is concerned than that which applies in relation to unfair dismissal claims. Thus, erroneous legal advice given to a claimant by an appropriately qualified person may in this context (but almost certainly not in relation to a claim of unfair dismissal) mean that the time limit can be extended.[141]

6.79 However, a claim which appears to be out of time may not in fact be so. There are three significant rules (set out in s 76(6) of the SDA 1975) for determining whether a claim is in time. They are as follows:

(1) 'any act extending over a period shall be treated as done at the end of that period';

(2) a deliberate omission is to be 'treated as done when the person in question decided upon it' ('and in the absence of evidence establishing the contrary a person shall be taken for the purposes of [s 76] to decide upon an omission when he does an act inconsistent with doing the omitted act or,

---

[135] *Miles v Gilbank* [2006] ICR 1297.
[136] Ibid.
[137] See SDA 1975, s 76. Time starts to run on the day on which 'the act complained of was done'. Thus the primary time limit for making a claim that a discriminatory act was done for example on 10 May will expire on 9 August.
[138] See para **2.36** above.
[139] See *BUPA Care Homes (BNH) Ltd v Cann* [2006] ICR 643.
[140] SDA 1975, s 76(5).
[141] See *Hawkins v Ball* [1996] IRLR 258.

if he has done no such inconsistent act, when the period expires within which he might reasonably have been expected to do the omitted act if it was to be done'); and

(3) 'where the inclusion of any term in a contract renders the making of the contract an unlawful act that act shall be treated as extending throughout the duration of the contract'.

6.80 The concept of an act extending over a period of time is not an easy one to apply. In *Commissioner of Police of the Metropolis v Hendricks*,[142] the Court of Appeal gave some useful guidance in that regard. There, the employer sought to strike out the claim on the basis that it could not succeed on the facts. The court ruled that she could pursue her claim. Mummery LJ made the following illuminating statement.

> '[The claimant] is, in my view, entitled to pursue her claim beyond this preliminary stage on the basis that the burden is on her to prove, either by direct evidence or by inference from primary facts, that the numerous alleged incidents of discrimination are linked one to another and that they are evidence of a continuing discriminatory state of affairs covered by the concept of "an act extending over a period". I regard this as a legally more precise way of characterising her case than the use of expressions such as "institutionalised racism", "a prevailing way of life", a "generalised policy of discrimination", or "climate" or "culture" of unlawful discrimination.'[143]

6.81 The case of *Amies v Inner London Education Authority*[144] provides a useful illustration of the distinction between an act which has continuing consequences and a continuing act.

Amies v Inner London Education Authority

In 1975 a female art teacher who was a deputy head of department applied for the job of head of that department. However, on 13 October 1975, a man was appointed instead. On 29 December 1975, the relevant provisions of the SDA 1975 came into force and on 1 January 1976, the teacher made a complaint to an industrial tribunal under that Act. She claimed that by appointing a man to the post of head of department, her employer had discriminated against her by reason of her sex contrary to ss 1(1)(a) and 6 of the Act. The only basis upon which in the circumstances she could bring her claim under the SDA 1975 was that the alleged discrimination constituted a continuing act extending over a period within the meaning of s 76(6) of the Act. The industrial tribunal decided that the alleged discrimination was not a continuing act. The claimant appealed to the EAT.

---

[142] [2003] ICR 530.
[143] Ibid, para 48.
[144] [1977] ICR 308.

Decision of the Employment Appeal Tribunal

The EAT dismissed the appeal. It decided that the failure to appoint the claimant to the position of head of department, and the appointment of a male teacher instead, was an act which had continuing consequences rather than a continuing act of discrimination.

6.82 The case of *Cast v Croydon College*[145] provides an interesting illustration of the manner in which an applicant to an employment tribunal may be able to argue that a claim which is on its face outside the three-month time limit, is in fact in time.

Cast v Croydon College

A woman worked full-time as the manager of a further education college's information centre. The college had a written policy of receptiveness to proposals for job sharing at all levels and this made no special provision for, or exception of, the employee's post. In early 1992, the employee became pregnant and in March 1992 she requested permission to work part-time and to share her job with another employee after her return from maternity leave. This request was refused. In May 1992 the employee wrote to the college, confirming that she intended to return to her employment after her maternity leave. On 1 March 1993 the employee returned to work from maternity leave, contractually complying with her full-time working commitments by using accrued leave of 33 days to enable her to work between one and two days a week. In March and May 1993 she again asked for permission to share her job with someone else, and on each occasion this was refused. She followed up those requests by a letter to a senior manager asking for the reasons for that decision and drawing his attention to the statement of policy in the college's corporate development plan of its objective 'to introduce job-sharing arrangements for posts at all levels throughout the college'.

The response of her manager was that it was essential for the holder of the post of information centre manager to work full time so as properly to co-ordinate the work of the centre's team of part-time employees.

The employee immediately took a week's sick leave and then returned to her pattern of working part time, still taking advantage of her accrued leave. On 7 June 1993 the employee wrote to her line manager giving one month's notice of her intention to leave because of his refusal to allow her to work part time and to share her job. She explained that she had taken the date of 6 July 1993 as the date of termination of her employment because up until that time she could continue to work part-time by making use of her accrued leave. On 13 August 1993, the employee presented a claim to an industrial tribunal complaining of unfair constructive dismissal and 'dismissal by sexual discrimination' on 6 July 1993.

The industrial tribunal decided that although the employer had made a fresh decision in relation to each of the claimant's requests, each refusal merely confirmed the original decision so that there was a single alleged discriminatory act in March 1992. Accordingly, the tribunal decided that the complaint was made outside the three-month time limit in s 76. The tribunal also decided that it was neither just nor equitable to extend that time limit. The claimant appealed to the EAT, but it dismissed her appeal. She appealed again to the Court of Appeal.

---

[145] [1998] ICR 500.

Decision of the Court of Appeal

The Court of Appeal allowed the appeal. The court stated that a decision in response to the repetition of an earlier request might constitute an act of discrimination for the purposes of ss 63(1) and 76(1) of the 1975 Act,[146] whether or not it was made on the same facts as before, if it resulted from a further consideration of the matter and was not merely a reference back to an earlier decision. Accordingly, the court ruled that the industrial tribunal, having found that the employer had reconsidered and looked at the matter again in 1993, had erred in failing to consider the implications of that finding for the purpose of the running of time under s 76. The court decided that, for the purposes of s 76(1), the most recent 'act complained of' under s 63 was the decision given on 10 May 1993, just over three months before the presentation of the complaint. However, in any event, the court said that the employee's complaint was of several decisions by her employer which indicated the existence of a discriminatory policy in relation to her post and the application of that policy to her, and that that constituted 'an act extending over a period' within the meaning of s 76(6). As a result, in the circumstances that act had to be treated as done at the end of her employment, and the complaint was presented in time.

Compensation

6.83 There is no upper limit on the amount of the compensation which may be awarded by an employment tribunal for discrimination on the ground of sex. Accordingly, an amount representing the true loss suffered by a complainant may be awarded by an employment tribunal. However, a successful claimant's losses may not be fully met by an award of compensation made by an employment tribunal in certain circumstances. In any event, the common law rules relating to mitigation of loss apply to an award of compensation for sex discrimination. Accordingly, a person who has been discriminated against will not receive compensation for the full amount of the loss if that person has failed to make reasonable efforts to mitigate the loss.

6.84 Compensation may be awarded for injury to feelings.[147] Such awards may range from a few hundred pounds to as much as £25,000 (or, in some circumstances, more), depending on the severity of the injury.[148]

6.85 However, where an employee is dismissed in part as a result of discrimination on the ground of her sex, it is not appropriate for an employment tribunal simply to award her compensation for all the losses which she has suffered as a result of the dismissal. Rather, it is necessary to decide to what extent the discrimination caused or contributed to her dismissal. This can

---

[146] SDA 1975, s 63 confers jurisdiction on employment tribunals to hear claims of discrimination contrary to s 6.
[147] SDA 1975, s 66(4).
[148] See *Vento v Chief Constable of the West Yorkshire Police* [2003] ICR 318 for the three broad 'bands' within which awards for injury to feelings should fall. These were stated to be £500–£5,000, £5,000–£15,000 and £15,000–£25,000. In *Miles v Gilbank* [2006] ICR 1297 the Court of Appeal declined to overturn an award of £25,000 for discrimination which was recognised by the court to have been bad, but not the worst imaginable.

be seen from the case of *Abbey National plc v Formoso*.[149] There, an employment tribunal decided that an employee who was dismissed for misconduct following a disciplinary hearing, which she was incapable of attending by reason of a pregnancy-related condition, had been discriminated against on the ground of her sex. The employment tribunal then awarded her compensation for all the losses flowing from the dismissal. The employer appealed to the EAT against both rulings and the appeal was dismissed regarding the ruling that the employee had been discriminated against on the ground of her sex, but allowed in relation to the award of compensation. The EAT decided that when determining what loss had been suffered by the employee, the employment tribunal should have considered the likelihood that the employee would have been retained in her employment if the discrimination had not occurred, and then awarded compensation by multiplying the full loss by that likelihood (expressed as a percentage). This assessment was to be made by the employment tribunal's considering whether the employee would have been dismissed if she had not been pregnant and had attended the disciplinary hearing.

Right to request flexible working

6.86 There are three sets of statutory provisions which are related to discrimination on the ground of sex in that claims concerning the subject-matter of the three sets of provisions were first made as claims of discrimination on the ground of sex. The first of these is the set of provisions concerning the right to request the adoption of flexible working requirements. The other two are the regulations relating to part-time workers and fixed-term workers, which are considered in the sections of this chapter immediately following this one.

6.87 The right to request 'flexible working' arises under ss 80F and 80G of the ERA 1996, read together with the Flexible Working (Procedural Requirements) Regulations 2002[150] and the Flexible Working (Eligibility, Complaints and Remedies) Regulations 2002.[151] Those provisions give employees no right to work flexibly. Rather, they give them the right to ask to work different hours, or to work some (or more) hours at home. An employee can ask to work differently in this way only if:

(1) the employee has more than 26 weeks' continuous employment with the employer, and

(2) the employee's purpose in asking to work differently is to enable him to care for another person in certain circumstances.[152]

---

[149] [1999] IRLR 222.
[150] SI 2002/3207.
[151] SI 2002/3236.
[152] See ERA 1996, s 80F(1) and reg 3 of the Flexible Working (Eligibility, Complaints and Remedies) Regulations 2002, SI 2002/3236.

The persons for whose care an employee can validly ask to change his contractual terms are either:

(a) a child where the employee:
 (i) is, at the time of the application, the 'mother, father, adopter, guardian, special guardian or foster parent' of the child, or
 (ii) is married to the 'civil partner or the partner of the child's mother, father, adopter, guardian, special guardian or foster parent',
 and (in both cases) the employee has or expects to have responsibility for the upbringing of the child, or

(b) an adult where the employee is or expects to be caring for a person in need of care who is either:
 (i) married to the partner or civil partner of the employee,
 (ii) a relative of the employee, or
 (iii) living at the same address as the employee.[153]

In the case of an application relating to the care of a child, the application must be made before the day on which the child reaches the age of 6 or, if disabled, 18.[154]

6.88 An employee whose contractual hours are changed in response to a request to work 'flexibly' has no right to change them back without his employer's agreement once the circumstances which gave rise to the request have ceased to exist. This is because the change takes the form of a contractual variation.

6.89 An initial meeting and if necessary an appeal hearing are required by the Flexible Working (Procedural Requirements) Regulations 2002.[155] The employer must allow the employee to be accompanied at the meeting by 'a single companion' who 'is a worker employed by the same employer as the employee', and who may address the meeting and confer with the employee during the meeting, but who may not answer questions on behalf of the employee.[156] A failure to permit the employee to be so accompanied may be made the subject of a complaint to an employment tribunal, and the tribunal may, if it finds the complaint well-founded, award the complainant compensation of no more than two weeks' pay, limited by reference to s 227 of the ERA 1996.[157]

6.90 The employer must 'give notice' to the employee of his decision after both the initial meeting and (if appropriate) the appeal meeting, and must do so within 14 days of the meeting.[158] If the employer refuses the request for a

---

[153] ERA 1996, s 80F(1) and regs 3 and 3B of SI 2002/3236.
[154] Ibid, reg 3A.
[155] See SI 2002/3207, regs 3, 6 and 8.
[156] See ibid, reg 14.
[157] See ibid, reg 15. The limit at the time of writing was £310 per week.
[158] See ibid, regs 4 and 9.

contract variation, then the employer must state the grounds for the decision and give 'a sufficient explanation as to why those grounds apply' to the request.[159] A failure to hold an initial or appeal meeting with the employee, or to notify the employee of the employer's decision appropriately within 14 days may lead to an award of a maximum of eight weeks' pay (capped at £310 per week currently) in favour of the employee.[160]

Discrimination against part-time workers

6.91 Part-time workers are protected against less favourable treatment as compared with comparable full-time workers (1) as regards the terms of their contracts of employment or (2) as a result of being subjected to 'any other detriment by any act, or deliberate failure to act,' by their employers on the ground of their part-time status, unless the less favourable treatment is 'justified on objective grounds'. This is the result of the Part-time Workers (Prevention of Less Favourable Treatment) Regulations 2000.[161] A worker for this purpose is either an employee or an 'individual' who works or at the material time worked under any contract other than a contract of employment:

> 'whether express or implied and (if it is express) whether oral or in writing, whereby the individual undertakes to do or perform personally any work or services for another party to the contract whose status is not by virtue of the contract that of a client or customer of any profession or business undertaking carried on by the individual'.[162]

Regulation 2 defines the terms 'full-time worker', 'part-time worker' and 'comparable full-time worker' in uncontroversial terms. Part-time and full-time workers are defined largely by reference to the manner in which workers are, 'having regard to the custom and practice of the employer in relation to workers employed by the worker's employer under the same type of contract', identified as part-time or full-time, as the case may be.

6.92 In deciding whether a part-time worker has been treated less favourably than a comparable full-time worker, a principle called the 'pro rata principle' must be applied 'unless it is inappropriate'.[163] That principle 'means that where a comparable full-time worker receives or is entitled to receive pay or any other benefit, a part-time worker is to receive or be entitled to receive not less than the proportion of that pay or other benefit that the number of his weekly hours bears to the number of weekly hours of the comparable full-time worker'.[164] It is of interest that in *McMenemy v Capita Business Services Ltd*,[165] the EAT decided on the facts of that case that a part-time employee at a call-centre which was open seven days a week who did not work on Mondays and who

---

[159] See SI 2002/3207, regs 5(b)(ii) and 10(b)(ii).
[160] See ERA 1996, ss 80I and 227(1)(za) and SI 2002/3236, regs 6 and 7.
[161] SI 2000/1551; see reg 5(1) and (2) for the prohibition.
[162] See ibid, reg 1.
[163] Ibid, reg 5(3).
[164] See SI 2000/1551, reg 1(2).
[165] [2006] IRLR 761.

therefore was entitled to fewer bank holidays pro rata than other employees, was not thereby discriminated against as a part-time worker. The fact that his line manager worked full-time but for the period when he worked Tuesday to Saturday did not receive time off in lieu was evidentially important.

6.93 A part-time worker who is paid at a lower rate for overtime worked by him in a period than a comparable full-time worker is or would be paid for overtime worked by him in the same period is not, for that reason, to be regarded as having been treated less favourably than the full-time worker. Only if the part-time worker works more than the full-time worker's required normal hours (thus disregarding absences from work and overtime) will there be less favourable treatment of the part-time worker in this regard.[166]

6.94 A part-time worker may ask his employer in writing for a written statement of the reasons for treatment which the worker believes may constitute discrimination on the ground of his part-time status. The employer must then give the employee such a statement within 21 days of the request. If in those circumstances the employer fails to provide such a statement and it appears to an employment tribunal that the failure was deliberate and without a reasonable excuse, then the tribunal may 'draw any inference which it considers just and equitable to draw, including an inference that the employer has infringed the right in question'.[167] The tribunal may draw the same inference if the employer provides a written statement and it is 'evasive or equivocal'.[168]

6.95 So far as relevant, the Part-time Workers (Prevention of Less Favourable Treatment) Regulations 2000 contain, or inserted in other employment legislation, protections which are parallel to those in the SDA 1975.[169]

Discrimination against fixed-term workers

6.96 Persons who are employed under fixed-term contracts are protected against less favourable treatment of them in relation to the terms of their contracts and otherwise by their employers as compared with 'comparable permanent' employees unless the less favourable treatment is 'justified on objective grounds'. This is the effect of the Fixed-term Employees (Prevention of Less Favourable Treatment) Regulations 2002.[170] It is to be noted that only employees are protected by those regulations. As with discrimination in relation to part-time workers, the pro rata principle applies 'unless it is inappropriate'.[171] In this context, the pro-rata principle 'means that where a comparable permanent employee receives or is entitled to pay or any other

---

[166] SI 2000/1551, reg 5(4).
[167] See ibid, reg 6.
[168] Ibid.
[169] See for example reg 7 concerning victimisation and unfair dismissal, reg 11 concerning the liability of employers and principals, and reg 8 concerning complaints to employment tribunals.
[170] SI 2002/2034. See regs 3 and 4 for the prohibition.
[171] See ibid, reg 3(5).

benefit, a fixed-term employee is to receive or be entitled to such proportion of that pay or other benefit as is reasonable in the circumstances having regard to the length of his contract of employment and to the terms on which the pay or other benefit is offered'.[172]

6.97 A 'comparable permanent employee' for these purposes must currently be 'engaged in the same or broadly similar work having regard, where relevant, to whether they have a similar level of qualification and skills'.[173] There is objective justification for the purposes of the Fixed-term Employees (Prevention of Less Favourable Treatment) Regulations 2002 concerning a particular contract term 'if the terms of the fixed-term employee's contract of employment, taken as a whole, are at least as favourable as the terms of the comparable permanent employee's contract of employment'.[174]

6.98 Where there are successive fixed-term contracts for a period of four or more years, the employee may need to be regarded as a permanent employee for the purposes of the Fixed-term Employees (Prevention of Less Favourable Treatment) Regulations 2002.[175] Only if there is objective justification for the employee remaining a fixed-term employee will the employee not then become a permanent employee.

6.99 In other respects, the Fixed-term Employees (Prevention of Less Favourable Treatment) Regulations 2002 are similar to the Part-time Workers (Prevention of Less Favourable Treatment) Regulations 2000.

Racial discrimination

6.100 There is no material difference between the main operative provisions of the RRA 1976 and those of the SDA 1975, except, of course, that there is no equivalent of the provisions concerning discrimination on the ground of marital status or civil partnership.

6.101 Mention nevertheless needs to be made here of several matters. Direct discrimination is discrimination 'on racial grounds'. The term 'racial grounds' is defined by s 3 of the RRA 1976 to mean 'any of the following grounds, namely colour, race, nationality or ethnic or national origins'. Further, indirect discrimination is defined for employment by s 1(1A) of the RRA 1976, and concerns the application to a person of a provision, criterion or practice 'to persons not of the same race or ethnic or national origins' as that person.

---

[172] See SI 2002/2034, reg 1(2).
[173] See ibid, reg 2.
[174] Ibid, reg 4(1).
[175] See ibid, regs 8 and 9.

Discrimination on grounds of religion or belief

6.102 Closely allied to, but quite distinct from, the RRA 1976, are the Employment Equality (Religion or Belief) Regulations 2003.[176] Those regulations mirror the provisions of the RRA 1976, but apply to less favourable treatment 'on grounds of religion or belief' and to indirect discrimination against persons of a particular religion or belief. Here it is necessary to note that for the purposes of those regulations, 'religion or belief' means 'any religion, religious belief, or similar philosophical belief'.[177]

6.103 The Employment Equality (Religion or Belief) Regulations 2003 do not affect the operation of ss 58–60 and 124A of the SSFA 1998.[178] One of the first reported cases concerning the application of the regulations co-incidentally involved a school. In *Azmi v Kirklees Metropolitan Borough Council*,[179] the EAT decided that an employer's decision to suspend a teaching assistant for refusing to obey an instruction not to wear her veil when in class with pupils and assisting a male teacher, was not direct discrimination on grounds of religion or belief. The EAT also held that although it was indirectly discriminatory on such grounds, it was not unlawful since it was a proportionate means of achieving a legitimate aim.

Discrimination on the ground of sexual orientation

6.104 Discrimination on the ground of sexual orientation is now unlawful by virtue of the Employment Equality (Sexual Orientation) Regulations 2003.[180] Their operative provisions are in almost precisely the same terms as those of the Employment Equality (Religion or Belief) Regulations 2003. They apply to discrimination against a person on the ground of his or her sexual orientation, which includes orientation towards the opposite sex as well as towards the same sex.

Discrimination on the ground of age

Introduction

6.105 At the time of writing, the Employment Equality (Age) Regulations 2006[181] had come into force relatively recently. Those regulations apply to treating a person less favourably 'on grounds of [that person's] age' (which for this purpose includes his apparent age),[182] and to the application of a provision, criterion or practice to persons not of the same 'age group' as the person in question, but which puts or would put persons of the same age group

---

[176] SI 2003/1660.
[177] See SI 2003/1660, reg 2.
[178] See reg 39 of the Employment Equality (Religion or Belief) Regulations 2003. See paras **4.78–4.85** above concerning ss 58–60 and 124A of the SSFA 1998.
[179] [2007] ICR 1154.
[180] SI 2003/1661.
[181] SI 2006/1031.
[182] SI 2006/1031, reg 3(1)(a) and (3)(b).

as that person at a particular disadvantage when compared with other persons, and which puts that person at that disadvantage.[183] For the latter purpose, 'age group' is defined to mean 'a group of persons defined by reference to age, whether by reference to a particular age or a range of ages'.[184]

Salient features of the age discrimination regulations

6.106 The Employment Equality (Age) Regulations 2006 are quite different in important respects from the other main sets of legislative prohibitions of discrimination. The salient features of the Employment Equality (Age) Regulations 2006 are as follows.

(1) It is possible to justify direct discrimination on the ground of age by showing that it is 'a proportionate means of achieving a legitimate aim'.[185]

(2) Causing a person to retire is on its face direct discrimination on the ground of age, but is not unlawful by virtue of the regulations as they stand, as long as the age of retirement is no less than 65.[186] Even if the normal age of retirement is below 65, the retirement will not constitute age discrimination if it is justified. There is, however, an obligation to notify an employee of the employer's intended date of retirement for the employee in accordance with requirements set out in Sch 6 to the Employment Equality (Age) Regulations 2006, and an obligation to consider any request made by the employee in accordance with Sch 6 to retire on a different date. A failure to comply with those requirements may make the employee's dismissal unfair, as a result of a complicated series of new provisions in part in Sch 6 to the Employment Equality (Age) Regulations 2006 and in part inserted by those regulations into the ERA 1996. These are discussed below.

(3) There is no discrimination against an employee in relation to service-related benefits where the employee has less than five years' service.[187] Where the employee's length of service exceeds five years, a difference in treatment may nevertheless be lawful. In order to be lawful:

> 'it must reasonably appear to [the employer] that the way in which he uses the criterion of length of service, in relation to the award in respect of which [the employee] is put at a disadvantage, fulfils a business need of his undertaking (for example, by encouraging the loyalty or motivation, or rewarding the experience, of some or all of his workers)'.[188]

---

[183] Ibid, reg 3(1)(b).
[184] Ibid, reg 3(3)(a).
[185] See ibid, reg 3(1).
[186] See ibid, reg 30.
[187] See ibid, reg 32.
[188] SI 2006/1031, reg 32(2).

(4) Enhanced redundancy payments are lawful under the Employment Equality (Age) Regulations 2006 only if they are calculated in the same way as statutory redundancy payments are calculated, although the multipliers may be increased.[189]

Retirements

Procedure to follow in relation to retirement

6.107 An employer who intends to retire an employee is now obliged to 'notify the employee in writing' of '(a) the employee's right to make a request [not to retire on the intended date]' and (b) 'the date on which he intends the employee to retire'.[190] This notification must take place 'not more than one year and not less than six months before that date'.[191] This duty to notify applies irrespective of the existence in the employee's contract of employment of any term indicating when his retirement is expected to take place, or any other communication from the employer to the employee of, or of information about, the employee's date of retirement or right to make a request.[192] If the employer fails to give the employee the requisite written notice in time, then the employer remains under a duty to give the employee such notice until the fourteenth day before the termination of the employment.[193]

6.108 The employee's request to retire on a date different from that which has been proposed by the employer must be made between three and six months before the employer's intended date of retirement where the employer has given due notice of that date, and where the employer has not given such notice the employee's request must be made before, but no more than six months before, the employer's intended date of the retirement.[194] The employee must say in the request whether he wants his retirement to be postponed indefinitely, for a stated period, or until a stated date.[195] He cannot make two such requests in relation to one proposed date of retirement.[196] Thus an employee cannot formally change his mind in relation to an altered date of retirement.

6.109 If the employer and the employee agree a different date of retirement, then there may be no need to give the employee a further notice of the sort referred to in para **6.107** above. There will be no such need if the agreed date is earlier than the originally proposed date, or no later than six months after the originally proposed date.[197]

---

[189] See ibid, reg 33.
[190] Employment Equality (Age) Regulations 2006, Sch 6, para 2(1).
[191] Ibid.
[192] Ibid, Sch 6, para 2(2).
[193] See ibid, Sch 6, para 4.
[194] See ibid, Sch 6, para 5(5).
[195] Ibid, Sch 6, para 5(2).
[196] Ibid, Sch 6, para 5(4).
[197] See Employment Equality (Age) Regulations 2006, Sch 6, para 3.

6.110 The employer must consider the employee's request, and must have a meeting with the employee within a reasonable time of receiving the request.[198] The parties must take 'all reasonable steps' to attend the meeting,[199] but the meeting need not take place if before the expiry of that reasonable period the parties agree that the employee's employment will continue either indefinitely or to a stated date, and (in both cases) the employer gives the employee notice in accordance with the newly agreed position.[200] The meeting also need not take place if it is 'not practicable to hold a meeting within the period that is reasonable' and the employer considers the request having considered any representations made by the employee.[201]

6.111 The employer must give the employee a notice in writing stating whether or not the request is accepted and, if so, the effect of the acceptance of the request.[202] If the employer refuses the request, then he must state that and the date when the employee will retire. There is no requirement to give reasons for either of these decisions. The employer must, however, give the notice of his decision as soon as is reasonably practicable after the meeting or, if there is no meeting, after the employer's consideration of the request.[203]

6.112 The employee has a right of appeal against a refusal to comply, or to comply fully, with his request, and if he exercises that right then the procedure is the same as that which applies to the initial request, suitably modified.[204] At both stages, the employee is entitled to be represented at the meeting (if one occurs) by a fellow employee of the employee's choice.[205] The fellow employee may address the meeting, but not answer questions on behalf of the employee, and may confer with the employee during the meeting.[206] The fellow employee is entitled to take paid time off for the purpose.[207] The employer must arrange for the meeting to take place at a time which is convenient for the fellow employee but within the period of seven days of the first proposed date for the meeting.[208]

6.113 The employment is continued after the dismissal if the dismissal takes effect before the employee's request is considered. The employment is then continued until the day following that on which notice of the employer's decision is duly given.[209]

---

[198] Ibid, Sch 6, paras 6 and 7(1).
[199] Ibid, Sch 6, para 7(2).
[200] Ibid, Sch 6, para 7(3).
[201] Ibid, Sch 6, para 7(4) and (5).
[202] Ibid, Sch 6, para 7(7).
[203] Ibid, Sch 6, para 7(6).
[204] Ibid, Sch 6, para 8.
[205] Ibid, Sch 6, para 9.
[206] Ibid.
[207] See ibid, Sch 6, paras 9(5) and (6).
[208] Ibid, Sch 6, para 9(3) and (4).
[209] Employment Equality (Age) Regulations 2006, Sch 6, para 10.

6.114 An employee may complain to an employment tribunal (a) that his employer has failed to give him proper notification of the intended date of his retirement and his right to request a different date, and (b) that his employer has wrongly refused to permit the employee to be accompanied at a meeting to discuss (i) the request or (ii) an appeal against a refusal of that request.[210] The employment tribunal may then award the employee compensation of no more than eight weeks' pay (capped by reference to s 227 of the ERA 1996, and therefore capped at £310 at the time of writing) or two weeks' pay (capped in the same way) respectively.[211]

6.115 The main financial disadvantage for an employer arising from the making of mistakes in relation to the retirement of an employee following the enactment of the Employment Equality (Age) Regulations 2006, is likely to arise where the employee's dismissal is automatically unfair as a result of a failure to comply with the provisions inserted by those regulations into the ERA 1996.

Unfair dismissal on retirement

6.116 *Retirement a potentially fair reason for dismissal.* There is now no upper age limit on claiming unfair dismissal, s 109 of the ERA 1996 having been repealed by the Employment Equality (Age) Regulations 2006. Nevertheless, retirement is now a potentially fair reason for the dismissal of an employee.[212]

6.117 *No normal retirement age.* However, if an employee does not have a normal retirement age and he is dismissed before the date when he achieves the age of 65, then the reason for the dismissal will not be retirement.[213] If the employee has no normal retirement age and he is dismissed at or after attaining the age of 65, but the employer has complied with the notice requirements described in the preceding paragraphs above and the employee's employment ends on the duly notified intended retirement date, then the only reason for the dismissal will be retirement and the employee will accordingly have been dismissed fairly.[214] In contrast, if the date of the termination of the employment is before the intended date of the retirement (whether or not as notified by the employer under Sch 6 to the Employment Equality (Age) Regulations 2006), then retirement 'shall not be taken to be the reason (or a reason) for the dismissal'.[215]

6.118 *Employee has a normal retirement age.* If an employee is dismissed before attaining his normal retirement age, then retirement will not be the (or a) reason for the dismissal.[216]

---

[210] See ibid, Sch 6, paras 11(1) and 12(1).
[211] See ibid, Sch 6, paras 11(3)–(5) and 12(3)–(5).
[212] ERA 1996, s 98(2)(ba).
[213] Ibid, s 98ZA.
[214] See ibid, s 98ZB(1) and (2).
[215] ERA 1996, s 98ZB(3) and (4).
[216] Ibid, s 98ZC.

6.119 If the employee is dismissed on or after the date when he attains his normal age of retirement, the employer has complied with the notice requirements in Sch 6 to the Employment Equality (Age) Regulations 2006 and the contract of employment terminates on the intended date of retirement, then the reason for the dismissal will (subject to what is said in the next paragraph below) be retirement only.[217] If the contract of employment terminates before the intended date of retirement (whether or not as notified by the employer under Sch 6 to the Employment Equality (Age) Regulations 2006), then the reason for the dismissal will not be retirement.[218]

6.120 If the employee's normal retirement age is below 65, and the employee is dismissed on or after the date when he attains the normal retirement age, then the dismissal will not be for retirement if the retirement age constitutes unlawful discrimination contrary to the Employment Equality (Age) Regulations 2006, which will be the case when it is not justified.[219]

6.121 In all other cases of dismissal (that is, when none of the circumstances dealt with in the preceding four paragraphs above exists) where the employer has not notified the employee of the intended date of retirement in accordance with para 2 of Sch 6 to the Employment Equality (Age) Regulations 2006, when deciding the reason, or principal reason, for the dismissal, the employment tribunal must have regard to:

(1) whether or not the employer has notified the employee in accordance with para 4 of Sch 6 to the regulations (which is the paragraph that imposes a continuing duty to inform employees of the intended date of retirement and of the right to make a relevant request until the fourteenth day before the date of dismissal),

(2) if so, how long before the notified retirement date (that is, notified under para 4 of Sch 6) the notification was given, and

(3) whether or not the employer has followed, or sought to follow, the procedures in para 7 of Sch 6 concerning the holding of a meeting.[220]

Fairness of a dismissal for retirement

6.122 An employee the reason, or principal reason, for whose dismissal was retirement will be unfairly dismissed if and only if the employer has failed to comply with one or more of the requirements of paras 4, 6, 7 and 8 of Sch 6 to the Employment Equality (Age) Regulations 2006.[221] Thus the dismissal will be unfair only if the employer has failed to:

---

[217] Ibid, ss 98ZD(1) and (2) and 98ZE(1) and (4).
[218] Ibid, ss 98ZD(3) and (4) and 98ZE (5) and (6).
[219] Ibid, s 98ZE(1) and (2).
[220] ERA 1996, s 98ZF.
[221] Ibid, s 98ZG.

(a) notify the employee of the intended date of retirement and of the employee's right to request an alternative date,

(b) consider the employee's request not to be retired on the employer's intended date, or

(c) allow the employee to appeal against a refusal to change the intended date of retirement.

Thus in any one of those three circumstances, the dismissal will be unfair, but in any other circumstances the dismissal will be fair.

6.123 A dismissal for retirement which was unfair would lead to a basic award calculated in accordance with s 119 of the ERA 1996,[222] but might not lead to a large compensatory award. This is because the employer might well be able to satisfy the employment tribunal that the employee would have been dismissed fairly soon afterwards.

Disability discrimination

Introduction

6.124 The law relating to disability discrimination is contained in the DDA 1995. In some respects, for example in relation to provisions concerning vicarious liability and aiding unlawful acts,[223] questionnaires,[224] victimisation,[225] and application not only to employees but also persons employed personally to execute any work or labour,[226] the DDA 1995 is in like or very similar terms to the SDA 1975 and the RRA 1976. Unlike the SDA 1975 and the RRA 1976, however, the DDA 1995 originally did not distinguish between direct and indirect discrimination. Further, the DDA 1995 as originally enacted did not contain an equivalent of the direct discrimination provisions in for example the SDA 1975 and the RRA 1976. Rather, it made unlawful the unjustified treatment of a disabled person less favourably for a reason related to his disability than a person who was not disabled, and it required the making of reasonable adjustments unless the failure to make such adjustments could be justified.

6.125 The concept of justifiably acting unreasonably was an odd one, and has now (that is, since the first edition of this book) gone. In addition, the now standard concepts of direct and indirect discrimination have been applied to disability discrimination, in order to implement Council Directive 2000/78/EC.

---

[222] Concerning which, see para **8.111** below.
[223] See ss 57 and 58 of the DDA 1995.
[224] See ibid, s 56.
[225] See ibid, s 55.
[226] See the definition of 'employee' in ibid, s 68(1).

6.126 Further important changes which have been made since the first edition of this book was published include the making of a new code of practice concerning the employment of disabled persons, and the issuing of new guidance by the Secretary of State under s 3 of the DDA 1995 about matters to be taken into account in determining whether a person is a disabled person for the purposes of that Act.

Definition of 'disability'

6.127 Generally, a person has a disability for the purposes of the DDA 1995 if he has a physical or mental impairment which has a substantial and long-term adverse effect on his ability to carry out normal day-to-day activities.[227] This definition is extended considerably by the provisions of Sch 1 to the DDA Act and the Disability Discrimination (Meaning of Disability) Regulations 1996.[228] Those regulations provide specifically that certain impairments are not disabilities for the purposes of the DDA 1995. For example, addiction to alcohol or to any other non-medicinal drug is not an impairment for the purposes of the 1995 Act.[229] Nor are:

(1) a tendency to set fires;

(2) a tendency to steal;

(3) a tendency to physical or sexual abuse of other persons;

(4) exhibitionism; and

(5) voyeurism.[230]

6.128 'Seasonal allergic rhinitis' (in other words, hay fever) is also not an impairment, although it may be taken into account where it aggravates the effect of another condition.[231]

Long-term effects

6.129 In order for an impairment to constitute a disability, it must (as stated above) have a substantial and long-term adverse effect. The effect of an impairment is long-term if:

(1) it has lasted at least 12 months;

(2) the period for which it lasts is likely to be at least 12 months; or

---

[227] DDA 1995, s 1.
[228] SI 1996/1455.
[229] Ibid, reg 3.
[230] Ibid, reg 4(1).
[231] Ibid, reg 4(2) and (3).

(3) it is likely to last for the rest of the life of the person concerned.[232]

6.130 Where an impairment ceases to have a substantial adverse effect on a person's ability to carry out normal day-to-day activities, it is to be treated as continuing to have that effect 'if that effect is likely to recur'.[233]

6.131 The Secretary of State's current guidance (issued on 29 March 2006 under s 3 of the DDA 1995) about matters to be taken into account in deciding whether an impairment has either a long-term effect, or a substantial adverse effect on a person's ability to carry out day-to-day activities, should be taken into account by a court or tribunal if it appears to be relevant.[234] However, certain impairments are expressly stated by the DDA 1995 (subject to exceptions set out in regulations) to be disabilities for the purposes of that Act.

Severe disfigurement

6.132 An impairment 'which consists of a severe disfigurement is to be treated as having a substantial adverse effect on the ability of the person concerned to carry out normal day-to-day activities'.[235] However, a severe disfigurement is not to be treated as having a substantial adverse effect on the ability of the person concerned to carry out normal day-to-day activities if it consists of a tattoo which has not been removed, or a body piercing for decorative or other non-medicinal purposes.[236]

Normal day-to-day activities

6.133 An impairment will be taken to affect the ability of a person to carry out normal day-to-day activities only if it affects:

(1) mobility;

(2) manual dexterity;

(3) physical co-ordination;

(4) continence;

(5) ability to lift, carry or otherwise move everyday objects;

(6) speech, hearing or eyesight;

(7) memory or ability to concentrate, learn or understand; or

---

[232] DDA 1995, Sch 1, para 2.
[233] Ibid, Sch 1, para 2.
[234] Ibid, s 3(3).
[235] Ibid, Sch 1, para 3.
[236] Disability Discrimination (Meaning of Disability) Regulations 1996, SI 1996/1455, reg 5.

(8) perception of the risk of physical danger.[237]

Progressive conditions

6.134 In order to come within the definition of a disability, an impairment must have a substantial adverse effect on the relevant person's ability to carry out normal day-to-day activities. The DDA 1995 originally provided (and still provides) that where a person has a progressive condition such as cancer, multiple sclerosis or muscular dystrophy or human immunodeficiency virus (HIV) infection, and as a result of that condition has an impairment which has (or had) an effect on his ability to carry out normal day-to-day activities, but that effect is not (or was not) a substantial adverse effect, then the person will be taken to have an impairment which has a substantial adverse effect if the condition is likely to result in his having such an impairment in the future.[238]

6.135 It is now provided for by an amendment to the DDA 1995 that a person who has cancer, HIV infection and multiple sclerosis is to be deemed to have a disability within the meaning of that Act, unless regulations provide otherwise.[239]

Effect of medical treatment

6.136 An impairment which would be likely to have a substantial adverse effect on the ability of the person concerned to carry out normal day-to-day activities but for the fact that measures (including medical treatment and the use of a prosthesis or other aid) are being taken to treat or correct it, is to be treated as having that effect.[240]

Past disabilities

6.137 A person who has previously had a disability within the meaning of the DDA 1995 is protected in the same way as is a person who currently has such a disability.[241]

Discrimination in relation to employment

6.138 Discrimination is defined for the purposes of the DDA 1995 in so far as it applies to employment by s 3A of that Act. There are now three principal ways in which an employer can discriminate against a disabled employee within the meaning of the DDA 1995. They are these:

---

[237] DDA 1995, Sch 1, para 4.
[238] Ibid, Sch 1, para 8.
[239] See ibid, Sch 1, para 6A as inserted with effect from 5 December 2005.
[240] Ibid, Sch 1, para 6(1) and (2). This does not apply to impairments of sight which are correctable by the use of spectacles, contact lenses 'or in such other ways as may be prescribed': para 6(3).
[241] See DDA 1995, s 2 and Sch 2.

(1) by unjustifiably treating the employee for a reason which relates to the employee's disability less favourably than the employer treats, or would treat, others 'to whom that reason does not or would not apply';

(2) by failing to make a reasonable adjustment for the employee's disability; and

(3) by directly discriminating against the employee by treating him less favourably 'on the ground of the [employee's] disability' than the employer treats or would treat a person not having that particular disability whose circumstances, 'including his abilities, are the same as, or not materially different from, those of the disabled person'.

6.139 These kinds of discrimination are made unlawful in relation to applicants for employment and existing employees by s 4 of the DDA 1995, which also makes it unlawful to harass a disabled employee or applicant for employment, in the same way that it is unlawful to harass (say) a woman employee or applicant.[242]

Deciding whether an employer has treated an employee less favourably for a reason related to the employee's disability

6.140 The Court of Appeal in *Clark v TDG Ltd t/a Novacold*[243] clarified the manner in which the question whether a person has been discriminated against contrary to the DDA 1995 is to be decided. This question is to be approached differently from the question whether there has been discrimination against a person on the ground of, for example, sex or race, where the treatment of that person is compared to the treatment of a real or hypothetical person of the other sex or different race. It is not necessary to find (or, alternatively, suppose) a person who has a difficulty which is not a disability within the meaning of the DDA 1995 but with which one could compare the claimant's disability, and then ask whether the employer treated the claimant less favourably than that other person. Rather, it is necessary to decide whether the claimant has been treated differently from a person who does not have a disability and then to decide whether the difference in treatment is justified.

6.141 So, to take an extreme example, if a blind person were refused a job as a teacher of physical education, then there would be less favourable treatment on the ground of disability. However, the less favourable treatment would probably be justified, with the result that there would not have been discrimination contrary to the DDA 1995.

6.142 In fact, the test for deciding whether less favourable treatment of a person for a reason related to his disability is justified is rather like that which is applied when deciding whether or not a dismissal was fair. The test is whether

---

[242] See ibid, s 3B for the definition of harassment; see paras **6.67–6.69** above concerning harassment on sexual grounds.
[243] [1999] ICR 951.

what was done or omitted to be done was within the range of reasonable responses of a reasonable employer.[244] In contrast, however, the question whether or not there has been a failure to make a reasonable adjustment falls to be decided by the employment tribunal without applying that test.[245]

6.143 It is specifically provided by the DDA 1995 that if an employer is under a duty to make reasonable adjustments in relation to a disabled employee but fails to make them, then the employer's treatment of the employee less favourably for a reason related to his disability cannot be justified unless it would have been justified even if the employer had complied with that duty.[246]

The duty to make reasonable adjustments

6.144 An employer's duty to make reasonable adjustments for a disabled employee or applicant for employment is imposed by s 4A of the DDA 1995. That provides that where '(a) a provision, criterion or practice applied by or on behalf of an employer, or (b) any physical feature of premises occupied by the employer, places the disabled person concerned at a substantial disadvantage in comparison with persons who are not disabled', the employer must take 'such steps as it is reasonable, in all the circumstances of the case, for him to have to take in order to prevent the provision, criterion or practice, or feature, having that effect'. However, no duty is imposed by s 4A in relation to an applicant or potential applicant for employment if the employer does not know and could not reasonably be expected to know that the disabled person is or may be an applicant for the employment in question or that that person has a disability and is likely to be affected as described in the second sentence of this paragraph.[247] In the case of an employee, no duty is imposed on an employer by s 4A if the employer does not know and could not reasonably be expected to know that the employee has a disability and is likely to be affected in that way.[248]

6.145 The employer's duty to make reasonable adjustments is dealt with also in several other sections of the DDA 1995. Section 18D(2) provides that the term 'provision, criterion or practice' includes 'any arrangements'. Section 18B provides that in deciding whether it is reasonable to require an employer to take any particular steps in order to comply with a duty to make reasonable adjustments, a court or tribunal must have regard to:

(1) the extent to which taking the step would prevent the effect in relation to which the duty is imposed;

(2) the extent to which it is practicable for the employer to take the step;

---

[244] *Post Office v Jones* [2001] ICR 805.
[245] See *Smith v Churchills Stairlifts plc* [2006] ICR 524; see further **6.147** below.
[246] DDA 1995, s 3A(6).
[247] See ibid, s 4A(3).
[248] DDA 1995, s 4A(3).

(3) the financial and other costs which would be incurred by the employer in taking the step and the extent to which taking it would disrupt any of the employer's activities;

(4) the extent of the employer's financial and other resources;

(5) the availability to the employer of financial or other assistance with respect to taking the step; and

(6) the nature of the employer's activities and the size of his undertaking.

6.146 Section 18B then sets out examples of steps which an employer might need to take in order to comply with a duty to make reasonable adjustments. They are these:

(1) making adjustments to premises;

(2) allocating some of the disabled person's duties to another person;

(3) transferring him to fill an existing vacancy;

(4) altering his hours of working or training;

(5) assigning him to a different place of work or training;

(6) allowing him to be absent during working hours for rehabilitation, assessment or treatment;

(7) giving, or arranging to be given, training or mentoring (whether for the disabled person or any other person);

(8) acquiring or modifying equipment;

(9) modifying instructions or reference manuals;

(10) modifying procedures for testing or assessment;

(11) providing a reader or interpreter; or

(12) providing supervision or other support.

6.147 The term 'arrangements' is a wide term, and it should be construed widely.[249] However, whether or not there has been a failure to make a reasonable adjustment is not to be decided by applying the 'range of reasonable

---

[249] See *Archibald v Fife* [2004] ICR 954.

responses of a reasonable employer' test. Rather, it is to be decided by the employment tribunal objectively,[250] sitting, one might say, as the 'industrial jury'.

6.148 Nevertheless, there are limits to the freedom of the tribunal to decide that there was (or was not) a failure to make a reasonable adjustment. For example, it is not open to an employment tribunal to decide that an employer failed to make a reasonable adjustment simply because he failed to consult an employee about the need (or otherwise) to make adjustments.[251] Similarly, failing to obtain a medical report concerning a disabled employee will not in itself give rise to a breach of the DDA 1995.[252] Further, only very rarely will it be necessary to pay a disabled employee full pay for disability-related absences.[253] However, an employee is not obliged to suggest any particular adjustments to an employer before the employer can come under a duty to make them.[254] Nor will an employer (at least normally) need to make available care for an employee's bodily functions.[255]

Code of practice

6.149 A code of practice has been issued by the Secretary of State concerning discrimination contrary to the DDA 1995 in employment.[256] It must be taken into account by a court or tribunal if it appears to the court or tribunal to be relevant to any question arising in any proceedings brought under the DDA 1995.[257] The code contains valuable guidance.

EQUAL PAY

Introduction

Equal Pay Act 1970

6.150 The EPA 1970 gives an employee a right to equal pay and other benefits under a contract of employment as compared with a person of the opposite sex employed by the same employer (or one which either controls or is controlled by the first employee's employer) at the same establishment.[258] This right to

---

[250] *Smith v Churchills Stairlifts plc* [2006] ICR 524.
[251] *Tarbuck v Sainsbury's Supermarkets Ltd* [2006] IRLR 664.
[252] *Spence v Intype Libra Ltd* UKEAT/0617/06.
[253] *O'Hanlon v Commissioners v HM Revenue & Customs* [2006] ICR 1579.
[254] *Cosgrove v Caesar and Howie* [2001] IRLR 653.
[255] *Kenny v Hampshire Constabulary* [1999] ICR 27.
[256] It was issued in 2004 and replaced the first such code, which was issued in 1996. It is currently available on the website of the Disability Rights Commission (www.drc.org.uk), whose functions will be undertaken in the near future by the Commission for Equality and Human Rights.
[257] DDA 1995, s 53A(8A).
[258] Or at an establishment which is one of a number of establishments in Great Britain which include that one and at which common terms and conditions of employment are observed either generally or for employees of the relevant classes.

equal pay is given effect by the deemed inclusion in a contract of employment of an 'equality clause'. The clause applies from the first day of employment since no period of continuous employment is required for the clause to apply. If a relevant difference in contractual terms can be shown to be genuinely due to a material factor which is not the difference of sex, then the equality clause will not apply to it. The EPA 1970 must be interpreted in the light of decisions of the ECJ on the original Art 119 of the Treaty of Rome.[259] Nevertheless, compensation may not be awarded under the EPA 1970 for injury to feelings.[260]

Equal pay for equal work

6.151 The EPA 1970 protects against discrimination on the ground of sex in relation to pay by giving employees the right to receive contractual benefits of equal value where they are engaged in 'like work',[261] 'work rated as equivalent',[262] and work of 'equal value'.[263] If an employee shows that her contract contains a provision which is less favourable than that of a man engaged on like work, work rated as equivalent or work of equal value, then she is entitled to the same benefit as the man receives, even if, overall, her terms and conditions before the change were of equal value. In other words, relevant employees can 'leapfrog' each other so as to obtain the best terms and conditions of both of them.[264] However, a claimant cannot compare herself with more than one other employee.[265]

Establishments with which comparisons can be made

6.152 The Education (Modification of Enactments Relating to Employment) (England) Order 2003[266] and its equivalent in Wales[267] do not make the governing body of a maintained school with a delegated budget the respondent to an employment tribunal claim for equal pay under the EPA 1970 brought by an employee of the LEA who is employed to work at the school. Accordingly, an employee who claims equal pay under that Act may compare his pay with that of any relevant employee in any other school maintained by the authority.

6.153 The question whether such a claim could be made for pay which is equal to that of an employee employed in a school which is maintained by a different LEA or which is a foundation, voluntary aided or foundation special school could, clearly, arise. According to the ECJ's judgment in *Lawrence v Regent Office Care Ltd*,[268] where the differences in pay of workers performing like work or work of equal value cannot be attributed to a single source, then there

---

[259] Now renumbered as Art 141.
[260] *Newcastle-upon-Tyne City Council v Allan* [2005] IRLR 504.
[261] EPA 1970, s 1(2)(a).
[262] Ibid, s 1(2)(b).
[263] Ibid, s 1(2)(c).
[264] See *Hayward v Cammell Laird Shipbuilders Ltd* [1988] ICR 464.
[265] *Degnan v Redcar and Cleveland Borough Council* [2005] IRLR 615.
[266] SI 2003/1964.
[267] SI 2006/1073.
[268] [2003] ICR 1092.

is no body which is responsible for the inequality and which could restore equal treatment, and therefore there will be no breach of Art 141. Thus, it will not be possible to compare pay in different schools maintained by different LEAs.[269]

Genuine material factor: justification generally

6.154 If a relevant inequality in contractual terms can be shown to be genuinely due to a material factor which is not the difference of sex, then the equality clause will not apply to it.[270] Although the inequality must be justified in the sense that the employer must prove that the inequality does not result from the difference of sex, the employer does not need to show that the inequality is objectively justified. This is well illustrated by the case of *Strathclyde Regional Council v Wallace*.[271]

Strathclyde Regional Council v Wallace

Nine women teachers employed by Strathclyde Regional Council brought claims for equal pay under the Equal Pay Act 1970 on the basis that they did like work to a principal teacher, but were paid at a lower rate. Each of the claimants selected a male comparator who was a principal teacher employed by the council, and claimed equality of pay with such comparator. The council sought to defend the claims by arguing that the inequalities in pay were 'genuinely due to a material factor which is not the difference of sex', and that s 1(3) of the 1970 Act therefore applied. An industrial tribunal held that the defence under s 1(3) of the 1970 Act had not been established because the council had failed to justify the reasons for the disparity. After that decision, the employment of the teachers was transferred to several successor local education authorities. Those authorities appealed to the EAT, which rejected the appeal. A further appeal, to the Court of Session, was made. That court allowed the appeal among other things on the ground that the difference in the treatment of the teachers as compared with that of their male comparators was not due to sex, but was due to a combination of the council's system of promotion coupled with financial constraints which amounted to a genuine material factor. The teachers appealed to the House of Lords.

Decision of the House of Lords

The House of Lords dismissed the appeal. It stated that the object of s 1 of the EPA 1970 is to eliminate sex discrimination in pay, and not to achieve fair wages. Accordingly, the House decided, if an inequality in pay is explained by genuine factors not trained by discrimination, then that will be sufficient to raise a valid defence under s 1(3). In such a case, the House of Lords decided, there is no further burden on the employer to justify the inequality. In the circumstances, the teachers' claims therefore failed.

6.155 One of the flurry of cases concerning the pay inequalities in local government employment decided in the last few years provides some comfort for employers in relation to equal pay claims. In *Redcar & Cleveland Borough*

---

[269] Compare *Armstrong v Newcastle-upon-Tyne NHS Hospital Trust* [2006] IRLR 124.
[270] EPA 1970, s 1(3).
[271] [1998] ICR 205.

Council v Bainbridge,[272] the EAT held that differences in pay can be objectively justified in part by reference to costs, although not where the purpose of the difference is simply to save money.

Remedies and time limit for claims

6.156 A successful complainant under the EPA 1970 is entitled under that Act to up to six years' back-pay (consisting of the amount by which the employee was underpaid by the employer contrary to the EPA 1970) and, where there was deliberate concealment by the employer of any fact which is relevant to the contravention to which the proceedings relate, all of the underpayments.[273] However, if the employment has ended then the claim must have been made within six months from the ending of the contract of employment, unless there was deliberate concealment of the same sort, in which case the claim must be made within 6 months of the date when the employee could with reasonable diligence have discovered it.[274]

6.157 An equality clause only applies where there is direct discrimination on the ground of sex. It does not apply to prevent indirect discrimination on the ground of sex in relation to pay and other contractual benefits. So, if a person is able to show that the conditions indicated above for indirect discrimination on the ground of sex exist in relation to a term in the contract of employment, there will be no remedy in UK law. Accordingly, the only possible basis for a claim in relation to that discrimination will be under Community law.[275]

HUMAN RIGHTS

6.158 Mention has already been made above of certain fundamental principles applicable where the HRA 1998 is relied upon. In the final part of this chapter, mention is made of the substantive Convention rights which are relevant to employment.

Relevant Convention rights

6.159 Only some of the Convention rights are likely to have an effect on employment law. They are as follows.

(1) A right not to be required to perform forced or compulsory labour (Art 4 of the Convention).

---

[272] [2007] IRLR 91.
[273] See EPA 1970, ss 2(5) and 2ZB. A person who is under a disability for limitation purposes is also catered for by s 2ZB.
[274] See ibid, ss 2(4) and 2ZA. A person who is under a disability for limitation purposes is also catered for by s 2ZA.
[275] See for example *Bilka-Kaufhaus v Weber von Hartz* [1987] ICR 110. See paras **6.6** and **6.12–6.18** above for the basic principles of Community law.

(2) A right to a fair trial in the determination of one's civil rights and obligations (Art 6(1) of the Convention). So far as relevant, Art 6(1) provides: 'In the determination of his civil rights and obligations . . . everyone is entitled to a fair and public hearing within a reasonable time by an independent and impartial tribunal established by law'.

(3) A right to respect for private and family life (Art 8 of the Convention). This is a limited right in that a public authority may interfere with it 'in accordance with the law and [to such an extent as is] necessary in a democratic society in the interests of national security, public safety or the economic well-being of the country, for the prevention of disorder or crime, for the protection of health or morals, or for the protection of the rights and freedoms of others'.

(4) A right to freedom of thought, conscience and religion, including a right to freedom to change one's religious belief, and freedom, either alone or in community with others and in public or private, to manifest one's religion or belief in worship, teaching, practice and observance (Art 9 of the Convention). The freedom to manifest one's religion or beliefs is subject to 'such limitations as are prescribed by law and are necessary in a democratic society in the interests of public safety, for the protection of public order, health or morals, or for the protection of the rights and freedoms of others'.

(5) A right to freedom of expression (Art 10 of the Convention). This right is also subject to limitations: it 'may be subject to such formalities, conditions, restrictions or penalties as are prescribed by law and are necessary in a democratic society, in the interests of national security, territorial integrity or public safety, for the prevention of disorder or crime, for the protection of health or morals, for the protection of the reputation or rights of others, for preventing the disclosure of information received in confidence, or for maintaining the authority and impartiality of the judiciary'.

(6) A right of freedom of assembly and association (Art 11 of the Convention). This includes a right to join or not to join a trade union. The right is 'to freedom of peaceful assembly and to freedom of association with others, including the right to form and to join trade unions for the protection of [one's] interests'. Restrictions may be placed on this right, but only 'such as are prescribed by law and are necessary in a democratic society in the interests of national security or public safety, for the prevention of disorder or crime, for the protection of health or morals or for the protection of the rights and freedoms of others'. Furthermore, 'This article shall not prevent the imposition of lawful restrictions on the exercise of these rights by members of the armed forces, of the police or of the administration of the State'.

(7) A right not to be discriminated against on the ground of 'sex, race, colour, language, religion, political or other opinion, national or social origin, association with a national minority, property, birth or other status' (Art 14 of the Convention).[276]

Application by the European Court of Human Rights of Convention rights

6.160 The ECHR has made a number of relevant decisions which are of importance to UK employment law, and there are several reported appellate cases concerning the Convention rights. Mention is made below of the decisions which remain of current interest. (Many decisions of the ECHR have now been given effect in UK law, and they are not mentioned below.)

Article 8: right to respect for private and family life

6.161 In *Halford v UK*,[277] the ECHR decided that Art 8(1) was contravened by the monitoring of the private telephone calls at work of the claimant, Ms Halford, in circumstances in which she had a reasonable expectation of privacy in relation to those calls. Her expectation of such privacy had been reinforced by the facts that (1) she was given two telephones, one of which was for private use, and (2) she had been told that telephone calls made in connection with a sex discrimination claim which she was making against her employer would not be intercepted. She was an Assistant Chief Constable of Police. Clearly, the principle in that case will apply to all public bodies. Clearly also, the principle may well apply to private e-mail messages. After all, the only difference is that the latter are more permanent than telephone calls. Nevertheless, if an employer informed all of its employees that all e-mails sent by them while at work might be read, and the employer then intercepted private e-mails sent while at work, there might well not be a breach Art 8 (although perhaps the communications of staff who routinely work very long hours might have to be exempted from such interception).

6.162 It is of note that in *McGowan v Scottish Water*,[278] the EAT decided that there was no breach of Art 8(1) where an employer carried out covert surveillance of an employee to see whether or not he was falsifying his timesheets.

Article 9: right to freedom of thought, conscience and religion

6.163 It is of interest that in *Ahmad v UK*,[279] the European Commission of Human Rights rejected a claim that an employee was entitled by Art 9 of the Convention to attend religious worship during his normal contractual working hours and be paid for doing so. It also rejected a claim that Art 14 had been

---

[276] See para **6.10** above for the manner in which Art 14 applies.
[277] [1997] IRLR 471.
[278] [2005] IRLR 167.
[279] (1982) 4 EHRR 126.

breached, on the basis that the employee was not treated less favourably than individuals or groups of individuals placed in comparable situations.

Article 10: freedom of expression

6.164 In *Vogt v Germany*,[280] the ECHR decided that the dismissal of a teacher in a German State school (who was a civil servant) simply because she was an active member of the German Communist Party, contravened Art 10. This is to be contrasted with the decisions of the ECHR in *Glasenapp v Germany*[281] and *Kosiek v Germany*,[282] where applicants for employment in the German civil service as teachers were held to have been properly refused such employment on the ground of their membership of, or support for, political parties whose policies were inimical to the constitution of the State. In *Vogt*, those decisions were distinguished because in *Vogt* the employee had already been employed for seven years before her dismissal. Furthermore, her job involved no security risks, and she had not been criticised for attempting to exert improper influence on her pupils. Her dismissal was therefore held to be a disproportionate response to the circumstances.

6.165 Moreover, in *Morissens v Belgium*,[283] the ECHR decided that the taking of disciplinary measures against a State school teacher who spoke out against her superiors in a television broadcast, did not contravene Art 10. This was because the Commission decided that a 'duty of moderation . . . arises from the duties and responsibilities which civil servants have as the agents through which the State operates'.

6.166 It should be noted also that the ECHR has decided that the current restrictions on political activity applicable in the local government sector do not contravene Art 10.[284]

---

[280] (1996) 21 EHRR 205.
[281] (1987) 9 EHRR 25.
[282] (1986) 9 EHRR 328.
[283] (1988) 56 DR 127.
[284] See *Ahmed v UK* [1999] IRLR 188.

Chapter 7

REDUNDANCY

INTRODUCTION

7.1 An employee is entitled to a redundancy payment if (1) he has been dismissed for redundancy, (2) he has more than two years' continuous employment, and (3) no relevant exception applies.

DEFINITION OF REDUNDANCY

7.2 An employee who has been dismissed is to be taken to have been dismissed for redundancy if the dismissal is wholly or mainly attributable to:

(1) the fact that his employer has ceased or intends to cease to carry on:
    (a) the business for the purposes of which the employee was employed by the employer; or
    (b) that business in the place where the employee was so employed; or

(2) the fact that the requirements of that business for employees to carry out:
    (a) work of a particular kind; or
    (b) work of a particular kind in the place where the employee was employed by the employer,

have ceased or diminished or are expected to cease or diminish.[1]

7.3 Thus the focus of the inquiry is not whether or not there is work of a particular kind still to be done, but whether the employer's requirements for employees to do work of that kind have ceased or diminished or are expected to cease or diminish.[2] In deciding whether there has been a cessation or diminution in the employer's requirements for employees to do work of a particular kind, it is normally necessary to consider only what the employee *actually* did before being dismissed, rather than what he *could* have been required to do under his contract of employment. It would normally only be permissible to consider what the employee could in theory have been required

---

[1] Section 139 of the ERA 1996.
[2] See *Huddersfield Parcels Ltd v Sykes* [1981] IRLR 115 and the approval by the EAT in *Burrell v Safeway Stores Ltd* [1997] ICR 523 of *Carry All Motors Ltd v Pennington* [1980] ICR 806. The analysis of the EAT in *Burrell* was specifically approved by the House of Lords in *Murray v Foyle Meats Ltd* [1999] ICR 827.

to do when deciding whether or not the dismissal was caused wholly or mainly by a cessation or diminution in the employer's requirements for employees to do work of a particular kind.[3]

7.4 One question which was raised in *Nottinghamshire County Council v Lee*[4] was whether the fact that an employer knows, at the time when an employee is engaged under a fixed-term contract of employment, that there will in the future be a diminishing need for employees to do this type of work, means that the employee will not be redundant when that diminution takes place. The Court of Appeal decided in that case that in that situation an employee will indeed be dismissed for redundancy when the fixed-term contract of employment ends.

7.5 In the case of schools, difficult questions may arise where the school's requirements for teaching staff alter, but the overall number of teaching staff required does not change. In that situation, as long as the requirements of the employer for employees to do work of the kind that the teacher carried out before his dismissal have ceased or diminished, the dismissal will be for redundancy. This question is most likely to arise where a teacher claims unfair dismissal. So, for example, if a teacher's main subject ceases to be required by the school but the teacher could do other work in an internal 'supply' teacher role, then if the school requires more specialist teaching in the only areas in which the teacher is now able to work and the teacher is dismissed as a result, it would be open to an employment tribunal to decide that the teacher had been dismissed because of redundancy.

REQUIREMENT FOR CONTINUOUS EMPLOYMENT

7.6 An employee will not have the right to a redundancy payment unless he has two or more years of continuous employment in the relevant post.[5] An employee cannot rely for the purposes of the ERA 1996 on an employer's promise to treat him as having continuous employment greater than that to which the relevant statutory provisions entitle him.[6] Furthermore, an employee who has within the previous two years been given a redundancy payment by his current employer or an associated employer in respect of his existing current continuous employment will not be entitled to a redundancy payment in respect of a dismissal from that employment. This is because such a payment breaks continuity for redundancy pay purposes.[7]

7.7 Continuity of employment is something which is determined by reference to some rather technical rules. Those rules as they apply generally are

---

[3] *Safeway Stores plc v Burrell* [1997] ICR 523.
[4] [1980] ICR 635.
[5] ERA 1996, s 155.
[6] *Secretary of State v Globe Elastic Thread Co Ltd* [1979] ICR 706.
[7] See ERA 1996, ss 145 and 214(2) and (4).

described in Chapter 8 below.[8] However, some rules which are specific to employment in local government and related employments might affect the position of an employee in a maintained school. Those rules are contained mainly in the Redundancy Payments (Continuity of Employment in Local Government etc) (Modification) Order 1999.[9] That Order has the effect that even if an employee has been in employment in a maintained school for less than two years, he may nevertheless have sufficient continuous service to be able to claim a redundancy payment.[10] This applies to employment which is continuous as between the employers named in the Order, which include LEAs, the governing bodies of foundation schools and the governing bodies of voluntary aided schools. Thus, a person may work as a teacher at one maintained school for one year and then, without a break, at another for a year and a half before being made redundant. The two periods of employment may then be combined so that the teacher can make a redundancy claim.

LOSING THE RIGHT TO A REDUNDANCY PAYMENT

7.8 An employee will not be entitled to a redundancy payment in respect of a dismissal if he has unreasonably refused an offer of suitable alternative employment made by either his current employer or an associated one,[11] before the dismissal, or if he has within four weeks of the dismissal commenced alternative employment (whether suitable or not) with either such employer, having been offered it before the dismissal.[12] In determining what is suitable alternative employment for this purpose, an employment tribunal would be both entitled and required to take into account the seniority of the alternative post offered, as well as the content of the duties.[13]

7.9 It should be noted, though, that if an employee has in the circumstances just described started a new post which is different from the original post, then the employee will have the right to a trial period of either four weeks or such longer period as may be agreed between the employer and the employee if (but only if) that longer trial period is for the purpose of retraining.[14] If the employee leaves the new employment during the trial period, then he will still be entitled to a redundancy payment unless the new employment was suitable alternative employment and he acted unreasonably in leaving it.[15]

---

[8] See para **8.7** below.
[9] SI 1999/2277.
[10] However this does not apply for unfair dismissal purposes.
[11] Which includes for this purpose one within the Redundancy Payments (Continuity of Employment in Local Government etc) (Modification) Order 1999, SI 1999/2277.
[12] ERA 1996, ss 138 and 141.
[13] *Taylor v Kent County Council* [1969] 2 QB 560.
[14] ERA 1996, s 138.
[15] See ibid, ss 138 and 141.

CALCULATION OF A REDUNDANCY PAYMENT

Method of calculation

7.10 A redundancy payment entitlement is calculated in very much the same way as a basic award for unfair dismissal.[16] The redundancy payment is calculated as follows.

7.11 An employee's continuous employment is calculated backwards in time from the date when the dismissal took effect. For each complete year during which the employee was over the age of 41, the employee is entitled to a week and a half's pay, capped (at the time of writing) at £310.[17] For every complete year during which the employee was above the age of 22 but below the age of 42, the employee is entitled to a week's pay capped at the same level. For every complete year of employment during which the employee was aged below 22, the employee is entitled to half a week's pay capped at £310. The calculation stops when 20 years' employment has been counted.

7.12 Two examples may be helpful. It is assumed in each case that the employee earns more than the maximum for calculation purposes of £310 per week.

(1) If a man has been employed for all of his working life for a local authority, his working life started at the age of 16 on 1 July 1981, his birthday is 30 June, and he is made redundant at the age of 35 on 30 September 2000, then the redundancy payment will be 13 x £310 + 6 x £155 = £4030 + £930 = £4960.

(2) If a woman has been employed as a teacher in various maintained schools, all employments being continuous, for 35 years, her birthday falls on 10 September, and she is made redundant at the age of 55 on 31 August 2000, then she will be entitled to a redundancy payment of 14 x £310 x 1.5 + 6 x £310 = £6510 + £1860 = £8370.

Calculation of redundancy pay

7.13 An employee's pay is calculated by reference to the 12-week period before the dismissal. The calculation of the payment may cause difficulty in some circumstances. For example, if an employee is employed under a series of fixed-term contracts, say for a term at a time, then the periods during which the employee was not working will often count for the purposes of continuity of employment[18] although they are unpaid. In that case, those weeks are ignored for the purpose of calculating pay.[19]

---

[16] See ERA 1996, s 162 for the calculation of a redundancy payment.
[17] See ibid, s 227, for the cap.
[18] See para **8.8** below.
[19] See ERA 1996, ss 221–224 and 228.

7.14 The case of *Cole v Birmingham City District Council*[20] is instructive in relation to the calculation of a redundancy payment.

Cole v Birmingham City District Council

An unqualified teacher was employed by an LEA to teach part-time at two schools at an hourly rate paid in respect of her actual attendances. As a result of an increased availability of qualified teachers, she was made redundant. Her employer calculated her redundancy payment on the basis of a reduced hourly rate, contending that part of her rate of pay related to holiday periods and should not be included for the purpose of calculating a redundancy payment. The teacher claimed to an industrial tribunal that her redundancy payment should have been calculated by reference to the actual hours which she worked, and not reduced by reference to holiday periods. The tribunal rejected her claim on the ground that the LEA was justified in relying on a scheme which in the LEA's view achieved parity between full-time and part-time teachers.

Decision of the Employment Appeal Tribunal

The EAT allowed the appeal. It said that in the absence of any agreement between the teacher and the LEA to vary the teacher's contract of employment, the teacher was entitled to a redundancy payment based on her average earnings calculated by reference to the full hourly rate and that her redundancy payment should be increased accordingly.

TIME OFF TO LOOK FOR ALTERNATIVE WORK OR UNDERGO TRAINING

7.15 An employee who has more than two years' continuous employment and who 'is given notice of dismissal by reason of redundancy' is entitled to be given a reasonable amount of time off with pay during his working hours in order either to look for new employment or to make arrangements for training for future employment.[21] The employee cannot simply take the time off: he must be given it. His remedy for a refusal by the employer to grant the relevant time off is to make a claim to an employment tribunal for compensation.[22] It should be noted that:

(1) this right to time off probably does not arise where a fixed-term contract is coming to an end;

(2) a warning of redundancy is not the same as being given notice of redundancy; and

(3) the right to compensation is limited to no more than two-fifths of a week's (uncapped) pay, no matter how much time the employee would like to be allowed off.

---

[20] [1978] ICR 1004.
[21] ERA 1996, s 52.
[22] Ibid, ss 53 and 54.

7.16 If an employee has greater rights under his contract of employment in respect of time off to look for alternative work if he is served with notice of redundancy, then those rights will prevail.

UNFAIR DISMISSAL

Right to claim unfair dismissal

7.17 An employee who is dismissed by reason of redundancy may claim unfair dismissal (see Chapter 8). In addition to the procedural rights granted to an employee in a maintained school in Wales by the regulations referred to in Chapter 8 below[23] and to all employees by the law of unfair dismissal,[24] an employee who is dismissed for redundancy can rely on certain substantive rights granted by case law concerning the law of unfair dismissal.

Substantive fairness

7.18 An employer is not obliged to satisfy an employment tribunal that it was economically necessary to make a member of staff redundant, for the redundancy to be fair.[25] However, the employer does need to be able to satisfy the tribunal that the dismissal was indeed for redundancy, and in doing so the employer may well need to adduce evidence to show that there was a perceived need to reduce the size of the workforce.[26]

SELECTION FOR REDUNDANCY

Method of selection

7.19 Dismissals for redundancy can occur in a number of ways. It may be that an employer has a number of employees doing the same kind of work, and there is a need to make one or more of those employees redundant. This need may arise because of a drop in the amount of work available, for example through a fall in the number of pupils at the school, or because of the employer's financial circumstances, for example because of a fall in a maintained school's delegated budget. Alternatively, it may be that an employee is the only person employed by an employer to do work of a particular sort, and that the employer no longer needs an employee to do work of that sort. This may well occur in the context of a reorganisation.

7.20 In the first situation, the employer will have to adopt a system for selecting the employee(s) to be made redundant, and the fairest way to do that would be to use a number of criteria by which to assess the employees in the 'pool' from which one or more are to be selected for redundancy. In order to

---

[23] See para **8.137** onwards below.
[24] See para **8.87** onwards below.
[25] *James W Cook & Co (Wivenhoe) Ltd v Tipper* [1990] ICR 716.
[26] Ibid.

maximise the chances of successfully defending a claim of unfair dismissal, those selection criteria must be as objective as possible, and, if not entirely objective, must be applied as objectively as possible. So, for example, a criterion such as the attitude of the employee to work would not be a safe one to use. Suitable criteria in the case of employees carrying out manual work might include timekeeping, length of service, disciplinary record, attendance record, and efficiency.

7.21 Teachers should be assessed by reference to rather more sophisticated criteria. For example, qualifications, or objectively assessed performance (possibly in terms of the number of students who obtain qualifications or do well in examinations) would be likely to be fair criteria to adopt. An Ofsted inspection report might be regarded as objective evidence of competence, but if reliance were sought to be placed on the report but its accuracy were contested then it might be best to call the inspector as a witness.

Reasonable efforts to redeploy

7.22 An employer is obliged to make reasonable efforts to redeploy an employee whom the employer proposes to dismiss as redundant. The importance of this cannot be overestimated, although, equally, it is essential to bear in mind the fact that the ultimate test of fairness in the context of dismissals for redundancy is the standard test of fairness in the law of unfair dismissal. That is whether or not the employer's actions were within the range of reasonable responses of a reasonable employer.[27] It might nevertheless be necessary to consider whether to offer an employee a job done by another member of staff, who would then be made redundant.[28] This process is called 'bumping', for obvious reasons. However, the bumped employee might then be able to claim unfair dismissal. Thus it will often be within the range of reasonable responses of a reasonable employer not to 'bump'.

Consultation

7.23 Before making an employee redundant, a reasonable employer will consult the employee about the proposed dismissal. It will only be fair to fail to consult an employee about his proposed dismissal by reason of redundancy where such consultation would be 'utterly futile' in the circumstances of the case.[29] If there has been a selection of one or more employees from a number of staff who are all doing work of the same sort, then consultation will need to be undertaken to ensure that the employer has not failed to take into account relevant information relating to the employee. Consultation will also need to be undertaken in order to ascertain whether the employee's personal circumstances are such that, if possible, some other employee should instead be made redundant (for example, a particular employee might be the only breadwinner in a family with ten children, and another employee might have a working

---

[27] See *Duffy v Yeomans & Partners Ltd* [1995] ICR 1.
[28] See *Thomas & Betts Manufacturing Ltd v Harding* [1980] IRLR 255.
[29] *Mugford v Midland Bank plc* [1997] ICR 399, 406G.

spouse and only two children). Further, an employee whose dismissal for redundancy is proposed might be able to suggest ways in which he could be redeployed. For example, an employer may not be obliged to assume that an employee would be willing to consider work at a lower status or level than that of the employee's present position,[30] and in consulting the employee, the employer will give the employee an opportunity to inform the employer of his willingness to consider work at such a lower status or level.[31]

7.24 Where an employee is the *only* person doing a particular kind of work, consultation will be required in order to allow the employee an opportunity to suggest ways in which he could be redeployed.

7.25 In any event, the consultation process may help to lessen the blow of being dismissed for redundancy. As will be appreciated, in many situations other than redundancy (most notably for capability or conduct) an employee will be likely to have had warning of the possibility of dismissal, and the dismissal will therefore be less of a shock.

7.26 At what stage should the consultation occur? Clearly, it should be before the dismissal takes effect. However, it should also be before a final decision has been made; if it were otherwise, then the consultation could be a sham. It is theoretically possible to give notice before consulting,[32] but if at all possible, it is best to avoid doing so. If notice *is* given before consulting an employee about the proposed dismissal, then it should be made clear that the notice is conditional and will be withdrawn if the consultation results in a decision not to make the employee redundant. One problem is that the giving of notice makes it look as if the employer has already made its decision. Another problem is that an employer cannot simply withdraw an unconditional notice of dismissal: the employee has to agree to such withdrawal. Nevertheless, an employee who refused to agree to a withdrawal of notice would be likely to be given fairly short shrift in an employment tribunal, either because the employer would have followed a fair procedure or, if the procedure were determined to have been unfair, because the employee would be likely to be awarded no compensation.[33]

The application of the statutory dismissal and discipline procedure to redundancies

7.27 There will in any event be a need to comply with the minimum requirements of the applicable statutory dismissal and discipline procedure in Sch 2 to the Employment Act 2002. The general requirements of those procedures are described in Chapter 2 above.[34] Extensive and helpful guidance

---

[30] *Barratt Construction Ltd v Dalrymple* [1984] IRLR 385.
[31] See for example *Huddersfield Parcels Ltd v Sykes* [1981] IRLR 115 and *Abbotts v Wesson-Glynwed Steels Ltd* [1982] IRLR 51.
[32] See for example *Mugford v Midland Bank plc* [1997] ICR 399.
[33] See further para **8.115** below.
[34] See para **2.41** onwards above.

has, however, been given by the EAT about the manner in which those procedures apply to dismissals for redundancy. In *Alexander v Brigden Enterprises Ltd*,[35] the EAT said that at step one of the standard procedure, it is necessary to give the employee an explanation 'as to why the employer is contemplating dismissing that particular employee'.[36] This 'will involve providing information as to both why the employer considers that there is, to put it colloquially, a redundancy situation and also why the employee is being selected.'[37] At step two, the employer 'should in advance of the meeting notify the employee of the selection criteria',[38] and 'the employee's own assessment'.[39] Informing the employee of the 'break point' will, however, not be required in order to satisfy the requirements of stage two.[40] Nor will it be necessary in order to satisfy the requirements of step two to tell an employee about other employees' scores, although the failure to do so might (depending on the circumstances) contravene 'general unfair dismissal law'.[41]

Automatically unfair selection

7.28 If an employee is selected to be made redundant for certain reasons, then the dismissal will be automatically unfair. These reasons are the same as those which apply to make dismissals automatically unfair (although the mechanism used in the statutory provisions is to make selection for redundancy for the prohibited reason automatically unfair).[42] No period of continuous employment is required for an employee to be able to claim unfair dismissal where he has been selected to be made redundant for one of these reasons.[43] In order to establish that the selection for redundancy was for such a reason, an employee would have to show to the satisfaction of the employment tribunal among other things that the circumstances constituting the redundancy applied equally to one or more other employees in the same undertaking who held positions similar to that of the dismissed employee, and that those other employees were not dismissed.[44]

---

[35] [2006] ICR 1277.
[36] Ibid, at para 41.
[37] Ibid.
[38] Ibid, at para 43.
[39] Ibid, para 45.
[40] Ibid, at para 46.
[41] Ibid. See further paras **8.38** and **8.95–8.96** below.
[42] See predominantly s 105 of the ERA 1996; see para **8.38** below for the kinds of dismissal which are automatically unfair.
[43] See ERA 1996, s 108(3)(h).
[44] Ibid, s 105(1)(b).

Chapter 8

DISCIPLINE AND DISMISSAL

UNFAIR DISMISSAL

Introduction

8.1 The area of employment law which is likely to be of most practical importance for a school is the law of unfair dismissal. There are several conditions for claiming unfair dismissal which have to be satisfied. Those which are most likely to be relevant are these:

(1) the person must be properly classifiable as an employee, and not be self-employed;

(2) the employee must have had sufficient length of service at the time of the dismissal to be able to claim unfair dismissal, unless the claim comes within a set number of exceptions;

(3) the contract must not have been tainted with illegality, for example through a deliberate joint attempt to defraud the Inland Revenue (although the likelihood of this in relation to a contract of employment of a teacher is minimal);

(4) the employee must not have validly signed away his right to claim unfair dismissal;

(5) the employee must show that he has been dismissed; and

(6) the employee must have made his claim within the time limit for doing so.

8.2 It is important to note that the governing body of a maintained school which has a delegated budget is the primary respondent to a claim of unfair dismissal, even where the employee's contractual employer was the LEA.[1] (The effects in employment law of a maintained school having a delegated budget are considered at length in Chapter 4 above.)

---

[1] See Education (Modification of Enactments Relating to Employment) (England) Order 2003, SI 2003/1964, arts 6(1) and (2) and Education (Modification of Enactments Relating to Employment) (Wales) Order 2006, SI 2006/1073, arts 6(1) and (2).

Conditions for claiming unfair dismissal

Employee or self-employed?

8.3 In most school situations, the employment status of staff will be straightforward, but not in every case. The label given by the parties to a relevant relationship is not conclusive. A number of factors have to be taken into account in determining for example whether or not a purportedly self-employed person actually is self-employed. The case of *Davis v New England College*[2] is illustrative of this.

Davis v New England College

A person who had been a self-employed freelance lecturer was engaged by New England College under an annual contract. Other lecturers were also employed under annual contracts, and the terms of all of the annual contracts were similar. After his appointment, the new lecturer asked to be treated as self-employed because he wished to retain that status for tax and national insurance purposes. The college paid his salary without deducting national insurance contributions or tax. His contract was renewed annually until he was employed under what was called a 'terminal contract'. That contract expired in May 1974 and the lecturer was not re-engaged. He claimed compensation for unfair dismissal. The industrial tribunal which heard his claim decided that he had failed to prove that he was employed under a contract of service and that he was therefore not entitled to claim unfair dismissal. The lecturer appealed against that ruling.

Decision of the Employment Appeal Tribunal

The EAT allowed the lecturer's appeal. It decided that, in determining whether the lecturer was engaged under a contract of service, it was necessary to look at the circumstances objectively. Looked at objectively, the tribunal decided, the relationship between the lecturer and the college was that of employee and employer. The EAT ruled that neither the lecturer's request to be treated as self-employed nor the fact that for fiscal purposes the college treated him as self-employed altered the contractual relationship between them. Accordingly, the EAT decided that the lecturer was an employee and that his claim for compensation for unfair dismissal should be heard on its merits.

8.4 *Davis v New England College* was a fairly extreme case, because the label of self-employment had been applied to a relationship which was clearly one of employment. In most cases there will be further factors which could be relied upon in arguing that the relationship is one of self-employment. It is necessary to consider a number of factors in deciding whether a relationship is one of employment or self-employment. Before referring to those factors, it is necessary to sound a note of caution. These factors result from the technicalities of the common law, and s 23 of the Employment Relations Act 1999 empowers the Secretary of State to introduce regulations giving to many of those people who are at present regarded by the common law as self-employed the right to claim unfair dismissal and other employment law

---

[2] [1977] ICR 6.

rights which have so far been available only to employees. However, there is no sign that that power will be acted upon.

8.5 The most relevant factors which are important in indicating that a person is an employee are that:

(1) he may not work for rivals of his employer (using that word in an informal and neutral sense);

(2) he is subject to his employer's disciplinary code; and

(3) he may not profit from his own efforts (his employer doing so instead).

8.6 On the other hand, if:

(1) a person assumes financial risk in relation to the work which he does for his employer (again using that word in a neutral manner);

(2) he has an opportunity to profit from sound management in the performance of his work;

(3) he owns his own tools or other equipment with which he carries out the tasks which he performs for his employer;

(4) he hires his own assistants;

(5) he works for a number of other employers;

(6) he is not obliged to work for the employer at the employer's request; and

(7) he may substitute someone else to carry out the work which he has agreed to do for his employer,

then the person will be self-employed.

Continuity of service

8.7 Since 1 June 1999,[3] the statutory requirement in the UK for being able to claim unfair dismissal has been one year's continuous service (except in certain circumstances, regarding which see below[4]). Continuity of employment is determined by reference to some rather technical rules. The main relevant rule is that an employee may have continuity of employment even though there have been gaps between periods of employment. Section 212 of the ERA 1996 contains the main rules relating to continuity of employment, and provides as follows:

---

[3] See the Unfair Dismissal and Statement of Reasons for Dismissal (Variation of Qualifying Period) Order 1999, SI 1999/1436.
[4] See paras **8.38–8.42** below.

'(1) Any week during the whole or part of which an employee's relations with his employer are governed by a contract of employment counts in computing the employee's period of employment. . . .

(3) Subject to subsection (4), any week (not within subsection (1)) during the whole or part of which an employee is –
   (a) incapable of work in consequence of sickness or injury,
   (b) absent from work on account of a temporary cessation of work, or
   (c) absent from work in circumstances such that, by arrangement or custom, he is regarded as continuing in the employment of his employer for any purpose,

counts in computing the employee's period of employment.

(4) Not more than twenty-six weeks count under subsection (3)(a) between any periods falling under subsection (1).'

8.8 Fixed-term contracts of employment for a term or an academic year are common in the education sector. In *Ford v Warwickshire County Council*,[5] the House of Lords ruled that the gaps between academic years will normally not break an employee's continuity of employment, there being merely a 'temporary cessation of work'.[6] However, in *Surrey County Council v Lewis*,[7] the House of Lords ruled that if an employee works under a series of contfracts each of which is for (say) an academic year, but the contracts are not to teach the same courses, then the gaps between these contracts will not be temporary cessations of work. Rather, the gaps will break continuity. The House of Lords stated that contracts of employment needed to be 'in the same series' for the approach in *Ford v Warwickshire County Council* to apply.

8.9 A further major factor to bear in mind when considering continuity of employment is the possibility that there has been a transfer of an undertaking or part of an undertaking to which the provisions of the Transfer of Undertakings (Protection of Employment) Regulations 2006[8] (TUPE) applied. Where TUPE applies (and that question is considered briefly below[9]) and there is such a transfer, then employees who are employed in the undertaking or part transferred are regarded as having been employed by the transferee from the beginning of their period of employment with the transferor. However, there are some complications in regard to the application of TUPE to the reorganisation of some State schools.[10] In any event, though, in some situations other statutory provisions can affect continuity of employment, for example, where a school became, or ceased to be, grant-maintained.

8.10 It may be necessary in certain circumstances to take into account the fact that an employee's continuous employment for the purpose of making a claim

---

[5] [1983] ICR 273.
[6] For the purpose of what is now s 212(3)(b) of the ERA 1996.
[7] [1987] ICR 982.
[8] SI 2006/246.
[9] See Chapter 10.
[10] See para **10.2** below.

of unfair dismissal is extended if he is summarily dismissed and the employer is not entitled by the employee's conduct to dismiss him in that way. The employee's employment is then extended by the period of the notice period to which he is entitled by virtue of s 86 of the ERA 1996.[11]

Illegality

8.11 The likelihood of a contract of employment in a school being tainted with illegality (and therefore preventing an employee from claiming unfair dismissal) is minimal. However, it should be noted that where:

(1) one person provides services to another person;

(2) the provider and the recipient of those services label the relationship of the provider as one of self-employment (and therefore subject to a more favourable tax régime than that relating to employment); and

(3) the relationship is subsequently decided by a court or tribunal to be in reality a relationship of employment,

the contract will not necessarily be illegal.[12] Only if the purpose of both the parties was to avoid paying tax would the contract necessarily be illegal.[13] However, the reported decisions are in some respects contradictory and no clear guidance can be given as to when an employment tribunal would be likely to decide that an employee could not claim unfair dismissal because of the illegality of his contract of employment.

Waiver of right to claim unfair dismissal

8.12 The general rule is that an employee may not validly waive his right to claim unfair dismissal. This is for the protection of employees who might otherwise be pressured into agreeing not to enforce their rights where they could not otherwise obtain employment. However, an employee may validly compromise a claim of unfair dismissal and thereby preclude himself from pursuing that claim before an employment tribunal if he has received independent advice as to the terms and effect of the proposed agreement and, in particular, its effect on his ability to pursue his rights before an employment tribunal.[14] The advice must have been given by:

(1) a qualified lawyer;

(2) an officer, official, employee or member of an independent trade union who has been certified in writing by the trade union as competent to give advice and as authorised to do so on behalf of the trade union;

---

[11] ERA 1996, s 97(2). See para **5.2** above concerning s 86.
[12] *Young & Woods Ltd v West* [1980] IRLR 201.
[13] See for example *Salveson v Simons* [1994] ICR 409.
[14] Under s 203 of the ERA 1996.

(3) a person who works at an advice centre (whether as an employee or a volunteer) and has been certified in writing by the centre as competent to give advice and as authorised to do so on behalf of the centre; or

(4) a person 'of a description specified in an order made by the Secretary of State' under s 203(3A)(d) of the ERA 1996.

8.13 There are some further detailed limitations on the power of an employee to compromise a claim under the ERA 1996 in order to ensure that the adviser is genuinely independent. An agreement to submit a relevant dispute to arbitration under a scheme which has effect by virtue of an order made under s 212A of the Trade Union and Labour Relations (Consolidation) Act 1992 also has the effect of precluding an employee from pursuing a claim arising under the ERA 1996 before an employment tribunal.

8.14 In order to be valid, an agreement entered into under s 203 of the ERA 1996:

(1) must be in writing;

(2) must relate to the particular proceedings; and

(3) there must have been in force, at the time when the independent adviser gave the necessary advice, a contract of insurance or an indemnity provided for members of a profession or professional body covering the risk of a claim by the employee or worker in respect of loss arising in consequence of the advice.

The agreement must also identify the adviser and state that the conditions regulating compromise agreements under the ERA 1996 are satisfied.

8.15 In practice, it has been known for an independent adviser to be asked to become a party to a compromise agreement entered into under s 203, or to warrant that he has given the necessary advice. This is not necessary for the agreement to have effect. If the agreement does not bind the employee because the necessary advice has not been given, then the employer can simply continue to defend the claim, and may either decline to pay the claimant the sum agreed to be paid under the compromise agreement or claim it back from the employee if it has already been paid. Furthermore, a claimant will not usually be able to require the adviser to become a party to the agreement or to warrant that the necessary advice has been given. In any event, if a claimant were paid a substantial sum pursuant to a compromise agreement which was in fact invalid and therefore not binding on the claimant (even if the invalidity did not result from any fault on the part of the claimant) and the claimant continued the proceedings, then the tribunal might be able properly to decline to grant the employee any further compensation. This would be by analogy with the approach taken by the industrial tribunal (with the clear approval of the EAT) in *Courage Take Home Trade Ltd v Keys*.[15] However, the facts of that case were unusual, and it seems likely that the best approach would be to offset any amount paid under the agreement against the total of any amounts determined by the tribunal to be payable by the employer to the employee. It is of note that the EAT took this approach in *NRG Victory Reinsurance Ltd v Alexander*,[16] despite having been referred to *Keys*.

Was the employee dismissed?

8.16 In order to be able to make a valid claim of unfair dismissal, the employee must show that he has been dismissed. This can occur only in three situations, set out in the following three paragraphs.[17]

Termination of the contract

8.17 The most common means by which a contract of employment is terminated is by the employer either giving notice of termination or terminating the contract of employment without notice (for example by dismissing the employee summarily for gross misconduct).

Ending of a limited-term contract

8.18 An employee will also be regarded as dismissed if he is employed under a contract which used to be called a fixed-term contract, but which is now called a 'limited-term contract', and the contract ends 'by virtue of the limiting event' without being renewed or extended.[18] The exact date for the ending of an employee's employment under a limited-term contract need not be known in advance if the contract will end on the happening of a particular event whose date *is* known. This principle is illustrated by *Wiltshire County Council v National Association of Teachers in Further and Higher Education*.[19]

> *Wiltshire County Council v National Association of Teachers in Further and Higher Education*
>
> An employee was engaged as a part-time teacher at a college of further education. She entered into fresh contracts of employment each year to teach specified subjects on specified occasions for each academic session, which ran from September to the end of June. The classes which she taught were subject to there being sufficient enrolments and did not necessarily continue until the end of the academic session. She was paid only for the hours which she taught. She was not offered a new contract at the end of an academic session and complained to an industrial tribunal that she had been dismissed unfairly. Her employer argued that she had not been dismissed, on the basis that no specific date for the ending of her contract of employment had been agreed since courses could be terminated prematurely. The tribunal decided that:

---

[15] [1986] ICR 874.
[16] [1992] ICR 675.
[17] See ERA 1996, s 95(1).
[18] Ibid, s 95(1)(b).
[19] [1980] ICR 455.

- she was employed under a contract for a fixed term,
- she had therefore been dismissed, and
- the tribunal accordingly had jurisdiction to hear her claim.

The employer appealed to the EAT, which dismissed the appeal. The employer appealed again, to the Court of Appeal.

Decision of the Court of Appeal

The Court of Appeal dismissed the employer's appeal. The court decided that since the employee was bound by her contract of employment to work for the period of the academic session if so required, it was a 'fixed term' contract within the meaning of what is now s 95(1)(b) of the ERA 1996. Accordingly, the court decided, since that contract had not been renewed, the employee had been dismissed for the purposes of s 95(1)(b).

'Constructive' dismissal

8.19 The employee may be dismissed 'constructively'.[20] An employee is 'constructively dismissed' where the employer either (1) repudiates the contract of employment (see the next paragraph below for what is meant by the word 'repudiate' in this context), or (2) or commits a fundamental or substantial breach of the contract of employment, and the employee terminates the contract in response to that repudiation or (as the case may be) breach.[21] The employee is said in that situation to have accepted the repudiation or (as appropriate) terminated the contract in response to the breach.

8.20 A repudiation of a contract occurs where a party to a contract shows an intention no longer to be bound by the terms of the contract in some essential respect. This may occur not only where the party is unwilling, but also where he is unable, to carry out the terms of the contract. A fundamental breach of contract is more or less self-explanatory. A repudiation may occur without a breach of the contract: all that is necessary is that the party in question indicates (whether by words or conduct) that he will not be performing the contract in some essential respect. (Sometimes, possibly a little confusingly, a breach of contract is said to constitute such an indication, in which case the breach is said to be repudiatory.)

8.21 The employee must not 'sit on his rights' where the employer has repudiated or fundamentally breached the contract of employment. If the employee delays acting for too long, then he will lose the right to claim unfair dismissal. Furthermore, where he leaves his employment (and that will occur in most cases[22]), he must make it clear that he is leaving his employment in response to the conduct of the employer, although the employee may rely on

---

[20] This term does not appear in the employment protection legislation, but has acquired meaning in relation to unfair dismissal.
[21] *Western Excavating (ECC) Ltd v Sharp* [1978] ICR 221.
[22] See para **8.24** below for the situation in which an employee need not do so in order to be able to claim constructive dismissal.

conduct which in the event is found not to have been repudiatory, as long as the employer was in fact in repudiation and the employee relied in some way on the repudiatory conduct.[23] Similarly, if an employee leaves one employment to commence another, then he is likely nevertheless to be able to claim to have been constructively dismissed by the first employer.[24]

8.22 In this context, the implied term of trust and confidence[25] is often of great relevance. However, even where an employee claims that his employer has breached that term and therefore 'constructively' dismissed him, it is not necessary to show that the employer has deliberately breached the contract of employment. Rather, all that is necessary is that the conduct of the employer, viewed objectively, was likely to destroy or seriously damage the relationship of trust and confidence.[26]

8.23 Any reduction or threatened reduction in the remuneration paid to an employee under a contract of employment will be a repudiation of the contract (except, possibly, but only possibly, a minor reduction).[27] It has been said that even a threat to terminate a contract of employment in accordance with its terms (in other words, usually, on notice) if an employee refuses to accept a reduction in the value of the benefits to which he is entitled under the contract, may be a constructive dismissal.[28] However, this was doubted in a later case,[29] and does not seem right. In any event, an employer may fairly impose such a reduction fairly (for some other substantial reason, regarding which see further below[30]), but a dismissal in those circumstances must be not only substantively but also procedurally fair.[31]

Changing of terms of employment

8.24 It is the ending of the *contract* of employment, and *not* the ending of the employment, which brings about a dismissal.[32] Accordingly, the fact that an employee remains in the employment of the employer does not by itself mean that he has not been dismissed. This was put beyond doubt by the decision of the EAT in *Hogg v Dover College*.[33] As a result, where an employer imposes new terms of employment on an employee, either by notice or otherwise, and the employee remains in the employment, the employee may nevertheless be able to claim unfair dismissal.

---

[23] *Meikle v Nottinghamshire County Council* [2005] ICR 1, para 33.
[24] Ibid.
[25] Concerning which, see paras **5.9–5.10** above.
[26] See *Omilaju v Waltham Forest London Borough Council* [2005] ICR 481, para 14(4).
[27] *Cantor Fitzgerald International v Callaghan* [1999] ICR 639.
[28] *Greenaway Harrison Ltd v Wiles* [1994] IRLR 380.
[29] *Kerry Foods Ltd v Lynch* [2005] IRLR 680.
[30] See para **8.82** onwards below.
[31] See para **8.85** below.
[32] See s 95(1)(a) of the ERA 1996.
[33] [1990] ICR 39, approved in this regard by the Court of Appeal in *Jones v Governing Body of Burdett Coutts School* [1999] ICR 38, at 42.

Mutually agreed termination or resignation

8.25 Sometimes, an employee and his employer may agree that the employee is to leave the employer's employment. Where that occurs, it is often said that there has been a mutually agreed termination of the employee's employment. The word 'mutually' is used to emphasise that an employer cannot for the purposes of the law of unfair dismissal force an employee validly to agree that his employment will end. The following passage from the judgment of Waite LJ in the case of *Jones v Mid-Glamorgan County Council*[34] indicates the effect of these principles (applied in fact to a retirement).

> 'Courts and tribunals have been willing, from the earliest days of the unfair dismissal jurisdiction, to look, when presented with an apparent resignation, at the substance of the termination for the purpose of inquiring whether the degree of pressure placed on the employee by the employer to retire amounted in reality to a dismissal. . . . At one end of the scale is the blatant instance of a resignation preceded by the employer's ultimatum "Retire on my terms or be fired" where it would not be surprising to find the industrial tribunal drawing the inference that what had occurred was a dismissal. At the other extreme is the instance of the long-serving employee who is attracted to early retirement by benevolent terms of severance offered by grateful employers as a reward for loyalty, where one would expect the industrial tribunal to draw the contrary inference of termination by mutual agreement. Between those two extremes there are bound to lie much more debatable cases to which, according to their particular circumstances, the industrial tribunals are required to apply their expertise in determining whether the borderline has been crossed between a resignation that is truly voluntary and a retirement unwillingly made in response to a threat. I doubt myself whether, given the infinite variety of circumstance, there can be much scope for assistance from authority in discharging that task: indeed attempts to draw analogies from other cases may provide more confusion than guidance. In cases where precedent is nevertheless thought to be of value, the authority that will no doubt continue to be cited is *Sheffield v Oxford Controls Co Ltd* [1979] I.C.R. 396.'

8.26 The facts and outcome of *Sheffield v Oxford Controls*[35] are particularly instructive, and are as follows.

> *Sheffield v Oxford Controls Co Ltd*
>
> An employee was both a director and an employee of an electronics company, which also employed his wife. The families of the employee and his co-director held an equal shareholding in the company until the co-director's family were able to put more money in the company and therefore increase their shareholding. Following a disagreement in which the employee's wife was threatened with dismissal, the employee threatened that he would leave his employment if his wife was dismissed. He was then told that if he did not resign voluntarily, he too would be dismissed. After some negotiation he signed an agreement to resign in return for certain financial benefits. He complained to an industrial tribunal that he had

---

[34] [1997] ICR 815, 818C–819A.
[35] [1979] ICR 396.

been unfairly dismissed. The tribunal rejected his complaint on the basis that he had resigned and had not been dismissed by the employers. The employee appealed against that ruling.

Decision of the Employment Appeal Tribunal

The EAT dismissed the appeal on its facts. The EAT stated, however, that where an employee was threatened that if he did not resign then he would be dismissed and the threat caused the employee to resign, there would be a dismissal in law. Nevertheless, where a resignation was brought about not by the threat of dismissal but by other factors such as an offer of financial benefits, there was no dismissal. Here, since the employee had agreed satisfactory terms upon which he was prepared to resign so that the threat of dismissal was not in fact the cause of his resignation, he had not been dismissed and the industrial tribunal's decision was correct.

8.27 In addition to *Sheffield v Oxford Controls*, *Birch v Liverpool University*[36] may be helpful in deciding whether a mutually agreed termination of a contract of employment has occurred. *Birch* concerned an early retirement scheme. The employer invited employees to apply for early retirement under the scheme, but stated that the scheme was not a redundancy scheme and that any application by an employee was subject to the final approval of the employer. Two employees took early retirement under the scheme and then claimed redundancy payments (which are payable only if the employee has been dismissed[37]). The employees were decided by the Court of Appeal not to have been dismissed.

Frustration

When is a contract ended by frustration?

8.28 In some situations, an employee's contract of employment may have been ended by what is called 'frustration'. A contract is frustrated where there is an event which was not foreseen or provided for by the parties to the contract at the time the contract was entered into, and which renders the performance of the contract radically different from that which the parties contemplated at the time when they entered into the contract. For example, this will occur in most cases if an employee is sent to prison.

Imprisonment

8.29 The facts of *Harrington v Kent County Council*[38] illustrate the application of the doctrine of frustration.

---

[36] [1985] ICR 470.
[37] See paras **7.1** and **7.2** above.
[38] [1980] IRLR 353.

Harrington v Kent County Council

Mr Harrington was employed as a teacher at a county primary school. He was suspended following allegations of indecent behaviour with some of the pupils. He was then convicted on two charges of indecent exposure and one of indecent assault and was sentenced to a total of 12 months' imprisonment. Leave to appeal against the conviction was granted but bail was refused. While he was in prison, his employer, the County Council, wrote to him, noting his convictions and sentence and saying that 'In the circumstances, I have to inform you that your appointment with the County Council at the Hollicondane County Primary School is regarded as automatically terminated by the sentence of imprisonment which, by its length, renders it impossible for you to perform your part of the contract.'

The teacher's appeal against his conviction for indecent assault was successful. On being released, he requested that he be re-engaged but the County Council made it clear that he would not be re-employed. The teacher made a complaint to an industrial tribunal of unfair dismissal. The tribunal decided that his complaint could not succeed because he had not been dismissed. According to the tribunal, when the teacher was sent to prison for 12 months, that 'automatically brought the employment to an end'. The subsequent appeal against conviction could not continue the existence of the contract because, by that time, it was already extinct. The teacher appealed to the EAT.

Decision of the Employment Appeal Tribunal

The EAT decided that the industrial tribunal had correctly decided that the County Council was entitled to treat the teacher's contract of employment as having come to an end through frustration when he was sentenced to 12 months' imprisonment, even though it was aware that he was appealing against that sentence. The EAT also decided that the industrial tribunal had approached the matter correctly when looking at the events at the time of the sentence of imprisonment. Where an employee is convicted and sentenced to a term of imprisonment, knowledge of an appeal does not prevent the contract from having been frustrated by the conviction and sentence of imprisonment.

In this case, at the date of conviction, the teacher had been found guilty of offences closely connected with his work and, as a result, had been sentenced to 12 months' imprisonment.[39] Allowing for remission for good conduct, this meant that he would be unable to perform his duties for a period of eight months. At that stage, said the EAT, the inevitable conclusion was that those events had so destroyed the foundation of the contract between the parties that it could no longer be regarded as being in existence. The fact that an appeal was launched, which eventually turned out to be successful, could not alter the position as it was at the date of conviction.

Long-term illness

8.30 A lengthy period of illness could have the effect of frustrating a contract of employment. This was expressly recognised by the Court of Appeal in

---

[39] It is not clear why the EAT thought that the fact that the offences were closely connected with the employee's work was relevant to the question of whether or not his contract of employment had been frustrated.

Notcutt v Universal Equipment Co (London) Ltd.[40] However, the doctrine of frustration was said by the lay members of the EAT in *Williams v Watsons Luxury Coaches Ltd*[41] to be 'one which, unless severely limited in its scope, can do harm to good industrial relations as it provides an easy escape from the obligations of investigation which should be carried out by a conscientious employer'. Furthermore, the Disability Discrimination Act 1995 may well make it difficult to argue that a contract of employment has been frustrated by the employee's illness. This is illustrated by the judgment of the EAT in *Williams v Watsons Luxury Coaches Ltd*, in which the proper approach to take in deciding whether there has been a frustration of a contract of employment in the event of the employee's illness was described in the following manner:

> 'First, ... the court must guard against too easy an application of the doctrine [of frustration], more especially when redundancy occurs and also when the true situation may be a dismissal by reason of disability. Secondly, ... although it is not necessary to decide that frustration occurred on a particular date, nevertheless an attempt to decide the relevant date is far from a useless exercise as it may help to determine in the mind of the court whether it really is a true frustration situation. Thirdly, ... there are a number of factors which may help to decide the issue as they may each point in one or other direction. These we take from the judgment of Phillips J. in *Egg Stores (Stamford Hill) Ltd v Leibovici* [1977] I.C.R. 260, 265:
>
>> "Among the matters to be taken into account in such a case in reaching a decision are these: (1) the length of the previous employment; (2) how long it had been expected that the employment would continue; (3) the nature of the job; (4) the nature, length and effect of the illness or disabling event; (5) the need of the employer for the work to be done, and the need for a replacement to do it; (6) the risk to the employer of acquiring obligations in respect of redundancy payments or compensation for unfair dismissal to the replacement employee; (7) whether wages have continued to be paid; (8) the acts and the statements of the employer in relation to the employment, including the dismissal of, or failure to dismiss, the employee; and (9) whether in all the circumstances a reasonable employer could be expected to wait any longer."
>
> To these we would add the terms of the contract as to the provisions for sickness pay, if any, and also, a consideration of the prospects of recovery. Fourthly – see *F.C. Shepherd & Co. Ltd. v. Jerrom* [1986] I.C.R. 802 – the party alleging frustration should not be allowed to rely upon the frustrating event if that event was caused by that party – at least where it was caused by its fault.'

Alternative employment in a redundancy situation

8.31 If an employee is given notice of dismissal by reason of redundancy, but before the notice expires the employee is offered a new job by his current employer or an associated employer to start within four weeks of the ending of his original contract of employment, then the employee may not be entitled to

---

[40] [1986] ICR 414.
[41] [1990] ICR 536, 542H.

a redundancy payment.[42] The reason for that is that where certain conditions are satisfied, the employee is treated for the purposes of the law of redundancy as not having been dismissed. However, the employee could nevertheless claim unfair dismissal by reason of the ending of his original contract of employment. This was confirmed by the Court of Appeal's decision in the case of *Jones v Governing Body of Burdett Coutts School*.[43] Nevertheless, this may be of little practical significance since the employee in that situation would be entitled (at the time of writing) to no more than £620 by way of a basic award and would be unlikely to obtain much by way of a compensatory award if the pay for the new job was commensurate with that of the original job.[44]

Time limit for claiming unfair dismissal

8.32 There is a three-month time limit for claiming unfair dismissal. This runs from the 'effective date of termination' of the contract of employment[45] which is not necessarily the same date as the date of the termination of that contract. It is very much a question of fact for the employment tribunal to decide what was the *effective* date of termination, but it is likely that if an employer makes it clear that it no longer regards a person as an employee, then the date when that occurs will be the effective date of termination.[46]

8.33 The 3-month time limit can be extended, but only where the employee can show that it was 'not reasonably practicable' to make the claim within that time limit. There is a considerable amount of case-law regarding what may and may not properly be regarded as 'not reasonably practicable'. One principle which is clear is that the negligence of an adviser will not suffice. (Instead, the employee is left with a claim in the law of negligence against the adviser.) The claim must be delivered to the relevant building – so a claim made by fax before midnight on the last day within the 3-month time limit will be in time.

Dismissals arising from a strike or other industrial action

8.34 An employee is given protection from dismissal for taking part in industrial action which is immune from liability in tort because it is 'official' (that is, because it has been approved by a ballot conducted in accordance with ss 226 to 235 of the Trade Union and Labour Relations (Consolidation) Act 1992[47]) if:

(1) the dismissal takes effect within a period called the 'protected period', which is a minimum of 12 weeks from the commencement of the industrial action,[48] or

---

[42] See paras **7.8** and **7.9** above.
[43] [1999] ICR 38; see especially at 43F.
[44] ERA 1996, s 121. See para **8.111** below regarding basic and compensatory awards.
[45] ERA 1996, s 97.
[46] See *Robert Cort & Son Ltd v Charman* [1981] ICR 816 and *BMK Ltd v Logue* [1993] ICR 601.
[47] See further paras **9.9–9.10** below in relation to official industrial action.
[48] Trade Union and Labour Relations (Consolidation) Act 1992, s 238A(3), and (7A)–(7D).

(2) the dismissal takes effect after the end of that 12-week period, but
 (a) the employee had stopped taking the industrial action in question during that period,[49] or
 (b) the employee had not stopped taking that action within that period, but the employer 'had not taken such procedural steps as would have been reasonable for the purposes of resolving the dispute to which the protected industrial action relates'.[50]

8.35 Certain matters are to be taken into account in deciding whether the employer failed to take steps of the sort just described. These include 'whether the employer or a union unreasonably refused, after the start of the protected industrial action, a request that conciliation services be used'.[51] However, the merits of the dispute are irrelevant for this purpose.[52] If, though, the union repudiates the action during the protected period and the employee continues the action on the working day after the next one after the day on which the repudiation takes place, then the protection is lost.[53]

8.36 The protection takes the form of the dismissal being automatically unfair,[54] and no qualifying period applies to the making of a claim of unfair dismissal on this basis.[55]

Employer's burden of proof

8.37 Where an employee claims unfair dismissal, the employer must prove the reason, or, if there was more than one, the principal reason, for the dismissal.[56] This means that in practice, as long as dismissal is admitted by the employer, the employer gives evidence first in the employment tribunal.

Automatically unfair dismissal

8.38 Certain dismissals are automatically unfair. The variety of automatically unfair dismissal which is most likely to occur in practice is that which occurs where the employer has failed to comply with the applicable dismissal and discipline procedure provided for by the Employment Act 2002.[57] Other automatically unfair dismissals include dismissals for pregnancy, childbirth or a related reason.[58] They also include dismissals in certain situations where health and safety matters are in issue, for example where there is no committee including health and safety representatives (whether from a recognised trade

---

[49] Trade Union and Labour Relations (Consolidation) Act 1992, s 238A(4).
[50] Ibid, s 238A(5).
[51] See ibid, s 238A(6).
[52] Ibid, s 238A(7).
[53] Ibid, s 238A(8). See s 21 of that Act for what is meant by the word 'repudiate' in this context.
[54] See ibid, s 238A(2).
[55] See ibid, s 239(1). See too s 239(2) concerning the time limit for claiming unfair dismissal, which is six months rather than three months.
[56] ERA 1996, s 98(1).
[57] See para **2.44** above.
[58] See further para **5.58** above.

union or elected by a ballot of employees), and an employee is dismissed for bringing to the employer's attention by reasonable means, circumstances connected with the employee's work which the employee reasonably believed were harmful or potentially harmful to health or safety.[59]

8.39 The dismissal of an employee for acting or proposing to act as an employee representative for the purposes of such a committee,[60] or for acting or proposing to act as an employee representative in relation to redundancies or the TUPE, is also automatically unfair.[61] A dismissal will also be automatically unfair where the employee is dismissed for asserting (in good faith) a statutory right of the sort referred to in s 104(4) of the ERA 1996.[62] Those include any right under the ERA 1996 the remedy for an infringement of which is by way of a complaint or reference to an employment tribunal.

8.40 If an employee is dismissed for having made a 'protected disclosure'[63] then the dismissal will also be automatically unfair.[64] A protected disclosure includes 'any disclosure of information which, in the reasonable belief of the worker making the disclosure, tends to show . . . (b) that a person has failed, is failing or is likely to fail to comply with any legal obligation to which he is subject'. This could have a wide effect in maintained schools. However, the disclosure must, for the protection to apply, have been made to one of a limited number of people. These include the worker's employer, although a worker is not obliged to disclose a relevant matter to his employer in certain circumstances.

8.41 Employees who are dismissed for being on jury service,[65] for refusing to work more than they are required by the Working Time Regulations 1998 to work,[66] for performing functions as trustees of occupational pension schemes relating to their employment,[67] for seeking to enforce the national minimum wage,[68] for seeking to enforce the right to tax credits under s 25 of the Tax Credits Act 2002,[69] and for seeking to work flexibly,[70] will all be dismissed automatically unfairly.

8.42 No period of continuous employment is required in order to be able to claim that a dismissal was automatically unfair for any of the reasons referred

---

[59] ERA 1996, s 100(1)(c).
[60] Ibid, s 100(1).
[61] Ibid, s 103.
[62] Ibid, s 104(1).
[63] Within the meaning of ibid, s 43B.
[64] Ibid, s 103A.
[65] Ibid, s 98B.
[66] Ibid, s 101A; see para **5.27** above concerning the Working Time Regulations 1998, SI 1998/1833.
[67] ERA 1996, s 102.
[68] Ibid, s 104A.
[69] Ibid, s 104B.
[70] Ibid, s 104C; see para **6.87** onwards above concerning the right to ask to work flexibly for this purpose.

to above, except the first one.[71] Thus an employee will need a year's continuous employment in order to claim that he has been automatically dismissed unfairly merely because of a failure to comply with a requirement of the applicable DDP.

Potentially fair reasons for dismissal

8.43 In order to be fair, a dismissal has to be for one of six reasons. These are:

(1) capability;

(2) conduct;

(3) retirement;

(4) redundancy;

(5) the fact that 'the employee could not continue to work in the position which he held without contravention (either on his part or on that of his employer) of a duty or restriction imposed by or under an enactment' (in other words, a statutory bar);[72] or

(6) 'some other substantial reason'.[73]

8.44 The first two of these reasons are at first sight straightforward (although they are referred to as capability and conduct rather than 'incapability' and 'misconduct'). However, difficulties can arise where an employee appears to be incapable, but is also refusing to carry out instructions designed to improve his performance. In that situation, the principal reason for the dismissal may well be the employee's conduct rather than his capability, although the reason for the refusal to follow the instructions may be a fear by the employee that he will be unable to comply with them. (The main principles of unfair dismissal law applicable to dismissals for conduct or capability are described in paras **8.52–8.79** below.)

8.45 Dismissals for retirement are considered in the chapter relating to discrimination, since they are most conveniently seen as protected primarily by the limited prohibition on discrimination on the ground of age conferred by the Employment Equality (Age) Regulations 2006.[74]

8.46 The definition of redundancy is set out and considered in para **7.2** above. Even if an employer could show that an employee's dismissal was for redundancy, on a complaint of unfair dismissal the employer would have to

---

[71] ERA 1996, s 108(3).
[72] These five reasons are contained in ibid, s 98(2).
[73] This sixth reason is set out in ibid, s 98(1)(b).
[74] SI 2006/1031. See para **6.107** onwards above for the law relating to dismissal on retirement.

show that the dismissal was reasonable in the circumstances. The employment tribunal would expect the employer to have followed a fair procedure (see paras **7.19–7.27** above).

8.47 There is no need to consider here at length the situation where there is a statutory bar (since that situation is considered in paras **8.79–8.81** below). However, it is worth mentioning here that if the Secretary of State were to bar a teacher in relevant employment,[75] then although the teacher's employer would be obliged to dismiss the teacher, the employer would still need to act reasonably in doing so in order to avoid a successful claim of unfair dismissal by the teacher.[76] However, even if a fair procedure were not followed, the teacher might not be awarded any compensation for the failure.[77]

8.48 A number of reasons may constitute 'some other substantial reason' for a dismissal. One is that there was a 'sound, good business reason' for the dismissal.[78] This may occur where the employer has to carry out a reorganisation of its activities. However, if the reorganisation results in what is often loosely called a 'redundancy situation', and an employee is dismissed for redundancy, then the reason for the dismissal will be redundancy. This is usually most important in relation to the potential entitlement of the employee to a redundancy payment.

8.49 In carrying out the reorganisation, the employer will often wish to impose changes to the terms and conditions of an employee. A simple imposition of such a change (without an express termination of the existing contract of employment) will often give rise to a right to claim unfair dismissal on the basis that the employer has 'constructively' dismissed the employee.[79] However, such a dismissal could in theory still be fair.[80] As should be clear from what is said in para **8.24** above, where the change is imposed by terminating the existing contract of employment (on notice) and offering new terms, the employee will have the clear right, subject to the conditions indicated above, to claim unfair dismissal.

Was the dismissal reasonable?

8.50 Even if a dismissal was for a potentially fair reason, it will still be necessary for the tribunal to determine whether it was reasonable in the circumstances to dismiss for that reason. This question must be determined by reference to s 98(4) of the ERA 1996, which provides as follows:

---

[75] Under s 142(1) of the Education Act 2002, concerning which, see para **3.15** onwards above.
[76] See further paras **8.79–8.80** below.
[77] See para **8.115** below.
[78] See *Hollister v NFU* [1979] ICR 542; see further para **8.82** onwards below.
[79] See paras **8.23** and **8.24** above.
[80] See para **8.83** below.

'Where the employer has fulfilled the requirements of subsection (1), the determination of the question whether the dismissal is fair or unfair (having regard to the reason shown by the employer):

(a) depends on whether in the circumstances (including the size and administrative resources of the employer's undertaking) the employer acted reasonably or unreasonably in treating it as a sufficient reason for dismissing the employee; and
(b) shall be determined in accordance with equity and the substantial merits of the case.'

8.51 The question of the reasonableness of the dismissal will therefore be determined in the light of the size and administrative resources of the employer, and in accordance with 'equity and the substantial merits of the case'. The test applied by employment tribunals is whether the dismissal of the employee was within the range of reasonable responses of a reasonable employer. Specific considerations apply to the five potentially fair reasons for dismissal, however, and they are discussed in the following paragraphs below.

Substantive fairness in capability dismissals

Proving incapability and offering an opportunity to improve

8.52 Capability dismissals are often the most difficult to defend successfully. This is because it is usually necessary to be able to put some substantial, objective evidence of incapability before the tribunal, in order to show that the dismissal was reasonable. Furthermore, it is usually necessary to be able to show that the employer has given the employee a reasonable opportunity to improve, and a warning must usually have been given. Moreover, the warning must have been sufficiently clear with regard to the consequences of a failure to comply with the warning. As it was put both helpfully and graphically in the case of *Winterhalter Gastronom v Webb*:[81]

'There are many situations in which a man's apparent capabilities may be stretched when he knows what is demanded of him; many do not know that they are capable of jumping the five-barred gate until the bull is close behind them.'

8.53 This is not to say that a dismissal will automatically be unfair if no warning and proper opportunity to improve is given. For example, in the exceptional case where an employee is constitutionally unable to change, it may be reasonable to dismiss the employee without warning him and affording him a proper opportunity to improve. In this context, appraisals made under the Education (School Teacher Appraisal) (England) Regulations 2001,[82] the

---

[81] [1973] ICR 245.
[82] SI 2001/2855.

Education (School Teacher Performance Management) (England) Regulations 2006,[83] or the Education (School Teacher Appraisal) (Wales) Regulations 2002,[84] may be relevant.

The competence of managers

8.54 The competence of managers may be particularly difficult to assess. However, the EAT has been generous to employers in this regard, as can be seen from *Cook v Thomas Linnell & Sons Ltd*.[85] In that case, in October 1974 the employee became the manager of his employer's depot concerned with the supply of food to retailers on a cash and carry basis. Before then, he had been the manager of another depot of his employer, which was concerned with the wholesale of hardware, and he had had no previous experience of supplying food. His employer was dissatisfied with the standard of his work at the food depot. Warnings and advice (which seem, from the report of the case, to have been only oral) were given to him about his performance but his performance did not improve. He was offered the managership of a non-food depot elsewhere at the same salary, but he declined the offer and was subsequently dismissed. He complained to an industrial tribunal that he had been unfairly dismissed. The majority of the tribunal determined that there had been a fall in the depot's profits which was due to the employee's poor management and that the employers were justified in dismissing him. The employee appealed to the EAT, which said this:

> 'A central theme in [counsel for the employee's] submission was that although there was plenty of contemporary evidence to show that the employers had lost confidence in the ability of the employee as a manager there was no hard factual evidence of a particular kind to support that judgment. Criticism and exhortation, he submitted, however strong, do not by themselves provide evidence of incapacity. It amounts to no more than the assertion of an opinion. It seems to us that this goes too far, although we accept that there is something in the point. When responsible employers have genuinely come to the conclusion over a reasonable period of time that a manager is incompetent we think that it is some evidence that he is incompetent. When one is dealing with routine operations which may be more precisely assessed there is no real problem. It is more difficult when one is dealing with such imponderables as the quality of management, which in the last resort can only be judged by those competent in the field. In such cases as this there may be two extremes. At one extreme is the case where it can be demonstrated, perhaps by reason of some calamitous performance, that the manager is incompetent. The other extreme is the case where no more can be said than that in the opinion of the employer the manager is incompetent, that opinion being expressed for the first time shortly before his dismissal. In between will be cases such as the present where it can be established that throughout the period of employment concerned the employers had progressively growing doubts about the ability of the manager to perform his task satisfactorily. If that can be shown, it is

---

[83] SI 2006/2661.
[84] SI 2002/1394.
[85] [1977] ICR 770.

in our judgement some evidence of his incapacity. It will then be necessary to look to see whether there is any other supporting evidence.'

Employees on probation

8.55 According to the EAT in *White v London Transport Executive*,[86] a probationer is probably entitled to more by way of appraisal than a non-probationer. The decision of the Court of Appeal in *Inner London Education Authority v Lloyd*[87] is to the same effect (*Lloyd* and *White* were decided at about the same time, but in each case without any reference to the other). This means that the induction period which is required by the Education (Induction Arrangements for School Teachers) (Consolidation) (England) Regulations 2001[88] and the Education (Induction Arrangements for School Teachers) (Wales) Regulations 2005[89] may have an effect which is favourable to new teachers. However, the approach taken in *White* would only be relevant to a claim of unfair dismissal if the probationary period were extended past the time when the employee was able to claim unfair dismissal. It is noted that it was decided in *White* that there is an implied term that an employer will take reasonable steps to maintain an appraisal of a probationer employee during the probationary period, giving guidance by advice or warning where necessary. It might be thought that an employee who did not have sufficient service to claim unfair dismissal would have a contractual claim for damages if the employer did not give such guidance, on the basis that the employee had lost the right to claim unfair dismissal where the giving of proper guidance would have led to the employee's employment being terminated later than it was and where at that later date the employee would have had the right to claim unfair dismissal. However, it seems clear that such a claim would not be valid.[90]

Incapability through ill-health

8.56 Dismissals because an employee is suffering from ill-health are usually justified on the basis that the employee has thus become incapable of doing his job. Such dismissals are usually fair only where the employer has consulted the employee about the position before dismissing him, and wherever possible has made reasonable efforts to redeploy the employee to other, suitable, employment. However, the possibility of a claim under the Disability Discrimination Act 1995[91] should be borne in mind before the employee is dismissed.

8.57 The EAT in *East Lindsey District Council v Daubney*[92] said this about dismissals for incapability through ill-health:

---

[86] [1981] IRLR 261.
[87] [1981] IRLR 394. See further para **8.80** below regarding *Lloyd*.
[88] SI 2001/2897, as amended, concerning which, see para **3.50** above onwards.
[89] SI 2005/1818 (W 146).
[90] See *Harper v Virgin Net Ltd* [2005] ICR 921.
[91] Concerning which, see para **6.124** onwards above.
[92] [1977] ICR 566, 571H.

'Unless there are wholly exceptional circumstances, before an employee is dismissed on the ground of ill health it is necessary that he should be consulted and the matter discussed with him, and that in one way or another steps be taken by the employer to discover the true medical position. . . . Discussions and consultation will often bring to light facts and circumstances of which the employers were unaware, and which will throw new light on the problem. Or the employee may wish to seek medical advice on his own account, which, brought to the notice of the employers' medical advisers, will cause them to change their opinion. There are many possibilities. Only one thing is certain, and that is that if the employee is not consulted, and given an opportunity to state his case, an injustice may be done.'

8.58 However, although the employer has a duty to keep himself informed of the employee's progress,[93] in *Mitchell v Arkwood Plastics (Engineering) Ltd*,[94] the EAT said that there is no equivalent duty placed on an employee who is absent from work on account of sickness to keep his employer informed of the prospects for his recovery.

Dismissals of head teachers for incapability

Recognising poor performance

8.59 One of the most difficult situations which may occur in a school context is where it is thought that the head teacher of a school is, or has become, incapable of doing the job of head teacher. In the case of State schools, for example, many members of the governing body will have little direct experience of the teaching profession. Furthermore, the head teacher is likely to be able to hide at least some matters from the governing body, in particular by stifling communications between members of the teaching staff and members of the governing body. In addition, there is usually a reluctance on the part of employees to complain about the under-performance of, or (worse) mistreatment of them by, their managers. Governing bodies will therefore be likely to benefit from the duty of an LEA to make a written report to the chairman of the governing body of a maintained school where the authority has 'serious concerns' about the performance of the head teacher of the school.[95]

Tackling the problem

8.60 A governing body would be well-advised to keep a record of any incidents of behaviour which it regards as examples of incapability on the part of the head teacher. A governing body should in addition be careful to avoid too many persons being involved in the initial stages of an investigation of a head teacher's performance (or, indeed, in any other situation which may lead

---

[93] See *Daubney*, at 571–2, which contains at 572 an interesting discussion concerning the situation where an employee's illness is 'in part at least, functional in nature', and where 'it is probable that the illness and [the employee's] conditions of work were connected'.
[94] [1993] ICR 471.
[95] See para **8.126** below regarding such reports.

to an employee's dismissal).[96] Accordingly, a sensible course of action might be for the chairman of the governing body, or the chairman of the personnel committee (if there is one), and one other governor to take action on receipt of a report from the LEA. The involvement of two governors is suggested in order to avoid allegations of personal bias or a personal vendetta against the head teacher. Furthermore, it may be easier for a head teacher to accept criticisms where they are made by more than one person.

8.61 The two governors might wish to arrange a meeting with the head teacher to discuss their concerns. It might help to set out an agenda in advance of the meeting, and to refer during the meeting to specific examples of what the governors regard as incapability or under-performance. The meeting would best be undertaken with a view to the head teacher remedying the perceived defects in his performance.

8.62 An employee cannot normally safely refuse to attend such a meeting.[97] Accordingly, if the head teacher refused to attend a meeting of the kind suggested, then that refusal would constitute misconduct, for which the head teacher could be disciplined. If he refused to attend outright, then that would be a good reason for his dismissal, and as long as a fair procedure was followed, the dismissal would be likely to be fair.[98]

8.63 It would be likely to be useful to set the head teacher clear targets in regard to the perceived deficiencies, and clear time limits for meeting those targets. Naturally, these targets would have to be reasonable, because if they were not then that could in itself be a 'constructive dismissal' by the governing body.[99]

Substantive fairness in conduct dismissals

Adequate investigation

8.64 A reasonable employer will not normally dismiss an employee for misconduct without having carried out an adequate investigation of the circumstances and given the employee an opportunity to answer the allegation and (if appropriate) plead that there were mitigating circumstances. This will normally involve giving the employee an opportunity to respond to the allegations in a disciplinary hearing.[100]

8.65 It could be argued that in misconduct dismissals, it is sufficient merely to call as a witness the person who made the decision to dismiss, so that the

---

[96] See para **8.91** below.
[97] See for example *Murray v British Rail* [1976] IRLR 382 and *Kramer v South Bedfordshire Community Health Care Trust* [1995] ICR 1066.
[98] See *Murray v British Rail*.
[99] Compare *BBC v Beckett* [1983] IRLR 43. See para **8.19** above concerning constructive dismissals generally.
[100] Regarding which, see para **8.92** below.

person can recount the investigation conducted and testify that he honestly believed what was told to him by witnesses of fact at the disciplinary hearing which led to the employee's dismissal. This is all that the leading case of *British Home Stores Ltd v Burchell*[101] is sometimes thought to require. However, if witnesses of the factual background are not called at the hearing in the employment tribunal, then it will be difficult for the tribunal to judge whether there were reasonable grounds for the conclusion that the employee committed such misconduct as to justify his dismissal, or whether the employer acted within the band of reasonable responses of a reasonable employer in deciding that the employee should be dismissed.

Warnings

8.66 A reasonable employer will not normally dismiss an employee for a first disciplinary offence: rather, a reasonable employer will normally give the employee a warning not to repeat the conduct in question. However, if an employee is caught committing gross misconduct, then it may be reasonable to dismiss him without first having given such a warning. A set of rules (for example, set out in a document such as a staff handbook) stating what will be regarded as gross misconduct will in any event usually suffice as a warning. However, the penalty of dismissal must nevertheless be reasonable in the circumstances for the dismissal to be fair.[102] Further, the mere fact that a particular kind of misconduct is stated by an employer to be regarded as gross misconduct will not suffice to justify the employer in dismissing an employee for that misconduct.[103]

Appeals

8.67 An employer should almost always give an employee an opportunity to appeal against a decision to dismiss him. Yet the mere granting of a right to appeal and the holding of a fair appeal hearing will not guarantee the fairness of a dismissal.[104]

Relevance of criminal conduct

8.68 One issue which may arise is whether an employer should have dismissed an employee for conduct which amounts to a criminal offence where the employee is facing criminal proceedings for that conduct. As long as the employer gives the employee an opportunity to respond in the normal way to the allegation that the employee has committed the misconduct and then considers the matter in the usual way (ignoring the fact that criminal proceedings are pending), the employer could (subject to the usual tests) dismiss the employee fairly.[105] Similarly, if an employee is prosecuted for a

---

[101] [1978] IRLR 379; [1980] ICR 303. See now *J Sainsbury plc v Hitt* [2003] ICR 111.
[102] See for example *Laws Stores Ltd v Oliphant* [1978] IRLR 251.
[103] See for example *Ladbroke Racing Ltd v Arnott* [1983] IRLR 154.
[104] See further para **8.93** below.
[105] *Harris (Ipswich) Ltd v Harrison* [1978] ICR 1256.

criminal offence but is acquitted, that does not preclude his employer from initiating disciplinary proceedings against him for that alleged conduct.[106]

8.69 A further issue which may arise is whether criminal conduct of a certain sort can routinely be taken by an employer as justification for the dismissal of employees. The cases of *Nottinghamshire County Council v Bowly*[107] and *Norfolk County Council v Bernard*[108] show that an employer cannot necessarily do that safely. In *Bowly*, the employee, who had been a schoolteacher for almost 30 years, was convicted after a plea of guilty of an offence of gross indecency with a man in a public lavatory. He was dismissed following a hearing before the Disciplinary Sub-Committee of the Council's Education Committee. An industrial tribunal decided that the dismissal was unfair, but the EAT allowed the employer's appeal against that decision. The EAT said this:

> 'There are some cases which are so obvious that only one course of action can be considered to be fair; whether to dismiss or not to dismiss. But there are many – and this in our judgment is one of them – where one cannot say that. Certainly, we do not purport to lay down that a teacher who has been convicted of an offence of this kind must automatically be dismissed. Equally, we do not purport to lay down – and if the Industrial Tribunal purported to lay it down, in our judgment they would be wrong – that for an employing authority to dismiss somebody for this kind of offence in the circumstances of this case is automatically unfair. In other words the facts of this case, in our judgment, lie within that grey or indeterminate area where, provided they approach the matter fairly and properly and direct themselves correctly, the Disciplinary Sub-Committee cannot be faulted in doing what in their judgment, being the responsible body, is the just and proper thing to do.'[109]

8.70 In *Bernard*, however, the employee, who was an advisory teacher of drama, was dismissed by Norfolk County Council after, on his own confession, he had been convicted of possession and cultivation of cannabis. An industrial tribunal held that his dismissal was unfair and made an order for his reinstatement. The County Council appealed against that decision. The industrial tribunal had said the following in its reasons for the decision:

> 'If a conviction for an offence outside employment seriously and genuinely affects the employee's relationship with his fellow employees then the dismissal might be justified. The same proposition is put forward if the nature of the offence upon which the conviction rests made the employee a danger to others particularly children. Certainly in that case dismissal would be justified. In certain circumstances dismissal for a criminal conviction might justify dismissal if the reputation or the business of an employer could be genuinely and seriously affected adversely. We cannot find in this case any of these conditions present. We find that the applicant is a man of high moral standards who finds himself in his present difficulty through the accident of a single transaction, the result of

---

[106] *Saeed v Inner London Education Authority* [1985] ICR 637.
[107] [1978] IRLR 252, approved by the Court of Appeal in *X v Y* [2004] IRLR 625, para 24.
[108] [1979] IRLR 220.
[109] [1978] IRLR 252, para 16.

foolishness and not vice. We find on the evidence that no reasonable person or committee properly directing themselves and weighing fairly and honestly the evidence which we know was put before them could arrive at a decision to dismiss.'[110]

8.71 Although the EAT seems to have thought that the decision of the industrial tribunal was a little generous to the employee, the EAT dismissed the appeal, implicitly approving this helpful passage. In that regard, the EAT said this:

'It may be, when one reads [the decision of the industrial tribunal] right through, as we all have done, that it does appear to lean rather heavily in favour of Mr Bernard. Be that as it may, everything that had to be considered by the Industrial Tribunal was considered. They applied the right principles of law that had to be applied.'[111]

Redeployment

8.72 Another issue which may arise in relation to a dismissal for misconduct is whether the employee could have been deployed to do another job where the misconduct would not be relevant. It may be hard to envisage circumstances where that could occur, but the facts of *P v Nottinghamshire County Council*[112] provide a good illustration of such circumstances. It should be said, however, that they are unlikely to recur, for the reasons which are set out after the following account of the facts of, and ruling in, that case. The case also illustrates the relevance of a guilty plea to a criminal offence.

P v Nottinghamshire County Council

P, an assistant groundsman, admitted indecently assaulting his daughter, aged 14, who was a pupil at the school at which he was employed. He was prosecuted for the offence, and indicated to his employer, the County Council, that he intended to plead guilty to the offence. The County Council suspended him on full pay pending a disciplinary hearing. He subsequently pleaded guilty to the charge asking for two offences of indecency with other daughters to be taken into account, and the matter was adjourned for sentence. Before the criminal proceedings were resumed, the County Council held a disciplinary meeting at which the employee stated that he had admitted the offence. The County Council indicated its concern as to the risk the employee represented in his current employment to other children, and his union representative inquired whether alternative work in another department was available. The County Council stated at that meeting that the employee would be dismissed but that the question of redeployment would be investigated. He was subsequently given formal notice of dismissal on 12 weeks' notice. Before the expiry of that notice period, the County Council found that alternative work was not available and informed the employee accordingly. He complained to an industrial tribunal that he had been unfairly dismissed, and sought re-engagement. By a majority the tribunal found that:

---

[110] See [1979] IRLR 220, para 12.
[111] [1979] IRLR 220, para 40.
[112] [1992] ICR 706.

(1) the County Council had not sufficiently investigated the circumstances of the employee's offence to enable it to assess the risk in retaining him;

(2) prior to notifying him of his dismissal it had failed to consider the question of alternative employment; and

(3) its subsequent attempts to arrange other work had been perfunctory.

The majority concluded that for these reasons, the employee had been unfairly dismissed. The County Council appealed to the EAT, which allowed the appeal. The employee appealed against that decision to the Court of Appeal.

Decision of the Court of Appeal

The Court of Appeal dismissed the appeal. It decided that where an employee pleaded guilty to or was found guilty of an offence, it was reasonable for his employer to believe that he had committed it. The industrial tribunal had not decided that the County Council was not reasonably entitled to believe that the employee had committed the offence. The court also decided that the County Council had sufficient material on which to assess the risks involved in continuing to employ the employee, and had no option but to remove him from his existing employment. As a result, the court decided, the finding by the majority of the industrial tribunal on the question of risk had been perverse. The court also decided that where an employee had become unsuitable for his current work, the possibility of alternative employment, depending on the size and administrative resources of his employer's undertaking, might be a relevant factor for it to take into account before dismissing him, but that what is now s 98(4) of the ERA 1996 did not require an employer to undertake that investigation prior to giving the employee notice of dismissal, provided that it did so before the notice took effect. Accordingly, the court decided, the finding of the majority of the industrial tribunal on the question of alternative employment could not be sustained.

8.73 The reasons why the facts of this case are unlikely to be repeated are these:

(1) the case arose before the delegation of budgets to maintained schools and the delegation to the governing bodies of such schools of the power to deploy and dismiss employees had occurred;[113] and

(2) as a result, if an employee at a school admitted indecent assault on a child, then there would be no position to which the governing body could deploy him which would not involve him coming into contact with children.

Was conduct misconduct?

8.74 One issue which may arise in connection with a dismissal for misconduct is whether the conduct for which the employee was dismissed was in fact

---

[113] See further paras **8.123**, **8.129–8.130**, and **8.134–8.144** below.

misconduct, and, if it was not misconduct, whether the dismissal was nevertheless fair. The facts of *Redbridge London Borough Council v Fishman*[114] illustrate this issue particularly well.

Redbridge London Borough Council v Fishman

Mrs Fishman, the employee, accepted an offer by the Redbridge London Borough Council (the LEA) to appoint her as a 'full time permanent teacher in charge of the resources centre, (scale 4.) at Wanstead High School, Redbridge Lane West, E.11. . . . or such other school as may be determined by the authority, with effect from September 1, 1973.' The employee had held other appointments with the authority, having been employed by it since 1965. The resources centre was built to encourage pupils to study video tapes, film strips, cassettes and other non-traditional teaching aids. The employee was told to work almost full-time at the centre, and only to do sufficient classroom teaching to enable her to keep in touch with practical requirements. In 1975, a new head teacher was appointed at the school. The new head teacher favoured more traditional teaching methods, and asked the employee to teach 12 English lessons a week in addition to her work at the centre. The employee was subsequently asked to teach 18 periods a week. She refused to do so, on the ground that it would interfere with her work at the centre. On 6 October 1976, she was suspended by the head teacher. In accordance with the relevant procedure, the matter came before the special education (teaching staff) sub-committee of the LEA. The sub-committee decided that the employee had refused to carry out the reasonable instructions of the head teacher, and she was dismissed 'for misconduct' with effect from the date of her suspension. She claimed unfair dismissal. The industrial tribunal decided that she had been dismissed unfairly because (1) she had been required to do work which was different from that which she was employed to do, and (2) she had acted reasonably in refusing to teach 18 English periods.

The Council appealed to the EAT against that decision.

Decision of the Employment Appeal Tribunal

The EAT dismissed the appeal, deciding that although a head teacher was entitled to require teachers to do work other than that for which they had been engaged provided that the request was reasonable, the employee had been specifically engaged as director of the resources centre and her teaching commitment was ancillary to that. In those circumstances, the EAT decided, the Council had not acted reasonably in treating her refusal to teach as a sufficient reason for dismissing her. The EAT also set out in its decision the following helpful statement of principle to be applied in this kind of case:[115]

> 'In truth, we think that the industrial tribunal perhaps paid too much attention to the contractual position. The jurisdiction based on paragraph 6(8) of Schedule 1 to the Trade Union and Labour Relations Act 1974 [which is now section 98(4) of the ERA 1996] has not got much to do with contractual rights and duties. Many dismissals are unfair although the employer is contractually entitled to dismiss the employee. Contrariwise, some dismissals are not unfair although the employer was not contractually entitled to dismiss the employee. Although the contractual rights and duties

---

[114] [1978] ICR 569.
[115] [1978] ICR 569 at 574.

are not irrelevant to the question posed by paragraph 6(8), they are not of the first importance. The question which the industrial tribunal had to answer in this case was whether the local authority could satisfy them that in the circumstances having regard to equity and the substantial merits of the case they acted reasonably in treating the employee's refusal to teach English for 18 periods as a sufficient reason for dismissing her. The industrial tribunal did not approach the matter in precisely this way, but there can be no doubt whatever that had they done so they would have answered the question in the negative, and found the dismissal to be unfair.'

8.75 What this statement hints at is the possibility of dismissing an employee for 'some other substantial reason' in cases where the employer is carrying out a reorganisation of its operations, and indeed the statement was applied in one of the cases mentioned below in that connection, *Farrant v The Woodroffe School*.[116]

Absence for religious worship

8.76 The case of *Ahmad v Inner London Education Authority*[117] is of interest in part because of the protections which are afforded to employees in a State school, as described in para **4.78** onwards above. It is also of interest because it shows how the ECHR has in the past applied Art 9 of the Convention.

Ahmad v Inner London Education Authority

Lord Denning set out the facts as follows. 'Mr. Ahmad is a schoolteacher. He was employed by the Inner London Education Authority ("I.L.E.A.") as a full-time teacher. This meant that he had to attend the school and teach the children on the five days, Monday to Friday, inclusive each week, with a break each day for luncheon from 12.30 p.m. to 1.30 p.m. But Mr. Ahmad was not only a schoolteacher. He was a devout Muslim. By his religion it was his duty every Friday to attend prayers at the nearest mosque. The time for these prayers was 1 p.m. to 2 p.m. and the mosque was about 15 to 20 minutes away. So when he went to the prayers he did not get back at 1.30 p.m. in time to teach his class. He only got back at 2.15 p.m. or 2.20 p.m. This meant that he missed about three-quarters of an hour of his teaching duty every Friday. One of the headmasters – at the school for maladjusted children – did his best to help and made arrangements to cope with his absence. But other headmasters in ordinary schools could not do so. His absence disrupted the classes too much. They could not fit it in with the rest of the work. But still he went to his Friday prayers. He said that he was entitled to do so and, notwithstanding his absences, he was entitled to full pay, just the same as if he had worked for the full five days.'

A provision in the staff code allowed teachers to have time off for special days in their religion when no work was to be done, such as Good Friday, the Day of Atonement, and Ramadan. The other members of the staff thought it was unfair for Mr Ahmad to have Friday afternoon off each week on full pay and the issue was referred to the I.L.E.A., which took the view that if Mr Ahmad wanted to take time off on Fridays for his prayers, then he could only be employed as a

---

[116] [1998] ICR 184, concerning which, see para **8.83** below.
[117] [1978] QB 36.

part-time teacher, working four days a week and being paid for those days. Mr Ahmad was unwilling to accept this and resigned in protest. He gave as his reason: 'I was exploited and humiliated by the I.L.E.A.' He then claimed constructive dismissal.

The industrial tribunal found unanimously that the employers were not being unreasonable. The EAT affirmed its decision,[118] again unanimously, but gave permission to appeal. Mr Ahmad relied heavily on s 30 of the Education Act 1944, which provided:

> '... no teacher ... shall be required to give religious instruction or receive any less emolument or be deprived of, or disqualified for, any promotion or other advantage by reason of the fact that he does or does not give religious instruction or by reason of his religious opinions or of his attending or omitting to attend religious worship: ...'

Equivalent provision to that in s 30 of the 1944 Act is now contained in 59(2) of the SSFA 1998.[119]

Decision of the Court of Appeal

The Court of Appeal dismissed the appeal. The majority of the court decided that the termination of the employee's full-time teaching contract was not 'by reason of his religious opinions or of his attending ... religious worship' within the meaning of s 30 of the Education Act 1944, and that that section did not permit an employee to break his contract of employment by absenting himself from school during school hours. The court also decided that, in the circumstances, the employers had acted reasonably and that the termination of the employee's contract was not due to their conduct, with the result that the employee had not been constructively dismissed.

However, Scarman LJ, the dissenting judge, said that s 30 of the 1944 Act should be broadly construed against the background of Art 9 of the European Convention on Human Rights and the policy of modern statute law, and that in the circumstances, the employee's 45 minutes' absence from class on Fridays to go to the mosque did not constitute a breach of his contract of employment.

The majority of the court decided that Art 9 of the Convention does not entitle an employee to absent himself from work for the purpose of religious worship in breach of his contract of employment. Lord Denning also said that s 30 of the 1944 Act entitles an employee to attend for religious worship during the working week only if it can be arranged consistently with performing his teaching duties under his contract of employment.

The employee applied to the European Commission of Human Rights on the basis that he had been treated contrary to the European Convention on Human Rights.

Decision of the European Commission of Human Rights

The European Commission of Human Rights dismissed the employee's complaint under the Convention.[120]

---

[118] [1976] ICR 461.
[119] See para **4.81** above.
[120] *Ahmad v UK* (1982) 4 EHRR 126.

Refusal to attend a disciplinary interview

8.77 It is not uncommon for an employee who has been suspended while alleged misconduct is investigated to refuse to attend a disciplinary interview because he is sick. Whether an employer could in that situation safely require the employee nevertheless to attend a disciplinary interview or hearing would depend on the illness from which the employee was suffering. In *Marshall v Alexander Sloan & Co Ltd*,[121] it was said that 'the employee is relieved of the obligation to perform such services as the sickness from which he is suffering prevents him from carrying out'.

8.78 Since it is clear that an employee may properly be required under a contract of employment to attend a disciplinary interview,[122] an employee could not safely refuse to attend a disciplinary interview merely on the ground of his sickness. Only if the sickness were such as to prevent him from attending could he safely do so. So, for example, an absence as a result of a broken leg would almost certainly not prevent an employee from attending a disciplinary interview.

Substantive fairness: statutory bar

8.79 The employment of staff in schools is subject to 'dut[ies] or restriction[s] imposed by or under an enactment' for the purposes of s 98 of the ERA 1996. Such duties include those imposed by s 142 of the Education Act 2002[123] and various sets of regulations the effects of which are described in Chapter 3 above. Accordingly, it would be potentially fair for an employer to dismiss a member of staff whose continued employment would breach any of those duties. However, a fair procedure would still need to be followed, and in any event the decision to dismiss would have to be reasonable in the circumstances. The case of *Sandhu v (1) Department of Education and Science and (2) London Borough of Hillingdon*[124] provides a good illustration of this.

> *Sandhu v (1) Department of Education and Science and (2) London Borough of Hillingdon*
>
> Mr Sandhu was employed by the London Borough of Hillingdon (the LEA) as a probationary teacher. Despite an extension of his probationary period, he was found by the Department of Education and Science to be unsuitable as a teacher. The LEA then took the view that it had no alternative but to dismiss him, and did so. The employee claimed that he had been unfairly dismissed. The LEA defended its decision to dismiss him by arguing that para 2(c) of Sch 2 to the then relevant regulations required his dismissal. That paragraph stated: 'If at the end of the probationary period [the Secretary of State] determines the teacher to be unsuitable for further employment as a qualified teacher, he shall not be so employed . . .'.

---

[121] [1981] IRLR 264, para 11.
[122] See *Murray v British Rail* [1976] IRLR 382. See also *Kramer v South Bedfordshire Community Health Care Trust* [1995] ICR 1066.
[123] See para **3.15** onwards above for s 142.
[124] [1978] IRLR 208.

The employee, however, maintained that his dismissal was due to racial discrimination and that he had never been given an opportunity to prove himself. An industrial tribunal held that his dismissal was fair. It said that 'once it is established that it would be unlawful for the employer to continue to employ a teacher who had been determined by the Secretary of State to be unsuitable for further employment, then it must follow that the provisions of para 6(8) [now section 98(4) of the ERA 1996] are met by the employers saying that it must be reasonable for them to comply with the law.' The employee appealed to the EAT against this decision.

Decision of the Employment Appeal Tribunal

The EAT allowed the employee's appeal, and remitted the case to a differently constituted industrial tribunal. The EAT decided that the industrial tribunal was mistaken in deciding that once the LEA had established that it was unlawful under the relevant regulations to employ the employee as a teacher after he had been deemed unsuitable by the Department of Education and Science, the employee's dismissal was automatically fair. The mere fact that the LEA could not have lawfully continued to employ the appellant as a teacher did not inevitably lead to the conclusion that he had not been unfairly dismissed and was not therefore entitled to compensation. If, as the employee contended, it were established that:

(1) he never really had a chance to prove himself;

(2) he was treated unreasonably during the probationary period;

(3) there was an element of race discrimination;

(4) there was a total lack of co-operation by the LEA; and

(5) the law was being used as a device to get rid of him,

then the industrial tribunal would have been entitled to consider whether the employers had acted reasonably in dismissing him and whether, for example, a reasonable employer would have discussed the matter with him and with the Department for Education and Science to see whether what had gone wrong could be put right so that he would have a fair trial and an opportunity to prove himself.

8.80 The decision of the Court of Appeal in *Inner London Education Authority v Lloyd*[125] is to the same effect. The same statutory requirement for a probationary period applied in that case as in *Sandhu*. The employer in *Lloyd* (the LEA) did not realise for the first 17 months of Mr Lloyd's employment that he was a probationer teacher. This was despite the fact that he had originally been employed as an unqualified teacher (unqualified, that is, in the sense that he was not qualified as a teacher, although he had a degree in mathematics). His period of employment as an unqualified probationer was two years, rather than the one year required for a qualified probationer. The employer did not realise that Mr Lloyd was a probationer until the Department of Education and Science asked for a report on his performance as a probationer. The employee did not receive any guidance as a probationer during that period, and although his probationary period was later extended so that it ended a year after the first report was requested, at the end of that

---

[125] [1981] IRLR 394.

extended period an inspector employed by the LEA was of the view that Mr Lloyd's employment should be terminated. An inspector within Her Majesty's Inspectorate concurred with that recommendation. Following the making of written representations by Mr Lloyd to the Department of Education and Science and a meeting of the governing body of the school at which he was employed (at which it appears that Mr Lloyd was not present and did not make representations), the LEA recommended to the Secretary of State that Mr Lloyd be deemed to be unsuitable to be employed further as a teacher. The Department of Education and Science accepted that recommendation, and Mr Lloyd was accordingly dismissed. He claimed unfair dismissal, and an industrial tribunal upheld his claim. This was on the basis that he had been entitled to appropriate advice and guidance, and that he had not received that because it had not been known during the first 17 months of his employment that he was a probationer. The LEA appealed against that ruling, and the EAT dismissed the appeal. The Court of Appeal dismissed a further appeal by the authority, deciding that the decision of the industrial tribunal was not unlawful.

8.81 It is of note that reg 13(2) of the Education (Induction Arrangements for School Teachers) (Consolidation) (England) Regulations 2001[126] provides that the 'duties assigned to a person serving an induction period [under those regulations], his supervision and the conditions under which he works shall be such as to facilitate a fair and effective assessment of his conduct and efficiency as a teacher'. Since the requirement for continuous service in order to be able to claim unfair dismissal is one year,[127] reg 13(2) and the cases of *Lloyd* and *Sandhu* may in some cases have a considerable impact.

Substantive fairness: some other substantial reason

Sound, good business reason

8.82 When dismissing an employee for a sound, good business reason which may cause an employer to impose new terms on the employee, the employer will need to consider the effect on the employee as compared with the advantages to be gained by the employer by the imposition of those terms.[128] However, the test remains whether the dismissal was within the range of reasonable responses of a reasonable employer in the circumstances as they existed at the time of the dismissal.

8.83 The case of *Farrant v The Woodroffe School*[129] provides a good illustration of a dismissal which was for 'some other substantial reason' and was fair.

---

[126] SI 2001/2897; see further para **3.56** above, including for the equivalent (but differently worded) provision applicable in Wales.
[127] See para **8.7** above.
[128] *Richmond Precision Engineering Ltd v Pearce* [1985] IRLR 179; *Catamaran Cruisers Ltd v Williams* [1994] IRLR 386.
[129] [1998] ICR 184.

Farrant v The Woodroffe School

A laboratory technician was dismissed from his employment in a grant-maintained school in Lyme Regis. His contract of employment required him to spend most of his time in the science laboratory, but also some time in helping service the craft design and technology area of the school. In November 1993, as part of a reorganisation of technical support services, the employee was required to transfer from the science department and divide his time between other departments. He refused to accept a new job description and was dismissed for gross misconduct. An industrial tribunal dismissed his complaint of unfair dismissal on the ground that, although the school was in breach of his contract of employment in removing him from laboratory work altogether, it had given him ample warning and had carried out sufficient consultation before dismissing him and had acted reasonably within the meaning of s 98(4) of the ERA 1996. The employee appealed against that decision.

Decision of the Employment Appeal Tribunal

The EAT dismissed the employee's appeal. The tribunal decided that, where on a complaint of unfair dismissal the employer was relying, as the ground for dismissal, on the employee's conduct in refusing to obey an instruction, the lawfulness of that instruction, although relevant, was not decisive when considering the reasonableness of the dismissal under s 98(4) of the ERA 1996. Furthermore, the EAT decided, the industrial tribunal's conclusion that the dismissal was fair was not perverse, and its decision would be upheld. The EAT quoted and applied the passage from *Redbridge London Borough Council v Fishman*[130] set out in para **8.74** above.

8.84 In *Fay v North Yorkshire County Council*,[131] it was held, perhaps surprisingly, that the expiry and non-renewal of a fixed-term contract could constitute 'some other substantial reason' for a dismissal. However, that was a decision on the particular facts of that case. Furthermore, in many cases, the expiry of what is now called (by s 95(1)(b) of the ERA 1996) a limited-term contract of employment will be for redundancy,[132] with the consequences that a redundancy payment will be payable and that the principles of unfair dismissal law applicable to dismissals for redundancy will apply. It is necessary in this context to bear in mind the possibility of breaching the requirement, imposed by the Fixed-term Employees (Prevention of Less Favourable Treatment) Regulations 2002,[133] not unjustifiably to discriminate against an employee who is employed under a fixed-term contract. However, the mere fact that a person is employed under a fixed-term contract will not constitute a breach of that requirement.[134]

---

[130] [1978] ICR 569.
[131] [1986] ICR 133.
[132] See for example *Nottinghamshire County Council v Lee* [1980] ICR 635 and *British Broadcasting Corporation v Farnworth* [1998] ICR 1116.
[133] SI 2002/2034, concerning which, see para **6.96** onwards above.
[134] See *Department for Work and Pensions v Webley* [2005] ICR 577; leave to appeal against that decision was refused by the House of Lords: see [2005] ICR 1161.

Following a fair procedure

8.85 In any event, even if there is some other substantial reason for an employee's dismissal, the dismissal may nevertheless be unfair. This is because of the need to act fairly in carrying out the dismissal. This is illustrated well by the case of *Beard v St Joseph's School Governors*.[135]

Beard v St Joseph's School Governors

The governors of an aided school employed an assistant needlework teacher under a fixed-term contract of employment from 1 January to 31 August 1977, with the possibility of a further period of employment. In May 1977 it was decided to engage a needlework teacher who could also teach modern languages or religious education, and the post was advertised. The employee, who had the necessary additional qualifications, applied for the post. However, she was not given an interview and her contract of employment was not renewed. She complained to an industrial tribunal that she had been dismissed unfairly. The tribunal decided that had the employers realised that the employee had the necessary qualifications, they would have been unreasonable not to interview her, but that they had genuinely overlooked the fact that the employee could teach modern languages. In those circumstances, the industrial tribunal decided, it was not possible to say that the governors had acted unreasonably within the meaning of para 6(8) of Sch 1 to the Trade Union and Labour Relations Act 1974 (now s 98(4) of the ERA 1996). Accordingly, the industrial tribunal decided, the dismissal was fair. The employee appealed against that decision.

Decision of the Employment Appeal Tribunal

The EAT allowed the appeal. The EAT said that where an employee was dismissed at the end of a fixed-term contract of employment, the reason for the dismissal, namely the expiry of the term, could be a substantial reason justifying dismissal within the meaning of para 6(1)(b) of Sch 1 to the Act of 1974, but that additionally, it was necessary to consider whether the employers had acted reasonably in dismissing the employee within the meaning of para 6(8) of Sch 1. The EAT decided that since a teacher applying for a different post in the same school who had notified her employers that she had the necessary qualifications ought at least to be considered for the post, and since the employers knew of the employee's ability to teach modern languages but had overlooked it, the governors had not acted reasonably within the meaning of para 6(8) in failing to interview the employee and in failing adequately to consider her application. Accordingly, the EAT decided, the dismissal was unfair.

Personality clash

8.86 Another reason which may be 'some other substantial reason' is a personality clash between two employees.[136] However, the employer must normally have made serious efforts to resolve the difficulty otherwise than by the dismissal of one employee.[137]

---

[135] [1978] ICR 1234.
[136] *Treganowan v Robert Knee & Co Ltd* [1975] ICR 405.
[137] *Turner v Vestric Ltd* [1980] ICR 528.

Procedural fairness

Relevance of contractual or statutory procedure

8.87 If a contract of employment contains a term or terms governing the procedure which should be followed in regard to an employee's dismissal, then that procedure will not only be enforceable in some circumstances,[138] but a failure to follow it will also be relevant to a claim of unfair dismissal. It was said by the Court of Appeal in *Stoker v Lancashire County Council*[139] that 'a reasonable employer could be expected to comply with the full requirements of the appeal procedure in its own disciplinary code'.[140] However, a failure to comply with a relevant requirement in the contract of employment will not in itself be determinative.[141]

Witnesses in disciplinary hearings

8.88 One question which could arise is whether or not the employer should call, or allow the employee to call, witnesses at a disciplinary hearing or meeting. Although the case-law is in some respects inconsistent, the safest route is (1) to allow an employee to call witnesses in his defence, and (2) to call witnesses to give evidence to the decision-maker, or at least to answer questions asked by the employee in 'cross-examination'.

8.89 However, if there are special considerations which make it undesirable that witnesses (or a particular witness) are called, then it may be regarded by an employment tribunal as reasonable not to have done so. One example of a good reason for not calling a person as a witness is that that person made disclosures on the basis that they would be kept confidential.[142]

8.90 In any event, the employee cannot realistically be said to have had an opportunity to respond to allegations on the basis of which an employer has dismissed him, unless the employer has given him sufficient information to do so. This will be particularly so in the case of dismissals for misconduct and capability, but it will also be so in the case of dismissals for other reasons. In the case of dismissals for redundancy, the information should be imparted as part of the consultation process described in paras **7.23–7.26** above. In the case of dismissals because of a statutory bar, the employer should give the employee an opportunity to correct the employer's preliminary conclusion and to say (if appropriate) why the employer should do something to help the employee before dismissing him. In the case of dismissals for some other substantial reason, the employer should indicate why the employee's dismissal is proposed.

---

[138] See paras **5.20** and **5.21** above.
[139] [1992] IRLR 75, para 20.
[140] See also *Westminster City Council v Cabaj* [1996] ICR 960.
[141] See for example *Hooper v British Railways Board* [1988] IRLR 517, para 54.
[142] See *Linfood Cash and Carry Ltd v Thompson* [1989] ICR 518, *Ramsey v Walkers Snack Foods Ltd* [2004] IRLR 754, and *Asda Stores v Thompson (No 2)* [2004] IRLR 598.

Separating the roles of 'prosecutor' and 'judge'

8.91 It is a fundamental principle of natural justice that the same person should not act as both 'prosecutor' and 'judge' in the same case. Accordingly, the involvement of the same individual as both accuser and decision-maker should be avoided if reasonably possible. However, courts and tribunals recognise that this (and other aspects of the rules of natural justice) cannot be applied rigidly, for example where the employer's organisation is too small for the decision-maker to be different from the accuser. Nevertheless, a recognition of the different roles is likely to be necessary if a decision to dismiss an employee is to be fair. The case of *Slater v Leicester Health Authority*[143] is instructive in this regard.

> *Slater v Leicester Health Authority*
>
> An employee, Mr Slater, was employed as a staff nurse in a hospital for the mentally ill. He was dismissed following an incident when it was alleged that he had slapped an elderly patient twice across the buttocks. The employee was suspended pending an investigation. The director of nursing services, Mr Sivewright, carried out a preliminary investigation into the incident. In the course of that investigation, he went to look at the patient. There was a red mark on the patient's body which Mr Sivewright concluded was consistent with a blow having been struck by an open hand upon the patient's buttocks. A doctor who was also present reached the same conclusion.
>
> The employee was subsequently called to a disciplinary hearing before Mr Sivewright and informed of the charges against him. The employee maintained that he had not slapped the patient but that he had had cause to restrain him by holding him down at the hips. Mr Sivewright decided on the evidence that he had heard that the employee had lost his temper with the patient and struck two gratuitous blows. He dismissed the employee for gross misconduct. The employee complained to an industrial tribunal that he had been unfairly dismissed.
>
> By a majority decision, the industrial tribunal dismissed his complaint of unfair dismissal. The majority rejected the argument that the dismissal was rendered unfair by the fact that Mr Sivewright was both a witness to the red mark found on the patient and the person who conducted the disciplinary hearing and reached the decision to dismiss. The employee appealed to the EAT, which dismissed his appeal. The EAT decided that it was open to Mr Sivewright to conduct the inquiry notwithstanding that he had seen the mark, and that it was open to the industrial tribunal to conclude that that was not contrary to the rules of natural justice. The employee appealed to the Court of Appeal.
>
> *Decision of the Court of Appeal*
>
> The Court of Appeal decided that the industrial tribunal and the EAT had not erred in holding that the employee's dismissal was not rendered unfair by the fact that the manager who had carried out a preliminary investigation also conducted the disciplinary hearing and took the decision to dismiss. The court said that it could not be decided that because the person conducting the disciplinary hearing had conducted the investigation, he was unable to conduct a fair inquiry. The

---

[143] [1989] IRLR 16. See also *Haddow v Inner London Education Authority* [1979] ICR 202.

court said that while it is a general principle that a person who holds an inquiry must be seen to be impartial, the rules of natural justice do not form an independent ground upon which a decision to dismiss may be attacked in the law of unfair dismissal, although a breach will clearly be an important matter when an industrial tribunal considers whether the dismissal was fair within the meaning of (now) s 98(4) of the ERA 1996. In the present case, therefore, the findings of both the industrial tribunal and the EAT that the dismissal was fair could be interfered with only if they were perverse, and there were no grounds for the court to hold that they were so.

Procedure to follow in a dismissal hearing

8.92 A useful guide to the procedure which should be followed in a hearing when considering whether to dismiss an employee, was provided by the industrial members of the EAT in *Clark v Civil Aviation Authority*.[144] There, the tribunal said that a suitable procedure might be as follows:

'. . . explain the purpose of the meeting; identify those present; if appropriate, arrange representation; inform the employee of the allegation or allegations being made; indicate the evidence whether in statement form or by the calling of witnesses; allow the employee and representative to ask questions; ask whether the employee wishes any witnesses to be called; allow the employee or the representative to explain and argue the case; listen to argument from both sides upon the allegations and any possible consequence, including any mitigation; ask the employee whether there is any further evidence or enquiry which he considers could help his case. After due deliberation the decision will almost certainly be reduced into writing, whether or not an earlier oral indication has been given.'

The opportunity to appeal

8.93 In many cases, irrespective of the requirement to allow an employee an opportunity to appeal against a decision to dismiss him where one of the two statutory dismissal and discipline procedures is being followed,[145] it will be advisable to afford an employee an opportunity to appeal against the decision to dismiss. This will be particularly so in the case of dismissals for conduct and capability, but less so in respect of dismissals for the other three potentially fair reasons. The advantage to an employer of allowing an employee to appeal against a decision to dismiss is that as a result of considering the whole of the procedure, including that which was followed on appeal, the dismissal may be fair when it would not have been if there had been no appeal.[146]

Time of determination of fairness of dismissal

8.94 As a matter of principle, the fairness of a dismissal where the employer has given the employee notice of the termination of his contract of

---

[144] [1991] IRLR 412, para 20.
[145] See para **2.37** onwards above for those procedures.
[146] See *Taylor v OCS Group Ltd* [2006] ICR 1602.

employment is to be considered at the time of the termination, and not at the time of giving notice. This is fundamental, but it appears that it is not always fully appreciated.[147]

Procedurally flawed dismissals may yet be fair

8.95 The Employment Act 2002 introduced into the ERA 1996 what has been called a partial reversal of the decision in *Polkey v AE Dayton Services Ltd*.[148] The effect of *Polkey* is stated in paras **8.114–8.115** below. The provision which brought about its partial reversal is s 98A(2) of the ERA 1996, which provides:

> 'Subject to subsection (1) [which has the effect that a dismissal following a failure to comply with one of the statutory discipline and dismissal procedures will be automatically unfair: see para **2.44** above], failure by an employer to follow a procedure in relation to the dismissal of an employee shall not be regarded for the purposes of section 98(4)(a) as by itself making the employer's action unreasonable if he shows that he would have decided to dismiss the employee if he had followed the procedure.'

8.96 Thus, if an employer can satisfy an employment tribunal on the balance of probabilities that he or it would have dismissed an employee even if he or it had followed a contractual procedure which was not in fact followed but which was not the applicable statutory dismissal and discipline procedure, then the employer will nevertheless have dismissed the employee fairly.[149] It is noted here that *Polkey* will still apply even if the dismissal is automatically unfair because of a breach of the applicable statutory dismissal and discipline procedure.[150]

Remedies for unfair dismissal

The remedies available

8.97 In theory, orders for reinstatement (which means being re-employed in the same job) or re-engagement (which means being re-employed in a similar job) are the primary remedies for a successful claim of unfair dismissal. However, in practice, the main remedy for unfair dismissal is compensation.

Reinstatement or re-engagement

Orders for reinstatement

8.98 An order for reinstatement is an order that the employer 'shall treat the complainant in all respects as if he had not been dismissed'.[151] The employee is

---

[147] The case-law which supports the proposition includes *Dyke v Hereford & Worcester County Council* [1989] ICR 800, *Mugford v Midland Bank plc* [1997] ICR 399, and *Parkinson v March Consulting Ltd* [1998] ICR 276.
[148] [1988] ICR 142.
[149] See *Alexander v Brigden Enterprises Ltd* [2006] ICR 1277, *YMCA Training v Stewart* [2007] IRLR 185, and *Kelly-Madden v Manor Surgery* [2007] ICR 203.
[150] *Alexander v Brigden Enterprises Ltd* [2006] ICR 1277, para 56.
[151] ERA 1996, s 114(1).

accordingly entitled to back pay and compensation for the loss of other contractual benefits (including pension rights) if an order for reinstatement is made. Furthermore, if there has been an improvement in the terms and conditions of employment which the employee would have benefited from if he had not been dismissed, then he must be treated as if he had benefited from that improvement from the date on which he would have done so if he had not been dismissed.[152]

8.99 However, wages received by a dismissed employee who has obtained new employment since the dismissal, wages in lieu of notice, and any ex gratia payments paid by the employer, are all deducted from the amount to be paid by way of compensation for pay and other benefits lost.[153]

8.100 An employer who fails to comply with an order for reinstatement is subject only to a financial penalty: an order for reinstatement is not like a normal court order in this regard since failure to comply with an order for reinstatement is not treated as a contempt of court. However, it is possible that even a financial penalty may not result (see below).

Orders for re-engagement

8.101 An order for re-engagement is an order that the unfairly dismissed employee be engaged by the employer, or by a successor of the employer, or by an associated employer, either in employment comparable to that from which he was dismissed or in other suitable employment.[154] In most other respects, an order for re-engagement is equivalent to an order for reinstatement (see below).

Circumstances in which orders may be made

8.102 Where a person successfully claims unfair dismissal, the employment tribunal is obliged[155] first to consider whether to make an order for his reinstatement. In doing so, it must take into account:

(1) whether the complainant wishes to be reinstated;

(2) whether it is practicable (note: not 'reasonably practicable') for the employer to comply with an order for reinstatement; and

(3) where the complainant caused or contributed to some extent to the dismissal, whether it would be just to order his reinstatement.[156]

---

[152] ERA 1996, s 114(3).
[153] Ibid, s 114(4).
[154] Ibid, s 115(1).
[155] Ibid, s 116.
[156] Ibid, s 116(1).

8.103 If the tribunal decides not to make an order for reinstatement, then it must decide whether to make an order for re-engagement and, if so, on what terms. In doing so, the tribunal must take into account:

(1) any wish expressed by the complainant as to the nature of the order to be made;

(2) whether it is practicable for the employer (or a successor or an associated employer) to comply with an order for re-engagement; and

(3) where the complainant caused or contributed to some extent to the dismissal, whether it would be just to order his re-engagement and (if so) on what terms.[157]

8.104 Except where the tribunal takes into account contributory fault, an order for re-engagement must be on terms which are, so far as is reasonably practicable, as favourable as an order for reinstatement.[158]

8.105 When deciding whether it is practicable for the employer to comply with an order for reinstatement or re-engagement, except in certain circumstances an employment tribunal is not permitted to take into account the fact that an employer has engaged a permanent replacement for a dismissed employee.[159] The circumstances in which it is lawful to take that fact into account are these:

(1) the employer shows 'that it was not practicable for him to arrange for the dismissed employee's work to be done without engaging a permanent replacement'; or

(2) the employer engaged the replacement after the lapse of a reasonable period without having heard from the dismissed employee that he wished to be reinstated or re-engaged and when the employer engaged the replacement, it was no longer reasonable to arrange for the dismissed employee's work to be done except by a permanent replacement.[160]

8.106 Orders for reinstatement or re-engagement are rare. The general principles to be applied in deciding whether these are practicable were stated by the Court of Appeal in a case concerning the commercial sector, *Port of London Authority v Payne*:[161]

> '[T]he test is [one of] practicability not possibility. The industrial tribunal, though it should carefully scrutinise the reasons advanced by an employer, should give due weight to the commercial judgment of the management unless of course the witnesses are disbelieved. The standard must not be set too high. The employer

---

[157] ERA 1996, s 116(3).
[158] Ibid, s 116(4).
[159] Ibid, s 116(5).
[160] Ibid, s 116(6).
[161] [1994] ICR 555, 574.

cannot be expected to explore every possible avenue which ingenuity might suggest. The employer does not have to show that reinstatement or re-engagement was *impossible*. It is a matter of what is practicable in the circumstances of the employer's business at the relevant time.' (Original emphasis)

8.107 In many cases, employment tribunals regard it as not practicable for the employer to re-employ the dismissed employee. For example, in *Wood Group Heavy Industrial Turbines Ltd v Crossan*,[162] the EAT, sitting in Scotland, said that where there is a breakdown in trust and confidence, reinstatement or re-engagement will be practicable only in the rarest of cases. In that case, an employee with 16 years' service was alleged to have used and dealt drugs in the workplace. His dismissal was found to have been unfair, because his employer had not carried out a sufficiently thorough investigation into the alleged conduct. However, the employer genuinely believed that the employee had committed the conduct in question. Despite this, the employment tribunal had ordered that the employee be re-engaged, and the EAT overturned that order.

8.108 Similarly, in *Meridian Ltd v Gomersall*,[163] an order for the reinstatement of two dismissed employees was overturned by the EAT in part because of a poisoning of the atmosphere in the workplace as a result of the conduct for which the employees were dismissed. Furthermore, if the employee distrusts the employer, then (perhaps surprisingly) that will be a lawful reason to decline to order reinstatement.[164]

8.109 Reinstatement was not ordered in *Redbridge London Borough Council v Fishman*.[165] This was because the reinstatement of the teacher would have involved a return to the policy the discarding of which had led to her dismissal.

8.110 Finally, in *Inner London Education Authority v Gravett*,[166] an order made by an industrial tribunal for the re-engagement of a man who was alleged to have committed indecent exposure and indecent assault on a 13-year old girl in the course of his employment, was overturned by the EAT. The man was employed as a temporary full-time swimming instructor, as a part-time temporary supervisor at a centre called the Ambler Centre (the nature of which is not clear from the report of the case), and as a part-time temporary assistant at a youth club. He allegedly committed the offences during the course of his employment at the Ambler Centre. He was dismissed, and claimed that his dismissal was unfair. The industrial tribunal decided that his dismissal was unfair because there had been insufficient investigation before the decision to dismiss him was made. However, the industrial tribunal accepted that the employer genuinely believed that the employee had committed the offences. In those circumstances, the EAT decided, the proper conclusion was that the order for re-engagement should not have been made.

---

[162] [1998] IRLR 680.
[163] [1977] ICR 597.
[164] *Nothman v London Borough of Barnet (No 2)* [1980] IRLR 65, Court of Appeal.
[165] [1978] ICR 569; see para **8.74** above for the facts of the case.
[166] [1988] IRLR 497.

Compensation

Normal awards

8.111 The normal award of compensation for unfair dismissal consists of two payments: the 'basic award',[167] which is calculated in essentially the same way as a redundancy payment,[168] and the 'compensatory award'.[169] The maximum which could, at the time of writing, be awarded by way of a normal basic award was £9,300.

8.112 Where a dismissal is in fact by reason of redundancy, an employee will not be entitled to a basic award as well as a redundancy payment.[170] Where an employee is dismissed by reason of redundancy but he is treated as not having been dismissed for the purposes of the law of redundancy, or he has unreasonably refused an offer of suitable alternative employment made before the dismissal took effect,[171] he will be entitled by way of a basic award to no more than 2 weeks' pay.[172] A week's pay is limited for this and many other purposes of the ERA 1996;[173] at the time of writing the limit was £310. The compensatory award payable in most cases is currently capped at £60,600. Both limits are index-linked and therefore are increased each year, in practice from 1 February onwards.

8.113 Only if an order for reinstatement or re-engagement is made and not complied with, may more be awarded in the usual case. In two kinds of case,[174] there is no limit on the compensatory award. These are cases concerning dismissals for having made a protected disclosure within the meaning of s 43A of the ERA 1996[175] and cases concerning dismissals related to certain health and safety matters.[176]

8.114 The amount of both a basic award and a compensatory award can be reduced, even to nil, if the dismissed employee's conduct caused or contributed to his dismissal.[177] Furthermore, a compensatory award should be made by an employment tribunal only if the tribunal considers that it is just and equitable for there to be such an award. Thus, the award can be reduced, even to nothing, if an employee's dismissal was unfair but conduct of his which did not cause or contribute to the dismissal was such that in the view of the tribunal he should receive no compensation.[178]

---

[167] Calculated in accordance with ss 119–122 of the ERA 1996.
[168] See para **7.10** onwards above regarding the calculation of a redundancy payment.
[169] See ERA 1996, ss 123–124A.
[170] Ibid, s 122(4); *Boorman v Allmakes Ltd* [1995] ICR 842.
[171] Regarding which possibility, see paras **7.8** and **7.9** above.
[172] ERA 1996, s 121.
[173] Ibid, s 227(1).
[174] See ibid, s 124(1A).
[175] That is, a dismissal which is contrary to ibid, s 103A or 105(6A).
[176] That is, dismissals contrary to ibid, ss 100 and 105(3).
[177] Ibid, ss 122(2) and 123(6).
[178] *Polkey v A E Dayton Services Ltd* [1988] ICR 142.

8.115 Similarly, if an employee proves that there has been a failure to consult properly in relation to his dismissal by reason of redundancy, then the employment tribunal must consider the likelihood (expressed as a percentage) that the employee would have been retained in employment if the employer had consulted properly before deciding how much, if anything, to award as a compensatory award.[179] So, for example, if the employer can satisfy the tribunal that there was a 40% chance that the employee would have been dismissed in any event, then the employee will be entitled to compensation for no more than 60% of his loss. It is clear that this approach should be applied to any finding of unfair dismissal where the unfairness was procedural, for example where an employee was dismissed because of a statutory bar.

8.116 As noted above,[180] even if a dismissal is automatically unfair because of a failure to comply with a requirement of the applicable statutory dismissal and discipline procedure, the application of *Polkey v AE Dayton Services Ltd*[181] may result in the reduction of the compensatory award, even to nothing.

8.117 Finally, the common law rules relating to mitigation of loss apply to compensatory awards. Thus, if a dismissed employee does not make what the employment tribunal concludes would have been reasonable efforts to find alternative work, then he will suffer a reduction in the compensation payable to him.

Additional awards

8.118 An 'additional award' of compensation may be made where an order for reinstatement or re-engagement is made. The additional award is 'an amount not less than 26 nor more than 52 weeks' pay'.[182] An additional award may be made only where:

(1) an order for reinstatement or re-engagement is made;

(2) the employer fails to comply with that order; and

(3) the employment tribunal decides that it remains practicable to comply with the order.

8.119 Thus, an additional award for a failure to comply with an order for reinstatement or re-engagement will not be payable if the employer can satisfy

---

[179] *Polkey v A E Dayton Services Ltd* [1988] ICR 142, para 163H. Although that specific statement was made in the speech of Lord Bridge, and not in that of Lord Mackay, with whom the other three Law Lords agreed, the approach of Lord Bridge was clearly treated as correct by the Court of Appeal in *Thornett v Scope* [2007] ICR 236, para 27. If the failures on the part of the employer which made the dismissal unfair are such that the employment tribunal is unable in practical terms to assess what would have happened if the failures had not occurred, then no percentage reduction should be made: *Thornett v Scope*, paras 28–34.

[180] See para **8.96** above.

[181] [1988] ICR 142.

[182] ERA 1996, s 117(3).

the tribunal that it was not practicable (again, it is helpful to note that it must be not practicable, not 'not reasonably practicable') to comply with the order. This, in effect, allows an employer a second opportunity to argue that it was not practicable to comply with the order, and the employer is not limited at this stage to arguing by reference only to matters which have arisen since the order was made.[183]

Maximum amount

8.120 Because of the rarity of additional awards (or indeed, orders for reinstatement or re-engagement), in practice the most that an employee can be awarded as compensation for unfair dismissal is £69,900. However, this limit is not often reached.

DAMAGES FOR BREACH OF CONTRACT

8.121 In addition to the above remedies, however, an employee can claim in the employment tribunal damages for breach of contract[184] as well as unfair dismissal. Accordingly, if the employee could, for example, show that he had suffered loss as a result of a breach of the implied term of mutual trust and confidence committed during the course of the employment,[185] then that loss would be recoverable in employment tribunal proceedings in addition to compensation for unfair dismissal.

COMPENSATION FOR FAILURE TO GIVE PAY IN LIEU OF NOTICE

8.122 Finally, if an employee is dismissed without notice in circumstances in which notice should have been given, or less notice pay is given than should have been paid, then an employment tribunal (or court) could order that damages for such failure, or a sum due under the contract in the form of lost wages[186] (as the case may be) be paid in addition to compensation for unfair dismissal. However, compensation will not be awarded for the same loss twice. In other words, there will not be double recovery.

---

[183] *Freemans plc v Flynn* [1984] ICR 874, EAT.
[184] Capped at £25,000 (see SI 1994/1623, art 10); but note that damages for personal injury and certain other matters cannot be claimed (see s 3(3) of the Employment Tribunals Act 1996). An employee who makes no valid claim for damages in the employment tribunal can claim in the county court unlimited damages for breach of the contract of employment (or other relevant contract).
[185] See para **5.09** above.
[186] Payable under s 13 of the ERA 1996, regarding which see para **5.32** onwards above.

DISCIPLINE AND DISMISSAL IN MAINTAINED SCHOOLS

Employment powers and responsibilities where a maintained school has a delegated budget

8.123 The governing body of a maintained school which has a delegated budget is obliged to 'establish procedures' for 'the regulation of conduct and discipline of staff at the school', for 'dealing with lack of capability on the part of staff at the school', and 'by which staff may seek redress for any grievance relating to their work at the school'.[187] The governing body (at least of such a school in Wales[188]) must also make these rules and procedures known to members of the staff. This might be done by issuing a staff handbook to employees. In England, it is implicit, and in Wales it is explicit, that the 'regulation of conduct and discipline in relation to the staff of the school . . . is . . . under the control of the governing body'.[189] The fact that in both England and Wales it is clearly stated in the regulations governing the employment of staff in maintained schools that the LEA must dismiss an employee who is employed to work solely at a community, voluntary controlled, community special or maintained nursery school if the governing body of the school decides that that person should cease to work at the school,[190] puts it beyond doubt that the governing bodies and not the LEA have ultimate control of the staff even of those schools (and not just voluntary aided, foundation and foundation special schools) where those schools have delegated budgets.

8.124 The governing body of any maintained school in Wales must, in determining the capability of members of the staff of the school, have regard to any guidance given from time to time by the National Assembly.[191] The guidance which may be issued by the Secretary of State or the National Assembly under ss 35(8) and 36(8) of the EA 2002 to which reference is made in para **4.39** above applies also to dismissals, and is therefore relevant here also. The governing bodies and head teachers of all maintained schools, and all LEAs, must have regard to such guidance. The best view is that a duty to have regard to guidance is not a duty follow that guidance slavishly, but, rather, merely a duty to take it into account where relevant.[192]

8.125 Where the implementation of any decision made by the governing body in relation to staff conduct and discipline requires action which is not within the functions exercisable by the governing body, but is within the power of the

---

[187] School Staffing (England) Regulations 2003, SI 2003/1963, regs 6(1) and 7; Staffing of Maintained Schools (Wales) Regulations 2006, SI 2006/873 (w 61), reg 7(2).
[188] See the concluding words of reg 7(2) of SI 2006/873, of which there is no equivalent in SI 2003/1963.
[189] See reg 7(1) of the Staffing of Maintained Schools (Wales) Regulations 2006.
[190] See reg 17 of both SI 2003/1963 and SI 2006/873.
[191] See reg 7(6) of SI 2006/873. There used to be, but is no longer, an equivalent obligation in England (see para 22(3) of Sch 16 to the SSFA 1998).
[192] The clearest authority on this issue is *De Falco v Crawley Borough Council* [1980] QB 460.

LEA, the LEA must take that action at the request of the governing body.[193] The position regarding discipline in the event of strike action may be thought to be problematic where the employer is the LEA. However, it seems clear that the power to determine whether to deduct pay in the event of, for example, a refusal to carry out a part only of a teacher's duties,[194] would lie with the governing body of the relevant school, and not the LEA.[195]

Report by local education authority on performance of head teacher

8.126 If the LEA has any serious concerns about the performance of the head teacher of a maintained school, it must make a written report to the chair of the governing body of the school and send a copy of it to the head teacher.[196] An LEA in Wales must, in determining whether to make such a report, have regard to any guidance given from time to time by the National Assembly.[197] The chair must then notify the authority in writing of the action which he proposes to take in the light of the report.[198]

Suspension of staff

8.127 The power to suspend an employee is given to both the governing body and the head teacher (but not to the LEA).[199] In order to exercise that power, the governing body or head teacher must be of the opinion that the employee's exclusion from the school is required, and when exercising the power, the governing body or the head teacher must inform the other and (in the case of a school which is a community, voluntary controlled or community special school) the LEA immediately. The suspension must be without loss of pay. Only the governing body can end the suspension, and when it does so, it must immediately inform the head teacher and (in the case of a school which is a community, voluntary controlled or community special school), the LEA.

---

[193] See reg 6(2) of SI 2003/1963 and reg 7(5) of SI 2006/873.
[194] See for example *Sim v Rotherham MBC* [1986] ICR 897, the effect of which is described in para **5.76** above. See also para **5.30** above regarding the impact of industrial action on the employee's entitlement to pay.
[195] This is because of reg 6(2) of SI 2003/1963 and reg 7(5) of SI 2006/873, interpreted in the light of (a) s 50(3) of the SSFA 1998 Act, which gives the power to spend the governing body's delegated budget – which includes the budget for staff – to the governing body, and (b) Sch 15 to the SSFA 1998, which empowers the LEA to suspend the governing body's right to a delegated budget in the event of mismanagement.
[196] See reg 5(a) of the School Staffing (England) Regulations 2003, SI 2003/1963, and reg 6(1)(a) of the Staffing of Maintained Schools (Wales) Regulations 2006, SI 2006/873.
[197] See reg 6(2) of SI 2006/873.
[198] See regs 5(b) and 6(1)(b) respectively.
[199] See regs 16 and 25 of SI 2003/1963 and regs 16 and 28 of SI 2006/873. All of the rest of the statements in the rest of this paragraph (**8.127**) are of the effects of those regulations.

8.128 It is possible for the governing body to delegate its powers in relation to suspension; the delegation may be to a committee, to a member of the governing body, or (if he is not a member of the governing body) to the head teacher.[200]

Dismissal of staff

Delegation of the power to dismiss

8.129 The governing body of a maintained school may delegate its function of deciding whether a person should be dismissed. In England, it may do so to (a) the head teacher, (b) one or more governors, or (c) one or more governors and the head teacher.[201] If the head teacher is not a decision-maker, then he is entitled to 'attend and offer advice at all relevant proceedings', and the governor or governors to whom the delegation has been made must consider that advice.[202] If the question is whether the head teacher should cease to work at the school or be dismissed from his employment at the school, then the power may be delegated to one or more governors.[203] There is no specific requirement in England for, or in relation to, an appeal against a decision that a person should cease to work at, or be dismissed from, employment in a maintained school. There will nevertheless be a need to comply with the requirements of the relevant DDP.[204]

8.130 In Wales, the power to decide whether an employee should cease to work, or be dismissed from employment, at a maintained school may be delegated only to a staff disciplinary and dismissal committee, which must have at least three members.[205] If the employee appeals against that decision, then a further committee, called the disciplinary appeal committee, must hear the appeal.[206] The committee must contain no fewer governors than the staff disciplinary committee whose decision is subject to appeal.[207]

8.131 If a disciplinary function has been delegated to a committee, one practical problem which may arise is that a member of the committee may be unable to attend on the date of a planned disciplinary hearing. However, unless there is a list of members of the governing body who sit as members of the committee if the standing members are unavailable, it would be unwise simply to choose another member of the governing body to sit in his place. This is because it would be the clerk who would have chosen a member of the governing body to sit on the disciplinary committee, and not the governing

---

[200] See reg 16 of the School Governance (Procedures) (England) 2003, SI 2003/1377 and reg 50 of the Government of Maintained Schools (Wales) Regulations 2005, SI 2005/2914 (W 211).
[201] See reg 4 of the School Staffing (England) Regulations 2003, SI 2003/1963.
[202] Ibid, reg 4(3).
[203] Ibid, reg 4(4).
[204] See para **2.41** above.
[205] See reg 55(1) and (3) of the Government of Maintained Schools (Wales) Regulations 2005, SI 2005/2914 (W 211).
[206] See ibid, reg 55(2).
[207] Ibid, reg 55(4).

body. It is likely that that would be regarded by a court as an unlawful act of delegation.[208] The effect in unfair dismissal cases might not, however, be fatal. Furthermore, a court might decline to grant a remedy in respect of the illegality, and would be likely to do so if no unfairness was caused to an employee who was dismissed by the relevant committee.

Involvement of staff governors in decisions

8.132 One question which is likely to arise in practice is whether or not teacher governors or other staff governors can take part in decisions to dismiss. There are two provisions applicable to maintained schools which indicate that, at least in certain situations, they may not be so involved. The provisions are in the School Governance (Procedures) (England) Regulations 2003[209] and the Government of Maintained Schools (Wales) Regulations 2005.[210] They have the effect that where there may be a conflict between:

(1) the interests of a member of the governing body, a member of a committee of the governing body, the head teacher or any person acting as the clerk to the governing body; and

(2) the interests of the governing body,

then the member, head teacher or clerk (as the case may be) must (subject to what is said in the final sentence of the next paragraph below) withdraw from the meeting (unless he is the clerk and his conduct is not in issue) and (in all cases) may not vote on the matter in question.[211]

8.133 Similarly, if a fair hearing is required and there is any reasonable doubt about the ability of a member of the governing body, a member of a committee of the governing body, the head teacher or any person acting as the clerk to the governing body to act impartially in relation to any matter, then the member, head teacher or clerk (as the case may be) must (subject to what is said in the final sentence of this paragraph) withdraw from the meeting (unless he is the clerk and his conduct is not in issue) and (in all cases) may not vote on the matter in question.[212] If there is a dispute about whether a person should be required to withdraw from a meeting and to be prohibited from voting on the matter in question, then that dispute is to be resolved by the other members of the governing body who are present at the meeting.[213] None of these prohibitions prevents a person appearing to give evidence to the governing

---

[208] Compare *Jones v Lee* [1980] ICR 310, 314B.
[209] SI 2003/1377, as amended by SI 2003/1916, SI 2004/450 and SI 2007/960, and applied to federations of schools by SI 2004/2042.
[210] SI 2005/2914 (W 211).
[211] See reg 14 of SI 2003/1377 and reg 63 of SI 2005/2914.
[212] Ibid.
[213] See regs 14(5) and 63(5) respectively.

body or committee, or to make representations if he is acting in a capacity other than as a member, the head teacher, or (as the case may be) the clerk.[214]

Further procedural requirements

8.134 *England.* There are now in England only one or two specific requirements in the education legislation governing the procedure to be followed in dismissing a member of the staff of a maintained school (in addition to those concerning delegation, the effects of which are described in para **8.129** above). Before turning to them, it is necessary to mention the legislation concerning the allocation of responsibility for the dismissal of school meals staff. The position in that regard is that where the governing body has a duty imposed by virtue of s 512A of the Education Act 1996 to provide school lunches or free school lunches, but the governing body has agreed with the LEA that the LEA will supply the lunches, then the LEA is responsible for the appointment, discipline, suspension and dismissal of school meals staff, but if the governing body decides that any school meals staff member should cease to work at the school, then it must notify the LEA in writing of that decision and the reason for it, and the LEA must then require that person to cease to work at the school.[215] Otherwise, the school meals staff members are treated in the same way as other members of the school's staff.[216]

8.135 The only statutory requirements in addition to those concerning delegation which apply generally to the procedure to be followed or otherwise in relation to the dismissal of a member of the staff of a maintained school in England which has a delegated budget, are regs 12, 17, 21 and 26 of the School Staffing (England) Regulations 2003.[217] Regulation 12 entitles a representative of the LEA to attend and offer advice at all proceedings relating to the dismissal of any teacher who is employed to work at a community, voluntary controlled or community special school, and obliges the governing body or any person or persons to whom the function of making the relevant decision has been delegated to consider such advice before making the decision. Regulation 17 as noted in para **8.123** above makes it clear that only the governing body of a community, voluntary controlled, community special or maintained nursery school with a delegated budget has the power to decide whether a person who is employed to work at the school should be dismissed from that employment. Regulation 17 is, however, merely mechanical in that it simply requires that, subject to reg 18 (concerning school meals staff, to which reference is made in the preceding paragraph above), where the governing body decides that any person employed or engaged by the LEA to work at the school should cease to work there, the governing body must 'notify the authority in

---

[214] See regs 14(3)(a) and 63(3)(a) respectively.
[215] See regs 18(2) and (3) of the School Staffing (England) Regulations 2003, SI 2003/1963.
[216] Regulation 18(4). It is difficult to see why reg 7 is not mentioned in reg 18(4).
[217] SI 2003/1963. Regulation 32 of, and Sch 9 to, the School Governance (Federations) (England) Regulations 2007, SI 2007/960, modify the School Staffing (England) Regulations 2003 so that they apply with appropriate modifications to the staffing of federations. The following paragraphs of the text should be read accordingly.

writing of its determination and the reasons for it', and the LEA must then take whichever is appropriate of two possible steps. If the person is not employed or engaged by the LEA to work solely at the school, then the LEA must require him to cease to work at the school. If the person is employed to work solely at the school and he does not resign, then the LEA must, within 14 days of the date when it was notified by the governing body of the decision that the employee should cease to work at the school, either give the employee notice in accordance with his contract of employment, or terminate that contract without notice if the circumstances are such that the LEA may lawfully do so by reason of the employee's conduct (which will be where he has committed a fundamental breach of, or repudiated, the contract).[218] This might be thought to have the (probably unintended) effect that even in the event of gross *incompetence*, a member of staff may be entitled under these statutory provisions to be given notice. However, it is unlikely that Parliament intended the ordinary law of contract to be ousted by implication.

8.136 For these purposes:

(1) 'a person employed by a local education authority is to be regarded as employed to work at a school if his employment with the authority for the time being involves work at that school'; and

(2) 'a person employed by a local education authority is to be regarded as employed to work solely at a school if his only employment with the authority (disregarding any employment under a separate contract with the authority) is for the time being at that school'.[219]

8.137 Regulations 21 and 26 of the School Staffing (England) Regulations 2003 apply to foundation, voluntary aided and foundation special schools with delegated budgets. Regulation 21 entitles an LEA to advise the governing body in relation to the exercise of any of the governing body's functions of dismissal to the same extent as in relation to the governing body's powers of appointment and engagement.[220] Regulation 26 simply applies regs 16 and 17 to support staff who are employed by the LEA rather than the governing body, pursuant to reg 24.[221]

8.138 *Wales*. In contrast, in Wales, if the governing body of a maintained school with a delegated budget is of the view that a member of the school's staff should be dismissed then, except in certain cases, it must follow the procedure and comply with the requirements set out in reg 17 or (as the case

---

[218] School Staffing (England) Regulations 2003, reg 17(2). See para **8.20** above for what constitutes a repudiation of contract. The LEA cannot delegate this function of dismissing to the governing body of the school: see para **8.146** below.
[219] See SSFA 1998, s 142(7), which applies here because of s 212(2) and (3) of the Education Act 2002, read with s 142(8) of the SSFA 1998 and s 11 of the Interpretation Act 1978.
[220] See para **4.58** above for the manner in which reg 21 applies.
[221] See the final sentence of para **4.59** above regarding reg 24.

may be) reg 29 of the Staffing of Maintained Schools (Wales) Regulations 2006.[222] However, this does not apply where the employee has less than a year's continuous employment, nor does it apply where the employee's dismissal will occur only because of the ending of the fixed-term contract under which he or she is employed.[223] Nor does it apply to a decision to terminate or not renew the contract of employment of a person (a) whose dismissal is required by reason of (1) a direction given under s 142(1) of the Education Act 2002 or (2) the current regulations concerning induction periods for newly-qualified teachers,[224] or (b) who is a teacher who is subject to a conditional registration, suspension or prohibition order made under Sch 2 to the Teaching and Higher Education Act 1998.[225]

Allegations against members of staff that involve issues of child protection

8.139 One major difference between the situation in England and that in Wales concerning the staffing of a maintained school is that if an allegation is made against a member of the staff of such a school in Wales which 'involve[s] issues of child protection', then the governing body of the school must 'appoint an independent investigator to investigate the allegations prior to the hearing of any proceedings relating to those allegations'.[226] Such an investigator may not be (a) a governor of the school, (b) a parent of a current or former pupil at the school, (c) a current or former member of the staff of the school, or (d) currently employed by the LEA which maintains the school.[227] Moreover, any staff disciplinary and dismissal committee which is considering whether to dismiss a person who is employed to work at a maintained school against whom allegations involving issues of child protection have been made, must include 'not less than two governors and an independent person who is not a governor'.[228] Similarly, any disciplinary and dismissal appeals committee which hears an appeal against a decision that a person should cease to work at a

---

[222] SI 2006/873. Regulation 17 applies to community, voluntary controlled, community special and maintained nursery schools. Regulation 29 applies to foundation, voluntary aided and foundation special schools. The effects of regs 17 and 29 are described in para **8.140** onwards below. In *Ryan v Blackburn with Darwen Borough Council* UKEAT/0928/03/DM, the EAT was not referred to any authority on the question of the manner in which the predecessor statutory obligations in the SSFA 1998 could be enforced – whether in public law or the law of contract. The EAT therefore (see para 28 of its judgment) preferred to express no view on that subject. However, the Court of Appeal in *Cornelius v Southwark London Borough Council* [1998] ELR 563 concluded, without the employee having been represented at the hearing, that the obligation was contractual.

[223] See regs 17(8) and 29(4).

[224] Currently the Education (Induction Arrangements for School Teachers) (Wales) Regulations 2005, SI 2005/1818 (W 146), concerning which see para **3.50** onwards above.

[225] See reg 17(11) and (12) and reg 31 of SI 2006/873. See paras **3.15** and **3.40** above respectively concerning s 142(1) and conditional registration, suspension and prohibition orders under Sch 2.

[226] Staffing of Maintained Schools (Wales) Regulations 2006, SI 2006/873, reg 7(3).

[227] See ibid, reg 7(4).

[228] See reg 55(3) of the Government of Maintained Schools (Wales) Regulations 2005, SI 2005/2914 (W 211). The conditions for a person to be independent for this purpose are set out in reg 55(4A), and are the same as those which are applied by reg 7(4) of the Staffing of Maintained Schools (Wales) Regulations 2006 in relation to an independent investigator.

maintained school where such allegations have been made must include an independent person who was not involved in the staff disciplinary committee's decision.[229]

Procedure in relation to the dismissal

8.140 Except in the circumstances indicated in the preceding paragraph above, the governing body must, before making a decision that an employee should cease to work at the school, give the employee an opportunity to make representations.[230] The governing body must then have regard to any such representations.[231] The governing body must also make arrangements for giving an opportunity to appeal against the decision before it notifies the LEA or (as the case may be) gives effect to it.[232] The EAT said in *Howard v Governor of Brixington Infants School*[233] in relation to what would now be a community school that the requirement to 'make arrangements' for giving an employee an opportunity to appeal means that the governing body must await the practical outcome of the appeal before notifying the LEA that it has decided to dismiss the employee. The EAT expressly rejected the argument advanced for the governing body in that case that merely telling an employee that he could appeal against a decision that he should cease to work at the school was sufficient. The tribunal stated[234] that it used the words:

> 'practical outcome . . . because whilst, no doubt, the practical outcome will generally be upon the determination of the appeal, there may be cases where a workable opportunity is afforded to the teacher but where the appeal is abandoned before the date for its hearing, or where it is, in practical terms, abandoned by a failure of the appellant to appear or be represented at the date and place appointed without good reason for that failure'.

8.141 If an employee does not appeal against the decision, then, in the case of a community, voluntary controlled or community special school, the governing body must notify the local education authority in writing of its decision and the reasons for it.[235] Similarly, if the employee appeals and subsequently withdraws the appeal, or he does not pursue it (in any of the ways described by the EAT in *Howard v Governor of Brixington Infants School*), or the appeal is rejected, the governing body must then notify the LEA of its decision and the reasons for it.[236]

---

[229] Government of Maintained Schools (Wales) Regulations 2005, reg 55(4). See further para **8.130** above concerning the appeal committee.
[230] Staffing of Maintained Schools (Wales) Regulations 2006, SI 2006/873, regs 17(6)(a) and 29(1)(a). See also para **8.130** above for the procedure which must be followed.
[231] Ibid, regs 17(6)(b) and 29(1)(b).
[232] Ibid, regs 17(7) and 29(2). See para **8.130** above for the requirement that the appeal is heard by a committee.
[233] [1999] ICR 1096.
[234] At page 1111.
[235] Reg 17(1) and (7) of SI 2006/873.
[236] Ibid, read in the light of *Howard v Governor of Brixington Infants School*.

8.142 If the employee is not employed or engaged to work solely at the school, then the LEA must require him to cease to work at the school with immediate effect.[237] If the employee is employed to work solely at the school and he does not resign, then the LEA must, within 14 days of the date when it was notified by the governing body of the decision that the employee should cease to work at the school, either give the employee notice in accordance with his contract of employment, or terminate that contract without notice if the circumstances are such that the LEA may lawfully do so by reason of the employee's conduct (which will be where he has committed a fundamental breach of, or repudiated, the contract).[238]

8.143 Where a notification is given by a relevant governing body to the LEA in respect of an employee who is not employed to work solely at the school, no part of the employee's wages relating to any period after the expiry of the employee's contractual notice period may be met from the governing body's delegated budget.[239] The notice period is treated as having commenced on the day when the authority was notified.[240]

8.144 In the case of a foundation, voluntary aided or foundation special school, where a decision has been made that an employee should have his or her contract of employment with the governing body terminated, subject to any appeal, the governing body must give that employee notice of the termination of the contract unless the governing body is entitled to terminate it without notice by reason of the employee's conduct.[241]

8.145 The head teacher (unless he is the person whose position the governing body is considering) and the chief education officer of the LEA (or a nominated officer of the authority) are entitled to attend all proceedings of 'the staff disciplinary committee' and 'the disciplinary appeal committee', for the purpose of giving advice.[242] Such committee must consider any resulting advice before making the decision.[243] Appropriate diocesan authorities may be given the same advisory rights in relation to a voluntary controlled school or foundation school which is a Church of England, Church in Wales or Roman Catholic School.[244] Such authorities automatically have such advisory rights in

---

[237] Regulation 17(3) of SI 2006/873. See para **8.136** above for the meaning in this context of the words 'employed to work solely at' a school.
[238] Ibid, reg 17(2). See para **8.20** above for what constitutes a repudiation of contract. As noted in para **8.135** above, this could (but probably does not) have the effect that even in the event of gross *incompetence*, a member of staff may be entitled under these statutory provisions to be given notice.
[239] See reg 17(4) of SI 2006/873.
[240] Ibid, reg 17(5).
[241] SI 2006/873, reg 29(3). See para **8.135** above concerning the circumstances in which no notice need be given. Note the specific provision for persons who are employed by the LEA to work at the school, made by reg 32, which applies regs 16–18 to such staff.
[242] Ibid, regs 17(9) and reg 30(1).
[243] Ibid, regs 17(10) and 30(2).
[244] See ibid, regs 19 and 23.

relation to a voluntary aided school which is a Church of England, Church in Wales or Roman Catholic Church School.[245]

8.146 The EAT expressly decided in *Howard v Governor of Brixington Infants School*[246] that it is not open to an LEA to delegate its functions in this context to the governing body of a school with a delegated budget. Accordingly, the purported delegation by the relevant LEA of the function of dismissing employees who were employed to work solely at a school with a delegated budget to the governing bodies of such schools, was unlawful and void. The practical impact of this did not, however, need to be worked out in that case.

EMPLOYMENT TRIBUNAL PROCEEDINGS WHERE THERE IS A DELEGATED BUDGET

8.147 Where there is a delegated budget in a maintained school, the governing body of the school (and not the LEA) will be the primary respondent to employment tribunal proceedings brought by a member or former member of the staff of the school in respect of a number of different types of claim. This is so even where the employee is or was employed by the LEA.[247] So, for example, a dismissal by an LEA following a notification to it by a governing body that a person should cease to work at the school, is treated for various employment law purposes as a dismissal by the governing body.[248] However, any award of the tribunal (except an order for reinstatement or re-engagement) in respect of such a person has effect against the authority.[249] The governing body must notify the LEA within 14 days of receiving notification of any employment tribunal proceedings and the authority is entitled, on written application to the tribunal, to be made an additional party to, and therefore to take part in, the proceedings.[250] The types of claim to which this applies include sex, race and disability discrimination claims, and claims of unfair dismissal.[251] However, the LEA is the only respondent to a claim made under the Equal Pay Act 1970 by an employee who is or was employed in a community, voluntary controlled or community special school.

---

[245] See SI 2006/873, reg 23(1) and (2).
[246] [1999] ICR 1096.
[247] This is a product of arts 3, 4, and 6(1) and (2) of (a) the Education (Modification of Enactments Relating to Employment) (England) Order 2003, SI 2003/1964, and (b) the Education (Modification of Enactments Relating to Employment) (Wales) Order 2006, SI 2006/1073.
[248] Ibid, art 3(1)(d).
[249] Ibid, art 6(3).
[250] Ibid, art 6(4).
[251] See the Schedule to both Orders for a full list of the relevant provisions. On one view, the failure to include in that Schedule a reference to the Transfer of Undertakings (Protection of Employment) Regulations 2006, SI 2006/246, is erroneous. In any event, the omission of such a reference has had the effect that those regulations appear not to apply to a reorganisation of community and/or voluntary controlled schools. See further para **10.2** below.

PAYMENTS IN RESPECT OF ANY MEMBER OF STAFF OF A MAINTAINED SCHOOL WITH A DELEGATED BUDGET

Dismissals and resignations

8.148 Where a maintained school has a delegated budget, that budget will of course extend to the costs of employing the staff of the school. However, the costs of dismissing or securing the resignation of a member of the staff of the school will not normally have to be met from the school's delegated budget.[252] The governing body has the power to decide whether any payment should be made by the LEA in respect of the dismissal, or for the purpose of securing the resignation, of any member of the staff of the school, and the amount of such payment.[253] The LEA must give effect to such a decision and may not make, or agree to make, a payment in respect of the dismissal or for the purpose of securing the resignation of a member of the staff of the school except in accordance with such a decision.[254] However the LEA may nevertheless decide to make a payment which is required to be made for some other reason.[255]

8.149 The wording of the s 37(2) of the EA 2002 appears to allow an LEA to enter into an agreement to compromise (that is, settle) a claim made by a person who has been employed at a maintained school with a delegated budget and who has been dismissed from that employment. However, s 37(1) indicates that Parliament intended the conduct of any such claim to be under the control of the governing body. But s 37(1) makes no reference to the making of a payment to settle a claim of, for example, sex discrimination where the claimant has not resigned or been dismissed, despite the fact that the governing body of a school with a delegated budget will be the primary respondent to such a claim brought by a person employed to work at the school.[256] Furthermore, s 37(2) would on any view not prevent the making of a payment by the LEA (against the governing body's wishes) to a member of staff who spontaneously resigned and who could not claim 'constructive dismissal' because he could not show a fundamental breach or repudiation of his contract of employment.[257]

8.150 The wording of s 37(5) is of particular importance here. It is this:

> 'Subject to subsection (7) [which concerns premature retirement costs, which are dealt with below], costs incurred by the local education authority in respect of the dismissal, or for the purpose of securing the resignation, of any member of the staff of a maintained school shall not be met from the school's budget share for

---

[252] See Education Act 2002, s 37(5).
[253] Ibid, s 37(1).
[254] Ibid, s 37(3).
[255] Ibid, s 37(2).
[256] See para **8.147** above.
[257] See para **8.19** onwards above for what constitutes a constructive dismissal. See para **8.152** below for a discussion concerning the responsibility for meeting the costs of employment law claims other than those arising from dismissals.

any funding period [in Wales, financial year] except in so far as the authority have good reason for deducting those costs, or any part of those costs, from that share.[258]

8.151 In contrast, costs incurred by the LEA in respect of the dismissal, or for the purpose of securing the resignation of, any member of the staff of a maintained school who is employed for community purposes under s 27 of the Education Act 2002, may be recovered by the LEA from the governing body (and not the school's delegated budget) unless the LEA agrees otherwise with the governing body in writing.[259]

Responsibility for payments in respect of claims where there is no dismissal or prior agreement to resign

8.152 There is no reference in s 37 to costs incurred otherwise than in securing the resignation, or in respect of the dismissal, of a member of staff. Accordingly Parliament can be inferred to have intended claims concerning the dismissal of staff (including for redundancy) to be under the control of the governing body of a school with a delegated budget (which would risk having to pay the costs arising out of such dismissal from that budget), and to have intended that other claims alleging breaches by the governing body of employment law could be compromised by the LEA without the consent of the governing body. This is presumably on the basis that the governing body would not be liable to meet the costs of any other kind of employment law claim from its delegated budget. However, that question is not specifically addressed in s 37. The complications caused by the delegation of the budget for meeting legal costs to the governing body are outside the scope of this book, as they are irrelevant to day-to-day employment matters in schools. However, those complications, and the fact that the regulations requiring such delegation[260] might, as a result of the practical difficulties which they could cause, be challengeable in judicial review proceedings, are noted here.

Premature retirements

8.153 Costs incurred by the LEA in respect of any premature retirement of a member of the staff of a maintained school with a delegated budget must be met from the school's budget share for one or more financial years 'except in so far as the authority agree with the governing body in writing (whether before or after the retirement occurs) that they shall not be so met'.[261]

---

[258] Section 37(6) provides that the fact that the authority has a policy precluding dismissals by reason of redundancy is not to be regarded as a good reason for the purposes of s 37(5).
[259] Education Act 2002, s 37(7).
[260] Those which apply in England are the School Finance (England) Regulations 2006, SI 2006/468.
[261] Education Act 2002, s 37(4) and (7).

PROBLEMATIC ISSUES

8.154 One matter which is likely to be problematic in England is who is the proper respondent to a claim of unfair dismissal where governing bodies which have delegated budgets have acted jointly. Presumably, they would all have to be respondents to such a claim unless they had previously designated one governing body as the employer.[262]

8.155 One question which will arise both in England and in Wales is what is the effect of a failure by the LEA to give notice to a teacher the governing body of the school at which he is employed has decided that he should be dismissed. The failure could be regarded as rendering a purported dismissal void, but that was not how the EAT regarded the situation in *Howard v Governor of Brixington Infants School*,[263] where it held that the failure should be regarded as a breach of contract. This would give rise only to a right to damages for the period during which the contract would have subsisted if it had not been determined prematurely.

---

[262] See the Education (Modification of Enactments Relating to Employment) (England) Order 2003, SI 2003/1964 and Pt 4 of the School Staffing (England) Regulations 2003, SI 2003/1963.
[263] [1999] ICR 1096, 1112G–H.

Chapter 9

STAFF REPRESENTATION

COLLECTIVE AGREEMENTS

9.1 From time to time representatives of one or other of the teaching unions or the non-teaching unions may negotiate employment issues on behalf of its members. The product of bargaining with unions (traditionally known as 'collective bargaining') is often a 'collective agreement'. There is a conclusive statutory presumption that such an agreement is not intended to be legally binding unless it is in writing and contains a statement that it is intended to be a legally enforceable contract.[1] Relevant terms of a collective agreement may, however, be incorporated in the terms of an individual employee's contract of employment, either expressly or impliedly.

RIGHT TO TIME OFF FOR UNION DUTIES AND ACTIVITIES

9.2 A trade union representative will have the right to a reasonable amount of time off during working hours for trade union activities. If the activity can be classified as a trade union 'duty',[2] then the representative will have the right to pay for that time off. Examples of such duties include:

(1) negotiating in relation to pay and conditions of employment, or the physical conditions in which any workers are required to work;

(2) suspension or dismissal of employees;

(3) matters of discipline;

(4) recognition of a union for collective bargaining purposes.

9.3 If the activity cannot be classified as a duty for that purpose, but does constitute a trade union activity, then the representative will be entitled to take a reasonable amount of time off, but without pay.

---

[1] Trade Union and Labour Relations (Consolidation) Act 1992 (TULRA 1992), s 179.
[2] Within the meaning of ibid, s 168.

9.4 In *Luce v Bexley London Borough Council*,[3] it was decided that when teachers took part in a lobby of Parliament organised by the Trades Union Congress in connection with proposed legislation which affected the teaching profession, they were not taking part in trade union activities. Accordingly, their absence from school was a breach of their contract of employment.

RIGHT NOT TO BE DISCRIMINATED AGAINST IN RESPECT OF TRADE UNION MEMBERSHIP OR ACTIVITIES

9.5 An employee (and a person who is not an employee but who works or seeks to work under a contract to do or perform personally any work or services for another party to the contract who is not a professional client of his) has the right under s 146 of TULRA 1992 not to have action short of dismissal taken against him:

(1) on the ground that he is, was, or proposes to become, a member of a trade union;

(2) on the ground that he is taking part, has taken part or intends to take part, in trade union activities at an appropriate time; or

(3) for the purpose of compelling him to be or become a member of a trade union.

9.6 Under s 152 of the TULRA 1992, the dismissal of an employee for any one of these reasons (suitable adapted) is automatically unfair. No qualifying period is required for a claim of unfair dismissal in breach of s 152.[4] Furthermore, more compensation may be awardable to an employee who is dismissed in breach of s 152 than is available to an employee who claims 'ordinary' unfair dismissal. This is because the minimum basic award will usually be (at the time of writing) £4,200.[5] However, the compensatory award is subject to the standard limit (£60,600 at the time of writing).[6]

9.7 Where:

(1) an employee has been dismissed and claims unfair dismissal contrary to s 152 of the TULRA 1992, and

(2) an authorised official of an independent trade union of which the employee was or proposed to become a member certifies in writing that

---

[3] [1990] ICR 591.
[4] TULRA 1992, s 154.
[5] Ibid, s 156. See para **8.111** above regarding the basic award.
[6] See para **8.111** above also for the compensatory award.

there appear to be reasonable grounds for supposing that the reason or principal reason for the dismissal was one which contravened s 152,

then the employee may apply to an employment tribunal for an order for the continuation of his contract of employment pending the final determination of the complaint.[7]

9.8 Under s 137 of the TULRA 1992, a person has the right not to be refused employment because:

(a) he is, or is not, a member of a trade union, or

(b) he is unwilling to take steps to become or cease to be, or remain or not to become, a member of a trade union.

The compensation for a breach of this right may include compensation for injury to feelings but may not exceed the compensation awardable for an 'ordinary' unfair dismissal (ie at the time of writing £60,600).[8] It is not entirely clear whether this prohibition extends to a refusal of employment to an employee on the ground of his previous trade union *activities*.[9]

STRIKES AND OTHER INDUSTRIAL ACTION

9.9 The law governing industrial action is highly complex. Industrial action will usually involve the individual employees who are taking it breaching one or more terms of their contracts of employment. They will therefore be vulnerable to being dismissed for misconduct. However, there is a considerable amount of protection in the law of unfair dismissal afforded to an employee against dismissal for industrial action where that action falls within s 219 of the TULRA 1992.[10] In order to fall within s 219, an act must (a) be 'done ... in contemplation or furtherance of a trade dispute [within the meaning of s 244 of the TULRA 1992]' and (b) have been approved by a ballot which complies with the requirements of ss 226–245 of the TULRA 1992. If those requirements are met, then, in addition to there being protection in the law of unfair dismissal for employees who participate in the industrial action, the trade union acquires protection against liability (which would otherwise arise) in the law of tort for inducing the employees to breach their contracts of employment. The details of the ballot requirements are outside the scope of this book, except to say that the ballot must support the action (in other words, there must be a majority in favour of the action) if the action is to be regarded as immune from civil liability and if the protection in the law of unfair dismissal is to arise.

---

[7] See ss 161–167 of TULRA 1992.
[8] See ibid, s 140.
[9] See *Harrison v Kent County Council* [1990] IRLR 15, [1995] ICR 431 (Note), and *Speciality Care plc v Pachela* [1996] ICR 633.
[10] See paras **8.34–8.36** above.

9.10 In order to determine whether any action is taken in contemplation or furtherance of a 'trade dispute', the question whether the relevant employee is obliged by his contract of employment to do those things which he refuses to do may be of particular importance. It is of interest that in *P (A minor) v National Association of Schoolmasters/Union of Women Teachers*,[11] the House of Lords ruled that a refusal to teach a pupil whose reinstatement had been ordered by an independent appeal panel was an act done in contemplation or furtherance of a trade dispute within the meaning of s 244 of the TULRA 1992. In contrast, in *Metropolitan Borough of Solihull v National Union of Teachers*,[12] no ballot had been held, and the employer sought an interim injunction, ordering the union to rescind its instruction to its members not to undertake certain actions pending a full trial of the issues. The union argued that its members were not contractually obliged to do those things which it had instructed them not to do, so that it was not liable for inducing its members to breach their contracts of employment, or any other contracts. The High Court held that it could not clearly be said that the members were not obliged to do those things which the union had instructed them not to do. Thus the union was ordered to rescind its instruction pending the trial of the matter.[13]

9.11 Often, the only practical remedy against strike action will be an injunction. Although an injunction could not, in practice, be obtained to compel an employee to comply with his contract of employment, an injunction could be obtained to compel a trade union to call off strike action which did not comply with the ballot requirements.

COLLECTIVE CONSULTATION

Definition of collective consultation

9.12 'Collective consultation' used to mean only consultation between the representatives of a recognised trade union and an employer regarding any employees of that employer. However, the term 'collective consultation' must now be regarded as applying also to consultation between elected employee representatives and the employer of those representatives, especially where there is no independent trade union recognised by the employer in respect of the kind of employees in question. The duty to consult collectively arises mainly so far as relevant in relation to redundancies, TUPE transfers and health and safety matters (see further below). The duty to inform and consult employees imposed by the Information and Consultation of Employees Regulations 2004[14] (the ICE Regulations 2004) is not imposed on the governing bodies of maintained schools which are not the contractual employers of their

---

[11] [2003] 2 AC 663.
[12] [1985] IRLR 211.
[13] See further Chapter 5 above regarding the obligations of teachers and other employees.
[14] SI 2004/3426. As from 6 April 2007 onwards those regulations have applied to employers with 100 or more employees, and as from 6 April 2008 they will apply to employers with 50 or more employees.

members of staff.[15] However, it should be noted that the ICE Regulations 2004 do not apply where the employer is obliged to inform and consult employee representatives under s 188 of the TULRA 1992 or reg 13 of TUPE (both of which are discussed below) and has stated that he or it will be complying with that other duty instead.[16]

What does consultation involve?

9.13 Consultation 'involves giving the body consulted a fair and proper opportunity to understand fully the matters about which it is being consulted, and to express its views on those subjects, with the consultor thereafter considering those views properly and genuinely'.[17] However, in cases of genuine and objectively justifiable urgency, an employment tribunal would be likely to accept that the timescale could be relatively short.

Redundancy consultation

9.14 A local education authority has certain obligations to consult in respect of redundancies at community, voluntary, controlled or community special schools. Collective consultation is required where an employer proposes to make 20 or more employees redundant within a period of 90 days or less.[18] For this purpose redundancy means dismissing an employee 'for a reason not related to the individual concerned or for a number of reasons all of which are not so related'.[19] This definition of 'redundancy' is for these purposes wider than that used for determining whether an individual has a claim for a redundancy payment.[20] The word 'dismiss' here means the same as for the purposes of the law of unfair dismissal,[21] and accordingly includes 'constructive' dismissal.

9.15 Consultation must take place within a period of 90 days of 100 or more proposed redundancies and within a period of 30 days of 20 to 99 proposed redundancies. The maximum penalty for an employer who fails to comply with these requirements is 90 days' gross pay for every employee in respect of whose proposed dismissal the employer should have consulted.[22]

---

[15] This is because the ICE Regulations 2004 are not included in the Schedule to the Education (Modification of Enactments Relating to Employment) (England) Order 2003, SI 2003/1964, or in the Schedule to the equivalent Order relating to Wales, SI 2006/1073.
[16] See reg 20 of the ICE Regulations 2004.
[17] *R v British Coal Corporation and Secretary of State, ex parte Price* [1994] IRLR 72, para 25.
[18] See s 188 of TULRA 1992, which is not included in the Schedule to the Education (Modification of Enactments Relating to Employment) (England) Order 2003, SI 2003/1964, or in the Schedule to the equivalent Order relating to Wales, SI 2006/1073.
[19] TULRA 1992, s 195.
[20] Contained in s 139 of the ERA 1996; see para **7.2** above.
[21] TULRA 1992, s 298. As for the definition, see para **8.16** onwards above.
[22] See s 190 of the TULRA 1992. It is not entirely clear whether the limit of £310 per week provided for in s 227 of the ERA 1996 applies here. Section 190(5) of the TULRA 1992 applies 'Chapter II of Part XIV of the Employment Rights Act 1996 . . . with respect to the calculation of a week's pay for the purposes of this section', which suggests that the limit in

9.16 The employer must also inform the Secretary of State of such dismissals for redundancy in certain circumstances.[23] This must be done within 30 days or 90 days of the time when the first dismissal is proposed to take effect, depending on the number of employees whose dismissal is proposed:

Number of employees	Period over which dismissals are proposed to take place	Notice period
20 or more but fewer than 100	90 days or less	At least 30 days
100 or more	90 days or less	At least 90 days

Consultation in relation to a TUPE transfer

9.17 Where a TUPE transfer (that is, a transfer within the meaning of the Transfer of Undertakings (Protection of Employment) Regulations 2006[24]) is going to occur,[25] an employer must at the earliest opportunity inform the relevant representatives of any affected employees[26] of certain matters (referred to below) and consult those representatives about any changes which the employer intends to make concerning employees as a result of the transfer.[27] Any such consultation must be conducted with a view to reaching agreement in respect of the measures intended to be taken.[28]

9.18 Both the transferor and the transferee must (among other things) inform relevant representatives of any affected employees of the fact that the transfer is to take place, its likely timing, the reasons for it, and the legal, social and economic implications for the affected employees.[29]

9.19 Where the employer is the transferor, the employer is also obliged to inform those representatives of the measures which the transferee intends to take in relation to the employees whose employment will be transferred. If no such measures are envisaged, then the transferor must inform them of that fact. The transferee must supply to the transferor the necessary information in this regard in sufficient time to allow the transferor to comply with this duty.[30]

9.20 It would be a defence to a claim that an employer had not complied with any of the duties imposed by TUPE described above that there were special

---

s 227 applies. However, there is no reference in s 227 of the ERA 1996 to s 190 of the TULRA 1992, and that might be thought to mean that s 227 does not apply to s 190.

[23] See s 193 of the TULRA 1992.
[24] SI 2006/246.
[25] See paras **10.1–10.2** below regarding what constitutes a TUPE transfer.
[26] Defined by reg 13(1) of TUPE to mean for this purpose 'any employees of the transferor or the transferee . . . who may be affected by the transfer or may be affected by measures taken in connection with it'.
[27] TUPE, reg 13(2) and (6). For a helpful definition of consultation, see para **9.13** above.
[28] Ibid, reg 13(6).
[29] Ibid, reg 13(2).
[30] Ibid, reg 13(4).

circumstances which rendered it not reasonably practicable for the employer to comply with the duty in question.[31] However, the employer must still 'take all such steps towards performing that duty as are reasonably practicable in the circumstances'.[32]

9.21 A failure to comply with any of the duties imposed by TUPE described above could result in an order being made by an employment tribunal that the employer pays up to 13 weeks' gross pay to each affected employee.[33] This pay is capped at £310.[34]

9.22 If a transferor fails to comply with the duty to inform but can show that that failure was caused by a failure by the transferee to provide the necessary information, then the transferee may be ordered to pay the relevant compensation.[35]

Health and safety consultation directly with representatives or staff

9.23 Where an employer has established a health and safety representatives' committee in response to a request to do so made under reg 9 of the Safety Representatives and Safety Committees Regulations 1977,[36] the employer is obliged to consult the committee in good time on matters relating to employees' health and safety at work.[37] Such matters include proposals to implement measures at work which may affect the health and safety of employees. These might include new procedures concerning the use of computers or arrangements to cope with building works on school premises. If there is no such committee, then the employer must consult on such matters with employees themselves.[38] However, the employees may elect representatives to be consulted on their behalf in relation to matters of health and safety, and if they do so then the employer can choose whether to consult the representatives or the employees directly.[39]

---

[31] TUPE, reg 13(9).
[32] Ibid.
[33] See ibid, regs 15 and 16(3).
[34] See ibid, reg 16(4), which applies 'Sections 220 to 228 of the 1996 Act . . . for calculating the amount of a week's pay' for this purpose. This more clearly applies s 227 than does the equivalent wording in relation to a protective award, concerning which see para **9.15**, n 22 above.
[35] See reg 15(8)(b) of TUPE.
[36] SI 1977/500.
[37] See the Safety Representatives and Safety Committees Regulations 1977, SI 1977/500, as amended, and the Health and Safety (Consultation with Employees) Regulations 1996, SI 1996/1513. For a helpful definition of consultation, see para **9.13** above.
[38] See SI 1996/1513, reg 4.
[39] See regs 3 and 4 of SI 1996/1513.

Chapter 10

TRANSFERS OF UNDERTAKINGS

APPLICATION OF THE TRANSFER OF UNDERTAKINGS (PROTECTION OF EMPLOYMENT) REGULATIONS 2006

10.1 The employers of staff in schools might think that they do not need to be aware of the Transfer of Undertakings (Protection of Employment) Regulations 2006[1] (TUPE) but that is not so. TUPE applies whenever a business, undertaking or part of an undertaking is transferred from one employer to another. TUPE also applies where there is a 'service provision change' within the meaning of reg 3 of TUPE. The details of for example reg 3 are outside the scope of this book. It is sufficient to know that there can be a transfer of an undertaking within the meaning of TUPE when there is the ending of a contract for the provision of, for example, cleaning services, and a new contractor takes over. This is so even if only one employee is carrying out the services in question.[2] TUPE provides some protection of the interests of the members of staff who are employed within ('assigned' to) the transferred business.

10.2 TUPE will clearly apply if for example a voluntary aided school is closed and a new school is opened, to which the majority of the pupils transfer. The question whether TUPE applies on the reorganisation of community and/or voluntary controlled schools is a difficult one to answer. This is because on one view, there is no change of employer: the contractual employer (ie the LEA) remains the same, although there is a change in the body responsible for claims of unfair dismissal (ie the governing body).[3] It could be argued that the European Community legislation which gave rise to TUPE, ie the Acquired Rights Directive,[4] should be used as an aid to the interpretation of TUPE, and that TUPE should be regarded as applying to the situation. It could also be argued that if TUPE does not apply to the situation, then the UK government has failed properly to implement the Acquired Rights Directive and that accordingly that Directive should be capable of being enforced directly.[5] However, the Court of Appeal rejected those arguments in *Governing Body of Clifton Middle School v Askew*.[6]

---

[1] SI 2006/246.
[2] See in particular reg 2(1) of TUPE.
[3] See para **8.147** above.
[4] Now 2001/23/EC.
[5] See paras **6.5–6.6** and **6.12–6.16** above for the principles concerning the direct effect of Community law.
[6] [2000] ICR 286. Lord Justice Chadwick dissented on the second of the two points.

10.3 However, if either TUPE or the Acquired Rights Directive does apply to the situation, then the requirement in Wales to advertise certain staff vacancies[7] will be in conflict with the obligations owed under TUPE to the staff who could claim to be entitled to fill those vacancies.

THE EFFECTS OF TUPE

10.4 Where TUPE applies, it operates to transfer to the transferee the employment of the staff in the undertaking in question who are employed by the transferor immediately before the transfer. This occurs through the contracts of employment of the transferring staff being treated as if they had been entered into by the transferee instead of the transferor. All rights, duties and liabilities under or in connection with the contract of employment also transfer. Any employee who has the right to claim unfair dismissal is automatically unfairly dismissed if the reason or principal reason for the dismissal (which may occur before or after the transfer) is the transfer, or a reason connected with it, unless (a) the reason for the dismissal is an economic, technical, or organisational one and (b) that reason entails changes in the workforce.[8] However, even where an employee is dismissed because of a TUPE transfer and those conditions are satisfied, the dismissal must still satisfy the normal conditions for a fair dismissal.

10.5 At one time it was thought that if a dismissal was automatically unfair because it was in breach of TUPE, then the dismissal was void and the employee's employment with the transferor was transferred to the transferee. However, it is now clear that even if:

(1) an employee is dismissed before the transfer and the reason for the dismissal is the transfer or a reason connected with it, and

(2) the reason is not an economic, technical or organisation one entailing changes in the workforce,

then the employee's dismissal is valid and not a nullity. Accordingly, in that situation the employee's employment is not transferred to the transferee. Nevertheless, it is now also clear that if the employee claims unfair dismissal, then the liability to meet the claim will lie with the transferee. Both of these propositions are drawn from the House of Lords' decision in *Wilson v St Helens Borough Council*.[9]

---

[7] Concerning which, see para **4.67** above. In England, there is a power to decline to advertise where there is 'good reason' not to do so: see para **4.49** above. Such good reason will include that TUPE applies.
[8] See reg 7 of TUPE.
[9] [1998] ICR 1141.

10.6 In contrast, if:

(1) the transferor or the transferee agrees with a transferring or transferred employee a change in the terms and conditions of the employee, and

(2) the reason for the change is either the transfer itself or a reason connected with the transfer that is *not* an economic, technical or organisational reason entailing changes in the workforce,

then the change will be void.[10] This does not prevent an employer from reorganising his or its workforce for a reason which is 'unconnected with the transfer'.[11]

10.7 The obligation to consult with representatives of the staff in relation to a TUPE transfer is merely noted here. It is considered in paras **9.17–9.22** above.

---

[10] TUPE, reg 4(4), which is subject to reg 9 of TUPE. Regulation 9 applies where the transferor is subject to certain kinds of insolvency proceedings. Such proceedings will almost certainly not apply to the employer of the staff of a maintained school.

[11] See reg 4(5) of TUPE, which spells out this arguably self-evident proposition.

INDEX

References are to paragraph numbers.

Adoption leave	5.62
right to	5.65
Adoption pay	
statutory	5.44
Advanced skills teacher standards	
pay and conditions, and	4.27, 4.28, 4.29, 4.30
Advertisements	
discrimination, and	1.8
Age discrimination	6.105
definitions	6.105
legislation	6.105
salient features of	6.106
retirements	6.107, 6.108, 6.109, 6.110, 6.111, 6.112, 6.113, 6.114, 6.115, 6.116, 6.117, 6.118, 6.119, 6.120, 6.121, 6.122, 6.123
Agency workers	
discrimination	6.71
sexual harassment	6.71
Annualised hours	5.15
extra hours	5.16
meaning	5.15
Ante-natal care	
time off for	5.50
Appeals	1.30
barring of persons from teaching	3.20, 3.21, 3.22, 3.23, 3.24
Care Standards Tribunal, to	3.23
conduct dismissals	8.67
dismissal	8.93
failure to complete induction period, and	3.60
flexible working, and	6.89
point of law, on	1.31
discerning	1.31
perverse decisions	1.32
register of teachers, and	3.39
restrictions on	1.30
Appointment	
member of staff	
maintained school, at	4.38
Appointment of staff	4.45
collaborating governing bodies	4.60
community, voluntary controlled, community special or maintained nursery school	
deputy head teacher	4.49, 4.50, 4.51
general requirements	4.46, 4.47, 4.48

Appointment of staff—*continued*	
community, voluntary controlled, community special or maintained nursery school—*continued*	
head teacher	4.49, 4.50, 4.51
support staff	4.54, 4.55, 4.56
teachers	4.52, 4.53
delegation of powers	4.61
foundation, voluntary aided or foundation special school	4.57, 4.58, 4.59
maintained school in Wales	4.63, 4.64, 4.65, 4.66, 4.67, 4.68, 4.69, 4.70
framework of regulations	4.71
non-school activities	4.74, 4.75, 4.76
religious education, and	4.79
religious opinions, and	4.84, 4.85
requirement to review staffing structure	4.72, 4.73
Appraisals	
teachers, of	4.77
Automatically unfair dismissals	8.38
Barring of persons from teaching	3.13
effect of barring direction	3.25
applying for work in regulated positions	3.26
criminal offences	3.25
'regulated position'	3.25
regulated position, definition	3.27
responsible person, definition	3.28
information to be given to	
Secretary of State	3.29
GTCE jurisdiction	3.33
information required	3.31
relevant issue, definition	3.30
Wales, in	3.32
Secretary of State's guidance	3.13, 3.14
statutory framework	3.15
appeals	3.20, 3.21, 3.22, 3.23, 3.24
application	3.15
circumstances for giving direction	3.18, 3.19
grounds for giving direction	3.16
power to vary directions	3.20, 3.21, 3.22, 3.23, 3.24
procedure for giving direction	3.17
revocations	3.20, 3.21, 3.22, 3.23, 3.24
scope	3.15
Bichard Inquiry	4.2

Breach of contract		Consideration—*continued*	
damages for	8.121	executory	5.45
Burden of proof		Constructive dismissal	8.19
direct discrimination	6.24, 6.25, 6.26, 6.28, 6.32	implied term of trust and confidence	8.22
burden of proof shifted	6.30	reduction of remuneration	8.23
case law	6.27	repudiation of contract	8.20
timing of two-stage test	6.31	'sit on his rights'	8.21
two-stage approach	6.29	Consultation	
race discrimination	6.39	selection for redundancy, and	7.23, 7.24, 7.25, 7.26
unfair dismissal	8.37	Contract of employment	
Burden of Proof Directive	6.24, 6.25, 6.26, 6.27, 6.28, 6.29, 6.30, 6.31, 6.32	come into existence, whether	4.10, 4.11
Burgundy Book	4.33	disciplinary procedures	5.20, 5.21
Dorling v Sheffield City Council	4.34	employees' obligations	5.73, 5.74, 5.75
entitlement to sick pay		employers' obligations after end of	5.25
dismissal because of incapacity, and	4.35, 4.36, 4.37	frustration of	8.28, 8.29, 8.30
		illegality, and	8.11
		implied obligations	5.78, 5.79, 5.80
Cancer		implied teachers' obligations	5.76, 5.77
disability discrimination	6.135	implied terms	5.9
Care Standards Tribunal	3.21	good faith	5.11
appeals to	3.23	hours of work	5.14
Child protection		safe place and system of work	5.12
allegations against members of staff	8.139	trust and confidence	5.9, 5.10
Civil partnership		maximum hours	5.17
discrimination, and	6.63, 6.64	notice obligations	5.2
Collaborating governing bodies		obligation to comply with	5.6
appointment of staff	4.60	alteration of terms	5.6
Collective agreements	9.1	imposition of new terms	5.7
Collective consultation	9.12	reduction of pay	5.7
Community facilities		obligations after end of	1.11
staffing	4.74, 4.75, 4.76	pay and conditions	4.19
Community schools		promotions and variations	5.45
appointment of head and deputy head teacher	4.49, 4.50, 4.51	consideration	5.45
appointment of staff	4.46, 4.47, 4.48	mutual termination of old contract	5.48
appointment of support staff	4.54, 4.55, 4.56	pay rise	5.46
appointment of teachers	4.52, 4.53	promotion	5.47
Community special schools		repudiation of	8.20
appointment of head and deputy head teacher	4.49, 4.50, 4.51	requirements	4.13
appointment of staff	4.46, 4.47, 4.48	scope	4.12
appointment of support staff	4.54, 4.55, 4.56	statement of terms and conditions	4.14, 4.15, 4.16, 4.17
appointment of teachers	4.52, 4.53	supply teachers, and	1.7
Compensation		termination of	8.17
damages for breach of contract	8.121	volunteers, and	1.7
failure to give pay in lieu of notice	8.122	Contract, law of	1.9
Sex Discrimination Act 1975, under	6.78, 6.79, 6.80, 6.81, 6.82, 6.83, 6.84, 6.85	Costs	
		award of	1.27, 1.28, 1.29
unfair dismissal	8.111	Costs orders	1.27
Complaints		Courts	
handling appropriately sex discrimination, and	6.49	hierarchy	1.18
Conduct dismissals		Criminal conduct	
substantive fairness in	8.64	conduct dismissals, and	8.68, 8.69, 8.70, 8.71
Consideration		Criminal Records Bureau (CRB)	
contracts, and	5.45	making of checks with	4.3, 4.4, 4.5
		register of checks	4.6, 4.7
		Damages	
		breach of contract, for	8.121
		failure to give notice	5.4

Index

Deductions
    pay and benefits, and   5.32, 5.33, 5.34, 5.35
Delegation of powers
    appointment of staff   4.61
Deputy head teacher
    appointment
        community, voluntary controlled, community special or maintained nursery school   4.49, 4.50, 4.51
Deputy head teachers
    acting   4.65
Direct discrimination   6.20
    proving   6.23
        burden of proof directive   6.24, 6.25, 6.26, 6.27, 6.28, 6.29, 6.30, 6.31
        case law   6.32
        employer's intention   6.33
        employment tribunal approach   6.35
        unreasonable behaviour, and   6.34
    Sex Discrimination Act 1975   6.45
Disability discrimination   6.124
    code of practice   6.149
    disability, definition   6.127
        addictions   6.127
        effect of medical treatment   6.136
        long term effects   6.129
        normal day-to-day activities   6.130, 6.133
        past disabilities   6.137
        progressive conditions   6.134, 6.135
        seasonal allergic rhinitis   6.128
        Secretary of State's guidance   6.131
        severe disfigurement   6.132
    employment, and   6.138
        forms of discrimination   6.138
        harassment, and   6.139
        justifiable less favourable treatment   6.141
        less favourable treatment   6.140
        reasonable adjustments, duty to make   6.143, 6.144, 6.145, 6.146, 6.147, 6.148
        test for deciding less favourable treatment   6.142
    justifiably acting unreasonably   6.125
    legislation   6.124
    new code of practice   6.126
    Secretary of State's guidance   6.126
Disciplinary action
    statutory grievance procedures, and   2.5
Disciplinary hearings
    witnesses   8.88, 8.89, 8.90
Disciplinary interview
    refusal to attend   8.77, 8.78
Disciplinary procedures
    contractual   5.20, 5.21
    maintained schools, at   4.43, 4.44
Discipline and dismissal
    maintainted schools, in   8.123

Discrimination
    age   6.105
    agency workers   6.71
    appellate decisions   6.3
    compensation   6.83, 6.84, 6.85
    definition
        application to employment   6.65
    direct   6.20
        meaning   6.20
        proving   6.23
        racial characteristics, and   6.21
    direct and indirect, distinction   6.19
    disability   6.124
    EC legislation   6.41
    equal opportunities policy   6.2
    fixed-term workers, against   6.96
    flexible working, and   6.86
    genuine occupational qualifications, and   6.72
    harassment   6.36
    indirect   6.1, 6.22
        definition   6.58
        meaning   6.22
    justified   6.1
    legislation   6.3
    part-time employees   5.8
    part-time workers, against   6.91
    positive   6.1
        schools with religious character, and   4.81, 4.82, 4.83
    pregnancy, and   6.51, 6.52, 6.53, 6.54, 6.55
    protection of employees   6.5
    racial   6.100
    recruitment, and   4.8, 4.9
    relationship between national and international prohibitions   6.5, 6.6
        European Community law   6.12, 6.13, 6.14, 6.15, 6.16, 6.17, 6.18
        human rights   6.7, 6.8, 6.9, 6.10, 6.11
    religion or belief, grounds of   6.102
    religious opinions in accordance with particular religion   4.84, 4.85
    self-employed workers   6.71
    sexual orientation   6.104
    time limits for claims
        SDA 1975, under   6.78, 6.79, 6.80, 6.81, 6.82
    UK legislation   6.42
        Sex Discrimination Act 1975   6.44, 6.45, 6.46, 6.47, 6.48, 6.49, 6.50, 6.51, 6.52, 6.53, 6.54, 6.55, 6.56, 6.57, 6.58, 6.59, 6.60, 6.61, 6.62, 6.63, 6.64
        subordinate legislation   6.43
    victimization   6.37
Dismissal
    compensation for discrimination, and   6.85
    incapacity, for
        entitlement to sick pay, and   4.35, 4.37
        required notice period   4.36
    maternity grounds, on   5.58

Dismissal and discipline procedures	
(DDPs)	2.37
application	2.38
'relevant disciplinary action'	2.40
retirement, and	2.39
compliance with	2.43
effect of failure to follow	
employee	2.45
employer	2.44
modified	2.41
application	2.42
requirements	2.46, 2.47, 2.48
standard	2.41
Dispute resolution procedures	2.1, 2.2
Employment Act 2002, in	2.1, 2.2
new statutory procedures	2.1, 2.2
sanctions for non-compliance	2.3, 2.4
statutory grievance procedures	2.5
types of	2.1, 2.2
EAT	
costs, and	1.27, 1.28, 1.29
members	1.24
Education action zone	
pay and conditions, and	4.21
Employees	
appointment	4.38
regulations	4.38, 4.39, 4.40, 4.41
defining	1.7
dismissal and discipline procedures	2.45
effect of failure to follow grievance	
procedures	2.29, 2.30, 2.31, 2.32, 2.33, 2.34
implied obligations	5.78, 5.79, 5.80
obligations	5.73, 5.74, 5.75
express terms of teacher's	
contract of employment	5.73, 5.74, 5.75
permanent or temporary	5.1
protection from discrimination	6.5
Employer	
attitude towards discrimination	6.35
defining	1.4, 1.5
governing body as	1.6
intention	
proving direct discrimination, and	6.33
Employers	
dismissal and discipline procedures	2.44
effect of failure to follow grievance	
procedures	2.35
obligations after contract of	
employment ended	5.25
Employment Act 2002	
dispute resolution procedures in	2.1, 2.2, 2.3
Employment Act 2002 grievance	
procedures	1.26
Employment law	
development of law	1.3
employees, defining	1.7
employer, defining	1.4, 1.5, 1.6

Employment law—*continued*	
generally	1.3, 1.9
applicable law	1.9
Health and Safety at Work etc Act 1974, and	1.10
termination of contract of employment, and	1.11
prospective employees	1.8
Employment tribunal	
direct discrimination, approach to	6.35
Employment tribunals	1.21
costs, and	1.27, 1.28, 1.29
creatures of statute, as	1.23
'industrial jury'	1.25
jurisdiction	1.23
lay members	1.24
members	1.24
Equal opportunities policy	6.2
Equal pay	6.150
comparisons	6.152
schools, in	6.153
Equal Pay Act 1970	6.150
equal work, for	6.151
genuine material factor	6.154, 6.155
remedies	6.156, 6.157
time limit for claims	6.156, 6.157
victimisation, and	6.38
Equality clauses	6.157
European Community law	
current prohibitions of	6.41
direct effect of	
discrimination, and	6.12, 6.13, 6.14, 6.15, 6.16
indirect effect of	
discrimination, and	6.17, 6.18
European Convention on Human Rights	3.46
European Court of Human Rights	
application of Convention rights	6.160, 6.161, 6.162, 6.163, 6.164, 6.165, 6.166
Excellent teacher standards	
pay and conditions, and	4.27, 4.28, 4.29, 4.30
Fast track teacher standards	
pay and conditions, and	4.27, 4.28, 4.29, 4.30
Fixed-term contracts	
non-renewal	
unfair dismissal, and	8.84
notice, and	5.3
unfair dismissal, and	8.8
Fixed-term workers	
discrimination against	6.96
comparable permanent employee	6.97
legislation	6.99
successive contracts for four or more years	6.98
Flexible working, right to request	6.86
appeal hearing	6.89

Index

Flexible working, right to request—*continued*
    changing back   6.88
    initial meeting   6.89
    notice of decision   6.90
    reasons for refusal   6.90
    statutory provisions   6.86, 6.87
Foundation schools
    appointment of staff   4.57, 4.58, 4.59
Foundation special schools
    appointment of staff   4.57, 4.58, 4.59
Freedom of expression   6.164, 6.165, 6.166
Freedom of thought, conscience and
    religion, right to   6.163
Frustration
    contract ended by   8.28
    imprisonment   8.29
    long-term illness   8.30

Gender reassignment
    harassment, and   6.70
General Teaching Councils   3.34
    advice   3.35
    disciplinary powers   3.40, 3.41
        abuse of process, test for   3.44
        employment tribunal findings,
            and   3.45
        European Convention on
            Human Rights, and   3.46
        Investigating Committee   3.42
        standards code   3.47
        unacceptable professional
            misconduct   3.43
    functions   3.34
    register of teachers   3.36, 3.37, 3.38, 3.39
    supply of information relating to
        teachers   3.48, 3.49
Genuine occupational qualifications
    discrimination, and   6.72
Grievance procedures   1.26
    appealing employers' decisions   2.14
    effect of failure to follow   2.28
        employee, on   2.29, 2.30, 2.31, 2.32, 2.33, 2.34
        employer, on   2.35
    extension of time   2.36
    general requirements   2.8
        meetings   2.8
        timetable   2.8
    grievance, meaning   2.9, 2.10, 2.11, 2.12
        modified procedure, and   2.13
    'modified'   2.7
        application   2.15
        non-compliance   2.16
    'appropriate representative'   2.26
    collective agreements   2.27
    failure to comply with statutory
        procedures   2.9, 2.17, 2.18, 2.20, 2.21, 2.22
    'relevant disciplinary action'   2.23, 2.24, 2.25
    'standard'   2.7
    statutory   2.5
        application   2.5

Grievance procedures—*continued*
    statutory—*continued*
        effect   2.6
Grievances
    employers' obligations   5.13

Harassment   6.36
    disabled employees   6.139
    sexual   6.67, 6.68, 6.69, 6.70
Head teacher
    qualification to be   3.63
        exceptions   3.64
        requirements   3.63
        Wales, in   3.65
Head teachers
    acting   4.65
    appointment
        community, voluntary
            controlled, community
            special or maintained
                nursery school   4.49, 4.50, 4.51
    dismissal for incapability
        unfair dismissal, and   8.59
    LEA concerns about
        maintained schools, at   4.42
    LEA report on performance of   8.126
Health and physical capacity
    teachers, of
        legislative requirements   3.9
        medical examination   3.12
        procedural requirements   3.11
        relevant activities   3.10
Health and safety   5.26
    collective consultation   9.23
High Court
    contractual disputes   1.22
    employment disputes in   1.21
HIV
    disability discrimination   6.135
Holidays
    paid   5.28
Homosexuals
    discrimination   6.104
Hours of work
    implied terms, and   5.14
Human rights   6.158
    Convention rights   6.159
        application by ECHR   6.160
        freedom of expression   6.164, 6.165, 6.166
        freedom of thought, conscience
            and religion   6.163
        relevant to employment law   6.159
        right to respect for private and
            family life   6.161, 6.162
    discrimination, and   6.7, 6.8, 6.9
        application of Convention
            rights   6.11
        Convention rights   6.10
Human Rights Act 1998
    discrimination, and   6.7, 6.8, 6.9, 6.10, 6.11

Ill-health	
incapability through	
unfair dismissal, and	8.56
Implied obligations	
all employees	5.78, 5.79, 5.80
teachers'	5.76, 5.77
Implied terms	
good faith	5.11
hours of work	5.14
safe place and system of work	5.12
trust and confidence	5.9, 5.10
constructive dismissal, and	8.22
Imprisonment	
frustration of contract, and	8.29
Independent schools	
employment in	1.14
relevant provisions	1.14
states schools contrasted	1.1
Indirect discrimination	6.22
definition	6.58, 6.59, 6.60, 6.61, 6.62
Induction periods	3.50
absence from work, and	3.55
appraisals during	3.57
charges for independent schools and sixth form colleges	3.61
completion of	3.58
English Induction Regulations	3.51
failure to satisfactorily complete	3.59, 3.60
length	3.54
National Assembly's Guidance	3.52
requirements	3.50
Secretary of State's Guidance	3.52
supervision and training during	3.56
Welsh Induction Regulations	3.52
Industrial action	9.9, 9.10, 9.11
dismissals arising from	
unfair dismissal, and	8.34, 8.35, 8.36
Judicial Committee of House of Lords	1.18
Judicial review	1.21
Law Lords	1.18
Legislation	
applicable	1.9
discrimination	6.42
Less favourable treatment	
meaning	6.46
Liability	
sex discrimination	6.73, 6.74, 6.75, 6.76, 6.77
Limited-term contract	
end of	
unfair dismissal, and	8.18
Local education authorities	
schools maintained by employer, and	1.4, 1.5
Long-term illness	
frustration of contract, and	8.30

Maintained nursery schools	
appointment of head and deputy head teacher	4.49, 4.50, 4.51
appointment of staff	4.46, 4.47, 4.48
appointment of support staff	4.54, 4.55, 4.56
appointment of teachers	4.52, 4.53
Maintained schools	
appointment of member of staff	4.38
delegated budget, with	
conduct, discipline and capability of staff	4.43, 4.44
LEA concerns about head teacher	4.42
staffing situation	4.42
delegated budget, with, in Wales	
acting head and deputy head teachers	4.65
additional powers and duties	4.63, 4.64, 4.65, 4.66, 4.67, 4.68, 4.69, 4.70
advice in relation to appointments	4.68, 4.69, 4.70
framework of regulations	4.71
independent investigation of child protection matter	4.64
requirement to advertise posts	4.67
selection panels	4.66
staffing situation	4.62
sufficiency of staff	4.63
discipline and dismissal in	8.123
child protection issues	8.139
delegation of power to dismiss	8.129, 8.130, 8.131
dismissal of staff	8.129
employment powers and responsibilities	8.123, 8.124, 8.125
involvement of staff governors	8.33, 8.132
LEA report on performance of head teacher	8.126
procedural requirements	8.134, 8.135, 8.137
suspension of staff	8.127, 8.128
Wales, in	8.138, 8.140, 8.141, 8.142, 8.143, 8.144, 8.145, 8.146
employment tribunal proceedings, and	8.147
failure to give notice	8.155
payments in respect of any member of staff	8.148
dismissals and resignations	8.148, 8.149, 8.150, 8.151, 8.152
premature retirements	8.153
respondents, identifying	8.154
Managers	
competence of	
unfair dismissal, and	8.54
Marital status	
discrimination, and	6.63, 6.64

Index

Maternity pay	5.38
notice	5.39
state maternity allowance	5.40
statutory maternity pay	5.38
suspension with pay on maternity grounds	5.41
Maternity rights	5.50
dismissal on maternity grounds	5.58
maternity leave, right to	5.52, 5.53, 5.54, 5.55, 5.56, 5.57
suitable alternative work	5.51
suspension with pay	5.51
time off for ante-natal care	5.50
Maximum hours	5.17
Misconduct	
definition	8.74
Mitigation of loss	8.117
Multiple sclerosis	
disability discrimination	6.135
National minimum wage	5.31
Negotiations	
without prejudice	2.49
Non-school activities	
staffing for	4.74, 4.75, 4.76
Notice	
obligation to give	5.2
contract of employment	5.2
damages for failure to give	5.4
fixed-term contracts	5.3
pay in lieu of notice	5.5
statutory right	5.2
Obiter dicta	1.17
Offers of employment	
discrimination, and	6.65
Parental leave	5.59
amount	5.61
pay	5.60
Part-time employees	
rights of	5.8
Part-time workers	
discrimination, and	6.91
definitions	6.92
legislation	6.95
less favourable treatment	6.91
overtime	6.93
pro rata principle	6.92
written statement of reasons	6.94
Paternity leave	5.62
availability	5.63
remuneration	5.64
terms and conditions of contract	5.64
Paternity pay	
statutory	5.42, 5.43
Pay and benefits	5.30
deductions	5.32, 5.33, 5.34, 5.35
maternity pay	5.38
national minimum wage	5.31
right to be paid	5.30
statutory adoption pay	5.44

Pay and benefits—*continued*	
statutory paternity pay	5.42, 5.43
statutory sick pay	5.36
suspension with pay on medical grounds	5.37
Pay and conditions	4.19
application of regulations	4.20
Burgundy Book	4.33, 4.34, 4.35, 4.36, 4.37
members of education action zone	4.21
school teacher's pay and conditions documents	4.22, 4.23, 4.24, 4.25, 4.26
advanced skills teacher standards	4.27, 4.28, 4.29, 4.30
application of	4.27, 4.28, 4.29, 4.30
excellent teacher standards	4.27, 4.28, 4.29, 4.30
fast track teacher standards	4.27, 4.28, 4.29, 4.30
performance thresholds	4.27, 4.28, 4.29, 4.30
temporary safeguarding of pay	4.31, 4.32
School Teachers' Review Body	4.22
Pay in lieu of notice	5.5
compensation for failure to give	8.122
Pension arrangements	
employers' obligations	5.18
Pensions	5.49
Performance thresholds	
pay and conditions, and	4.27, 4.28, 4.29, 4.30
Personality clash	
dismissal for	8.86
Positive discrimination	
schools with religious character	4.81, 4.82, 4.83
Precedent, doctrine of	1.2
application	1.16
effect	1.20
importance of	1.15
Judicial Committee of House of Lords, and	1.18
obiter dicta, and	1.17
persuasive authorities	1.19
ratio decidendi, and	1.17
Pregnancy	
discrimination on ground of	6.51, 6.52, 6.53, 6.54, 6.55
Private and family life, right to respect for	6.161, 6.162
Pro rata principle	6.92
Probation	
employees on	
unfair dismissal, and	8.55
Probationers	
employers' obligations	5.19
Promotion	
discrimination, and	6.66
Protected disclosure	
unfair dismissal, and	8.40
Protection from detriment	5.72

Qualified teachers	3.5
health and physical capacity	3.9, 3.10, 3.11, 3.12
regulations	3.5
requirement to be registered as	3.6, 3.7
Wales, in	3.8
requirements for	3.5
specified work, and	3.3
Questionnaires	
sex discrimination, and	6.50
Racial discrimination	6.100
burden of proof	6.39
definitions	6.101
Ratio decidendi	1.17
Re-engagement	
orders for	8.101
Reasonable adjustments	
disability discrimination, and	6.143, 6.144, 6.145, 6.146, 6.147, 6.148
Recruitment	4.1
Bichard Inquiry	4.2
Criminal Records Bureau	4.5
register of checks	4.6, 4.7
discrimination, and	1.8
legal issues	4.8
contract of employment	4.10, 4.11, 4.12, 4.13
discrimination	4.8, 4.9
Rehabilitation of Offenders Act 1974, and	4.18
statement of terms and conditions	4.14, 4.15, 4.16, 4.17
need for caution	4.2
non-school activities	4.74, 4.75, 4.76
pay and conditions	4.19
requirement to review staffing structure	4.72, 4.73
Secretary of State's guidance	4.3, 4.4
Redundancy	7.1
alternative employment unfair dismissal, and	8.31
calculation of payment	7.10
examples	7.12
method of	7.10, 7.11
collective consultation	9.14
notification to Secretary of State	9.16
time frame for	9.15
definition	7.2, 7.3
employer's knowledge schools requirements for teaching staff	7.4
	7.5
dismissal and discipline procedures, and	2.38
entitlement to payment	7.1
losing right to	7.8, 7.9
redundancy pay, calculation of	7.13
case law	7.14
requirement for continuous employment	7.6
rules	7.7

Redundancy—*continued*	
requirement for continuous employment—*continued*	
statutory provisions	7.6
selection for	7.19
automatically unfair selection	7.28
consultation	7.23, 7.24, 7.25, 7.26
method of	7.19, 7.20, 7.21
reasonable efforts to redeploy	7.22
statutory dismissal and discipline procedure	7.27
time off to look for alternative work	7.15, 7.16
training, time off for	7.15, 7.16
unfair dismissal, and	7.17, 8.46
right to claim	7.17
substantive fairness	7.18
Reference	
refusal to give	6.38
Register of teachers	3.36, 3.37
appeals to High Court regarding	3.39
fees	3.38
Registration	
teachers, of	3.6, 3.7
Wales, in	3.8
Regulation of employment in schools	3.1
bans and suspensions	3.2
health requirements	3.2
qualification requirements	3.2
'specified work'	3.3
Regulations	
number affecting schools	1.1
Rehabilitation of Offenders Act 1974	
work in regulated position, and	4.18
Reinstatement	
orders for	8.98
Relevant disciplinary action	
definition	2.40
Religious character	
schools with	4.78
positive discrimination	4.81, 4.82, 4.83
Religious discrimination	6.102
application of regulations	6.103
definitions	6.102
legislation	6.102
Religious education	
appointment of reserved teachers, and	4.79
'effeciently and suitably'	4.80
fitness and competence to give	4.78
teachers, and	4.78
Religious opinions	
in accordance with particular religion	
discrimination, and	4.84, 4.85
protection of staff regarding	4.81, 4.82, 4.83
Religious worship	
absence for	
conduct dismissals	8.76
Remedies	
damages for breach of contract	8.121

Index

Remedies—*continued*
    equal pay, and   6.156, 6.157
    unfair dismissal   8.97
Resignation
    unfair dismissal, and   8.25, 8.26, 8.27
Retirement
    age discrimination, and   6.107
    dismissal and discipline procedures, and   2.39
    fairness of dismissal for   6.122
        basic award   6.123
        requirements   6.122
    premature   8.153
    procedure for   6.107
        acceptance of request   6.111
        appeal against refusal to comply   6.112
        continuation of employment after dismissal   6.113
        different date, right to request   6.108
        failure to comply with provisions   6.115
        meeting   6.110
        notice   6.109
        potential complaints   6.114
    unfair dismissal on   6.116
        employee has normal retirement age   6.118, 6.119, 6.120, 6.121
        no normal retirement age   6.117
        retirement fair reason for dismissal, as   6.116
Revocations
    barring of persons from teaching   3.20, 3.21, 3.22, 3.23, 3.24
Right to be paid   5.30

School Teachers Review Body
    pay and conditions, and   4.22
Selection panels
    Wales, in   4.66
Self-employed workers
    discrimination   6.71
    sexual harassment   6.71
    unfair dismissal, and   8.3, 8.4, 8.5, 8.6
Self-employment   1.7
Sex discrimination
    employer's general attitude, and   6.35
    flexible working, and   6.86
    genuine occupational qualifications   6.72
    marital status, and   6.63, 6.64
Sex Discrimination Act 1975   6.44
    application of definition of discrimination   6.65
    appropriate comparison   6.48
    civil partnership   6.63, 6.64
    comparator   6.47
    compensation   6.83
        dismissal, and   6.85
        injury to feelings   6.84
    direct discrimination   6.45

Sex Discrimination Act 1975—*continued*
    discrimination on ground of
        pregnancy   6.51, 6.52, 6.53, 6.54, 6.55
    genuine occupational qualifications   6.72
    handling complaints appropriately   6.49
    harassment   6.67, 6.68, 6.69, 6.70
    indirect discrimination   6.58
        'proportionate means of achieving a legitimate aim'   6.61, 6.62
        'provision, criterion or practice', meaning   6.59
        putting at a disadvantage   6.60
    less favourable treatment   6.46
    liability   6.73, 6.74, 6.75, 6.76, 6.77
        employees and agents, for   6.73, 6.74, 6.75, 6.76, 6.77
        secondary parties, of   6.73, 6.74, 6.75, 6.76, 6.77
    marital status   6.63, 6.64
    offers of employment   6.65
    promotion, transfer and training   6.66
    questionnaires   6.50
    sexual harassment   6.67, 6.68, 6.69, 6.70
    time limits for claims   6.78, 6.79, 6.80, 6.81, 6.82
    victimization   6.56, 6.57
Sexual harassment   6.67
    agency workers   6.71
    conduct   6.68
    gender reassignment, and   6.70
    men   6.69
    self-employed workers   6.71
Sexual orientation discrimination   6.104
Sick pay
    entitlement to
        dismissal for incapacity, and   4.35, 4.36, 4.37
    statutory   5.36
Specified work   3.3
    meaning   3.3
    requirements to carry out   3.3
    skills, expertise and experience   3.4
Staff governors
    involvement in dismissals   8.33, 8.132
Staff representation   9.1
    collective agreements   9.1
    collective consultation   9.12
        definition   9.12
        health and safety   9.23
        redundancy consultation   9.14, 9.15, 9.16
        scope   9.13
        TUPE transfer   9.17, 9.18, 9.19, 9.20, 9.21, 9.22
    strikes and industrial action   9.9, 9.10, 9.11
    union duties and activities
        right not to be discriminated against   9.5, 9.6, 9.7, 9.8
        right to time off for   9.2, 9.3, 9.4

Staffing structure	
requirement to review	4.72, 4.73
State maternity allowance	5.40
State schools	
employment in	1.12
relevant provisions	1.12
independent schools contrasted	1.1
Statement of terms and conditions	4.14, 4.15
failure to comply with obligations	4.16, 4.17
Statutory adoption pay	5.44
Statutory grievance procedures	2.5
Statutory paternity pay	5.42, 5.43
Statutory sick pay	5.36
Strikes	9.9, 9.10, 9.11
dismissals arising from	
unfair dismissal, and	8.34, 8.35, 8.36
Supply staff	
CRB checks, and	4.5
Supply teachers	1.7
Support staff	
appointment	
community, voluntary	
controlled, community	
special or maintained	
nursery school	4.54, 4.55, 4.56
Suspension on medical grounds	
maternity grounds	5.41
right to pay	5.37
Teachers	
appointment	
community, voluntary	
controlled, community	
special or maintained	
nursery school	4.52, 4.53
appraisals	4.77
implied obligations	5.76, 5.77
Temporary employees	
obligations	5.1
Temporary safeguarding of pay	
legality	4.31, 4.32
Terms and conditions	
changing	
unfair dismissal, and	8.24
Time limits	
equal pay, and	6.156, 6.157
unfair dismissal, claiming	8.32, 8.33
Time off for dependents	5.66
complaint about refusal of	5.69
dependant, meaning	5.68
employee obligations	5.67, 5.71
extent of rights	5.70
qualified right to	5.66
Time off for public duties	5.22
penalties for breach	5.23
Time off for trade union duties	5.24
Tort, law of	1.9

Trade unions	
right not to be discriminated	
against in respect of	
membership or activities	9.5, 9.6, 9.7, 9.8
right to time off for activities and	
duties	9.2, 9.3, 9.4
Training, discrimination, and	6.66
Transfer of undertakings	10.1
application of TUPE Regulations	10.1, 10.2, 10.3
collective consultation	9.17, 9.18, 9.19, 9.20, 9.21, 9.22
TUPE, effects	10.4, 10.6
consultations	10.7
unfair dismissal, and	10.5
unfair dismissal, and	8.9
Transfers	
discrimination, and	6.66
Unacceptable professional misconduct	
General Teaching Councils, and	3.43
Unfair dismissal	8.1
automatically unfair	8.38
continuity of employment, and	8.42
employee representatives	8.39
flexible work	8.41
jury service	8.41
national minimum wage	8.41
'protected disclosures'	8.40
tax credits	8.41
trustees of occupational	
pension schemes	8.41
working hours	8.41
'buying off' right to claim	1.29
conditions for claiming	8.1
continuity of service	8.7, 8.10
employee or self-employed	8.3, 8.4, 8.5, 8.6
fixed-term contracts	8.8
illegality	8.11
transfer of undertakings, and	8.9
employee dismissed, whether	8.16
alternative employment and	
redundancy	8.31
changing of terms of	
employment	8.24
'constructive' dismissal	8.19, 8.20, 8.21, 8.22, 8.23
ending of limited-term contract	8.18
frustration	8.28, 8.29, 8.30
mutually agreed termination or	
resignation	8.25, 8.26, 8.27
termination of contract	8.17
employer's burden of proof	8.37
fair dismissals	8.43
capability	8.44
reasonableness	8.50, 8.51
redundancy	8.46
reorganisation of activities	8.48, 8.49
retirement	8.45
six reasons for	8.43
'some other substantial reason'	8.48

Index

Unfair dismissal—*continued*
  fair dismissals—*continued*
    statutory bar   8.47
    incapability of head teachers   8.59
      meeting to discuss concerns   8.61
      recognizing poor performance   8.59
      refusal to attend meeting   8.62
      tackling the problem   8.60
      targets   8.63
    incapability through ill-health   8.56
      case law   8.57
      employer's duties   8.58
    opportunity to appeal   8.93
    procedural fairness   8.87
      procedure for dismissal hearing   8.92
      'prosecutor' and 'judge'   8.91
      relevance of contractual or statutory procedure   8.87
      witnesses in disciplinary hearings   8.88, 8.89, 8.90
    procedurally flawed dismissals
      fairness   8.95, 8.96
    redundancy, and   7.17
    remedies   8.97
      additional awards   8.118, 8.119
      automatically unfair dismissal   8.116
      circumstances for making orders   8.102, 8.103, 8.104, 8.105, 8.106, 8.107, 8.108, 8.109, 8.110
      compensation   8.111
      compensation for lost benefits   8.99
      contractual benefits   8.98
      damages for breach of contract   8.121
      failure to comply with order for reinstatement   8.100
      failure to consult for redundancy   8.115
      failure to give pay in lieu of notice   8.122
      maximum amount   8.120
      mitigation of loss   8.117
      normal awards   8.111, 8.113
      order for re-engagement   8.101
      orders for reinstatement   8.97, 8.98
      reduction of awards   8.114
      redundancy payments, and   8.112
    retirement, on   6.116
    schools' primary respondent   8.2
    some other substantial reason   8.82
      case law   8.83
      following fair procedure   8.85
      non-renewal of fixed-term contract   8.84
      personality clash   8.86
      sound, good business reason   8.82
    statutory bar   8.79
      case law   8.79, 8.80, 8.81
    strikes and industrial action   8.34, 8.35, 8.36

Unfair dismissal—*continued*
  substantive fairness in capability dismissals   8.52
    competence of managers   8.54
    employees on probation   8.55
    opportunity to improve   8.52, 8.53
    proving incapability   8.52, 8.53
  substantive fairness in conduct dismissals   8.64
    absence for religious worship   8.76
    adequate investigation   8.64
    appeals   8.67
    conduct misconduct, whether   8.74, 8.75
    criminal conduct   8.68, 8.69, 8.70, 8.71
    redeployment   8.72, 8.73
    refusal to attend disciplinary interview   8.77, 8.78
    warnings   8.66
    witnesses   8.65
  time limit for claiming   8.32
    extension   8.33
  time of determination of fairness   8.94
  TUPE transfers, and   10.5
  waiver of right to claim   8.12
    detailed limitations   8.13
    independent advice   8.12
    independent adviser as party to agreement   8.15
    validity of agreement   8.14
Unreasonable behaviour
  discrimination, whether   6.34

Victimisation   6.37
  end of relationship of employment   6.40
  equal pay   6.38
  House of Lords decisions   6.37
  racial grounds, on   6.39
  refusal to give reference   6.38
  SDA 1975, under   6.56, 6.57
Voluntary aided schools
  appointment of staff   4.57, 4.58, 4.59
Voluntary controlled schools
  appointment of head and deputy head teacher   4.49, 4.50, 4.51
  appointment of staff   4.46, 4.47, 4.48
  appointment of support staff   4.54, 4.55, 4.56
  appointment of teachers   4.52, 4.53
Volunteers   1.7

Warnings
  conduct, and   8.66
Without prejudice negotiations   2.49
Witnesses
  disciplinary hearings   8.88, 8.89, 8.90
Working Time Regulations 1998   5.27
  enforcement   5.29
  paid holiday   5.28